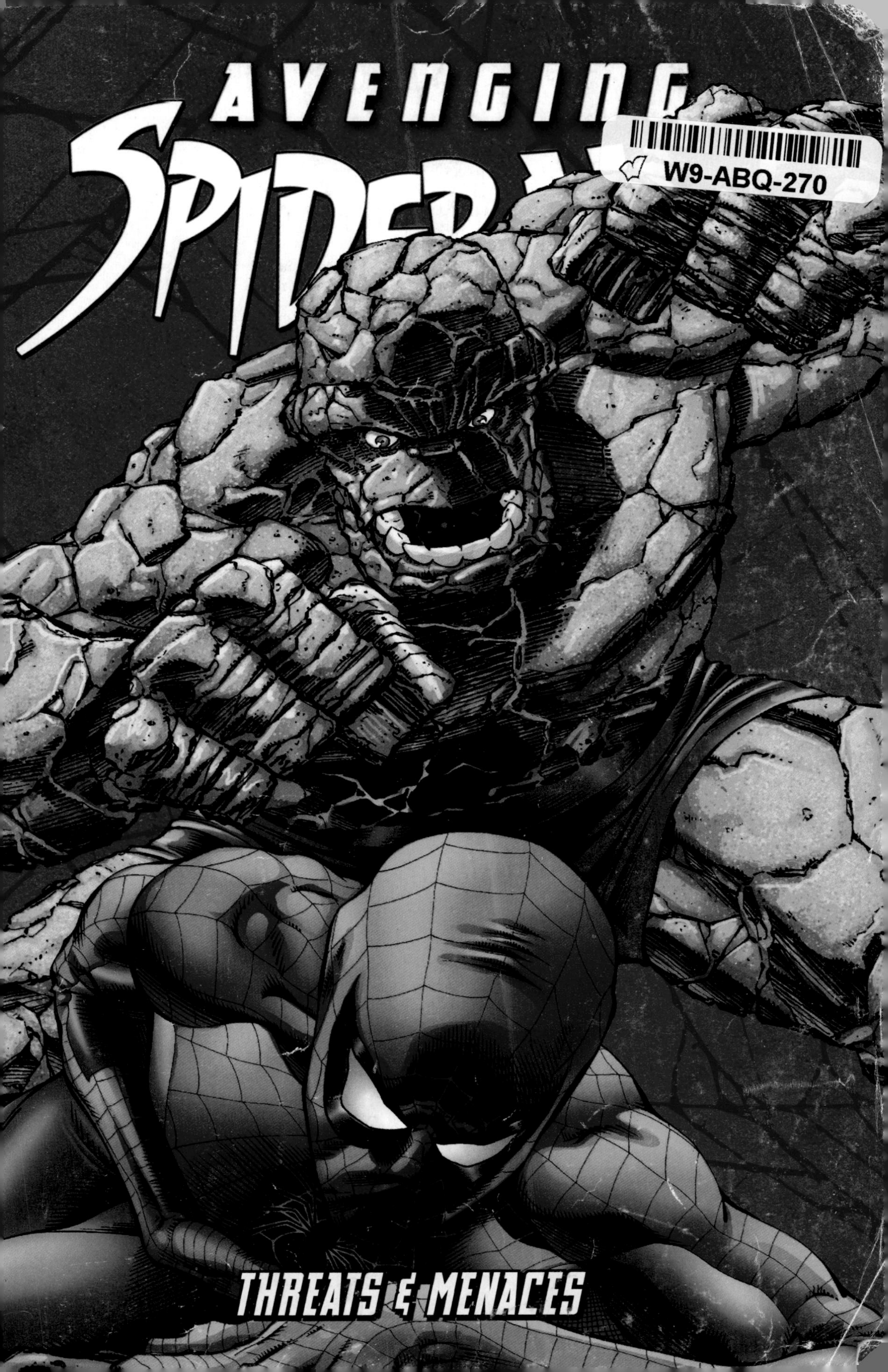
AVENGING
THREATS & MENACES

AVENGING SPIDER-MAN

THREATS & MENACES

AVENGING SPIDER-MAN #14-15

WRITER CULLEN BUNN	**ARTIST** GABRIELE DELL'OTTO
COLOR ARTIST DOMMO AYMARA	**LETTERER** VC'S JOE CARAMAGNA
COVER ART GABRIELE DELL'OTTO	**ASSISTANT EDITOR** ELLIE PYLE
EDITOR STEPHEN WACKER	**EXECUTIVE EDITOR** TOM BREVOORT

AVENGING SPIDER-MAN ANNUAL #1

WRITER ROB WILLIAMS	**PENCILER** BRAD WALKER
INKER JOHN LIVESAY	**COLORIST** CHRIS SOTOMAYOR
LETTERER VC'S JOE CARAMAGNA	**COVER ART** PATCH ZIRCHER & MARTE GRACIA
EDITOR TOM BRENNAN	**SENIOR EDITOR** STEPHEN WACKER

AMAZING SPIDER-MAN ANNUAL #39

WRITER
BRIAN REED

PENCILER
LEE GARBETT

INKER
JOHN LUCAS

COLORIST
ANTONIO FABELA

LETTERER
VC'S JOE CARAMAGNA

COVER ART
LEE GARBETT, KARL KESEL & WIL QUINTANA

EDITOR
ELLIE PYLE

SENIOR EDITOR
STEPHEN WACKER

"SPIDER-MAN FOR A NIGHT"
FROM AMAZING SPIDER-MAN #692

WRITER & ARTIST
DEAN HASPIEL

COLOR ARTIST
GIULIA BRUSCO

LETTERER
VC'S CHRIS ELIOPOULOS

ASSISTANT EDITOR
ELLIE PYLE

EDITOR
STEPHEN WACKER

"JUST RIGHT"
FROM AMAZING SPIDER-MAN #692

WRITER
JOSHUA HALE FIALKOV

ARTIST
NUNO PLATI

LETTERER
VC'S CLAYTON COWLES

ASSISTANT EDITOR
ELLIE PYLE

EDITOR
STEPHEN WACKER

SPIDER-MAN VS. VAMPIRES #1

WRITER
KEVIN GREVIOUX

PENCILER
ROBERTO CASTRO

INKERS
**WALDEN WONG
& SANDU FLOREA**

COLORISTS
**SOTOCOLOR, JOHN KALISZ,
ANTONIO FABELA & ANDRES MOSSA**

LETTERER
DAVE SHARPE

COVER ART
CHAD HARDIN & CHRIS SOTOMAYOR

EDITOR
TOM BRENNAN

Collection Editor: Cory Levine
Assistant Editors: Alex Starbuck & Nelson Ribeiro
Editors, Special Projects: Jennifer Grünwald & Mark D. Beazley
Senior Editor, Special Projects: Jeff Youngquist
SVP of Print & Digital Publishing Sales: David Gabriel
Book Design: Jeff Powell

Editor in Chief: Axel Alonso
Chief Creative Officer: Joe Quesada
Publisher: Dan Buckley
Executive Producer: Alan Fine

AVENGING SPIDER-MAN: THREATS & MENACES. Contains material originally published in magazine form as AVENGING SPIDER-MAN #14-15 and ANNUAL #1, AMAZING SPIDER-MAN ANNUAL #39, AMAZING SPIDER-MAN #692, and SPIDER-MAN VS. VAMPIRES #1. First printing 2013. ISBN# 978-0-7851-6573-6. Published by MARVEL WORLDWIDE, INC., a subsidiary of MARVEL ENTERTAINMENT, LLC. OFFICE OF PUBLICATION: 135 West 50th Street, New York, NY 10020. Copyright © 2010, 2012 and 2013 Marvel Characters, Inc. All rights reserved. All characters featured in this issue and the distinctive names and likenesses thereof, and all related indicia are trademarks of Marvel Characters, Inc. No similarity between any of the names, characters, persons, and/or institutions in this magazine with those of any living or dead person or institution is intended. and any such similarity which may exist is purely coincidental. **Printed in the U.S.A.** ALAN FINE. EVP - Office of the President, Marvel Worldwide, Inc. and EVP & CMO Marvel Characters B.V.; DAN BUCKLEY, Publisher & President - Print, Animation & Digital Divisions; JOE QUESADA, Chief Creative Officer; TOM BREVOORT, SVP of Publishing; DAVID BOGART, SVP of Operations & Procurement, Publishing; C.B. CEBULSKI, SVP of Creator & Content Development; DAVID GABRIEL, SVP of Print & Digital Publishing Sales; JIM O'KEEFE, VP of Operations & Logistics; DAN CARR, Executive Director of Publishing Technology; SUSAN CRESPI, Editorial Operations Manager; ALEX MORALES, Publishing Operations Manager; STAN LEE, Chairman Emeritus. For information regarding advertising in Marvel Comics or on Marvel.com, please contact Niza Disla, Director of Marvel Partnerships, at ndisla@marvel.com. For Marvel subscription inquiries, please call 800-217-9158. **Manufactured between 3/7/2013 and 4/9/2013 by QUAD/GRAPHICS, VERSAILLES, KY, USA.**

10 9 8 7 6 5 4 3 2 1

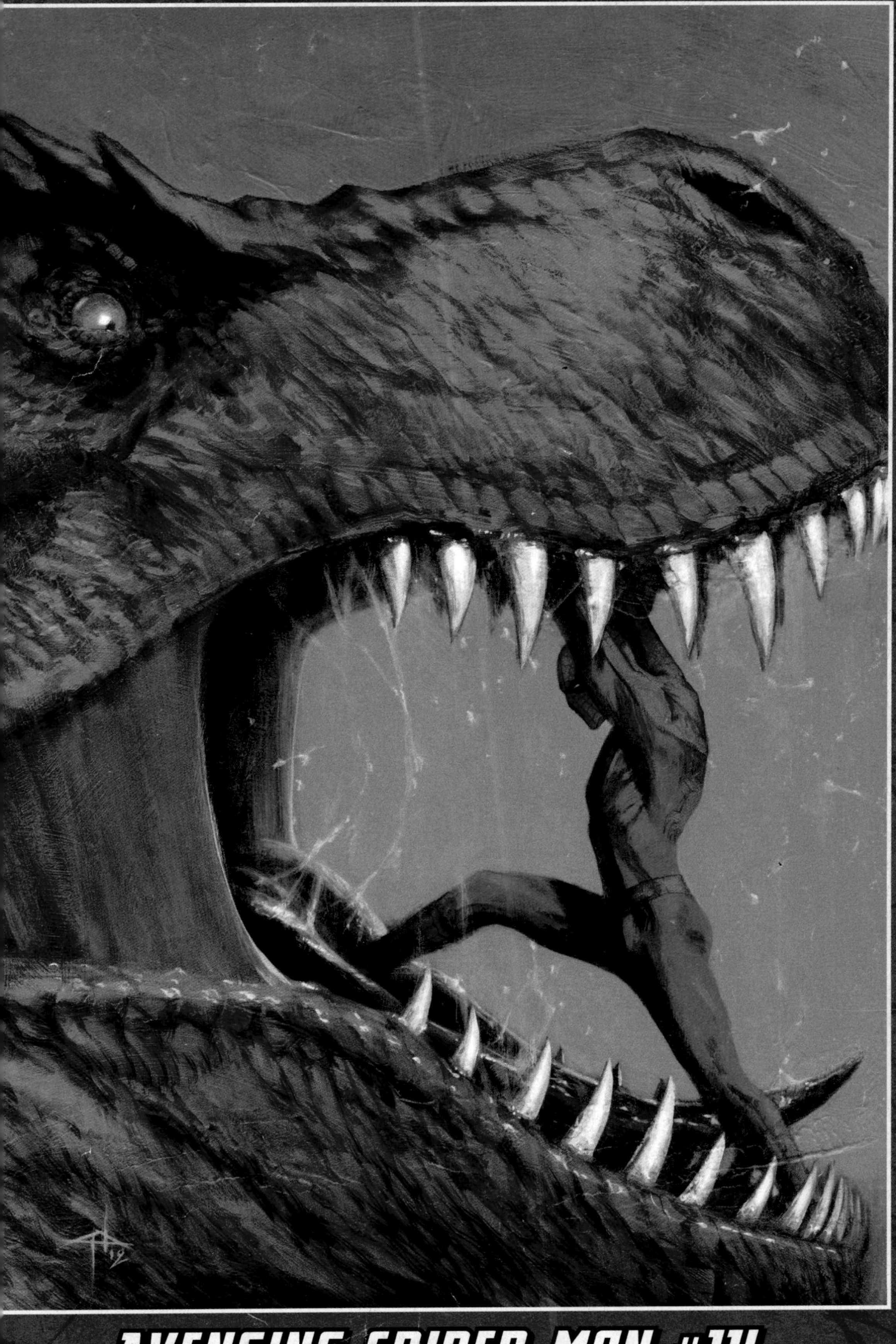

AVENGING SPIDER-MAN #14

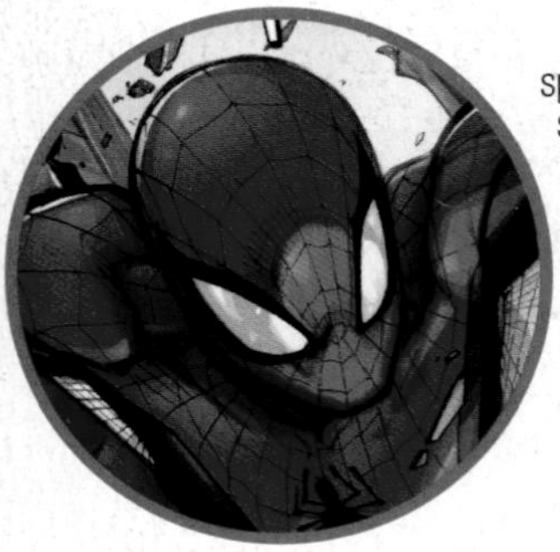

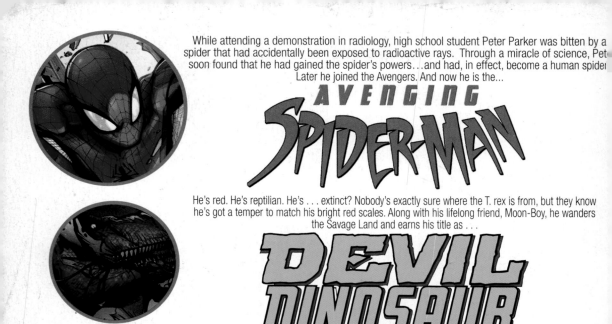

While attending a demonstration in radiology, high school student Peter Parker was bitten by a spider that had accidentally been exposed to radioactive rays. Through a miracle of science, Pet soon found that he had gained the spider's powers…and had, in effect, become a human spidei Later he joined the Avengers. And now he is the...

AVENGING SPIDER-MAN

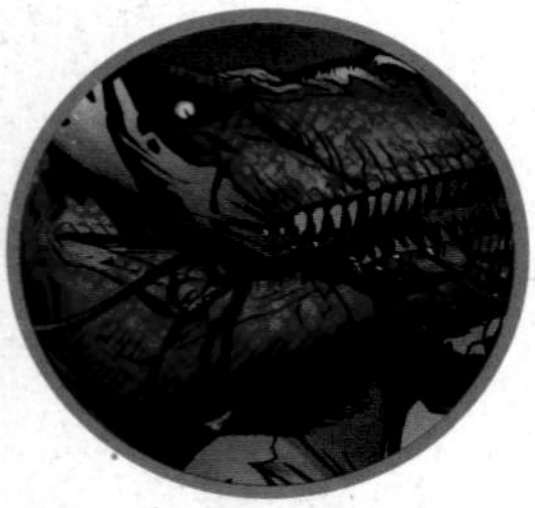

He's red. He's reptilian. He's . . . extinct? Nobody's exactly sure where the T. rex is from, but they know he's got a temper to match his bright red scales. Along with his lifelong friend, Moon-Boy, he wanders the Savage Land and earns his title as . . .

DEVIL DINOSAUR

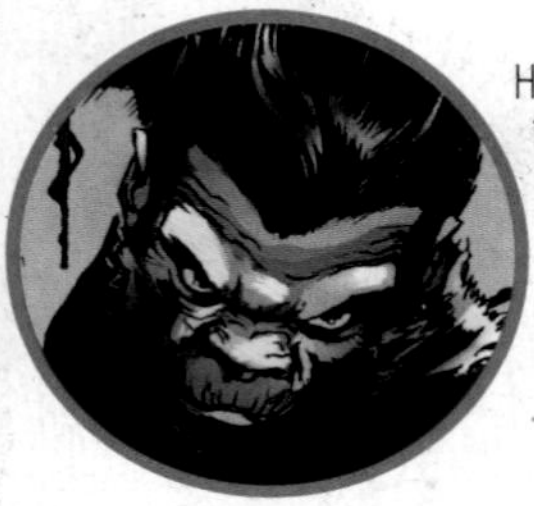

He may be out of his evolutionary element, but this Neanderthal is no dumb ape. After saving Devil Dinosa from the Killer-Folk, he bonded with the secretly sweet dino and together, they defend the Savage Land fron invaders. This hairy hero only speaks lizard language, but you can call him . . .

MOON-BOY

AVENGING SPIDER-MAN

PREVIOUSLY...

Spider-Man was seeing stars and psychedelic colors while being Hypno-hustled through prison with Deadpool. But hey—you want that story, buy issue #13. For now, Spider-Man's swinging through the jungle, the mighty jungle, but sleeping lions are the least of his problems...and you have stunning art waiting for you! **JUST TURN THE PAGE!**

WRITER: **CULLEN BUNN** ART: **GABRIELE DELL'OTTO**

COLORIST: **DOMMO AYMARA** LETTERER: **VC's JOE CARAMAGNA** COVER: **GABRIELE DELL'OTTO**

ASSISTANT EDITOR: **ELLIE PYLE** VELOCIWACKER: **STEPHEN WACKER**

EXECUTIVE EDITOR: **TOM BREVOORT** EDITOR IN CHIEF: **AXEL ALONSO**

CHIEF CREATIVE OFFICER: **JOE QUESADA** PUBLISHER: **DAN BUCKLEY** EXECUTIVE PRODUCER: **ALAN FINE**

THE SAVAGE LAND.

IN A WORLD OF GLASS AND STEEL...OF SKY-FIRE HARNESSED TO DO THE BIDDING OF MAN...THERE IS NO OTHER PLACE LIKE IT.

HERE IS LIFE AND DEATH...FLESH AND BLOOD...BEGINNINGS AND ENDINGS.

HERE IS HONESTY.

THIS IS THE STORY OF HOW THE MAN-SPIDER HELPED US SAVE THE SAVAGE LAND FROM A FESTERING EVIL AT ITS CORE.

IT DID NOT GO SMOOTHLY.

"I'M GONNA LET YOU GUYS IN ON A *LITTLE SECRET*..."

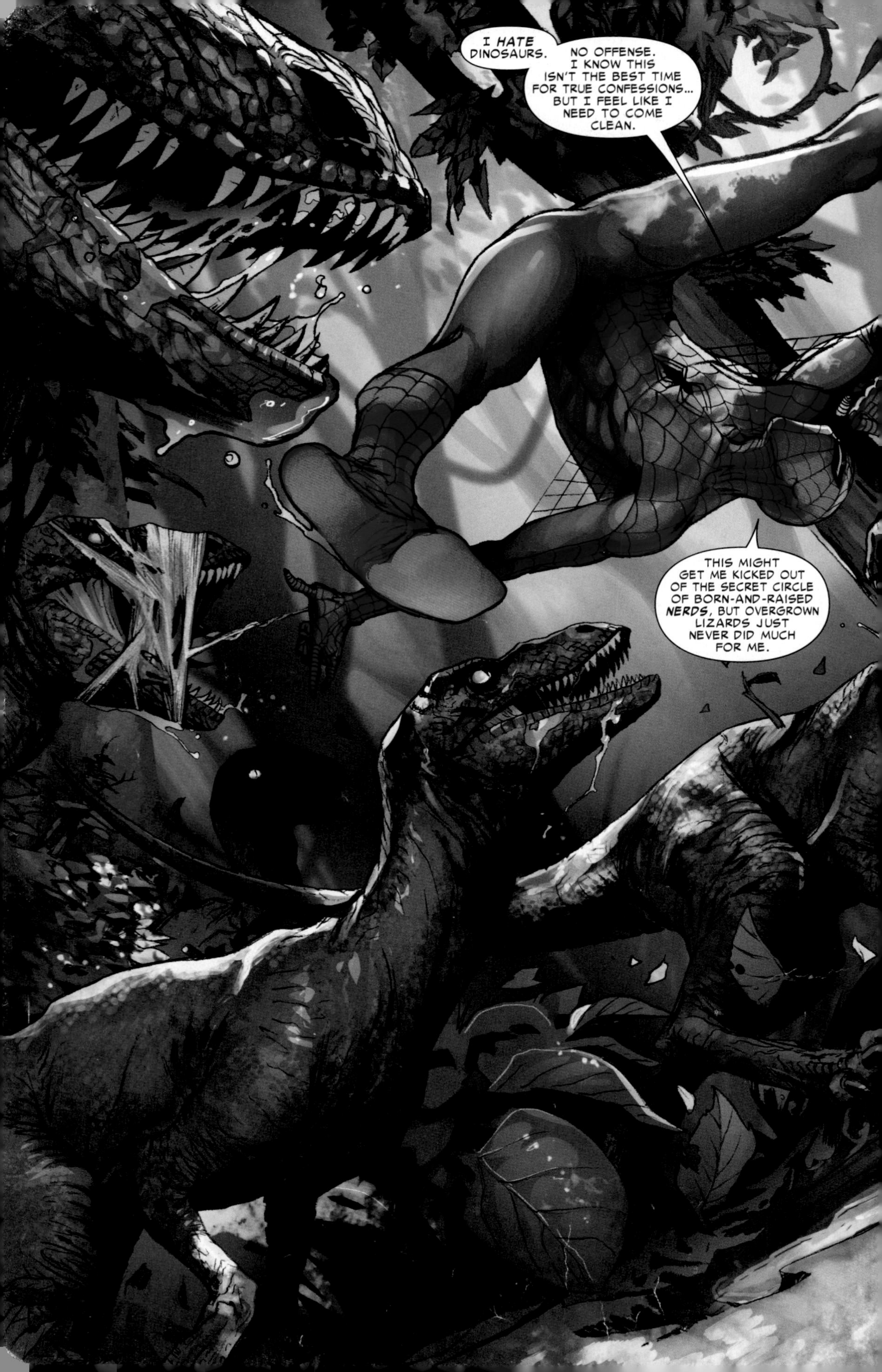
I *HATE* DINOSAURS.
NO OFFENSE. I KNOW THIS ISN'T THE BEST TIME FOR TRUE CONFESSIONS... BUT I FEEL LIKE I NEED TO COME CLEAN.
THIS MIGHT GET ME KICKED OUT OF THE SECRET CIRCLE OF BORN-AND-RAISED ***NERDS***, BUT OVERGROWN LIZARDS JUST NEVER DID MUCH FOR ME.

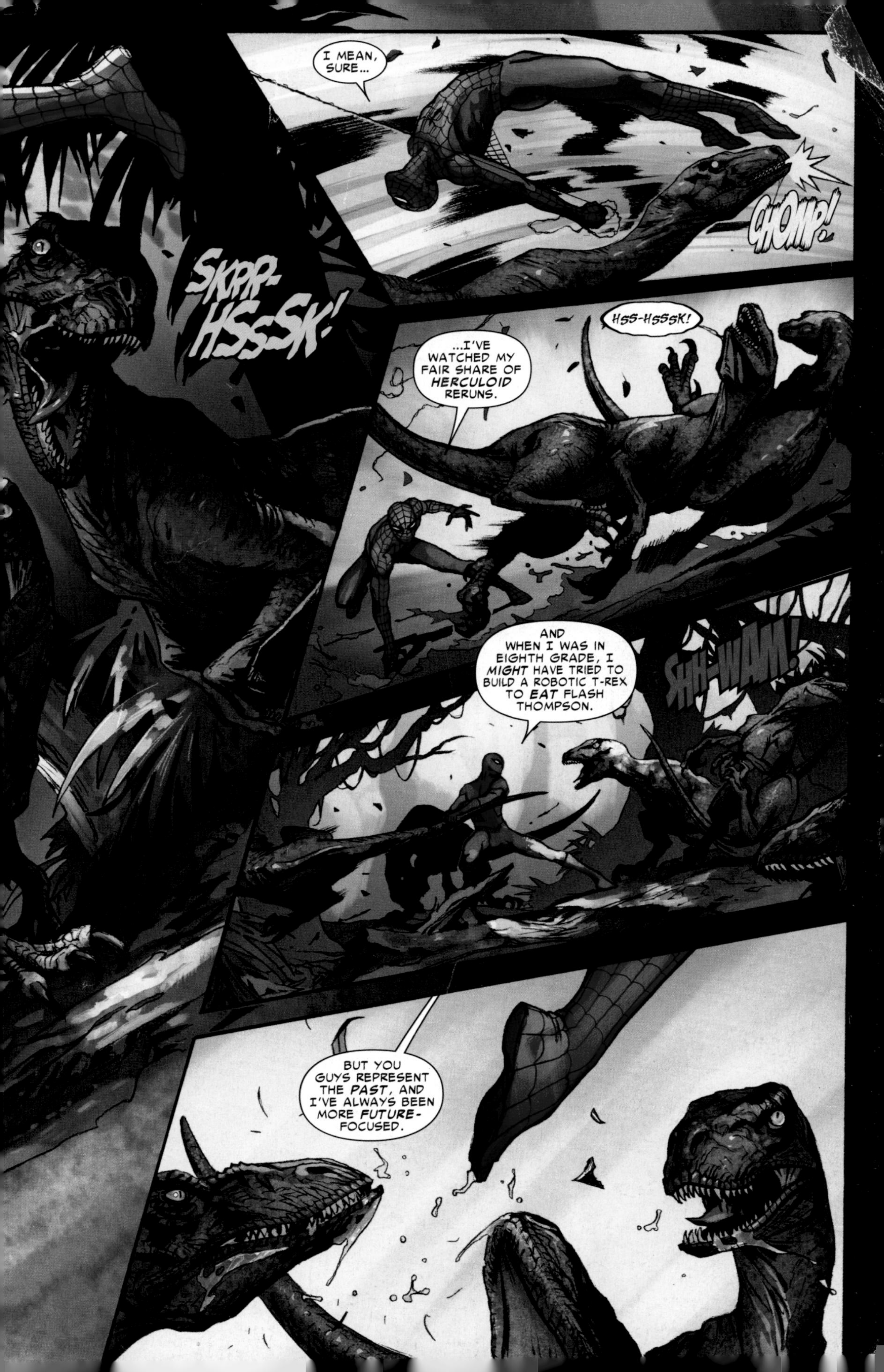
I MEAN, SURE...
CHOMP!
SKRR-HSSSK!
...I'VE WATCHED MY FAIR SHARE OF HERCULOID RERUNS.
HSS-HSSSK!
AND WHEN I WAS IN EIGHTH GRADE, I MIGHT HAVE TRIED TO BUILD A ROBOTIC T-REX TO EAT FLASH THOMPSON.
SHH-WAM!
BUT YOU GUYS REPRESENT THE PAST, AND I'VE ALWAYS BEEN MORE FUTURE-FOCUSED.

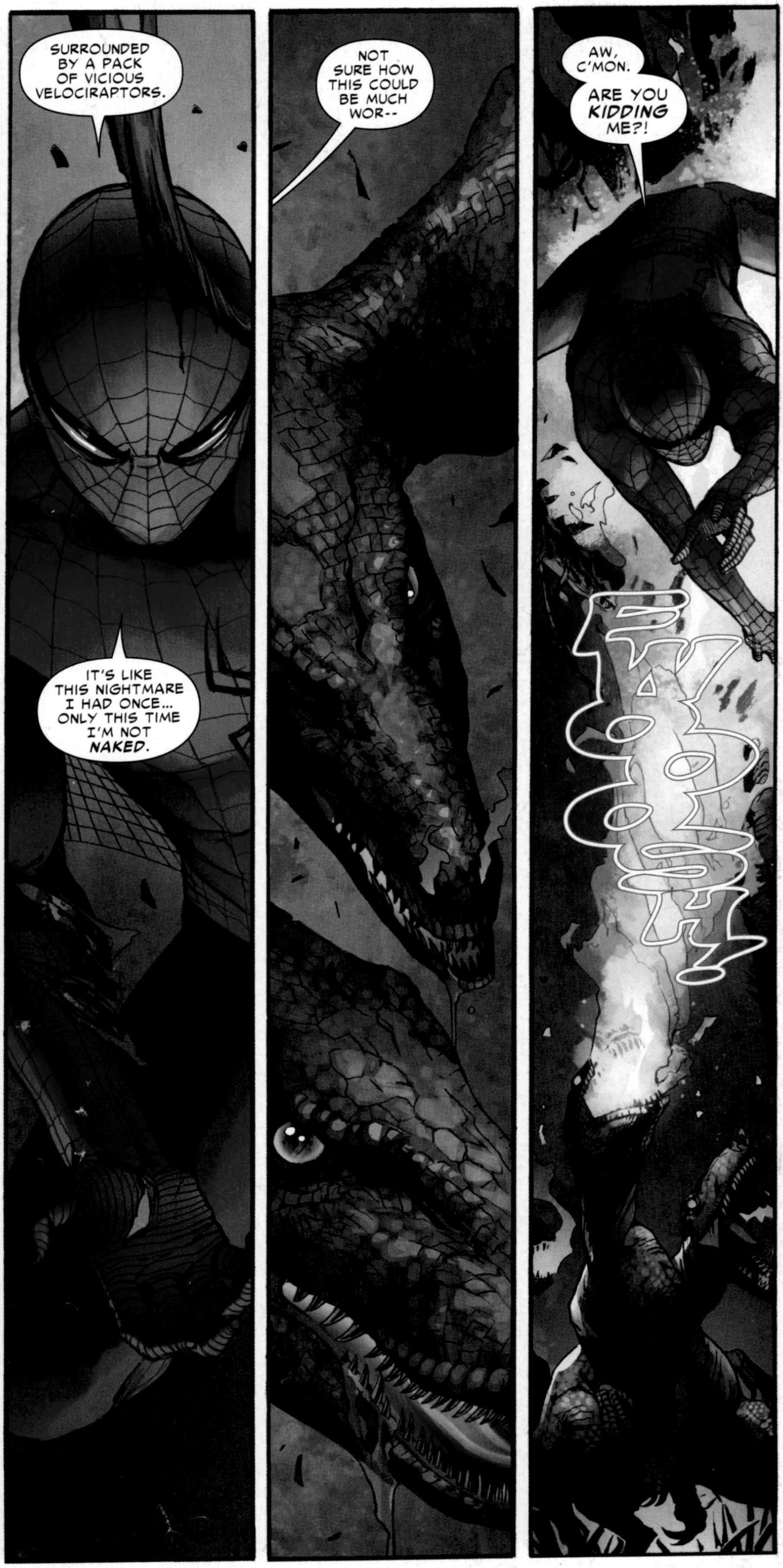
SURROUNDED BY A PACK OF VICIOUS VELOCIRAPTORS.
IT'S LIKE THIS NIGHTMARE I HAD ONCE... ONLY THIS TIME I'M NOT NAKED.
NOT SURE HOW THIS COULD BE MUCH WOR--
AW, C'MON.
ARE YOU KIDDING ME?!
FWOOOSH!

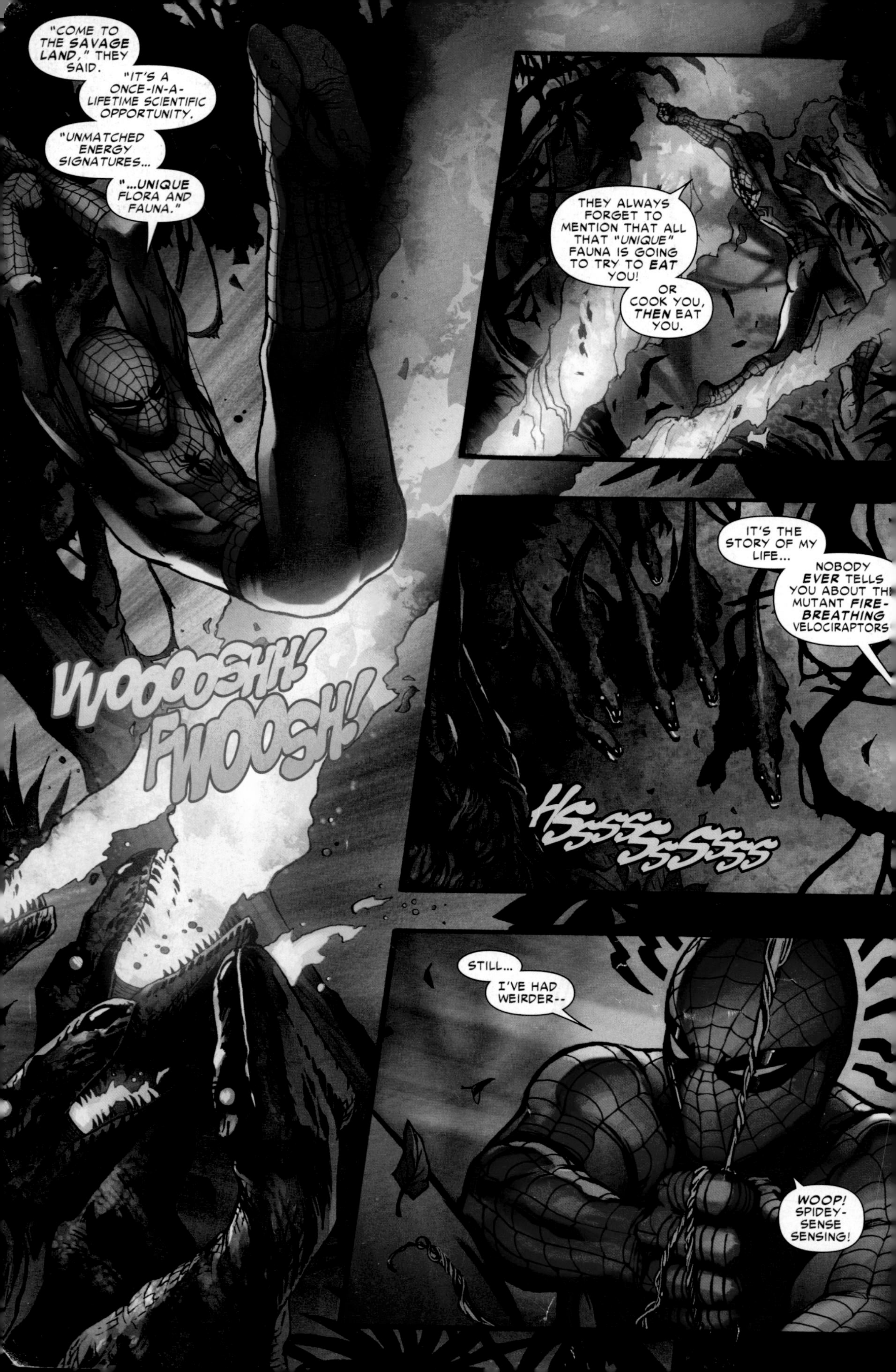
"COME TO THE SAVAGE LAND," THEY SAID.
"IT'S A ONCE-IN-A-LIFETIME SCIENTIFIC OPPORTUNITY.
"UNMATCHED ENERGY SIGNATURES...
"...UNIQUE FLORA AND FAUNA."
VVOOOOSHH! FWOOSH!
THEY ALWAYS FORGET TO MENTION THAT ALL THAT "UNIQUE" FAUNA IS GOING TO TRY TO EAT YOU!
OR COOK YOU, THEN EAT YOU.
IT'S THE STORY OF MY LIFE...
NOBODY EVER TELLS YOU ABOUT TH MUTANT FIRE-BREATHING VELOCIRAPTORS
HSSSSSSSSS
STILL... I'VE HAD WEIRDER--
WOOP! SPIDEY-SENSE SENSING!

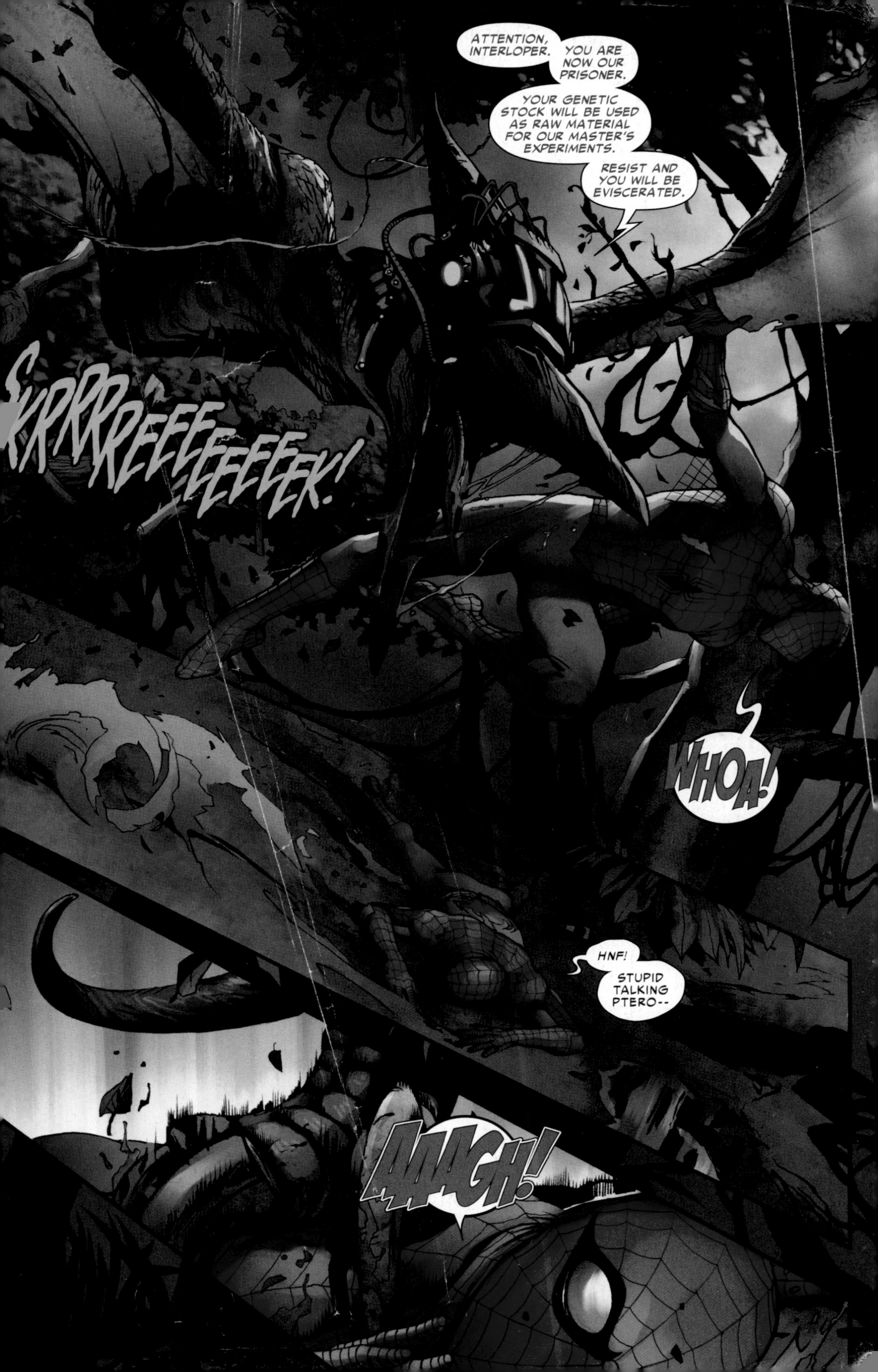
ATTENTION, INTERLOPER.
YOU ARE NOW OUR PRISONER.
YOUR GENETIC STOCK WILL BE USED AS RAW MATERIAL FOR OUR MASTER'S EXPERIMENTS.
RESIST AND YOU WILL BE EVISCERATED.
SKRRRREEEEEEEEEK!
WHOA!
HNF!
STUPID TALKING PTERO--
AAAGH!

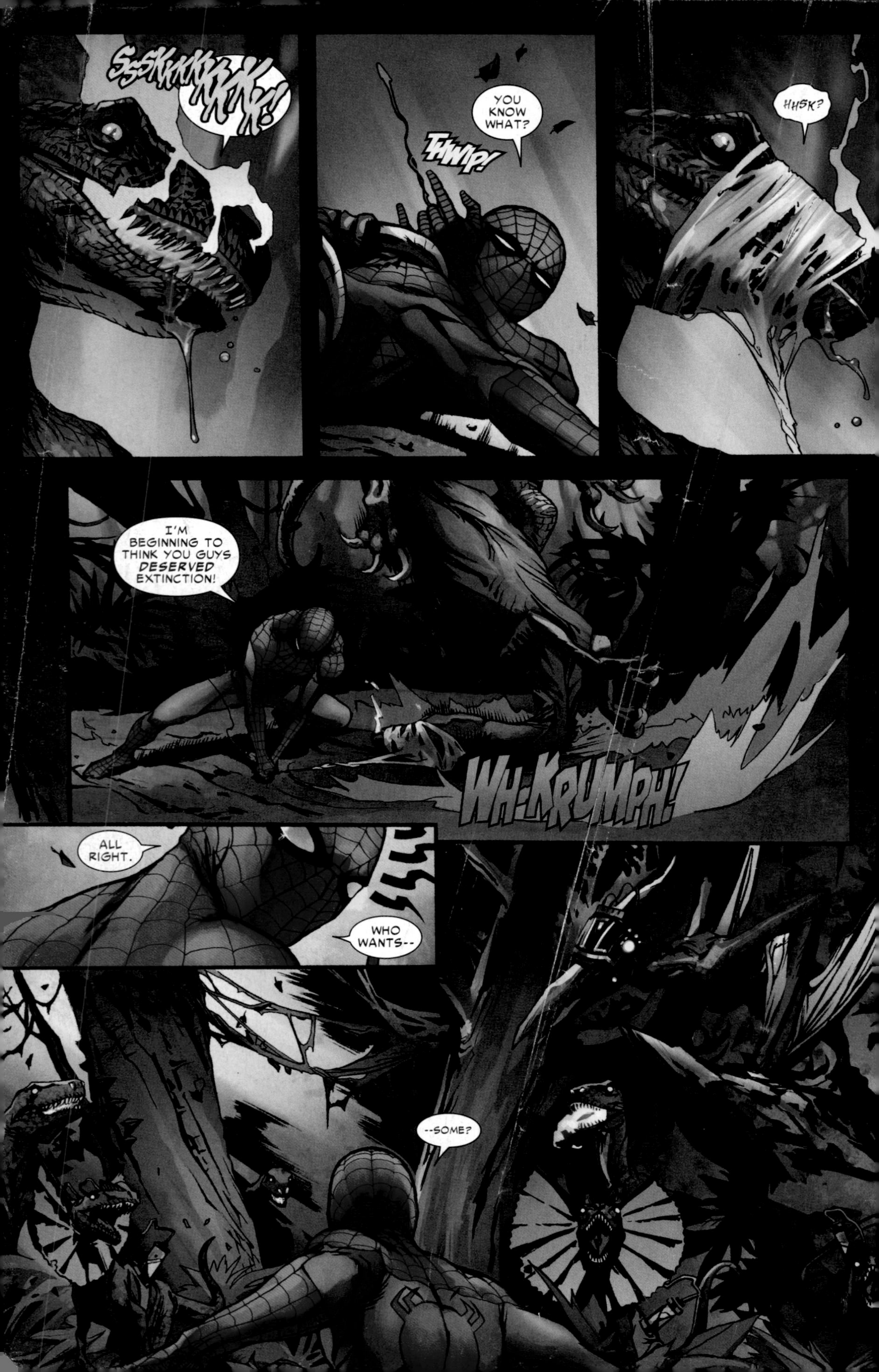
SSSKKKKKKKK!
YOU KNOW WHAT?
THWIP!
HHSK?
I'M BEGINNING TO THINK YOU GUYS *DESERVED* EXTINCTION!
WH-KRUMPH!
ALL RIGHT.
WHO WANTS--
--SOME?

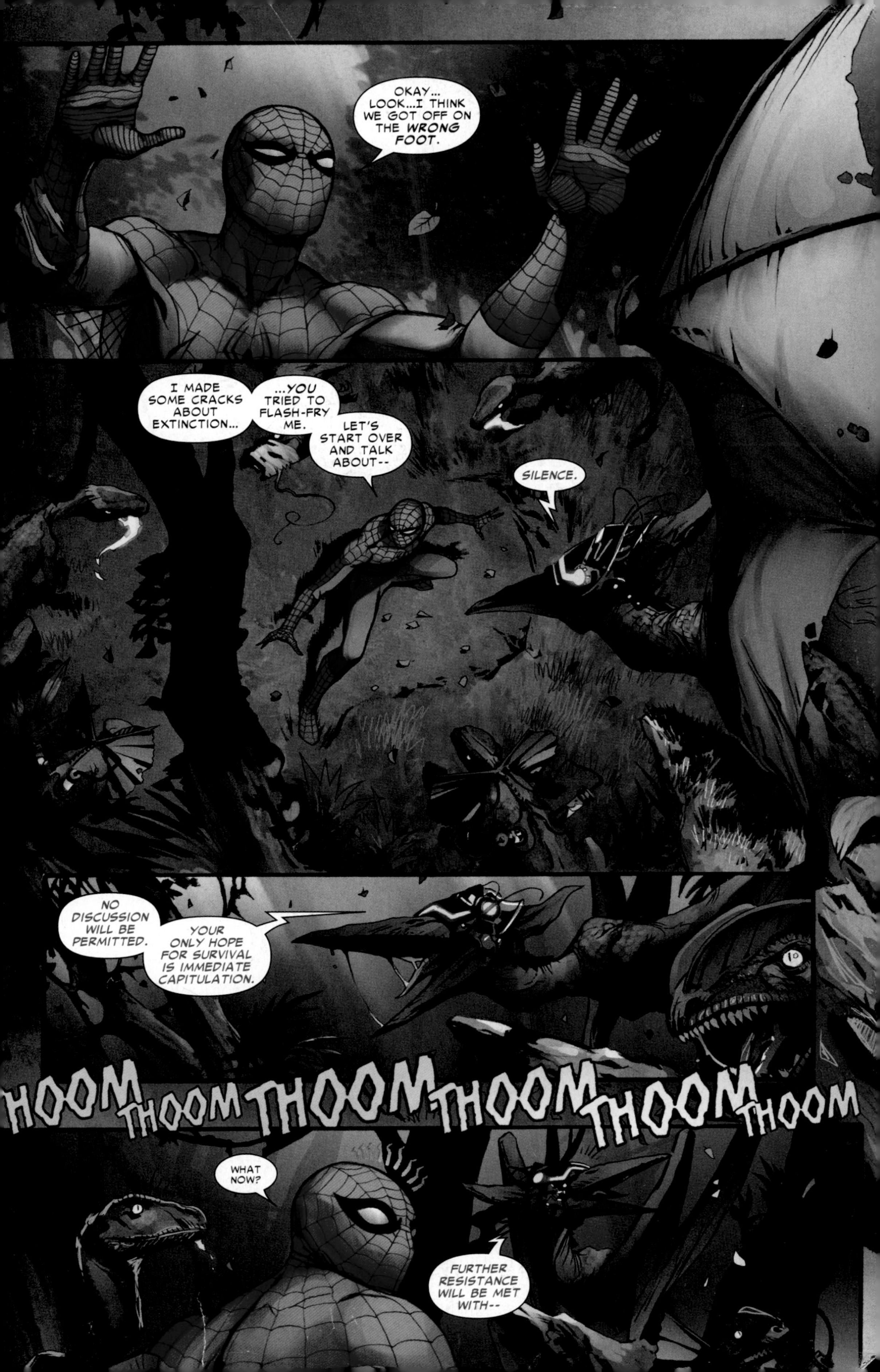
OKAY... LOOK...I THINK WE GOT OFF ON THE WRONG FOOT.
I MADE SOME CRACKS ABOUT EXTINCTION...
...YOU TRIED TO FLASH-FRY ME.
LET'S START OVER AND TALK ABOUT--
SILENCE.
NO DISCUSSION WILL BE PERMITTED.
YOUR ONLY HOPE FOR SURVIVAL IS IMMEDIATE CAPITULATION.
HOOM THOOM THOOM THOOM THOOM THOOM
WHAT NOW?
FURTHER RESISTANCE WILL BE MET WITH--

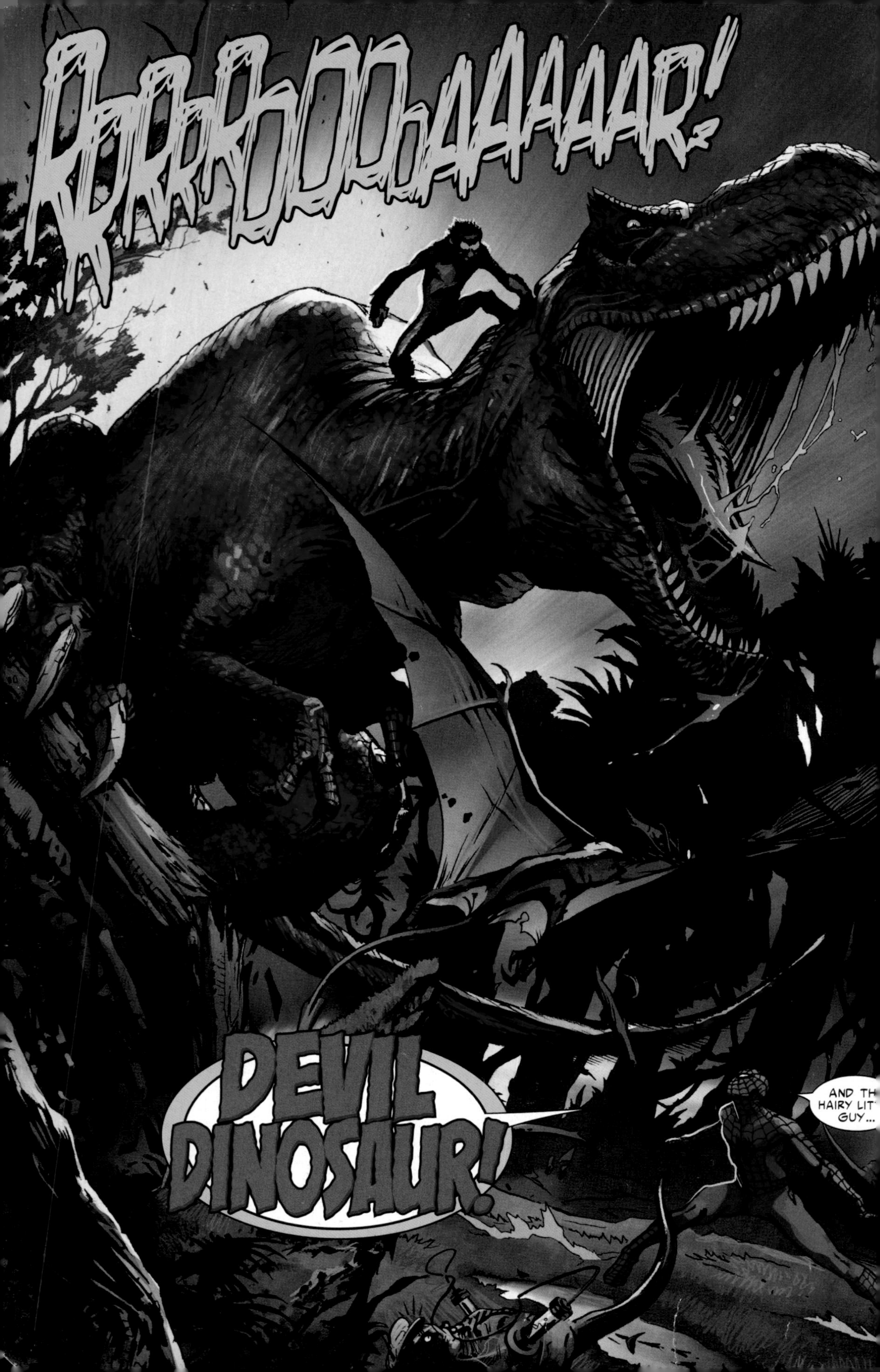
RRRROOOAAAAAR!
DEVIL DINOSAUR!
AND TH HAIRY LIT GUY...

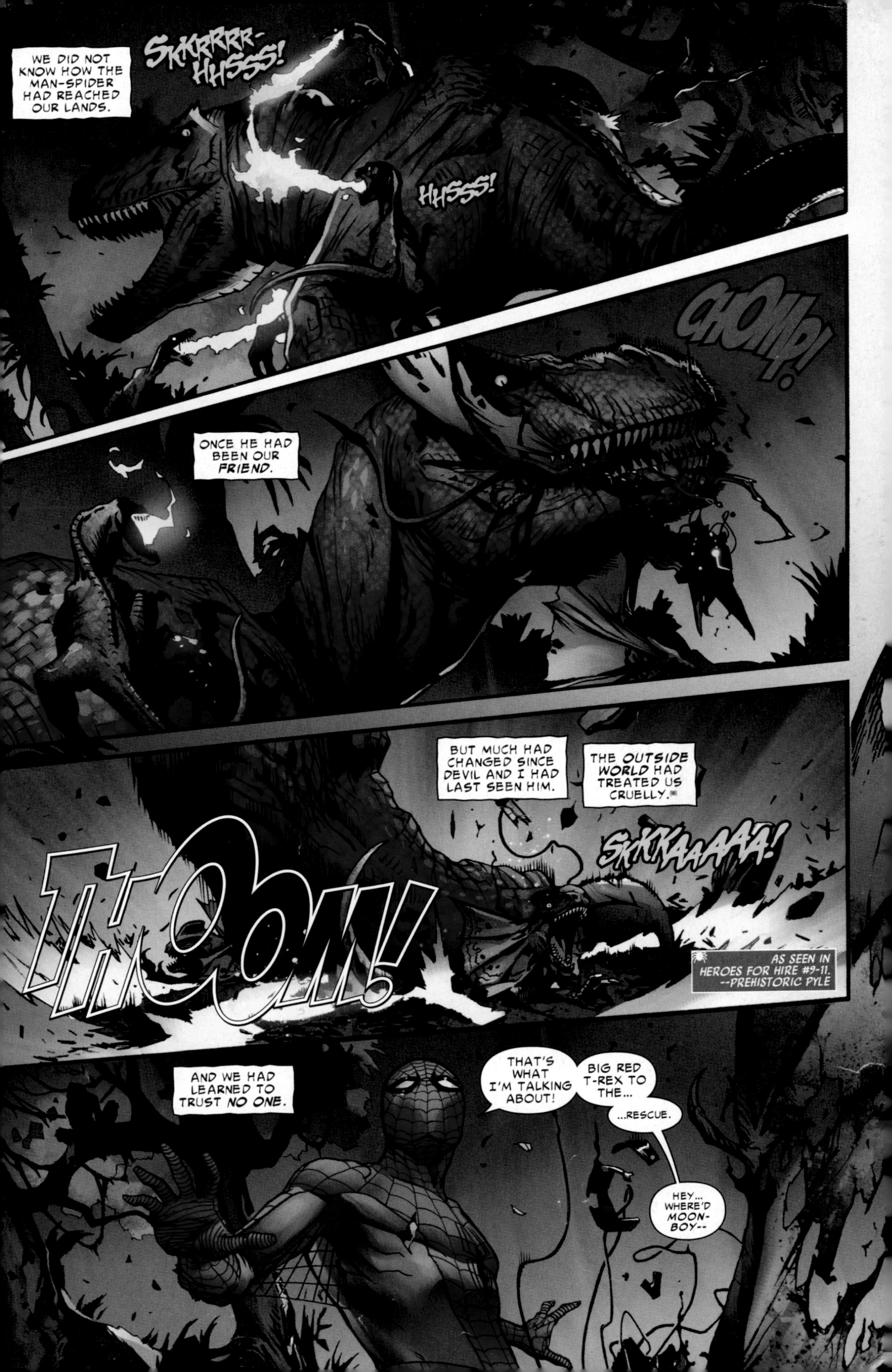
WE DID NOT KNOW HOW THE MAN-SPIDER HAD REACHED OUR LANDS.
SKKRRRR-HHSSS!
HHSSS!
CHOMP!
ONCE HE HAD BEEN OUR FRIEND.
BUT MUCH HAD CHANGED SINCE DEVIL AND I HAD LAST SEEN HIM.
THE OUTSIDE WORLD HAD TREATED US CRUELLY.*
SKKKAAAAAA!
THOOOM!
AS SEEN IN HEROES FOR HIRE #9-11. --PREHISTORIC PYLE
AND WE HAD LEARNED TO TRUST NO ONE.
THAT'S WHAT I'M TALKING ABOUT!
BIG RED T-REX TO THE...
...RESCUE.
HEY... WHERE'D MOON-BOY--

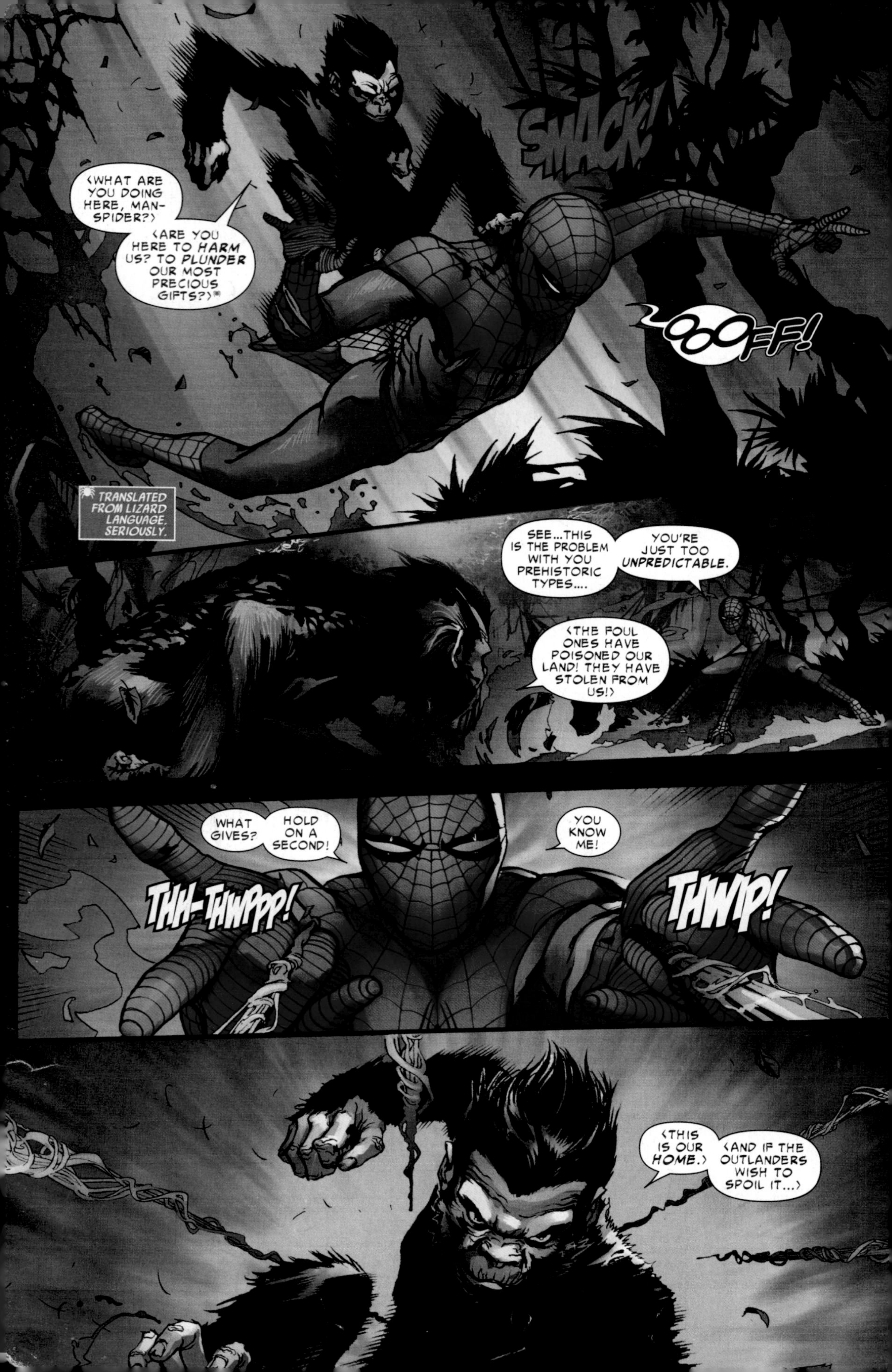
SMACK!
‹WHAT ARE YOU DOING HERE, MAN-SPIDER?›
‹ARE YOU HERE TO *HARM* US? TO *PLUNDER* OUR MOST PRECIOUS GIFTS?›*
OOOFF!
*TRANSLATED FROM LIZARD LANGUAGE. SERIOUSLY.
SEE...THIS IS THE PROBLEM WITH YOU PREHISTORIC TYPES....
YOU'RE JUST TOO *UNPREDICTABLE*.
‹THE FOUL ONES HAVE POISONED OUR LAND! THEY HAVE STOLEN FROM US!›
WHAT GIVES?
HOLD ON A SECOND!
YOU KNOW ME!
THH-THWPPP!
THWIP!
‹THIS IS OUR *HOME*.›
‹AND IF THE OUTLANDERS WISH TO SPOIL IT...›

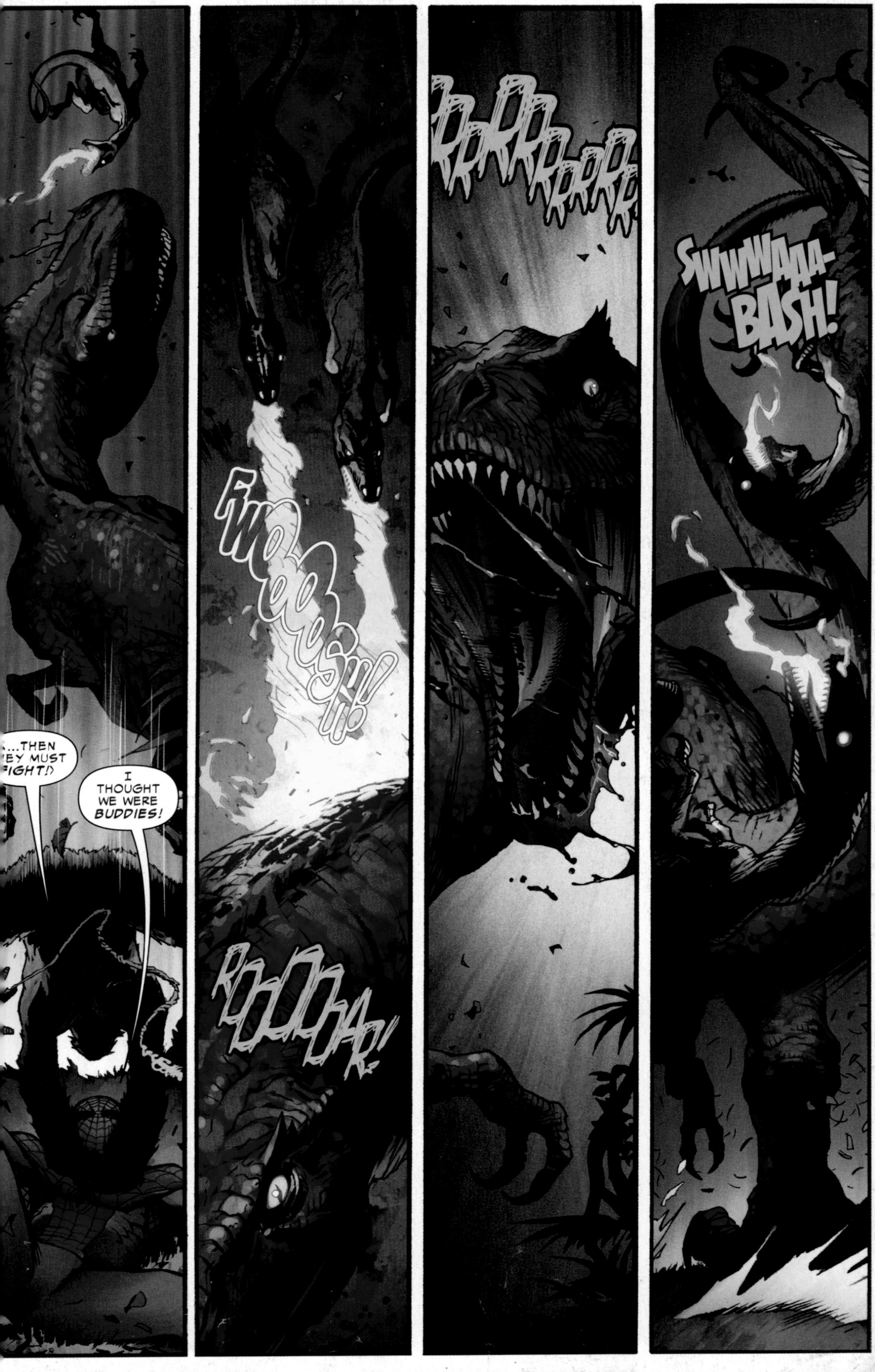

...THEN EY MUST FIGHT!
I THOUGHT WE WERE BUDDIES!
FWOOOSH!
ROOOOAR!
RRRRRRRRRRRR
SWWWAAA-BASH!

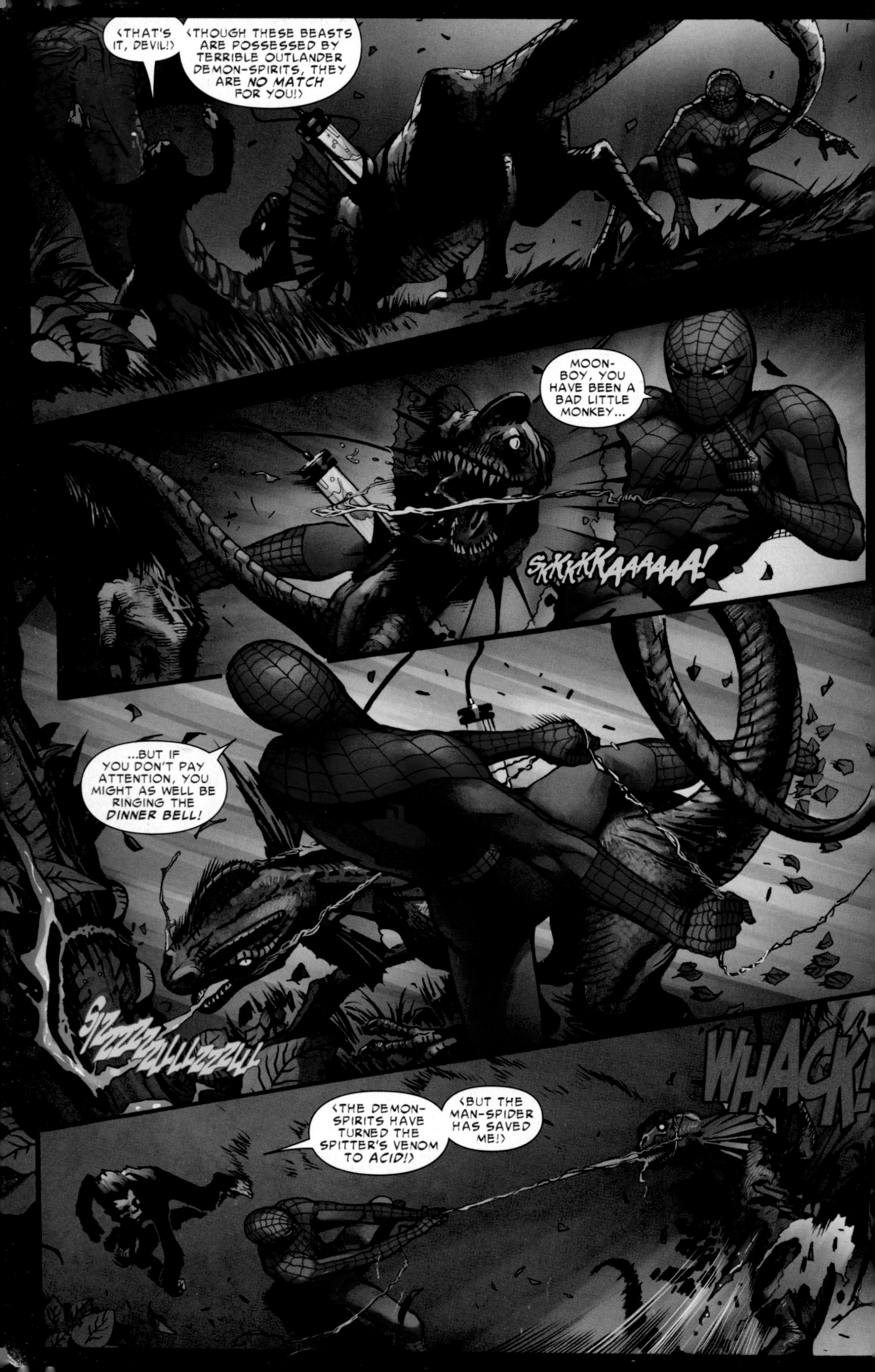

‹THAT'S IT, DEVIL!›
‹THOUGH THESE BEASTS ARE POSSESSED BY TERRIBLE OUTLANDER DEMON-SPIRITS, THEY ARE *NO MATCH* FOR YOU!›
MOON-BOY, YOU HAVE BEEN A BAD LITTLE MONKEY...
SKKKKKAAAAAA!
...BUT IF YOU DON'T PAY ATTENTION, YOU MIGHT AS WELL BE RINGING THE *DINNER BELL!*
SIZZZZZZLLLZZZLLL
WHACK!
‹THE DEMON-SPIRITS HAVE TURNED THE SPITTER'S VENOM TO *ACID!*›
‹BUT THE MAN-SPIDER HAS SAVED ME!›

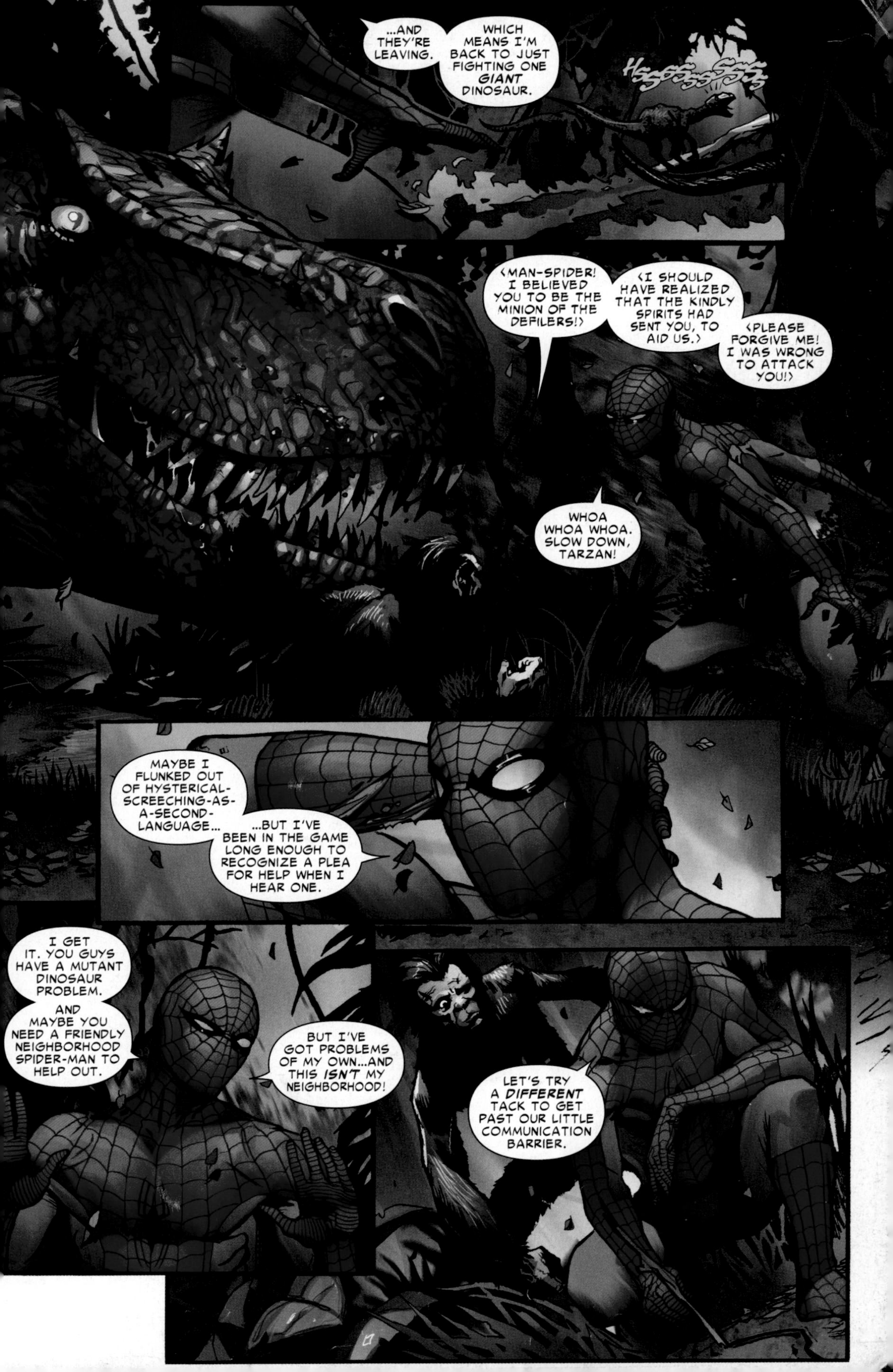
...AND THEY'RE LEAVING.
WHICH MEANS I'M BACK TO JUST FIGHTING ONE GIANT DINOSAUR.
HSSSSSSSSSS
‹MAN-SPIDER! I BELIEVED YOU TO BE THE MINION OF THE DEFILERS!›
‹I SHOULD HAVE REALIZED THAT THE KINDLY SPIRITS HAD SENT YOU, TO AID US.›
‹PLEASE FORGIVE ME! I WAS WRONG TO ATTACK YOU!›
WHOA WHOA WHOA. SLOW DOWN, TARZAN!
MAYBE I FLUNKED OUT OF HYSTERICAL-SCREECHING-AS-A-SECOND-LANGUAGE...
...BUT I'VE BEEN IN THE GAME LONG ENOUGH TO RECOGNIZE A PLEA FOR HELP WHEN I HEAR ONE.
I GET IT. YOU GUYS HAVE A MUTANT DINOSAUR PROBLEM.
AND MAYBE YOU NEED A FRIENDLY NEIGHBORHOOD SPIDER-MAN TO HELP OUT.
BUT I'VE GOT PROBLEMS OF MY OWN...AND THIS ISN'T MY NEIGHBORHOOD!
LET'S TRY A DIFFERENT TACK TO GET PAST OUR LITTLE COMMUNICATION BARRIER.

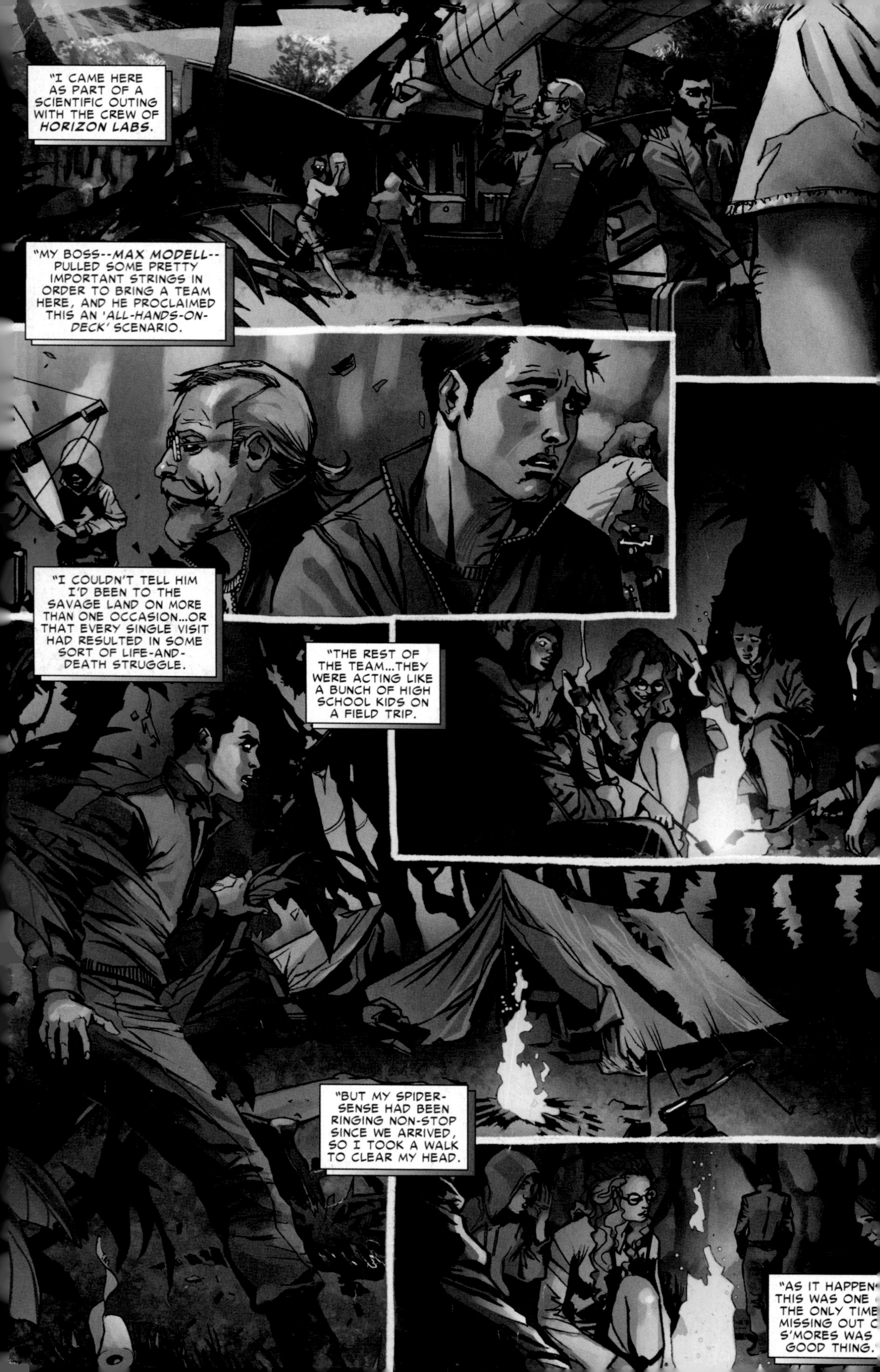
"I CAME HERE AS PART OF A SCIENTIFIC OUTING WITH THE CREW OF HORIZON LABS.
"MY BOSS--MAX MODELL--PULLED SOME PRETTY IMPORTANT STRINGS IN ORDER TO BRING A TEAM HERE, AND HE PROCLAIMED THIS AN 'ALL-HANDS-ON-DECK' SCENARIO.
"I COULDN'T TELL HIM I'D BEEN TO THE SAVAGE LAND ON MORE THAN ONE OCCASION...OR THAT EVERY SINGLE VISIT HAD RESULTED IN SOME SORT OF LIFE-AND-DEATH STRUGGLE.
"THE REST OF THE TEAM...THEY WERE ACTING LIKE A BUNCH OF HIGH SCHOOL KIDS ON A FIELD TRIP.
"BUT MY SPIDER-SENSE HAD BEEN RINGING NON-STOP SINCE WE ARRIVED, SO I TOOK A WALK TO CLEAR MY HEAD.
"AS IT HAPPEN THIS WAS ONE THE ONLY TIME MISSING OUT S'MORES WAS GOOD THING.

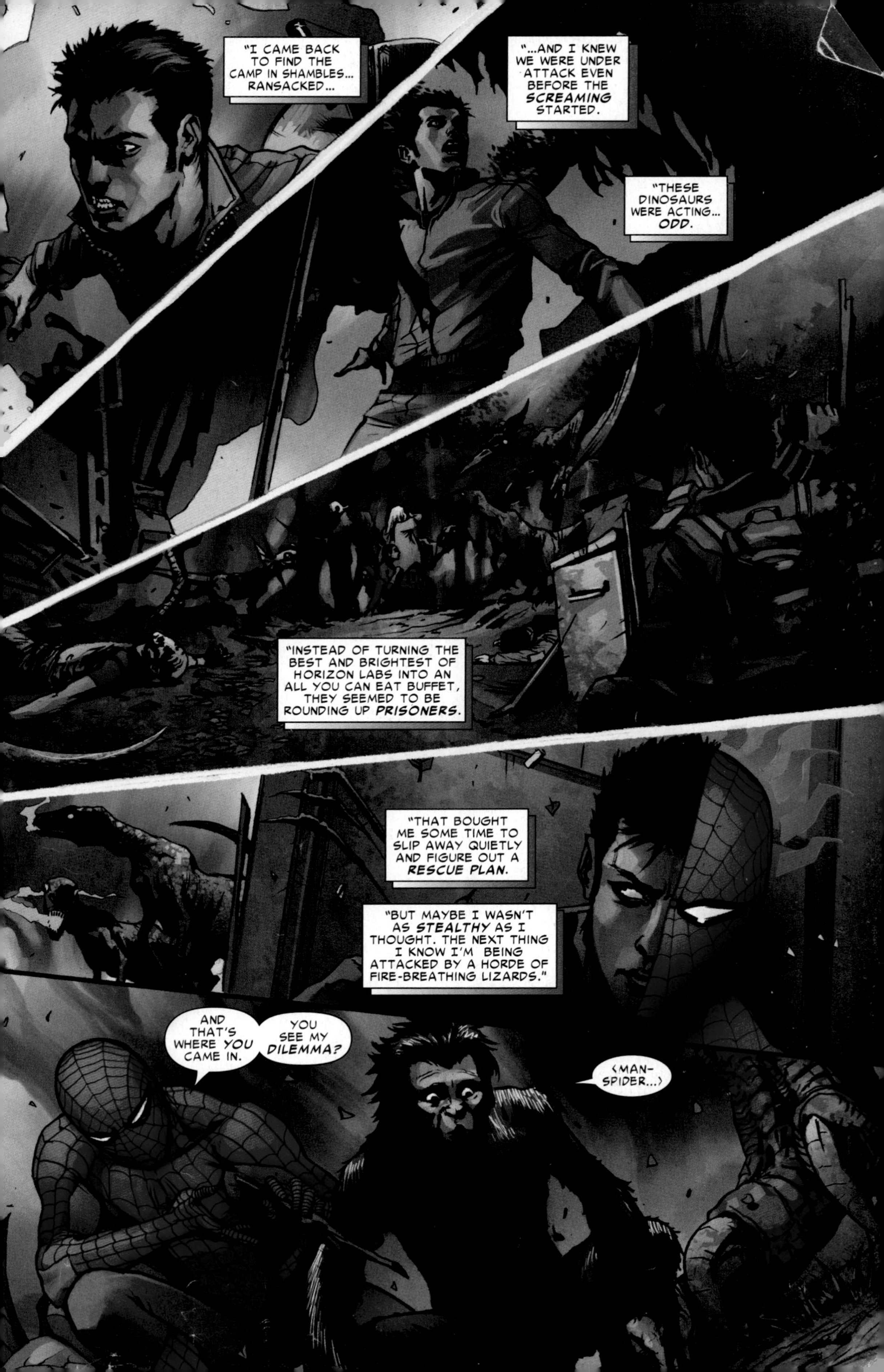
"I CAME BACK TO FIND THE CAMP IN SHAMBLES... RANSACKED...
"...AND I KNEW WE WERE UNDER ATTACK EVEN BEFORE THE SCREAMING STARTED.
"THESE DINOSAURS WERE ACTING... ODD.
"INSTEAD OF TURNING THE BEST AND BRIGHTEST OF HORIZON LABS INTO AN ALL YOU CAN EAT BUFFET, THEY SEEMED TO BE ROUNDING UP PRISONERS.
"THAT BOUGHT ME SOME TIME TO SLIP AWAY QUIETLY AND FIGURE OUT A RESCUE PLAN.
"BUT MAYBE I WASN'T AS STEALTHY AS I THOUGHT. THE NEXT THING I KNOW I'M BEING ATTACKED BY A HORDE OF FIRE-BREATHING LIZARDS."
AND THAT'S WHERE YOU CAME IN.
YOU SEE MY DILEMMA?
<MAN-SPIDER...>

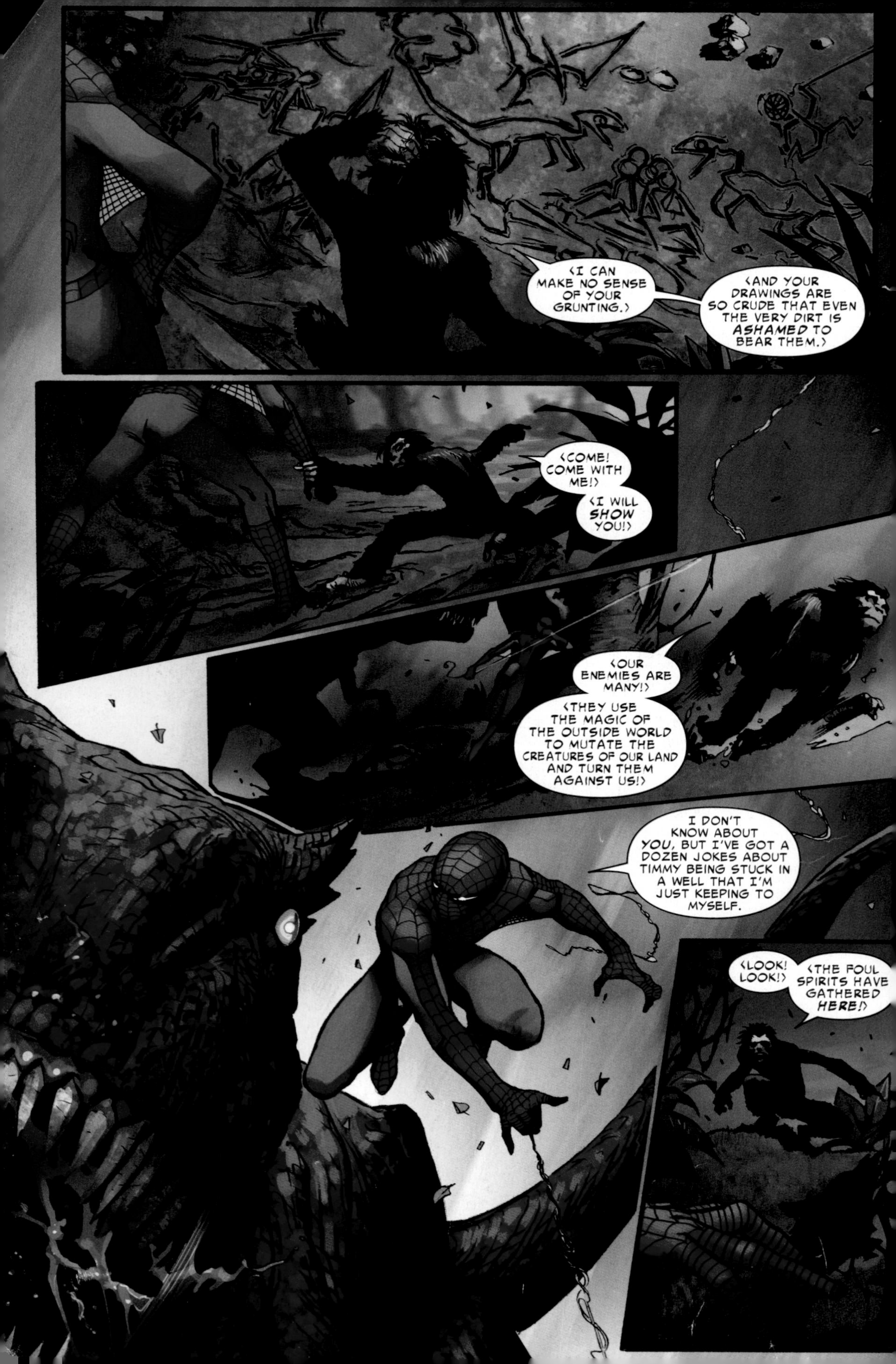

‹I CAN MAKE NO SENSE OF YOUR GRUNTING.›
‹AND YOUR DRAWINGS ARE SO CRUDE THAT EVEN THE VERY DIRT IS ASHAMED TO BEAR THEM.›
‹COME! COME WITH ME!›
‹I WILL SHOW YOU!›
‹OUR ENEMIES ARE MANY!›
‹THEY USE THE MAGIC OF THE OUTSIDE WORLD TO MUTATE THE CREATURES OF OUR LAND AND TURN THEM AGAINST US!›
I DON'T KNOW ABOUT YOU, BUT I'VE GOT A DOZEN JOKES ABOUT TIMMY BEING STUCK IN A WELL THAT I'M JUST KEEPING TO MYSELF.
‹LOOK! LOOK!›
‹THE FOUL SPIRITS HAVE GATHERED HERE!›

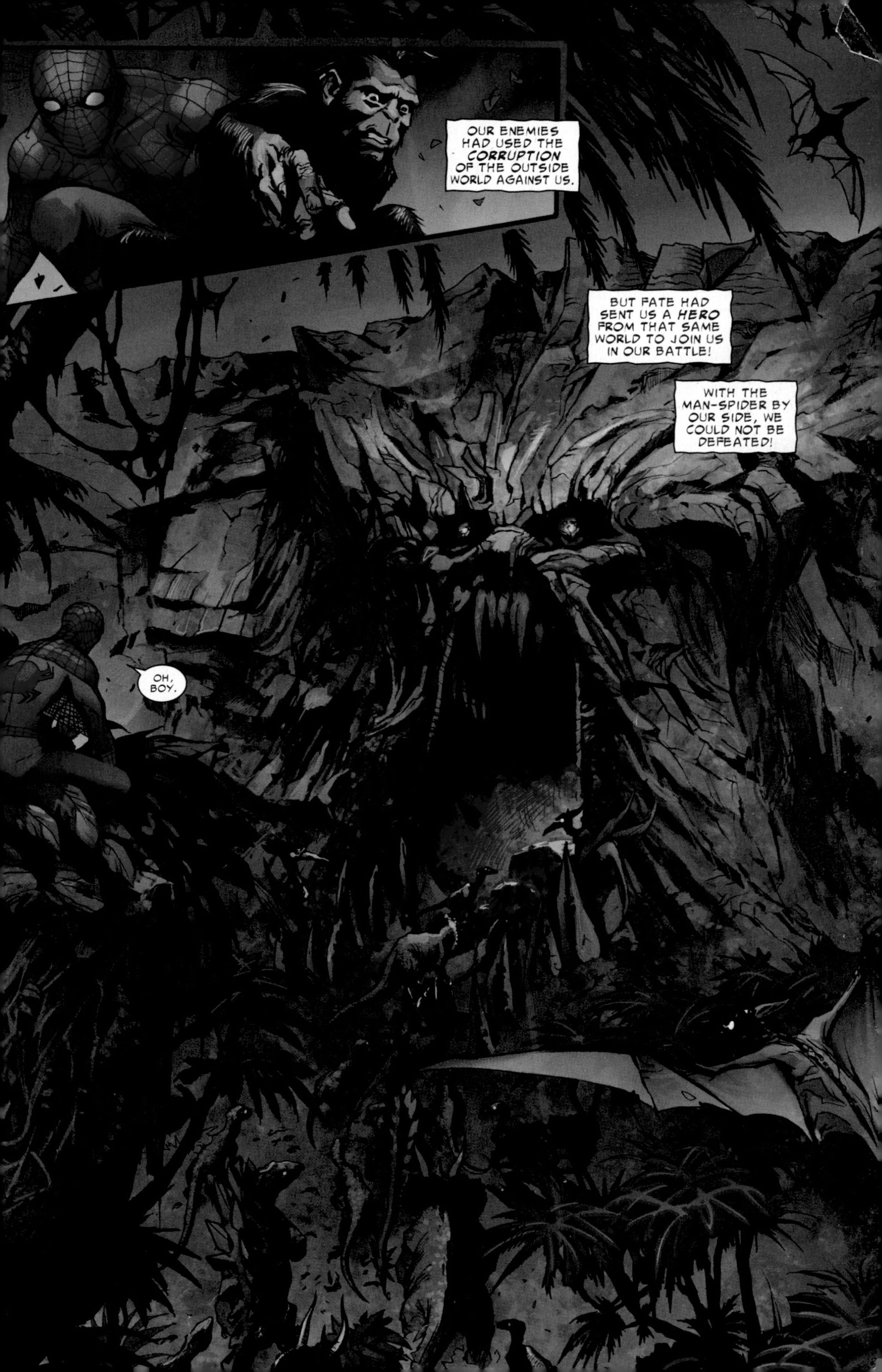
OUR ENEMIES HAD USED THE CORRUPTION OF THE OUTSIDE WORLD AGAINST US.
BUT FATE HAD SENT US A HERO FROM THAT SAME WORLD TO JOIN US IN OUR BATTLE!
WITH THE MAN-SPIDER BY OUR SIDE, WE COULD NOT BE DEFEATED!
OH, BOY.

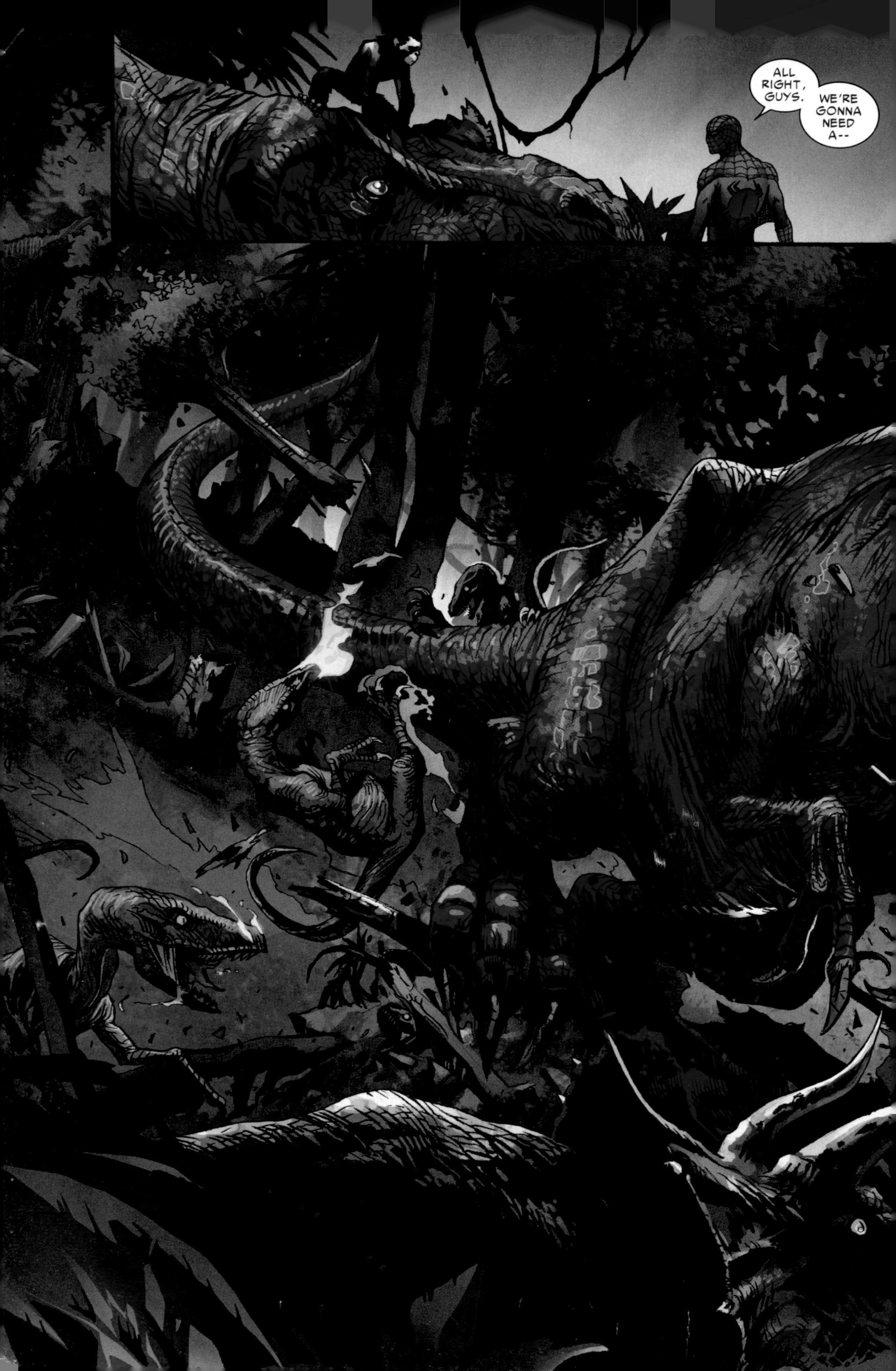
ALL RIGHT, GUYS.
WE'RE GONNA NEED A--

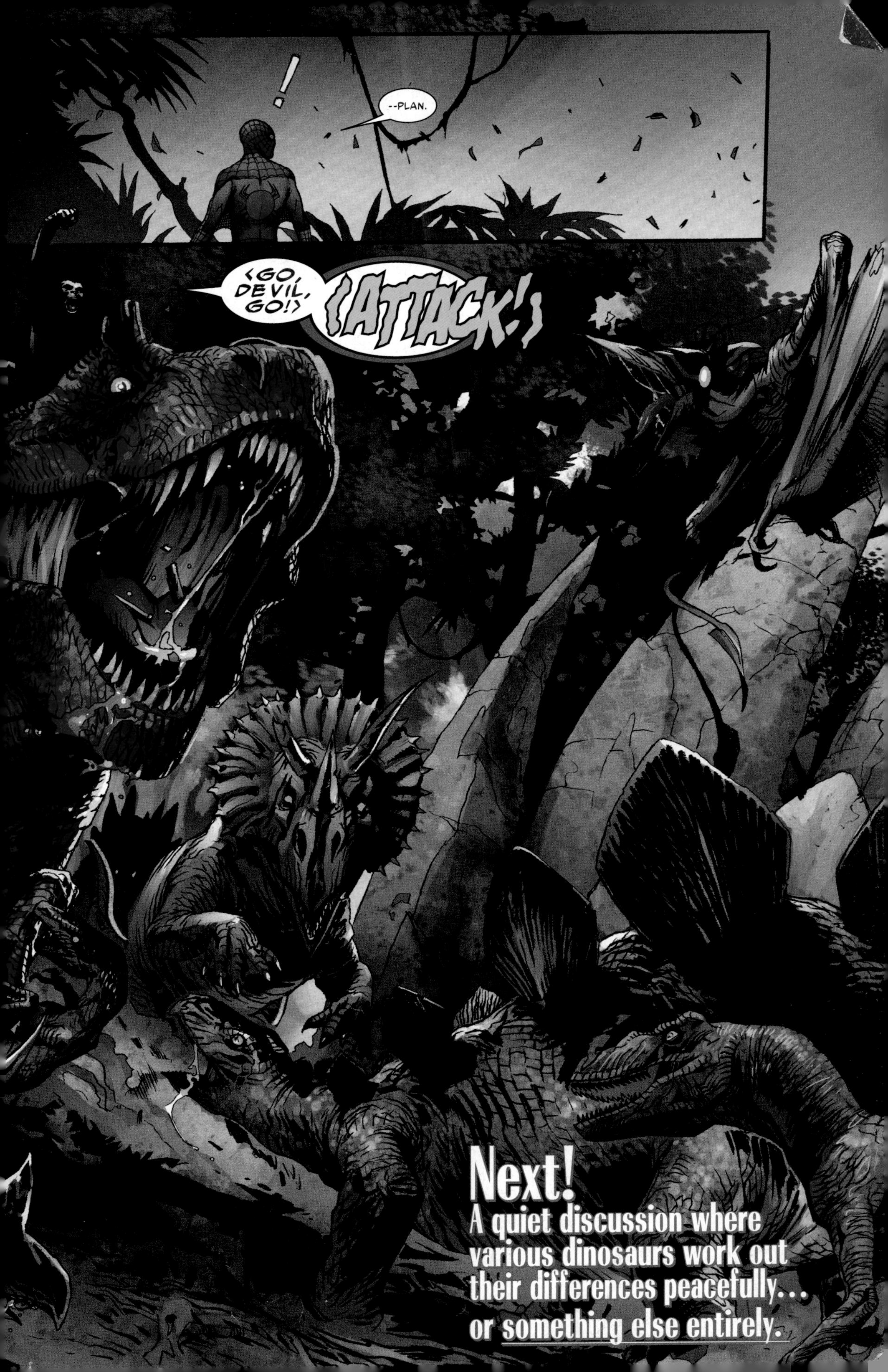
!
--PLAN.
<GO, DEVIL, GO!>
<ATTACK!>
Next!
A quiet discussion where various dinosaurs work out their differences peacefully...
or something else entirely.

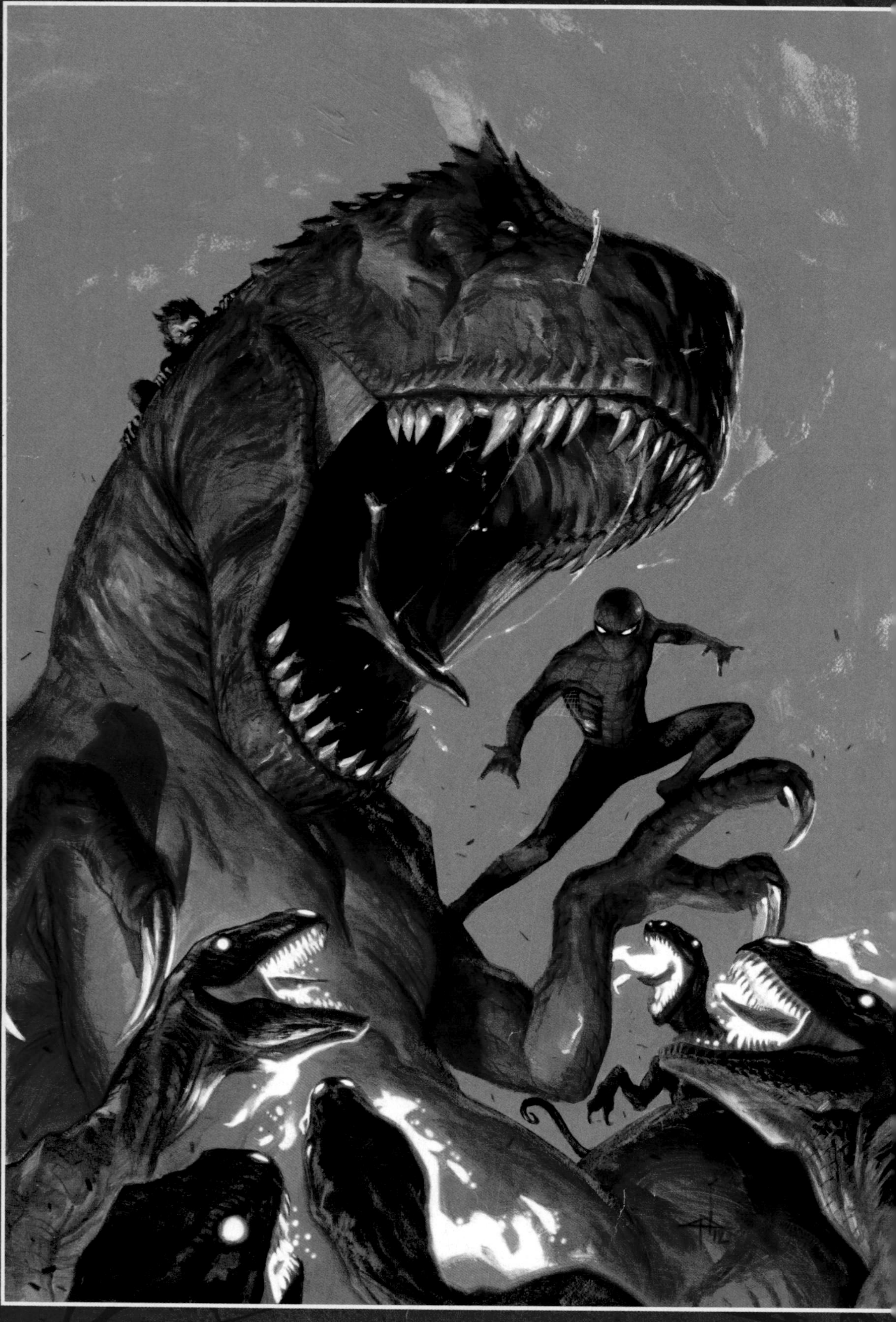

AVENGING SPIDER-MAN #15

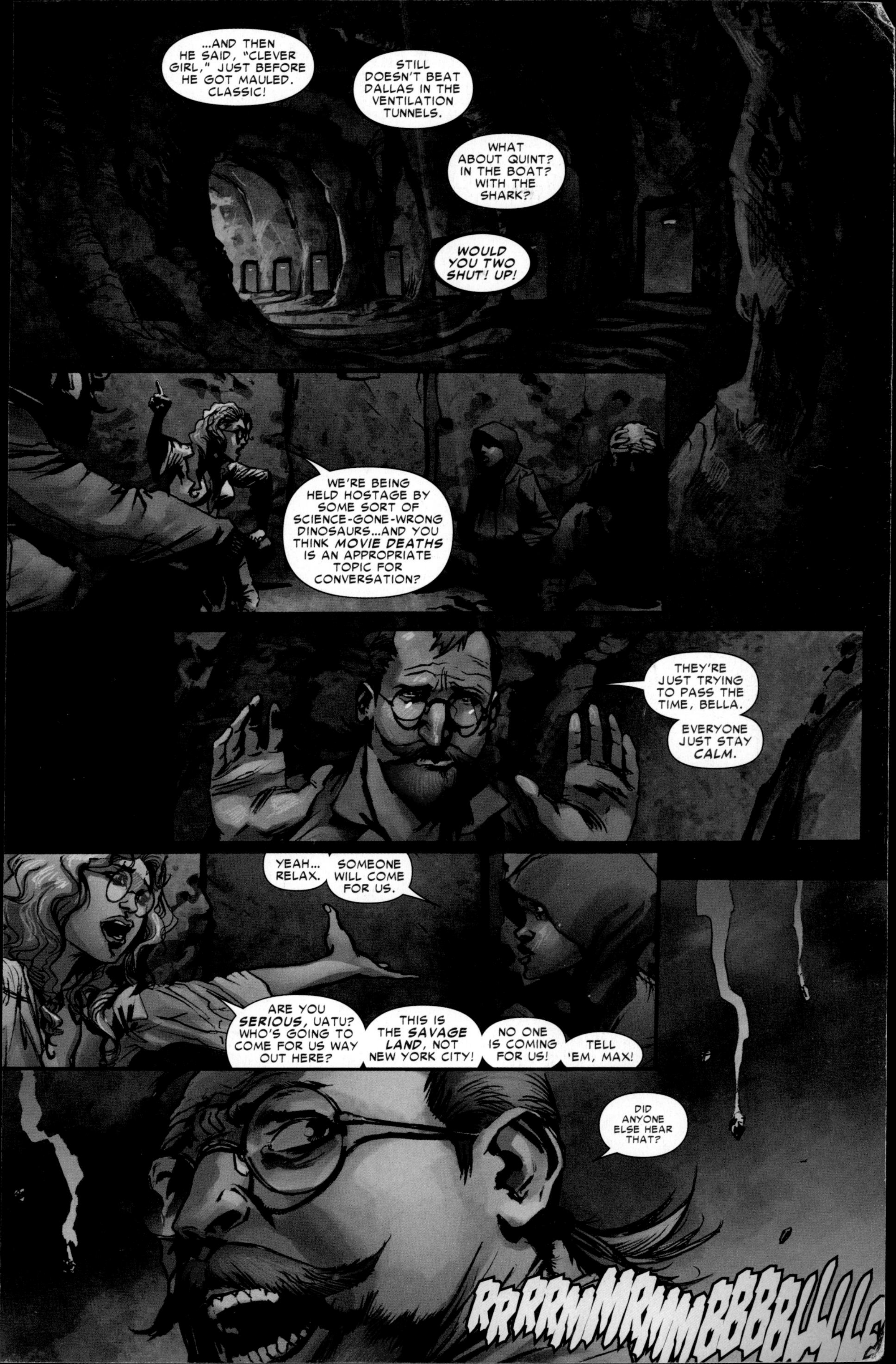
...AND THEN HE SAID, "CLEVER GIRL," JUST BEFORE HE GOT MAULED. CLASSIC!
STILL DOESN'T BEAT DALLAS IN THE VENTILATION TUNNELS.
WHAT ABOUT QUINT? IN THE BOAT? WITH THE SHARK?
WOULD YOU TWO SHUT! UP!
WE'RE BEING HELD HOSTAGE BY SOME SORT OF SCIENCE-GONE-WRONG DINOSAURS...AND YOU THINK MOVIE DEATHS IS AN APPROPRIATE TOPIC FOR CONVERSATION?
THEY'RE JUST TRYING TO PASS THE TIME, BELLA.
EVERYONE JUST STAY CALM.
YEAH... RELAX.
SOMEONE WILL COME FOR US.
ARE YOU SERIOUS, UATU? WHO'S GOING TO COME FOR US WAY OUT HERE?
THIS IS THE SAVAGE LAND, NOT NEW YORK CITY!
NO ONE IS COMING FOR US!
TELL 'EM, MAX!
DID ANYONE ELSE HEAR THAT?
RRRRMMRMMMBBBBLLLL

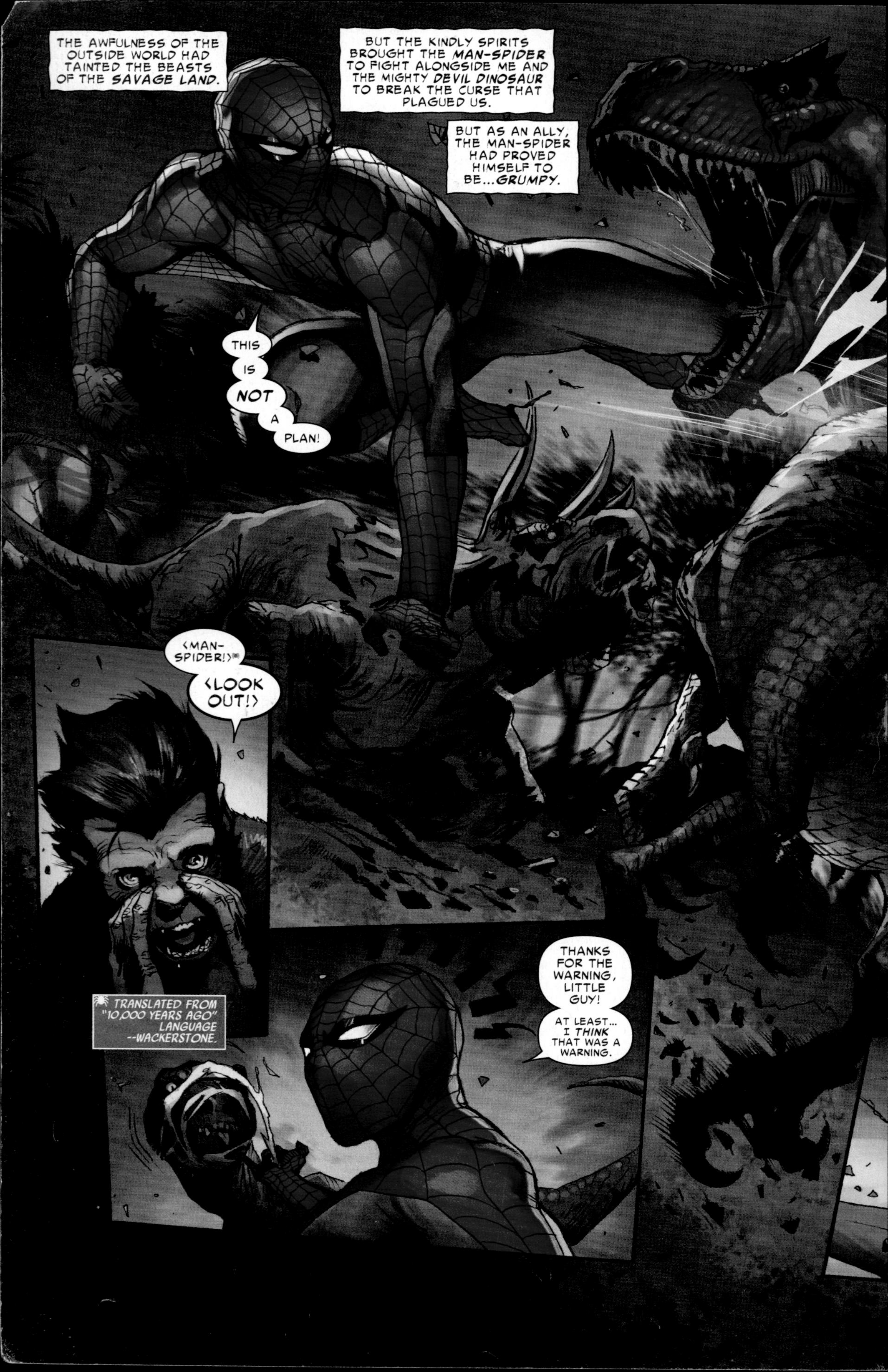
THE AWFULNESS OF THE OUTSIDE WORLD HAD TAINTED THE BEASTS OF THE SAVAGE LAND.
BUT THE KINDLY SPIRITS BROUGHT THE MAN-SPIDER TO FIGHT ALONGSIDE ME AND THE MIGHTY DEVIL DINOSAUR TO BREAK THE CURSE THAT PLAGUED US.
BUT AS AN ALLY, THE MAN-SPIDER HAD PROVED HIMSELF TO BE...GRUMPY.
THIS IS NOT A PLAN!
‹MAN-SPIDER!›
‹LOOK OUT!›
TRANSLATED FROM "10,000 YEARS AGO" LANGUAGE --WACKERSTONE.
THANKS FOR THE WARNING, LITTLE GUY!
AT LEAST... I THINK THAT WAS A WARNING.

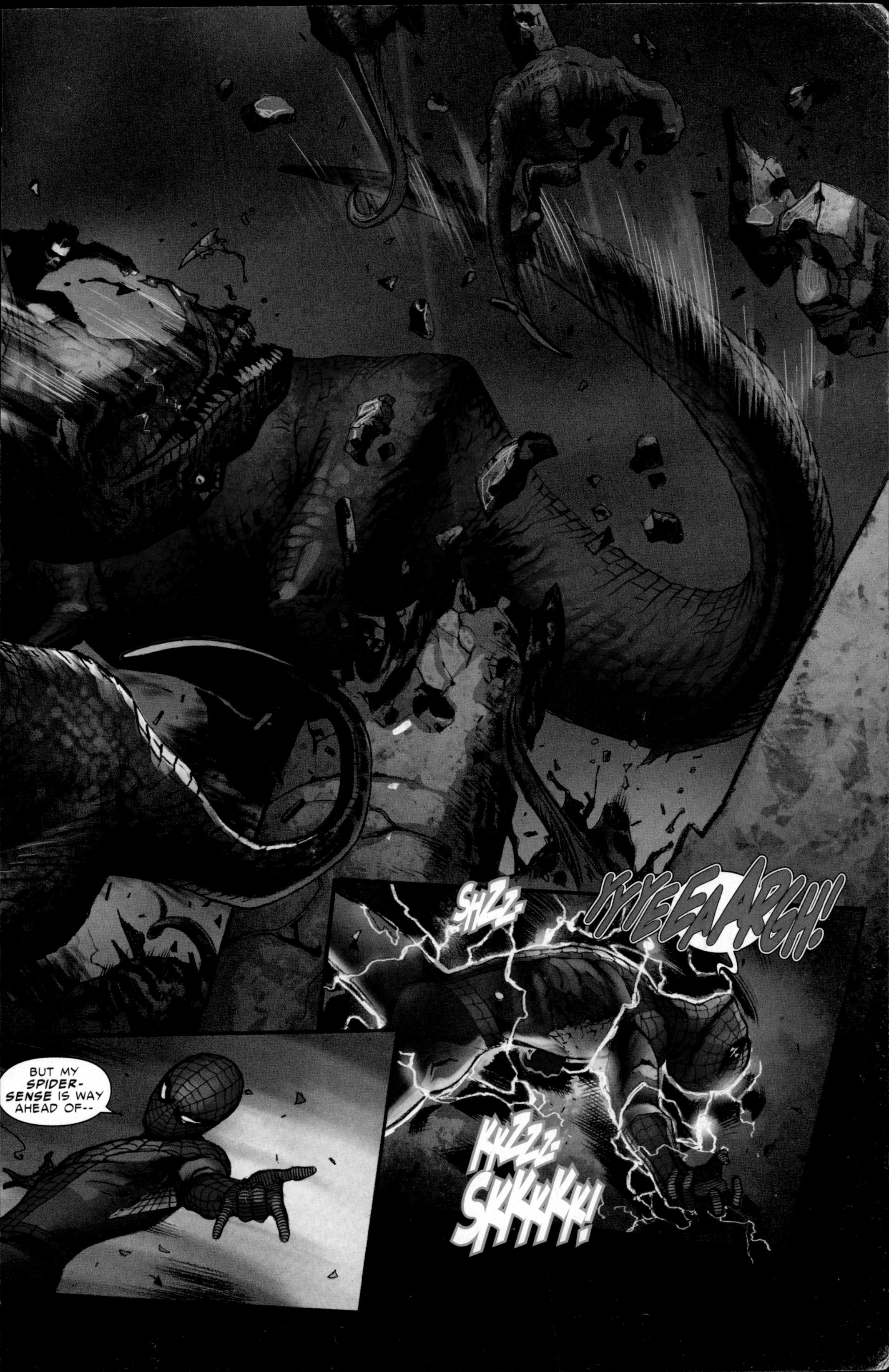
SHZZZ-
YYYYEEAAARGH!
BUT MY SPIDER-SENSE IS WAY AHEAD OF--
KKZZZZ-SKKKKKK!

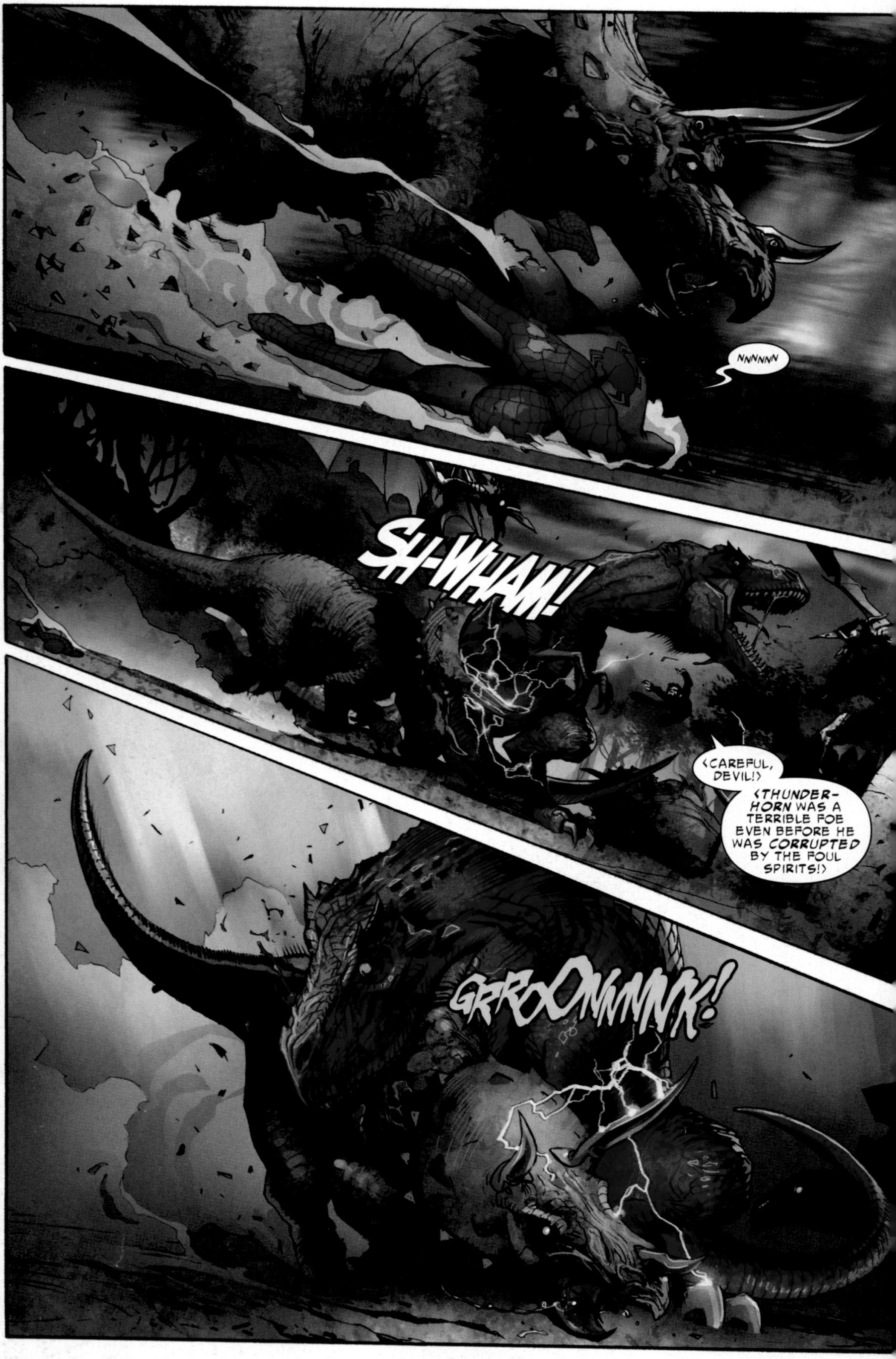
NNNNNN
SH-WHAM!
‹CAREFUL, DEVIL!›
‹THUNDER-HORN WAS A TERRIBLE FOE EVEN BEFORE HE WAS CORRUPTED BY THE FOUL SPIRITS!›
GRROONNNNK!

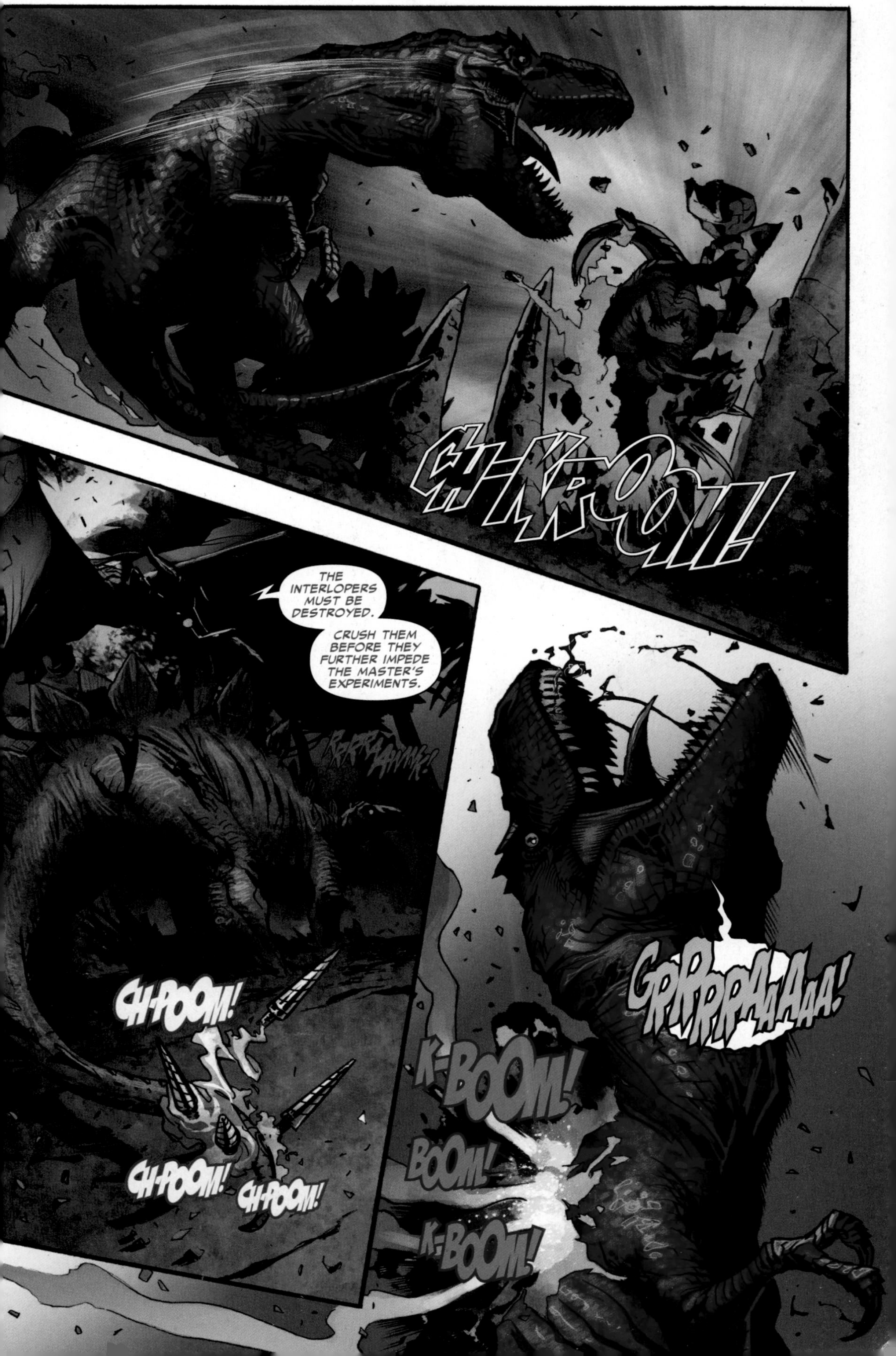
CH-KROOM!
THE INTERLOPERS MUST BE DESTROYED.
CRUSH THEM BEFORE THEY FURTHER IMPEDE THE MASTER'S EXPERIMENTS.
CH-POOM!
CH-POOM!
CH-POOM!
GRRRRAAAAA!
K-BOOM!
BOOM!
K-BOOM!

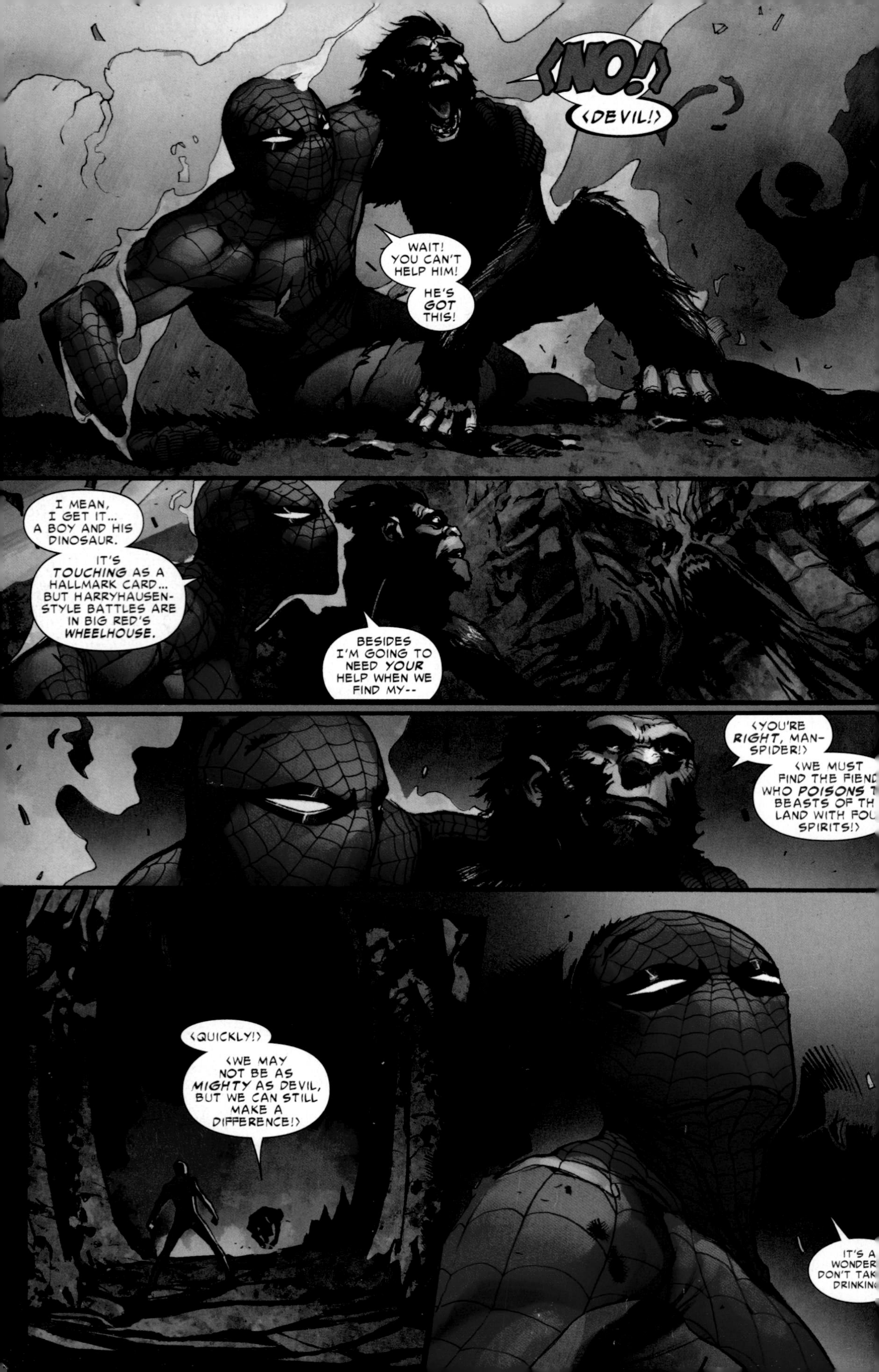

‹NO!›
‹DEVIL!›
WAIT! YOU CAN'T HELP HIM!
HE'S GOT THIS!
I MEAN, I GET IT... A BOY AND HIS DINOSAUR.
IT'S TOUCHING AS A HALLMARK CARD... BUT HARRYHAUSEN-STYLE BATTLES ARE IN BIG RED'S WHEELHOUSE.
BESIDES I'M GOING TO NEED YOUR HELP WHEN WE FIND MY--
‹YOU'RE RIGHT, MAN-SPIDER!›
‹WE MUST FIND THE FIEND WHO POISONS T BEASTS OF TH LAND WITH FOU SPIRITS!›
‹QUICKLY!›
‹WE MAY NOT BE AS MIGHTY AS DEVIL, BUT WE CAN STILL MAKE A DIFFERENCE!›
IT'S A WONDER DON'T TAK DRINKIN

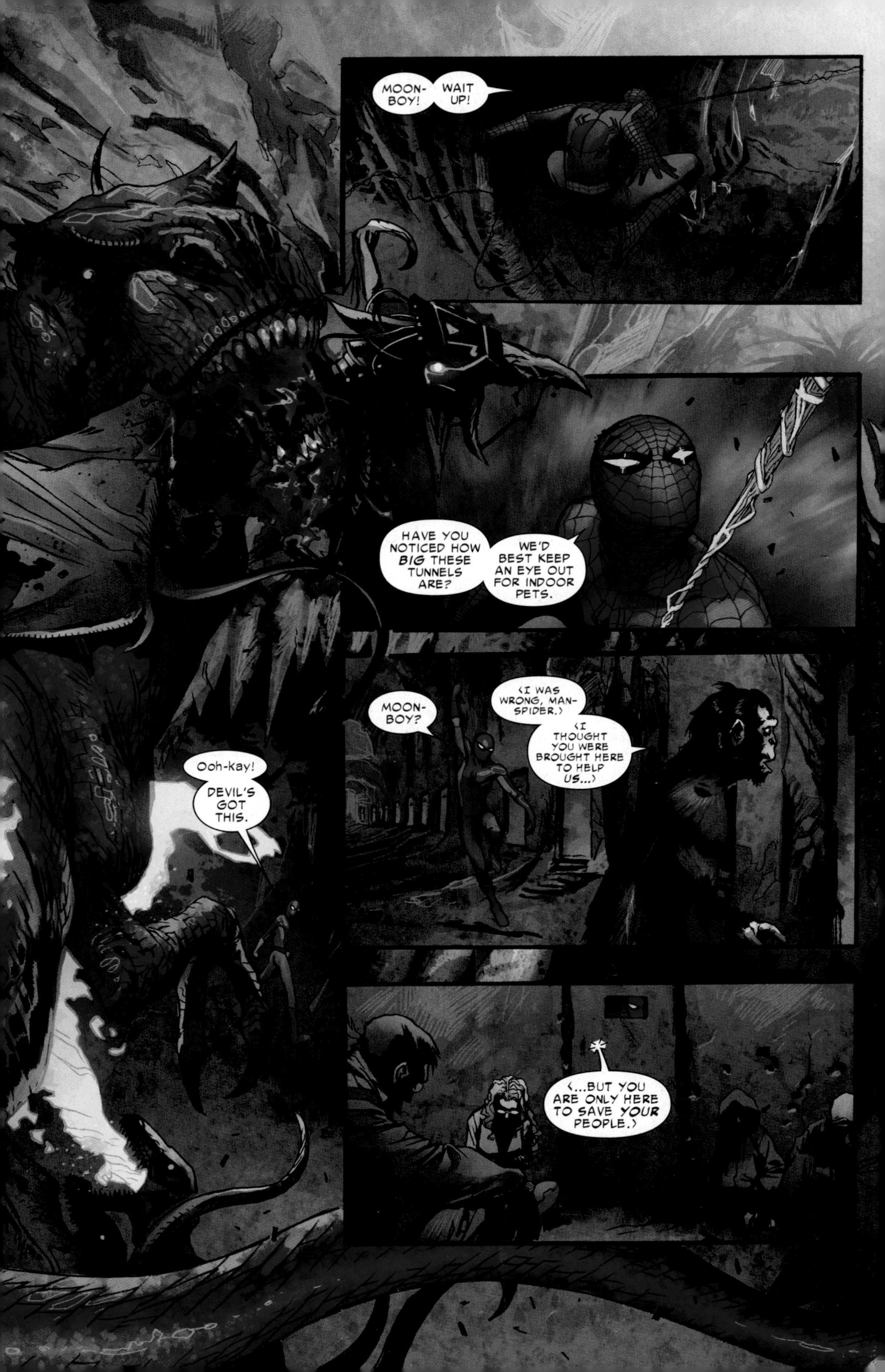
MOON-BOY!
WAIT UP!
HAVE YOU NOTICED HOW *BIG* THESE TUNNELS ARE?
WE'D BEST KEEP AN EYE OUT FOR INDOOR PETS.
MOON-BOY?
‹I WAS WRONG, MAN-SPIDER.›
‹I THOUGHT YOU WERE BROUGHT HERE TO HELP *US*...›
‹...BUT YOU ARE ONLY HERE TO SAVE *YOUR* PEOPLE.›
Ooh-kay!
DEVIL'S GOT THIS.

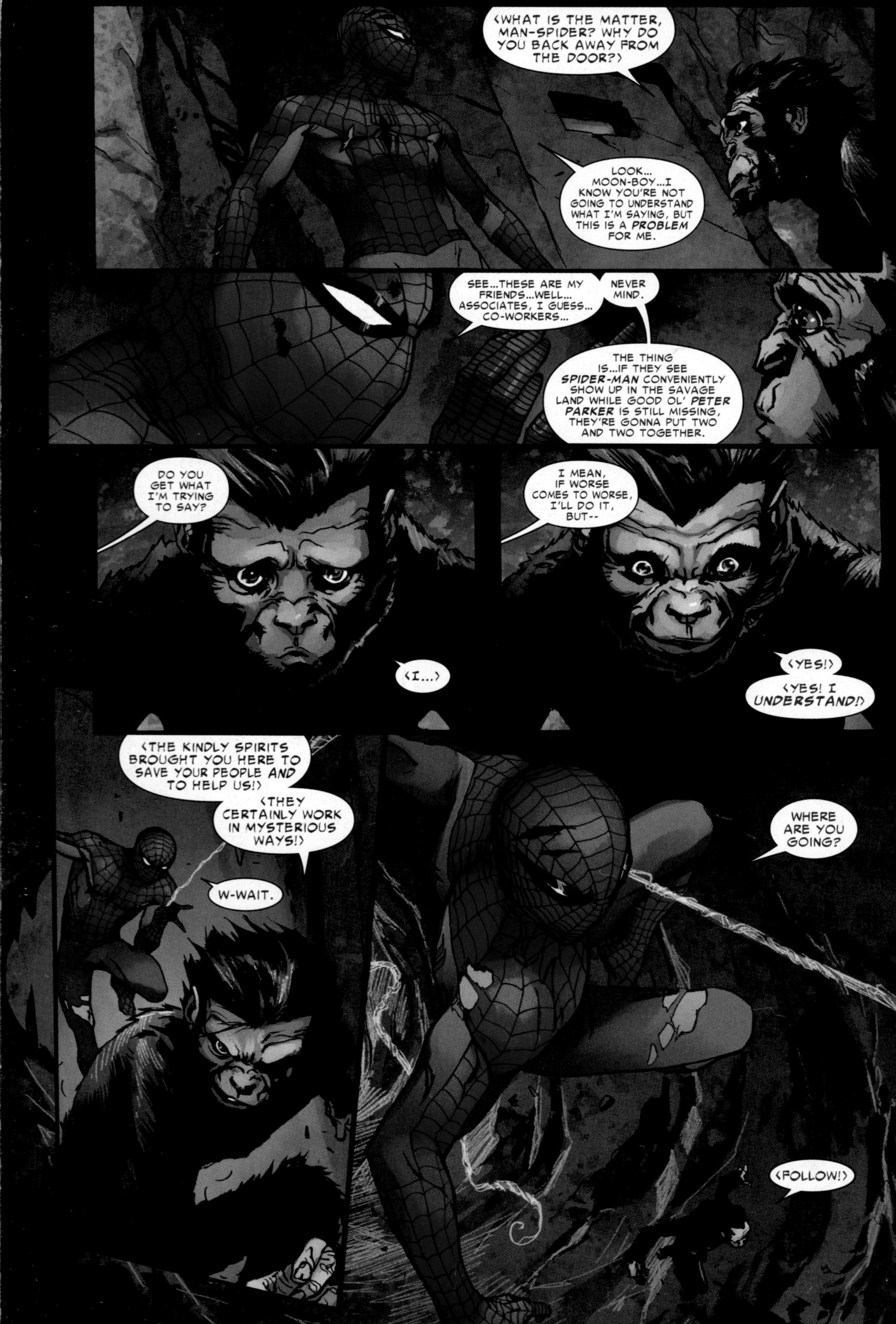

‹WHAT IS THE MATTER, MAN-SPIDER? WHY DO YOU BACK AWAY FROM THE DOOR?›
LOOK... MOON-BOY...I KNOW YOU'RE NOT GOING TO UNDERSTAND WHAT I'M SAYING, BUT THIS IS A *PROBLEM* FOR ME.
SEE...THESE ARE MY FRIENDS...WELL... ASSOCIATES, I GUESS... CO-WORKERS...
NEVER MIND.
THE THING IS...IF THEY SEE *SPIDER-MAN* CONVENIENTLY SHOW UP IN THE SAVAGE LAND WHILE GOOD OL' *PETER PARKER* IS STILL MISSING, THEY'RE GONNA PUT TWO AND TWO TOGETHER.
DO YOU GET WHAT I'M TRYING TO SAY?
I MEAN, IF WORSE COMES TO WORSE, I'LL DO IT, BUT--
‹I...›
‹YES!›
‹YES! I *UNDERSTAND!*›
‹THE KINDLY SPIRITS BROUGHT YOU HERE TO SAVE YOUR PEOPLE *AND* TO HELP US!›
‹THEY CERTAINLY WORK IN MYSTERIOUS WAYS!›
W-WAIT.
WHERE ARE YOU GOING?
‹FOLLOW!›

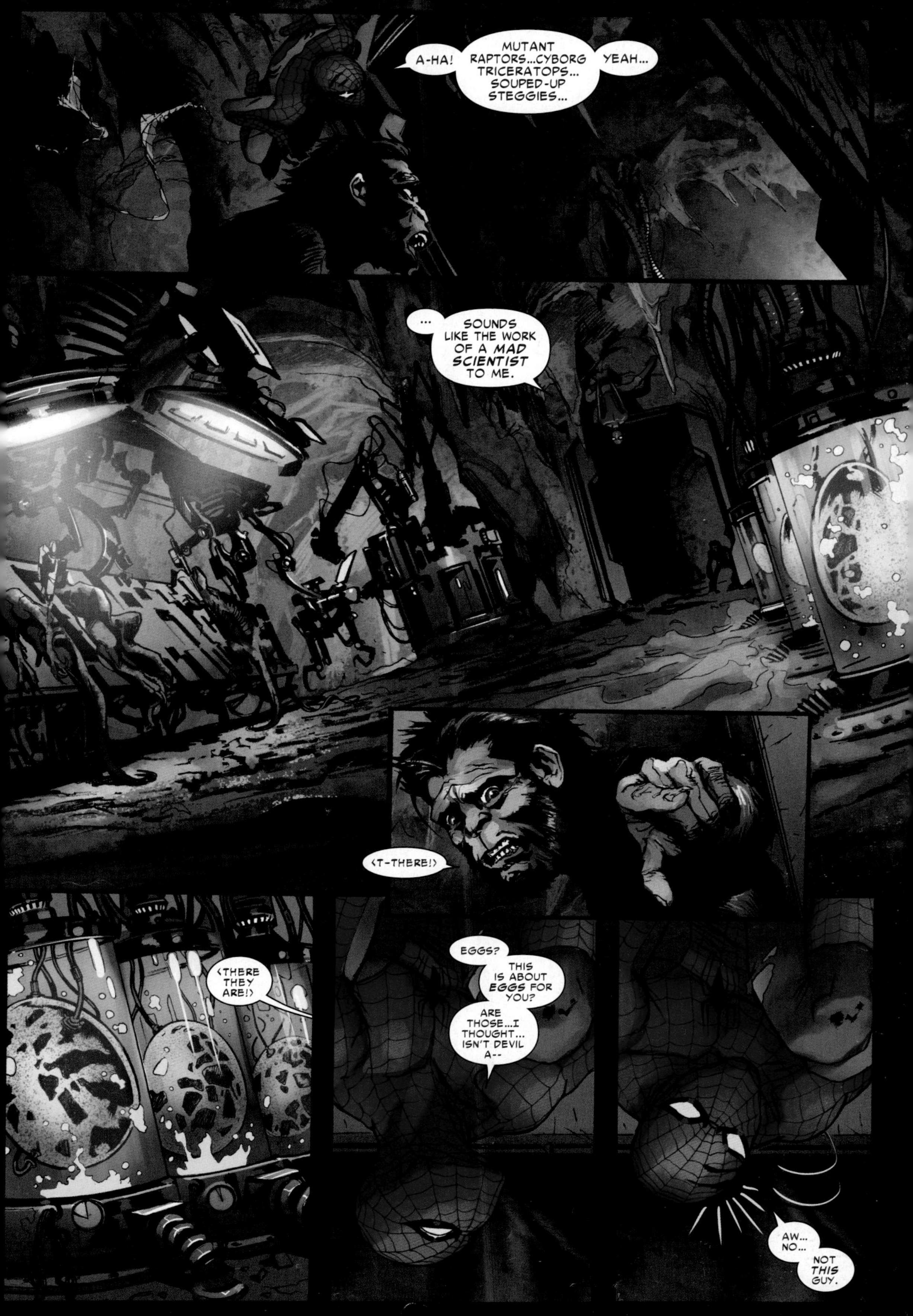
A-HA!
MUTANT RAPTORS...CYBORG TRICERATOPS... SOUPED-UP STEGGIES...
YEAH...
...
SOUNDS LIKE THE WORK OF A *MAD SCIENTIST* TO ME.
‹T-THERE!›
‹THERE THEY ARE!›
EGGS?
THIS IS ABOUT *EGGS* FOR YOU?
ARE THOSE...I THOUGHT... ISN'T DEVIL A--
AW... NO...
NOT *THIS* GUY.

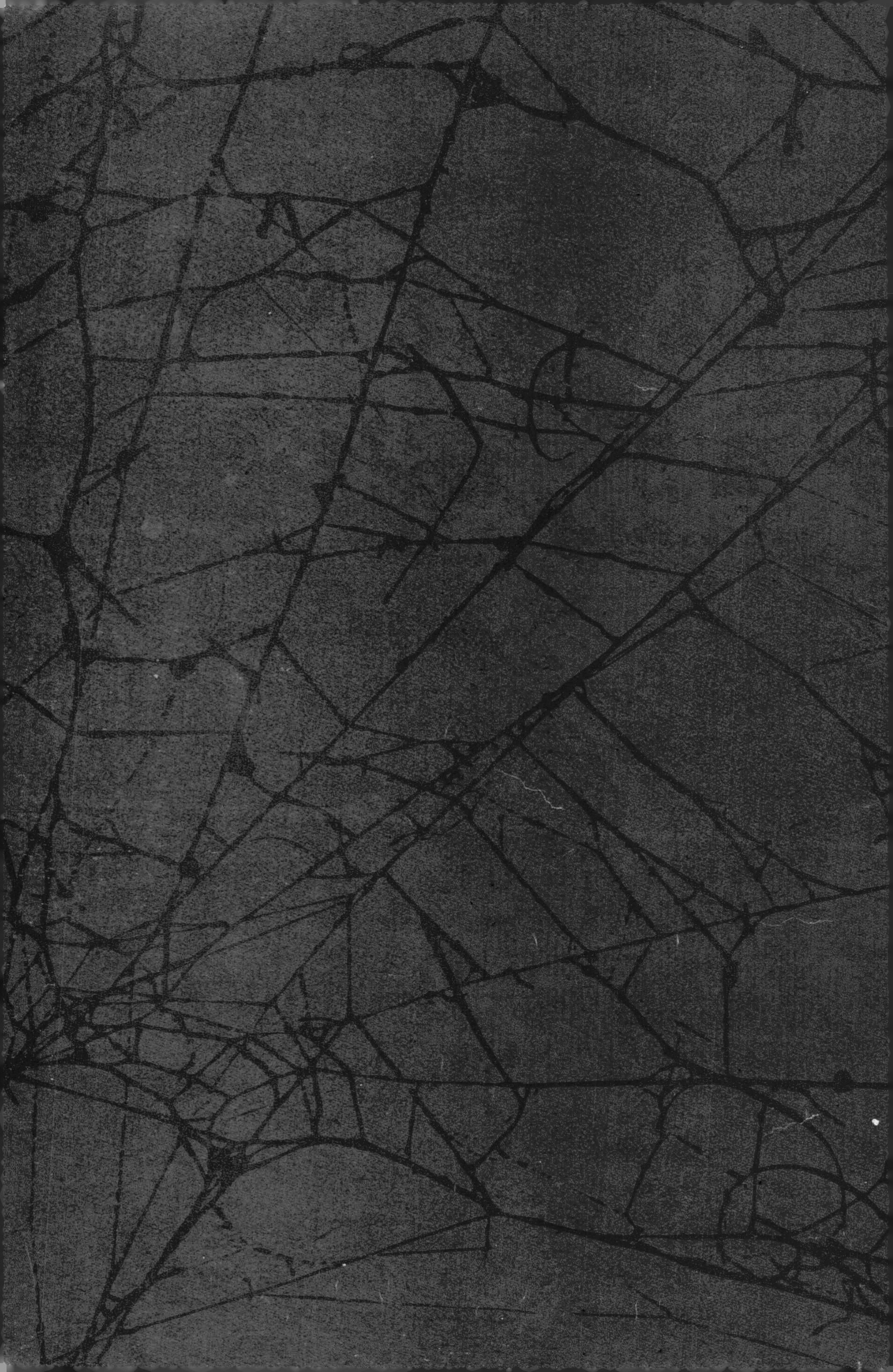

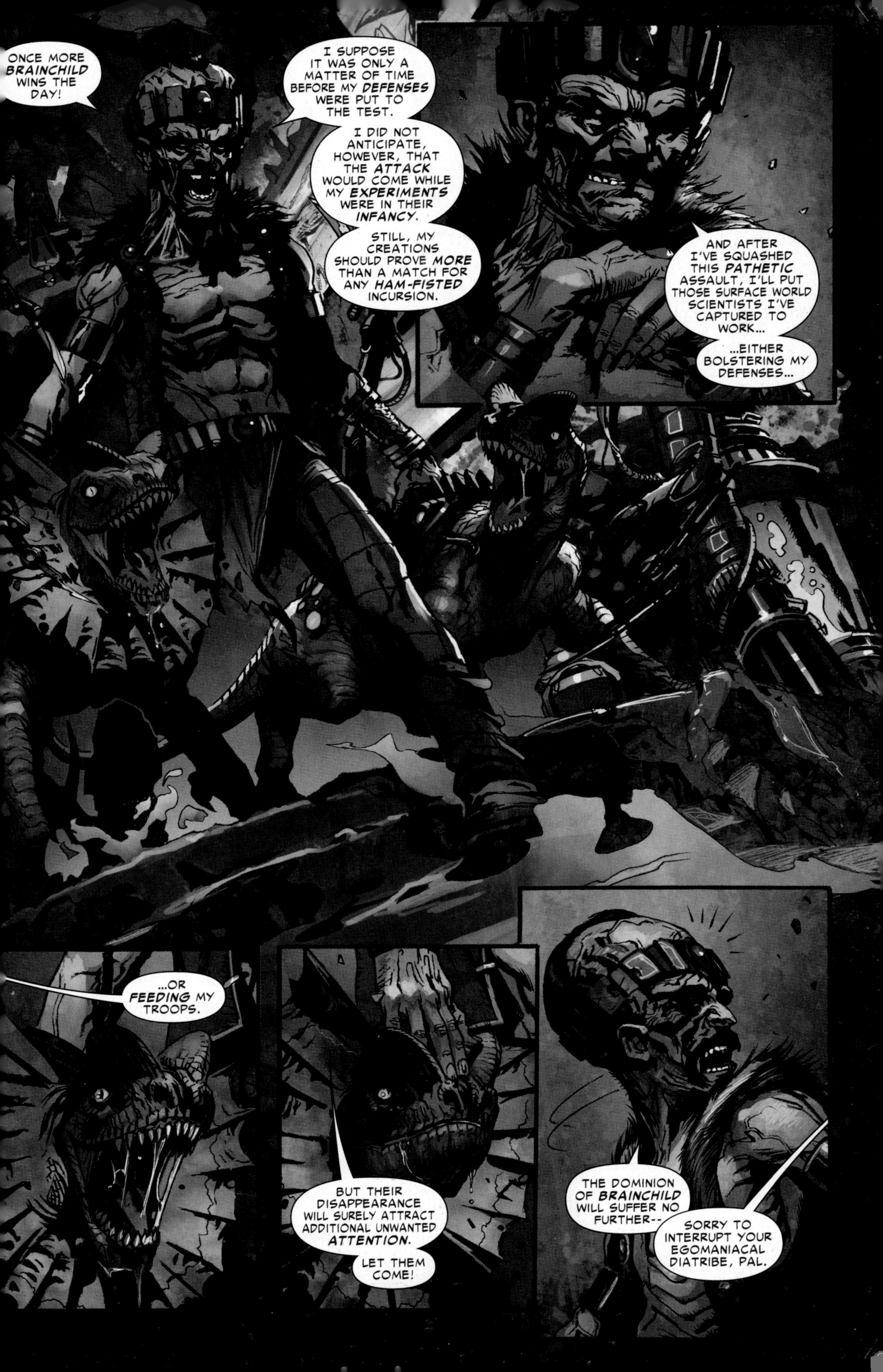
ONCE MORE BRAINCHILD WINS THE DAY!
I SUPPOSE IT WAS ONLY A MATTER OF TIME BEFORE MY DEFENSES WERE PUT TO THE TEST.
I DID NOT ANTICIPATE, HOWEVER, THAT THE ATTACK WOULD COME WHILE MY EXPERIMENTS WERE IN THEIR INFANCY.
STILL, MY CREATIONS SHOULD PROVE MORE THAN A MATCH FOR ANY HAM-FISTED INCURSION.
AND AFTER I'VE SQUASHED THIS PATHETIC ASSAULT, I'LL PUT THOSE SURFACE WORLD SCIENTISTS I'VE CAPTURED TO WORK...
...EITHER BOLSTERING MY DEFENSES...
...OR FEEDING MY TROOPS.
BUT THEIR DISAPPEARANCE WILL SURELY ATTRACT ADDITIONAL UNWANTED ATTENTION.
LET THEM COME!
THE DOMINION OF BRAINCHILD WILL SUFFER NO FURTHER--
SORRY TO INTERRUPT YOUR EGOMANIACAL DIATRIBE, PAL.

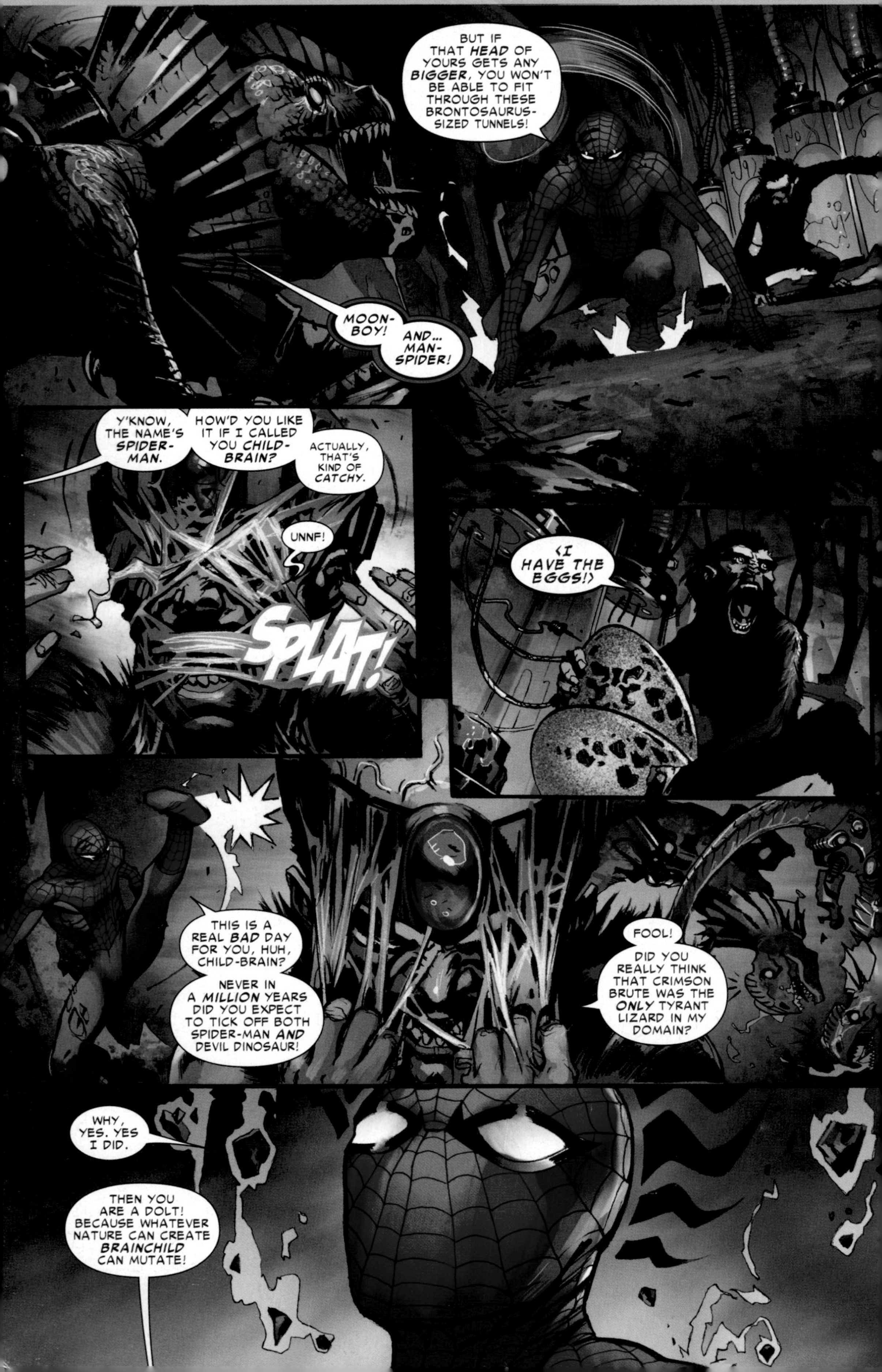
BUT IF THAT HEAD OF YOURS GETS ANY BIGGER, YOU WON'T BE ABLE TO FIT THROUGH THESE BRONTOSAURUS-SIZED TUNNELS!
MOON-BOY!
AND... MAN-SPIDER!
Y'KNOW, THE NAME'S SPIDER-MAN.
HOW'D YOU LIKE IT IF I CALLED YOU CHILD-BRAIN?
ACTUALLY, THAT'S KIND OF CATCHY.
UNNF!
SPLAT!
‹I HAVE THE EGGS!›
THIS IS A REAL BAD DAY FOR YOU, HUH, CHILD-BRAIN?
NEVER IN A MILLION YEARS DID YOU EXPECT TO TICK OFF BOTH SPIDER-MAN AND DEVIL DINOSAUR!
FOOL!
DID YOU REALLY THINK THAT CRIMSON BRUTE WAS THE ONLY TYRANT LIZARD IN MY DOMAIN?
WHY, YES. YES I DID.
THEN YOU ARE A DOLT! BECAUSE WHATEVER NATURE CAN CREATE BRAINCHILD CAN MUTATE!

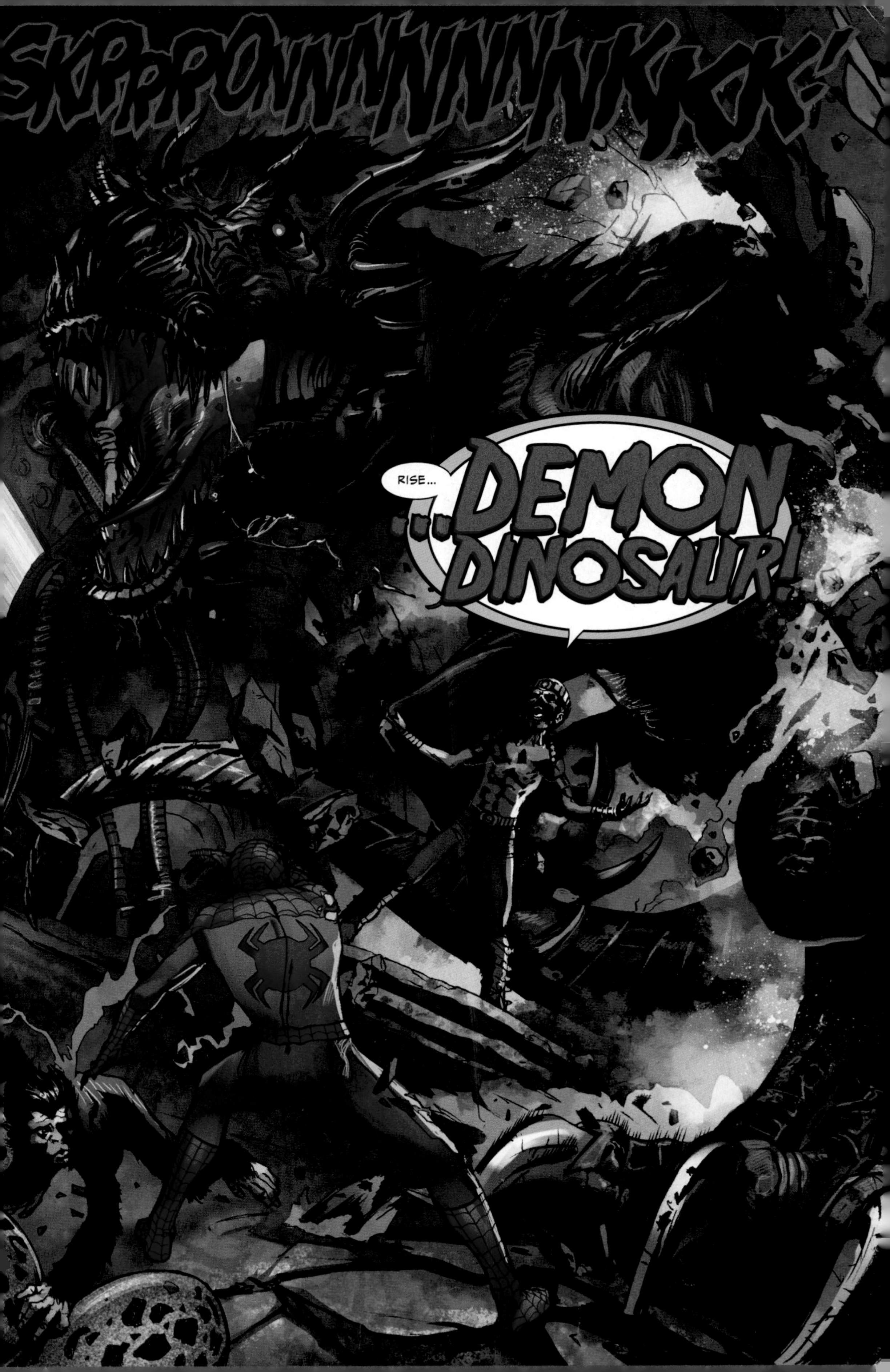
SKRRRONNNNNNNKKK!
RISE... ...DEMON DINOSAUR!

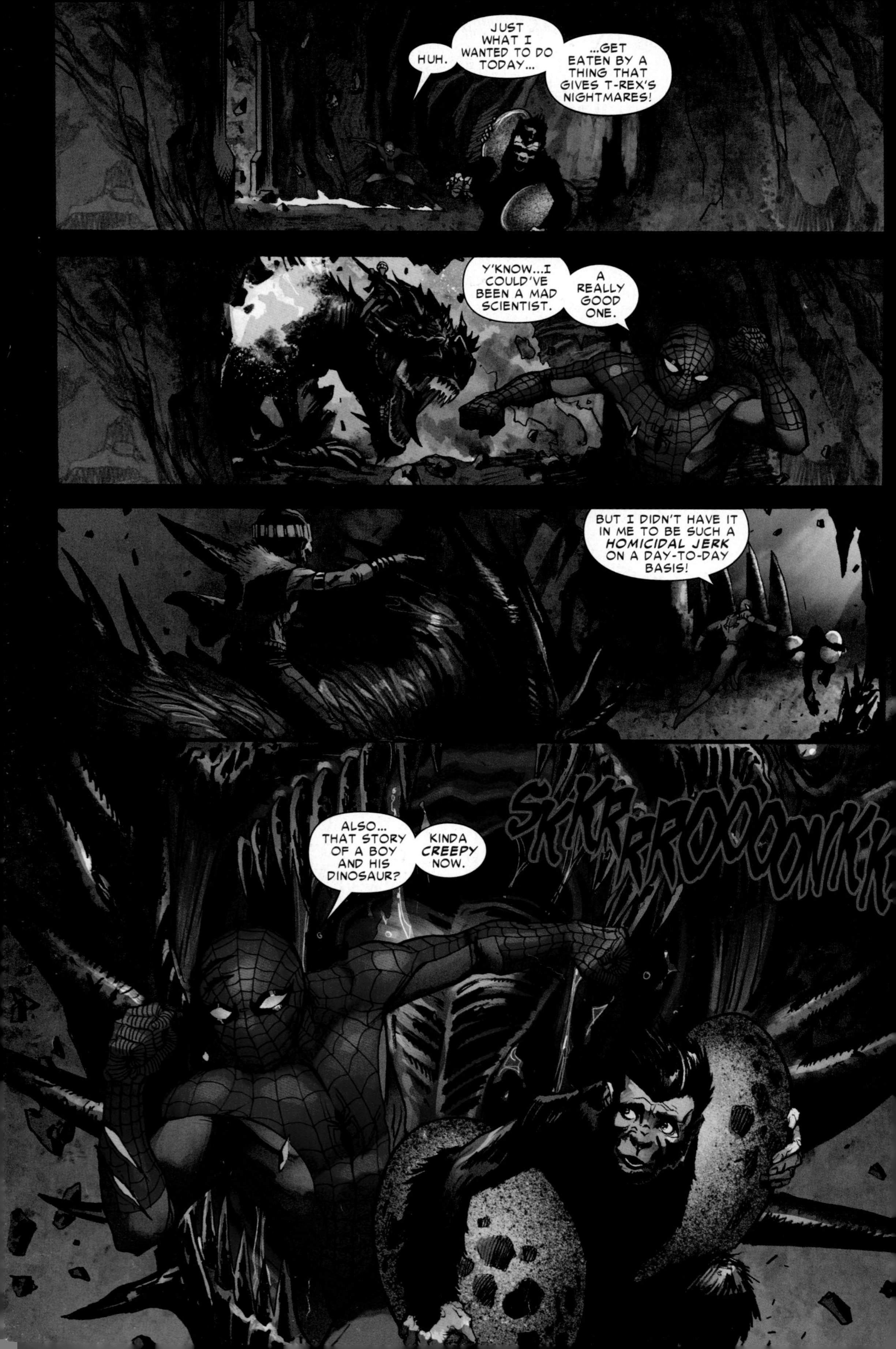
HUH.
JUST WHAT I WANTED TO DO TODAY...
...GET EATEN BY A THING THAT GIVES T-REX'S NIGHTMARES!
Y'KNOW...I COULD'VE BEEN A MAD SCIENTIST.
A REALLY GOOD ONE.
BUT I DIDN'T HAVE IT IN ME TO BE SUCH A HOMICIDAL JERK ON A DAY-TO-DAY BASIS!
SKRRROOOONKK
ALSO... THAT STORY OF A BOY AND HIS DINOSAUR?
KINDA CREEPY NOW.

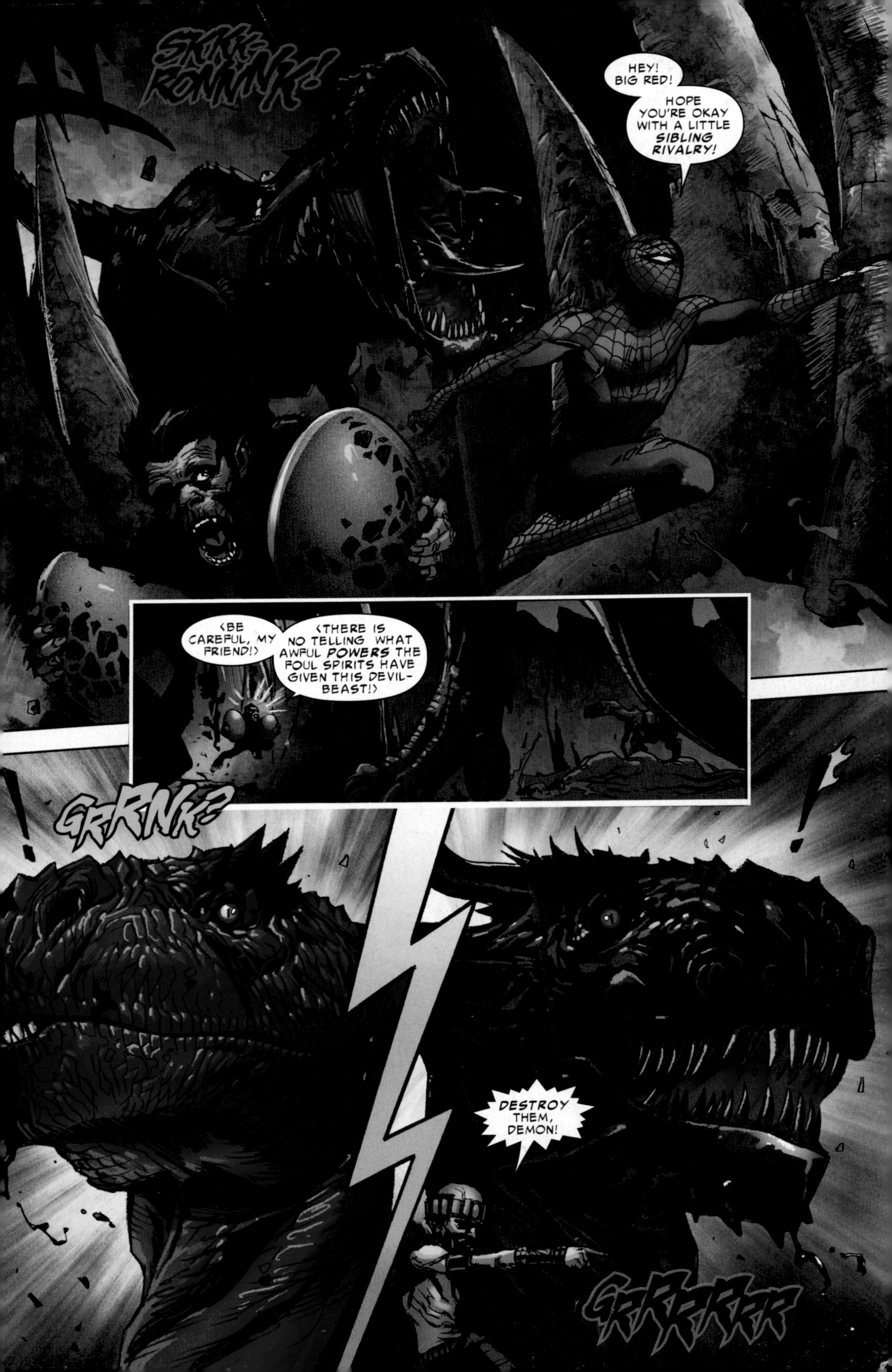
SKRRK-RONNNK!
HEY! BIG RED!
HOPE YOU'RE OKAY WITH A LITTLE SIBLING RIVALRY!
‹BE CAREFUL, MY FRIEND!›
‹THERE IS NO TELLING WHAT AWFUL POWERS THE FOUL SPIRITS HAVE GIVEN THIS DEVIL-BEAST!›
GRRNK?
DESTROY THEM, DEMON!
GRRRRRR

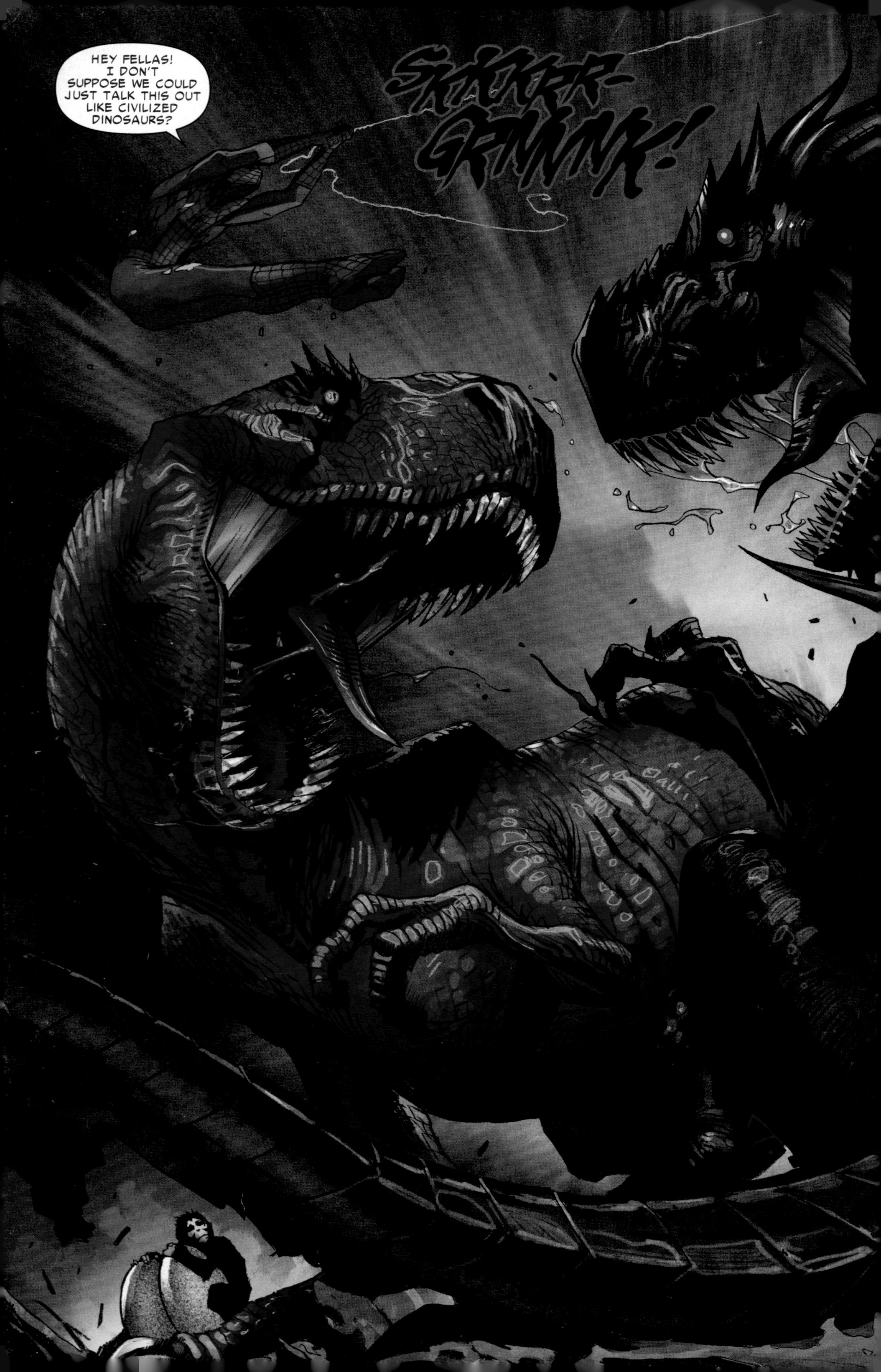
HEY FELLAS! I DON'T SUPPOSE WE COULD JUST TALK THIS OUT LIKE CIVILIZED DINOSAURS?
SKRKRR-GRNNNK!

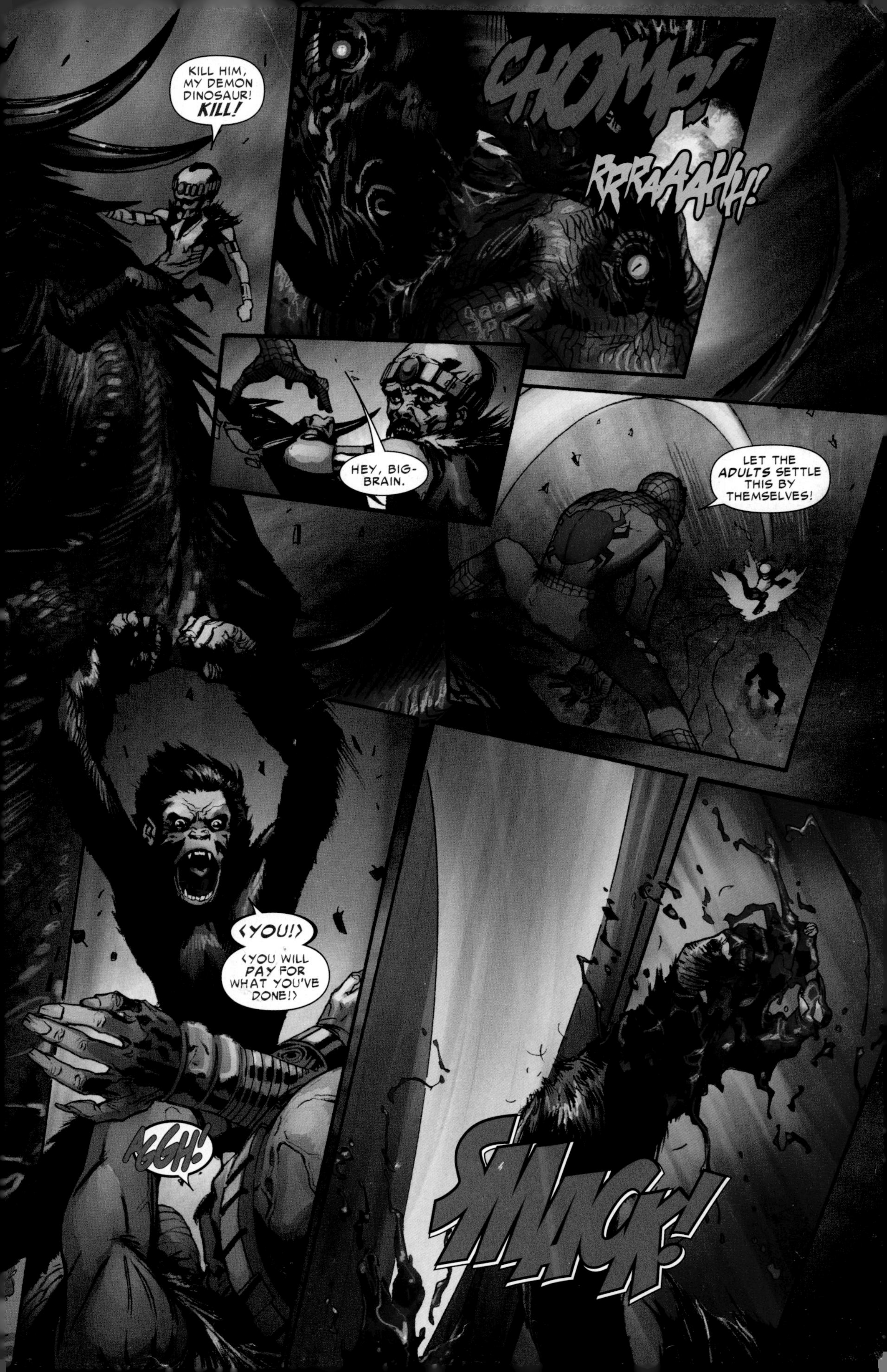
KILL HIM, MY DEMON DINOSAUR! **KILL!**
CHOMP!
RRRAAAHH!
HEY, BIG-BRAIN.
LET THE **ADULTS** SETTLE THIS BY THEMSELVES!
‹YOU!›
‹YOU WILL **PAY** FOR WHAT YOU'VE DONE!›
AGGH!
SMACK!

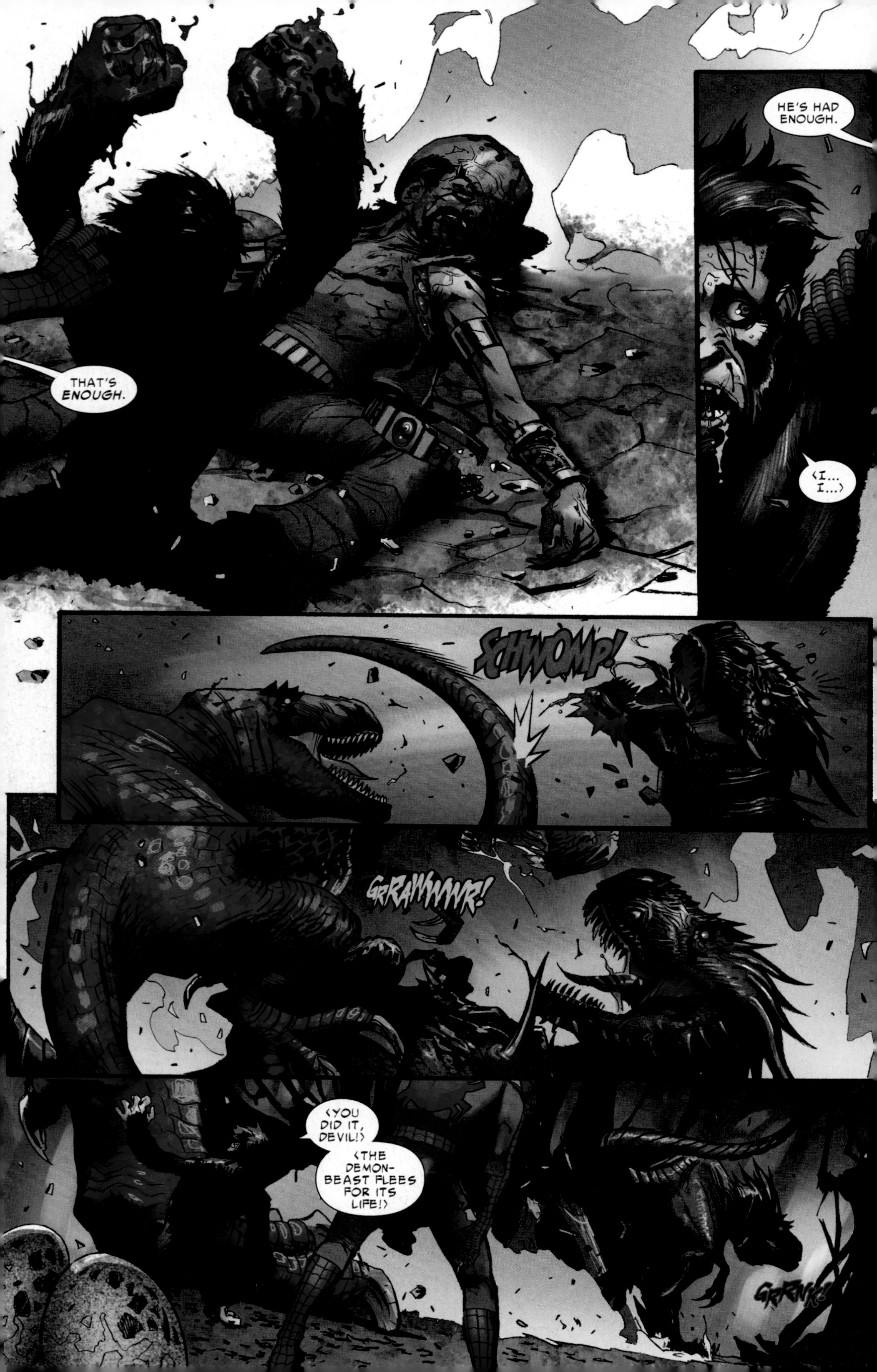
HE'S HAD ENOUGH.
THAT'S ENOUGH.
‹I... I...›
SCHWOMP!
GRRAWWWR!
‹YOU DID IT, DEVIL!›
‹THE DEMON-BEAST FLEES FOR ITS LIFE!›
GRRNK!

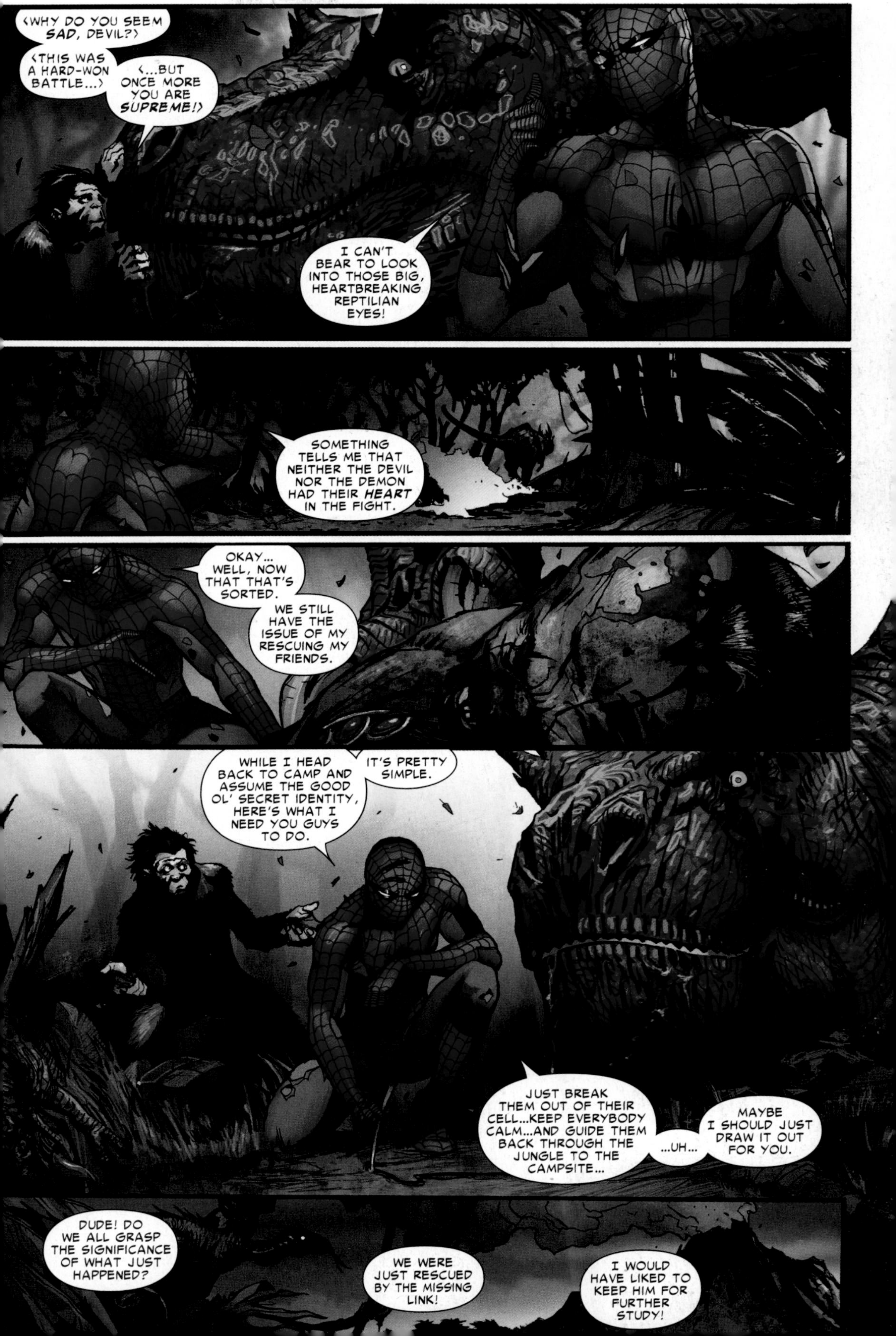
‹WHY DO YOU SEEM SAD, DEVIL?›
‹THIS WAS A HARD-WON BATTLE...›
‹...BUT ONCE MORE YOU ARE SUPREME!›
I CAN'T BEAR TO LOOK INTO THOSE BIG, HEARTBREAKING REPTILIAN EYES!
SOMETHING TELLS ME THAT NEITHER THE DEVIL NOR THE DEMON HAD THEIR HEART IN THE FIGHT.
OKAY... WELL, NOW THAT THAT'S SORTED.
WE STILL HAVE THE ISSUE OF MY RESCUING MY FRIENDS.
IT'S PRETTY SIMPLE.
WHILE I HEAD BACK TO CAMP AND ASSUME THE GOOD OL' SECRET IDENTITY, HERE'S WHAT I NEED YOU GUYS TO DO.
JUST BREAK THEM OUT OF THEIR CELL...KEEP EVERYBODY CALM...AND GUIDE THEM BACK THROUGH THE JUNGLE TO THE CAMPSITE...
...UH...
MAYBE I SHOULD JUST DRAW IT OUT FOR YOU.
DUDE! DO WE ALL GRASP THE SIGNIFICANCE OF WHAT JUST HAPPENED?
WE WERE JUST RESCUED BY THE MISSING LINK!
I WOULD HAVE LIKED TO KEEP HIM FOR FURTHER STUDY!

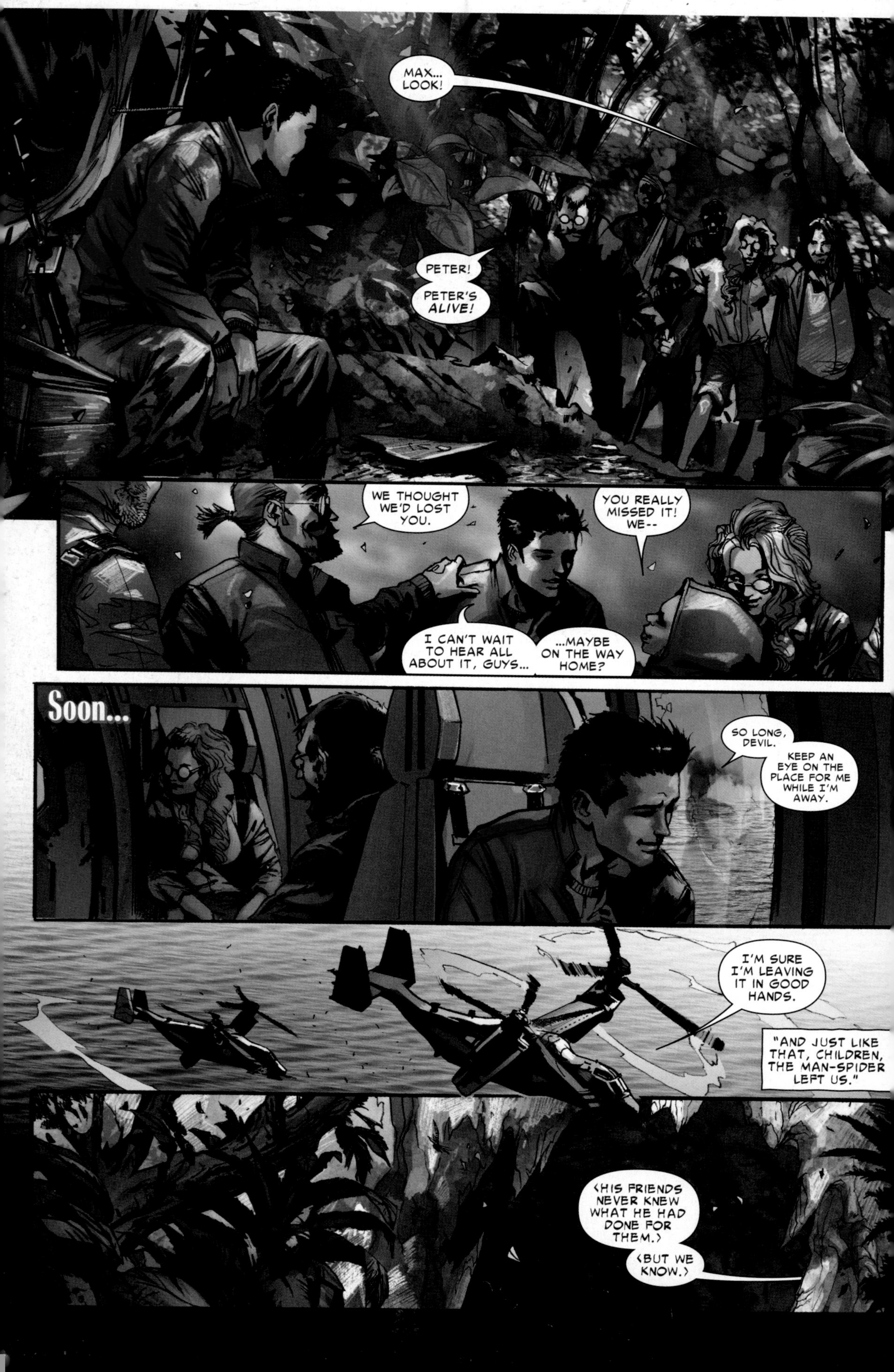

MAX... LOOK!
PETER!
PETER'S ALIVE!
WE THOUGHT WE'D LOST YOU.
YOU REALLY MISSED IT! WE--
I CAN'T WAIT TO HEAR ALL ABOUT IT, GUYS...
...MAYBE ON THE WAY HOME?
Soon...
SO LONG, DEVIL.
KEEP AN EYE ON THE PLACE FOR ME WHILE I'M AWAY.
I'M SURE I'M LEAVING IT IN GOOD HANDS.
"AND JUST LIKE THAT, CHILDREN, THE MAN-SPIDER LEFT US."
‹HIS FRIENDS NEVER KNEW WHAT HE HAD DONE FOR THEM.›
‹BUT WE KNOW.›

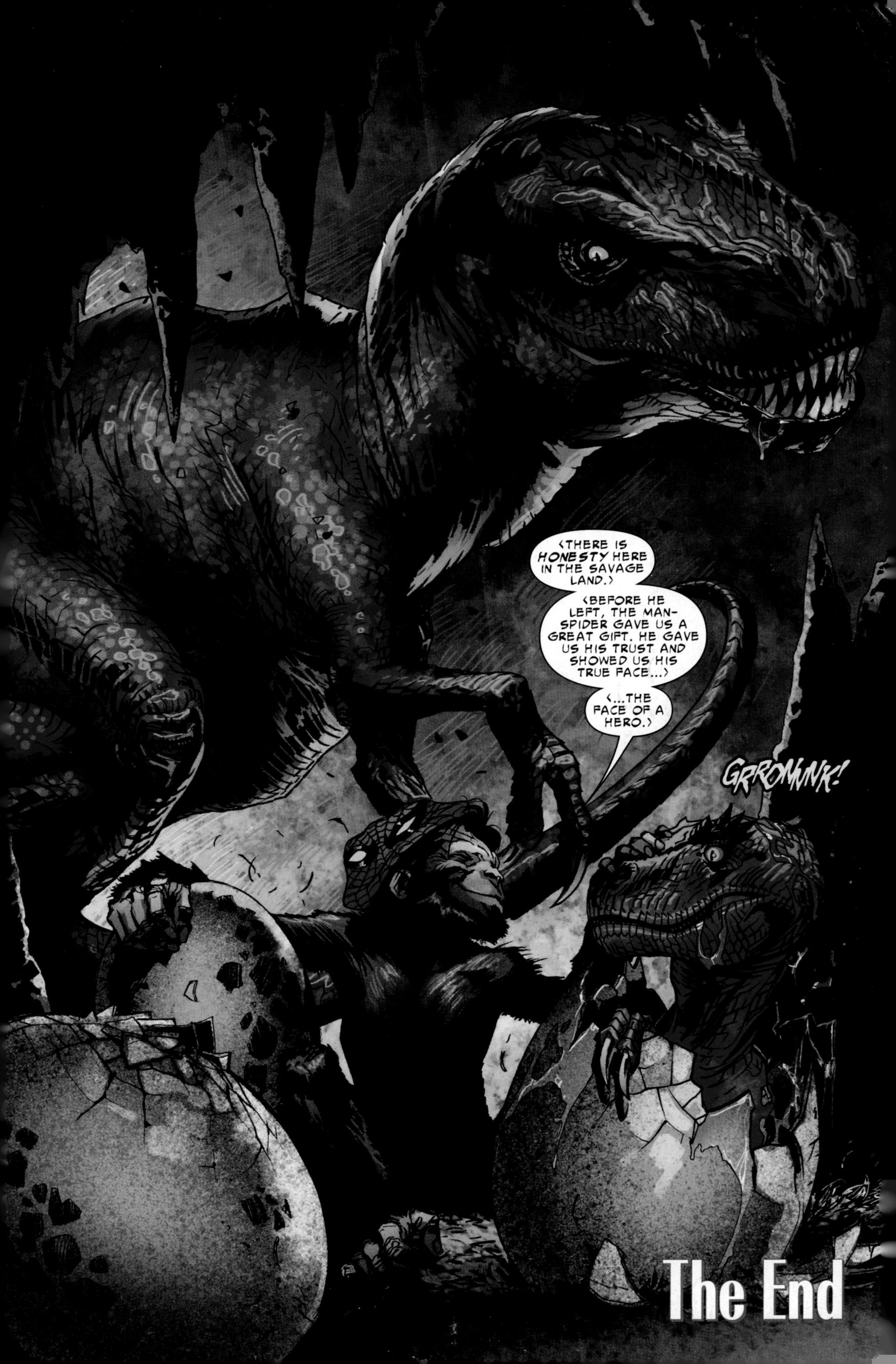

‹THERE IS HONESTY HERE IN THE SAVAGE LAND.›
‹BEFORE HE LEFT, THE MAN-SPIDER GAVE US A GREAT GIFT. HE GAVE US HIS TRUST AND SHOWED US HIS TRUE FACE...›
‹...THE FACE OF A HERO.›
GRROMMNK!
The End

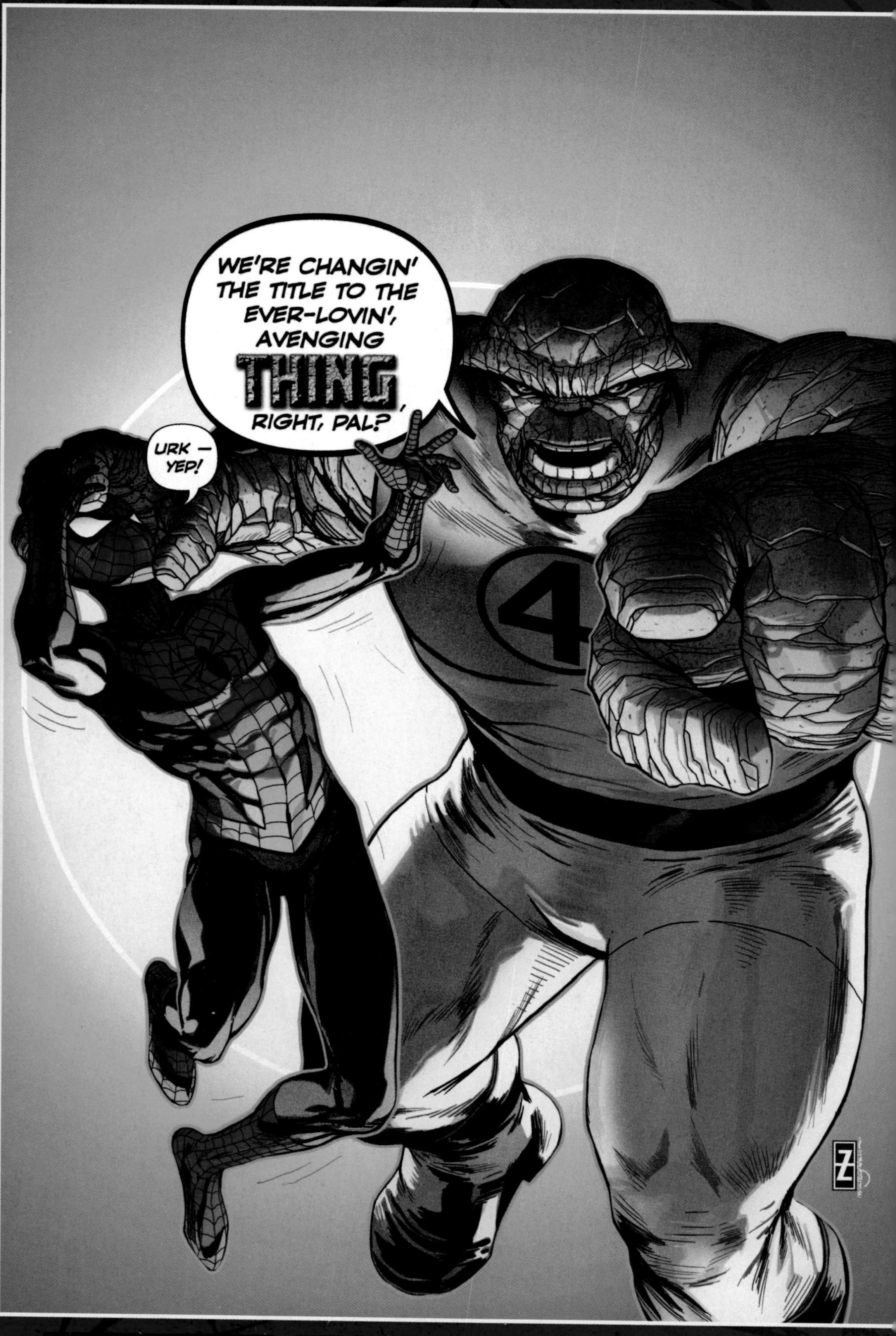
WE'RE CHANGIN' THE TITLE TO THE EVER-LOVIN', AVENGING THING, RIGHT, PAL?
URK — YEP!

AVENGING SPIDER-MAN ANNUAL #1

While attending a demonstration in radiology, high school student Peter Parker was bitten by a spider which had accidentally been exposed to radioactive rays. Through a miracle of science, Peter soon found that he had gained the spider's powers . . . and had, in effect, become a human spider! Later he joined the Avengers. And now he is...

AVENGING SPIDER-MAN

Ben Grimm used to be known for his boxing stance and blue eyes, but these days, he's recognized more for his rocky muscles and big-hearted belligerence. After getting blasted by cosmic rays, along with his friends, Ben quit street fighting and joined the big leagues as a member of the Fantastic Four. Between saving Earth and teaching at the Future Foundation, this muscle-bound softie barely has time for Spider-Man. But somehow, he manages to make it work as . . .

THE THING

AVENGING SPIDER-MAN

PREVIOUSLY...

Spider-Man and the Thing recently worked together in both the New Avengers and the FF. Sheesh, makes you wonder how they have time to do everything they do in a comic book, right? Boy. Super heroes.

WRITER: **ROB WILLIAMS**   PENCILS: **BRAD WALKER**

INKER: **JOHN LIVESAY**   COLORS: **CHRIS SOTOMAYOR**

LETTERER: **VC's JOE CARAMAGNA**   COVER: **PATCH ZIRCHER & MARTE GRACIA**

YOUNG & HIP EDITOR: **TOM BRENNAN**   OLDER EDITOR: **STEPHEN WACKER**   EDITOR IN CHIEF: **AXEL ALONSO**

CHIEF CREATIVE OFFICER: **JOE QUESADA**   PUBLISHER: **DAN BUCKLEY**   EXECUTIVE PRODUCER: **ALAN FINE**

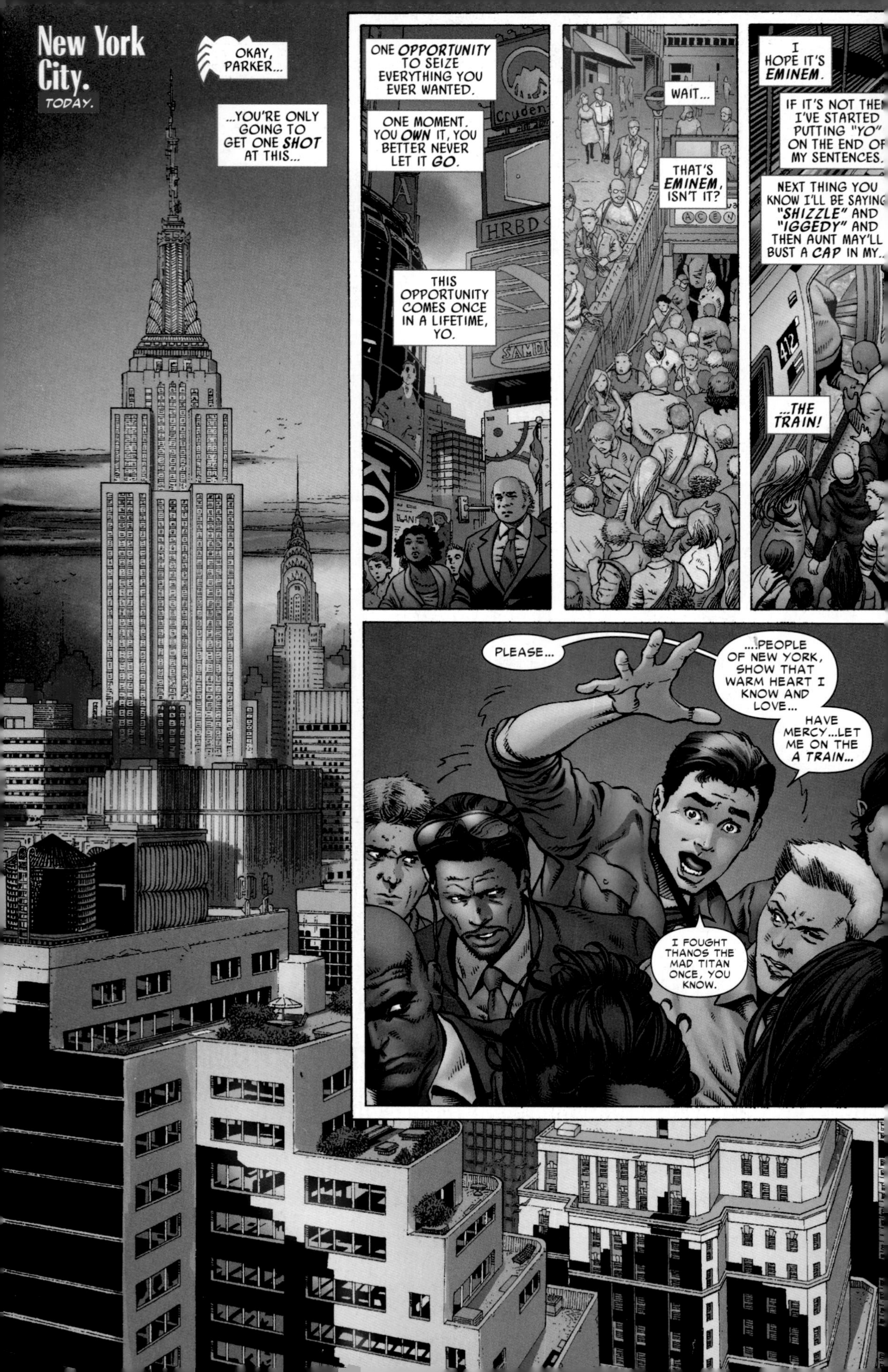
New York City.
TODAY.
OKAY, PARKER...
...YOU'RE ONLY GOING TO GET ONE SHOT AT THIS...
ONE OPPORTUNITY TO SEIZE EVERYTHING YOU EVER WANTED.
ONE MOMENT. YOU OWN IT, YOU BETTER NEVER LET IT GO.
THIS OPPORTUNITY COMES ONCE IN A LIFETIME, YO.
WAIT...
THAT'S EMINEM, ISN'T IT?
I HOPE IT'S EMINEM.
IF IT'S NOT THEN I'VE STARTED PUTTING "YO" ON THE END OF MY SENTENCES.
NEXT THING YOU KNOW I'LL BE SAYING "SHIZZLE" AND "IGGEDY" AND THEN AUNT MAY'LL BUST A CAP IN MY...
...THE TRAIN!
PLEASE...
...PEOPLE OF NEW YORK, SHOW THAT WARM HEART I KNOW AND LOVE...
HAVE MERCY...LET ME ON THE A TRAIN...
I FOUGHT THANOS THE MAD TITAN ONCE, YOU KNOW.

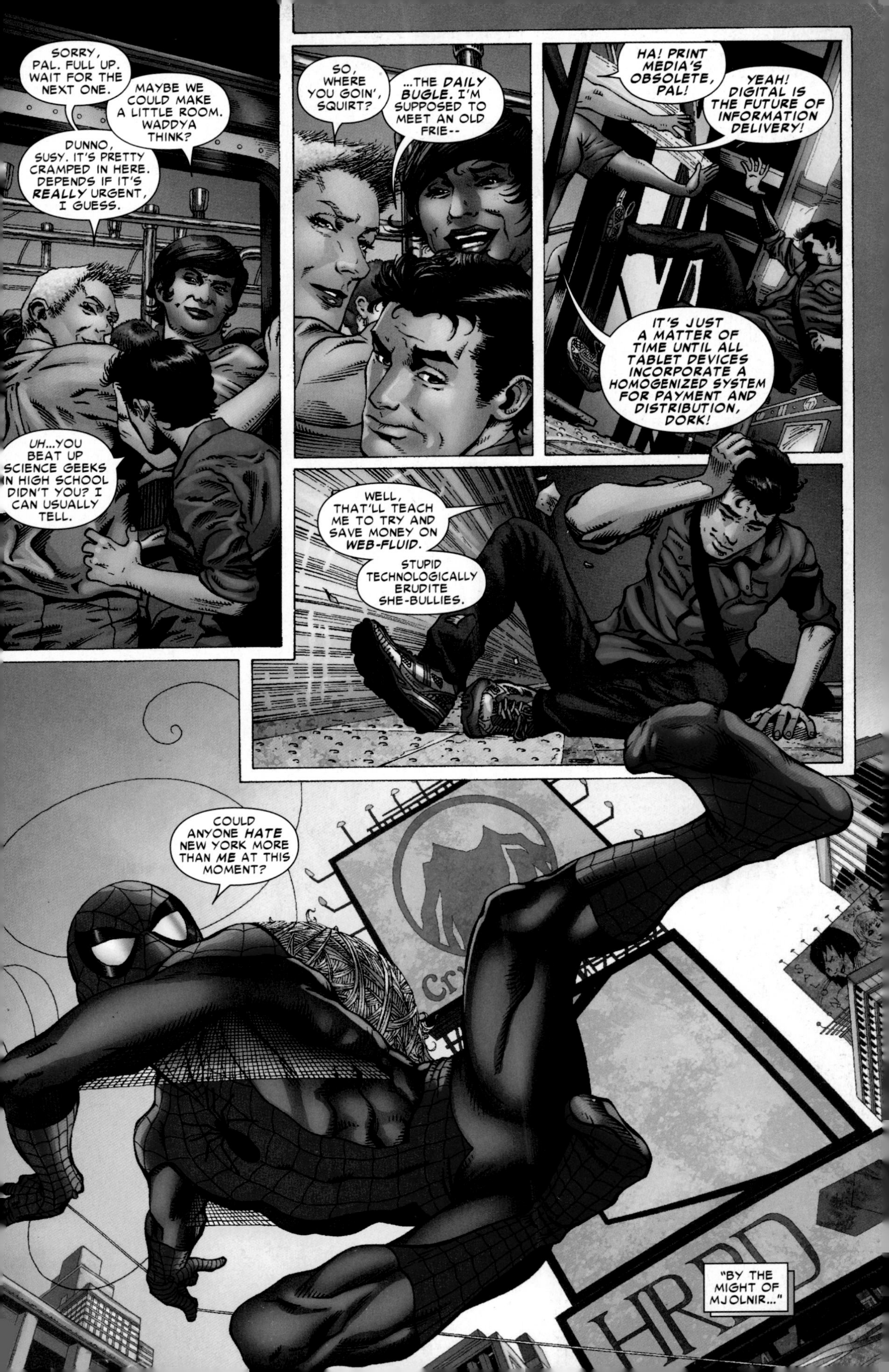

SORRY, PAL. FULL UP. WAIT FOR THE NEXT ONE.
MAYBE WE COULD MAKE A LITTLE ROOM. WADDYA THINK?
DUNNO, SUSY. IT'S PRETTY CRAMPED IN HERE. DEPENDS IF IT'S REALLY URGENT, I GUESS.
UH...YOU BEAT UP SCIENCE GEEKS IN HIGH SCHOOL DIDN'T YOU? I CAN USUALLY TELL.
SO, WHERE YOU GOIN', SQUIRT?
...THE DAILY BUGLE. I'M SUPPOSED TO MEET AN OLD FRIE--
HA! PRINT MEDIA'S OBSOLETE, PAL!
YEAH! DIGITAL IS THE FUTURE OF INFORMATION DELIVERY!
IT'S JUST A MATTER OF TIME UNTIL ALL TABLET DEVICES INCORPORATE A HOMOGENIZED SYSTEM FOR PAYMENT AND DISTRIBUTION, DORK!
WELL, THAT'LL TEACH ME TO TRY AND SAVE MONEY ON WEB-FLUID.
STUPID TECHNOLOGICALLY ERUDITE SHE-BULLIES.
COULD ANYONE HATE NEW YORK MORE THAN ME AT THIS MOMENT?
"BY THE MIGHT OF MJOLNIR..."

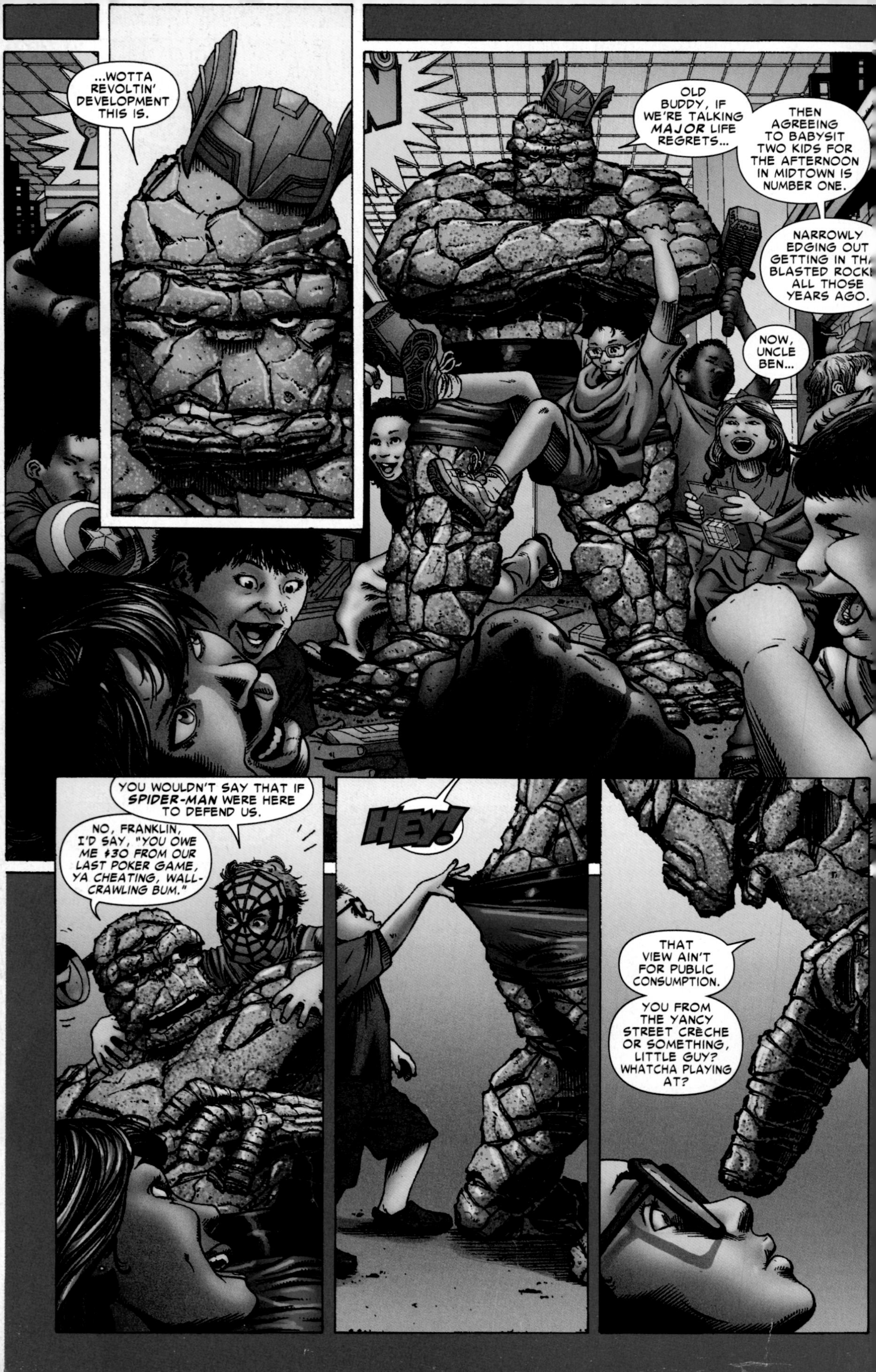
...WOTTA REVOLTIN' DEVELOPMENT THIS IS.
OLD BUDDY, IF WE'RE TALKING MAJOR LIFE REGRETS...
THEN AGREEING TO BABYSIT TWO KIDS FOR THE AFTERNOON IN MIDTOWN IS NUMBER ONE.
NARROWLY EDGING OUT GETTING IN THA BLASTED ROCK ALL THOSE YEARS AGO.
NOW, UNCLE BEN...
YOU WOULDN'T SAY THAT IF SPIDER-MAN WERE HERE TO DEFEND US.
NO, FRANKLIN, I'D SAY, "YOU OWE ME $30 FROM OUR LAST POKER GAME, YA CHEATING, WALL-CRAWLING BUM."
HEY!
THAT VIEW AIN'T FOR PUBLIC CONSUMPTION.
YOU FROM THE YANCY STREET CRÈCHE OR SOMETHING, LITTLE GUY? WHATCHA PLAYING AT?

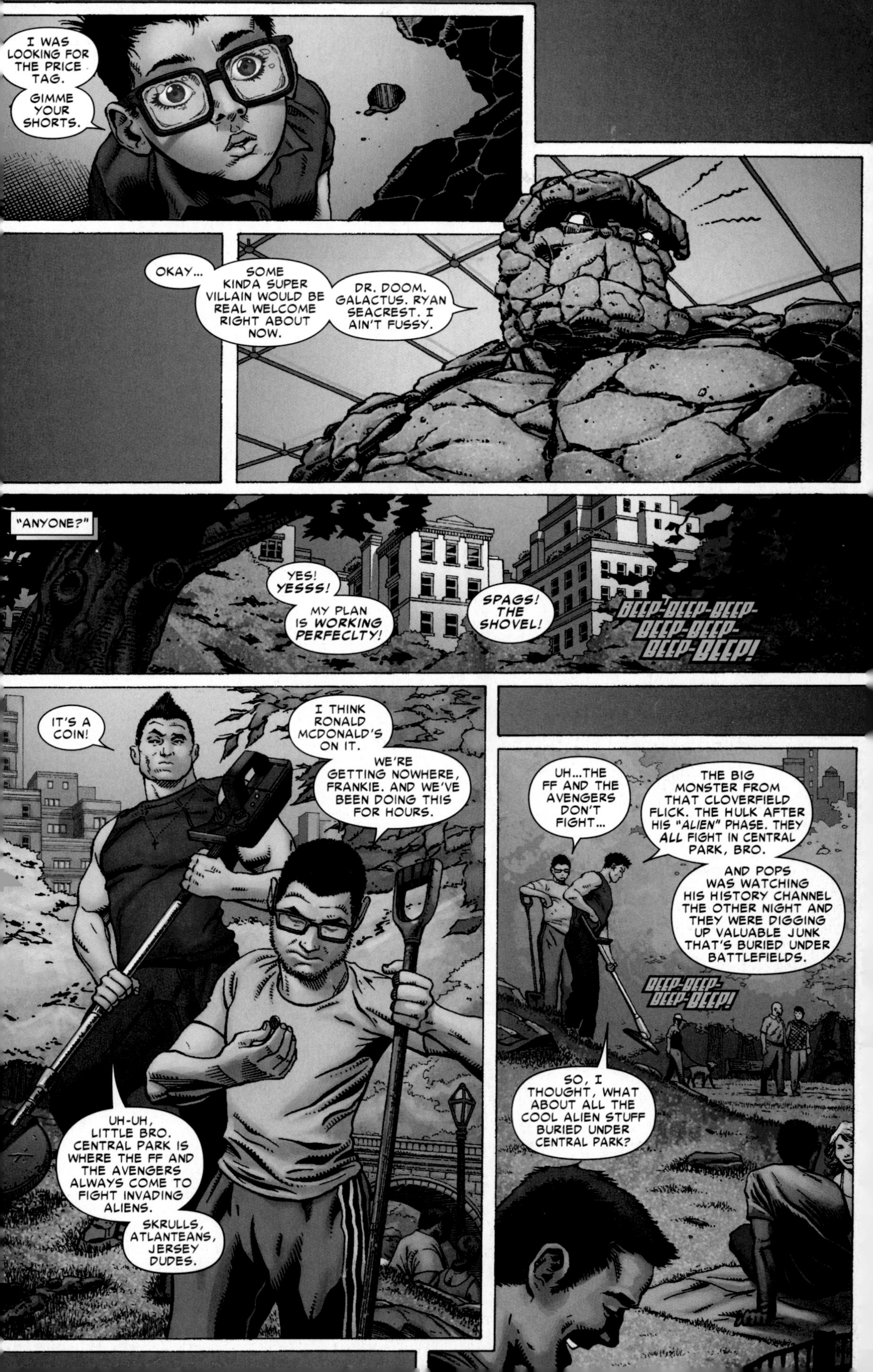
I WAS LOOKING FOR THE PRICE TAG.
GIMME YOUR SHORTS.
OKAY...
SOME KINDA SUPER VILLAIN WOULD BE REAL WELCOME RIGHT ABOUT NOW.
DR. DOOM. GALACTUS. RYAN SEACREST. I AIN'T FUSSY.
"ANYONE?"
YES! YESSS!
MY PLAN IS WORKING PERFECLTY!
SPAGS! THE SHOVEL!
BEEP-BEEP-BEEP-BEEP-BEEP-BEEP-BEEP!
IT'S A COIN!
I THINK RONALD MCDONALD'S ON IT.
WE'RE GETTING NOWHERE, FRANKIE. AND WE'VE BEEN DOING THIS FOR HOURS.
UH-UH, LITTLE BRO. CENTRAL PARK IS WHERE THE FF AND THE AVENGERS ALWAYS COME TO FIGHT INVADING ALIENS.
SKRULLS, ATLANTEANS, JERSEY DUDES.
UH...THE FF AND THE AVENGERS DON'T FIGHT...
THE BIG MONSTER FROM THAT CLOVERFIELD FLICK. THE HULK AFTER HIS "ALIEN" PHASE. THEY ALL FIGHT IN CENTRAL PARK, BRO.
AND POPS WAS WATCHING HIS HISTORY CHANNEL THE OTHER NIGHT AND THEY WERE DIGGING UP VALUABLE JUNK THAT'S BURIED UNDER BATTLEFIELDS.
BEEP-BEEP-BEEP-BEEP!
SO, I THOUGHT, WHAT ABOUT ALL THE COOL ALIEN STUFF BURIED UNDER CENTRAL PARK?

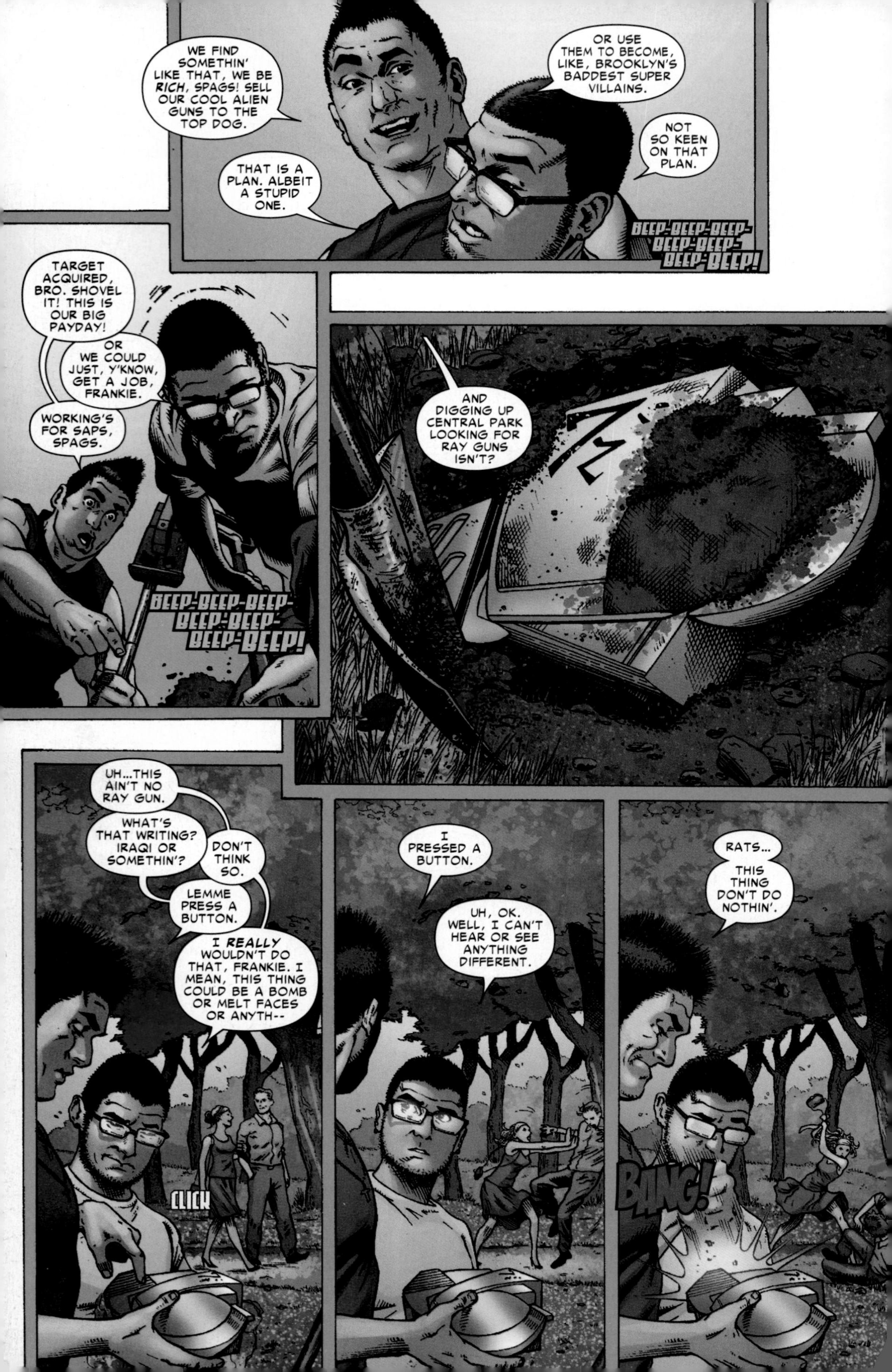

WE FIND SOMETHIN' LIKE THAT, WE BE RICH, SPAGS! SELL OUR COOL ALIEN GUNS TO THE TOP DOG.
OR USE THEM TO BECOME, LIKE, BROOKLYN'S BADDEST SUPER VILLAINS.
THAT IS A PLAN. ALBEIT A STUPID ONE.
NOT SO KEEN ON THAT PLAN.
BEEP-BEEP-BEEP-BEEP-BEEP-BEEP-BEEP!
TARGET ACQUIRED, BRO. SHOVEL IT! THIS IS OUR BIG PAYDAY!
OR WE COULD JUST, Y'KNOW, GET A JOB, FRANKIE.
WORKING'S FOR SAPS, SPAGS.
BEEP-BEEP-BEEP-BEEP-BEEP-BEEP-BEEP!
AND DIGGING UP CENTRAL PARK LOOKING FOR RAY GUNS ISN'T?
UH...THIS AIN'T NO RAY GUN.
WHAT'S THAT WRITING? IRAQI OR SOMETHIN'?
DON'T THINK SO.
LEMME PRESS A BUTTON.
I REALLY WOULDN'T DO THAT, FRANKIE. I MEAN, THIS THING COULD BE A BOMB OR MELT FACES OR ANYTH--
CLICK
I PRESSED A BUTTON.
UH, OK. WELL, I CAN'T HEAR OR SEE ANYTHING DIFFERENT.
RATS... THIS THING DON'T DO NOTHIN'.
BANG!

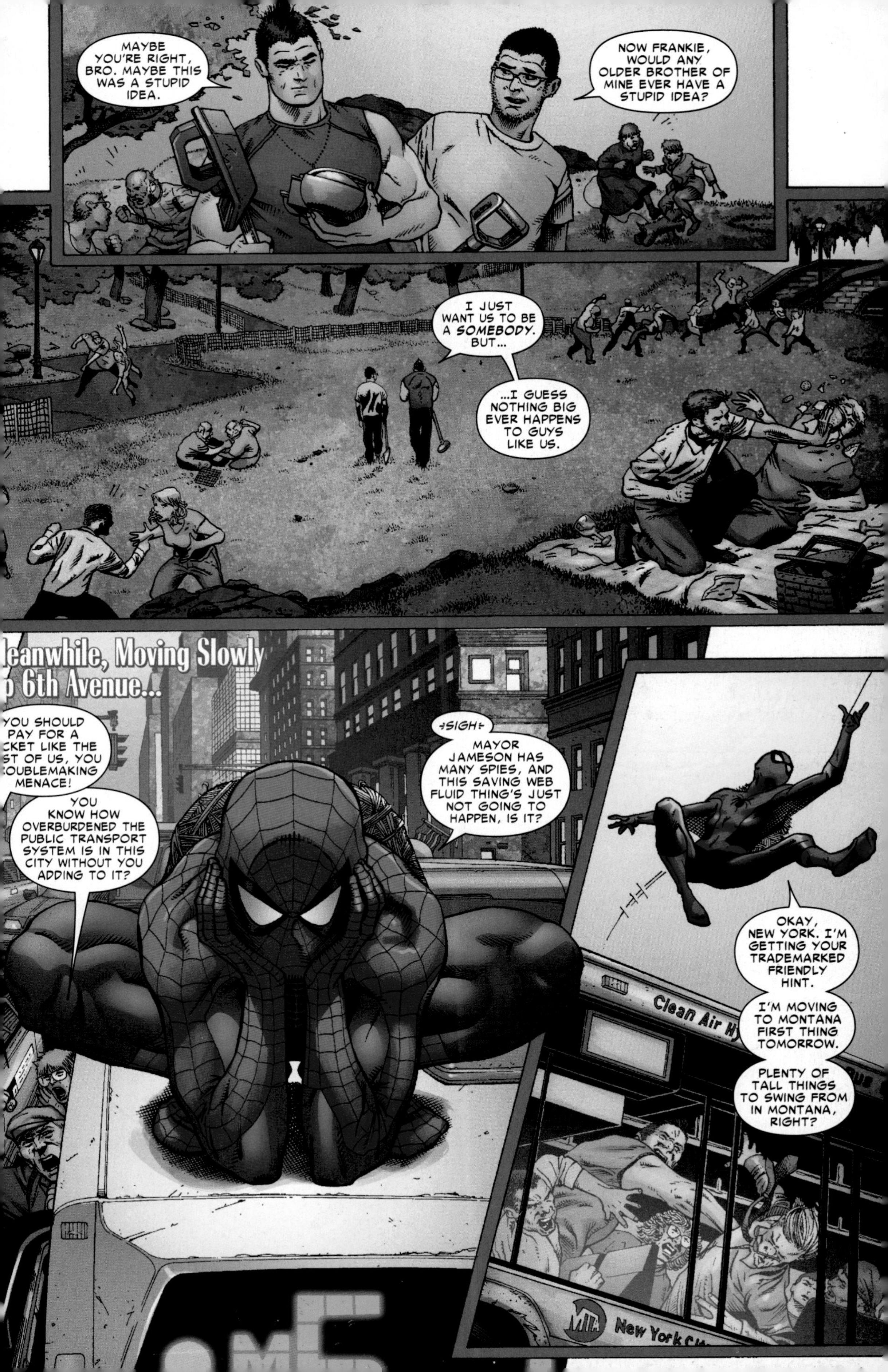

MAYBE YOU'RE RIGHT, BRO. MAYBE THIS WAS A STUPID IDEA.
NOW FRANKIE, WOULD ANY OLDER BROTHER OF MINE EVER HAVE A STUPID IDEA?
I JUST WANT US TO BE A SOMEBODY. BUT...
...I GUESS NOTHING BIG EVER HAPPENS TO GUYS LIKE US.
leanwhile, Moving Slowly p 6th Avenue...
YOU SHOULD PAY FOR A CKET LIKE THE ST OF US, YOU OUBLEMAKING MENACE!
YOU KNOW HOW OVERBURDENED THE PUBLIC TRANSPORT SYSTEM IS IN THIS CITY WITHOUT YOU ADDING TO IT?
SIGH
MAYOR JAMESON HAS MANY SPIES, AND THIS SAVING WEB FLUID THING'S JUST NOT GOING TO HAPPEN, IS IT?
OKAY, NEW YORK. I'M GETTING YOUR TRADEMARKED FRIENDLY HINT.
I'M MOVING TO MONTANA FIRST THING TOMORROW.
PLENTY OF TALL THINGS TO SWING FROM IN MONTANA, RIGHT?
Clean Air
New York Ci

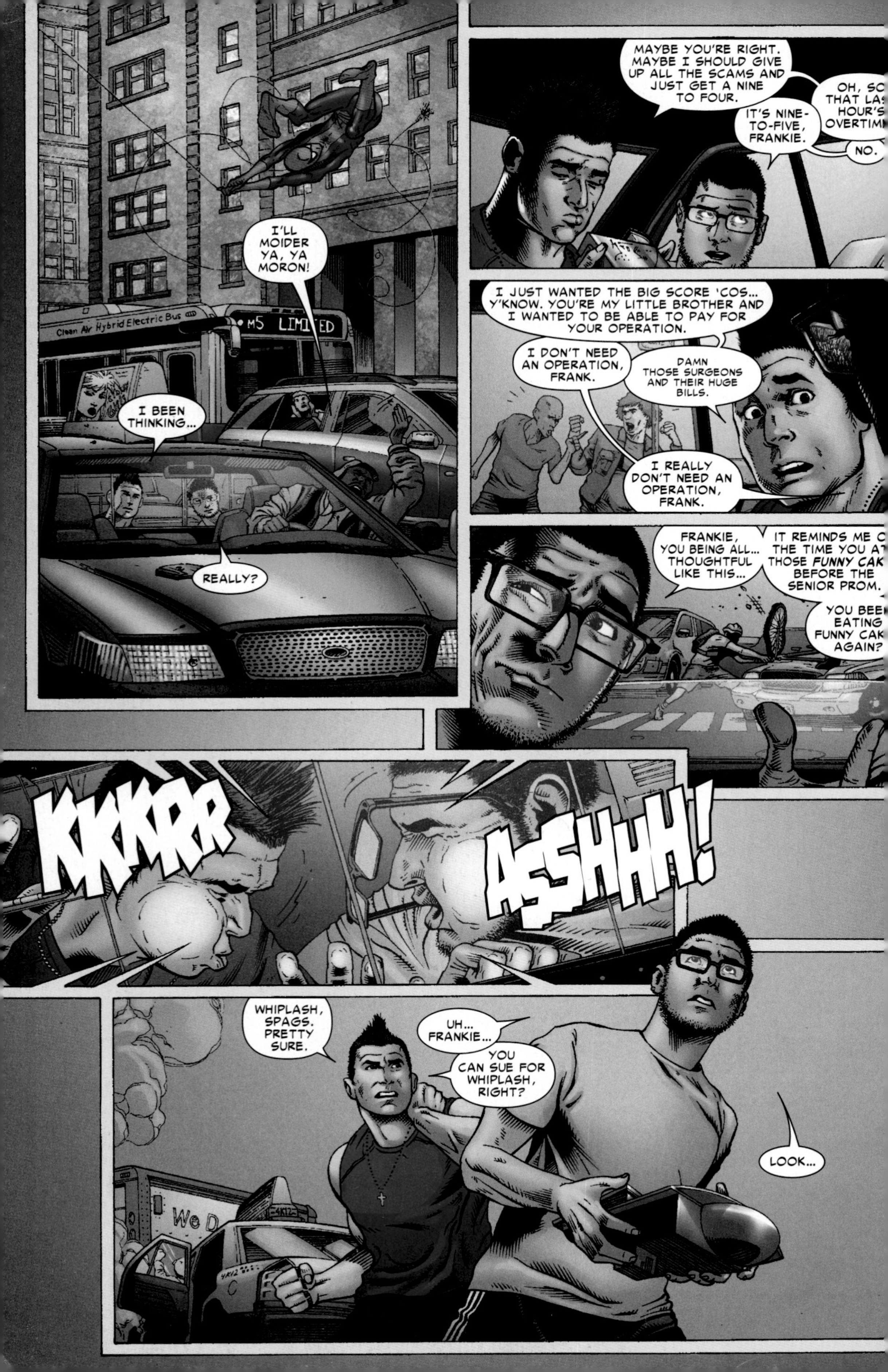

Clean Air Hybrid Electric Bus
M5 LIMITED
I'LL MOIDER YA, YA MORON!
I BEEN THINKING...
REALLY?
MAYBE YOU'RE RIGHT. MAYBE I SHOULD GIVE UP ALL THE SCAMS AND JUST GET A NINE TO FOUR.
IT'S NINE-TO-FIVE, FRANKIE.
OH, SO THAT LAS HOUR'S OVERTIM
NO.
I JUST WANTED THE BIG SCORE 'COS... Y'KNOW. YOU'RE MY LITTLE BROTHER AND I WANTED TO BE ABLE TO PAY FOR YOUR OPERATION.
I DON'T NEED AN OPERATION, FRANK.
DAMN THOSE SURGEONS AND THEIR HUGE BILLS.
I REALLY DON'T NEED AN OPERATION, FRANK.
FRANKIE, YOU BEING ALL... THOUGHTFUL LIKE THIS...
IT REMINDS ME O THE TIME YOU AT THOSE FUNNY CAK BEFORE THE SENIOR PROM.
YOU BEE EATING FUNNY CAK AGAIN?
KKKRR
ASSHHH!
WHIPLASH, SPAGS. PRETTY SURE.
UH... FRANKIE...
YOU CAN SUE FOR WHIPLASH, RIGHT?
LOOK...

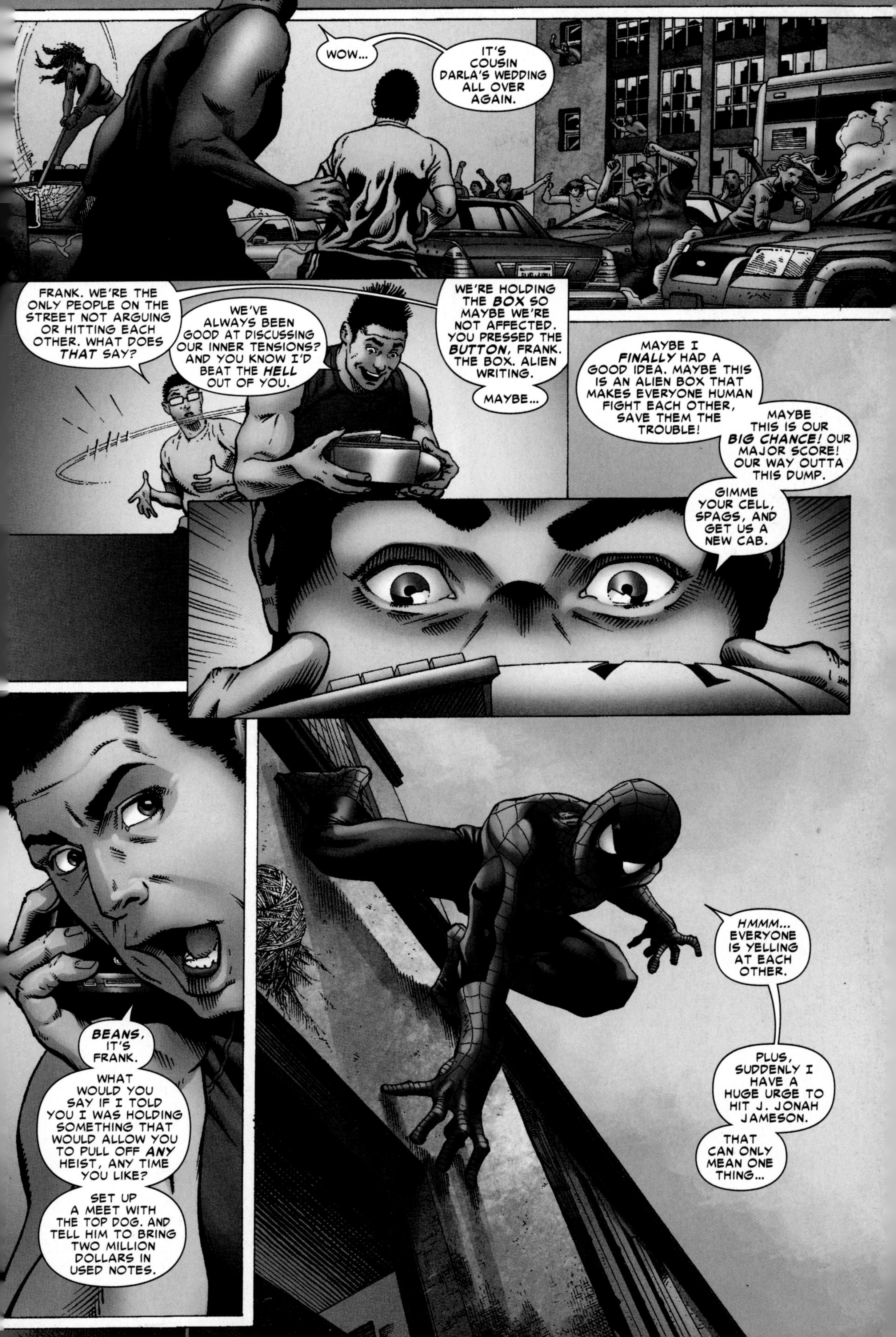
WOW...
IT'S COUSIN DARLA'S WEDDING ALL OVER AGAIN.
FRANK. WE'RE THE ONLY PEOPLE ON THE STREET NOT ARGUING OR HITTING EACH OTHER. WHAT DOES THAT SAY?
WE'VE ALWAYS BEEN GOOD AT DISCUSSING OUR INNER TENSIONS? AND YOU KNOW I'D BEAT THE HELL OUT OF YOU.
WE'RE HOLDING THE BOX SO MAYBE WE'RE NOT AFFECTED. YOU PRESSED THE BUTTON, FRANK. THE BOX. ALIEN WRITING.
MAYBE...
MAYBE I FINALLY HAD A GOOD IDEA. MAYBE THIS IS AN ALIEN BOX THAT MAKES EVERYONE HUMAN FIGHT EACH OTHER, SAVE THEM THE TROUBLE!
MAYBE THIS IS OUR BIG CHANCE! OUR MAJOR SCORE! OUR WAY OUTTA THIS DUMP.
GIMME YOUR CELL, SPAGS, AND GET US A NEW CAB.
BEANS, IT'S FRANK.
WHAT WOULD YOU SAY IF I TOLD YOU I WAS HOLDING SOMETHING THAT WOULD ALLOW YOU TO PULL OFF ANY HEIST, ANY TIME YOU LIKE?
SET UP A MEET WITH THE TOP DOG. AND TELL HIM TO BRING TWO MILLION DOLLARS IN USED NOTES.
HMMM... EVERYONE IS YELLING AT EACH OTHER.
PLUS, SUDDENLY I HAVE A HUGE URGE TO HIT J. JONAH JAMESON.
THAT CAN ONLY MEAN ONE THING...

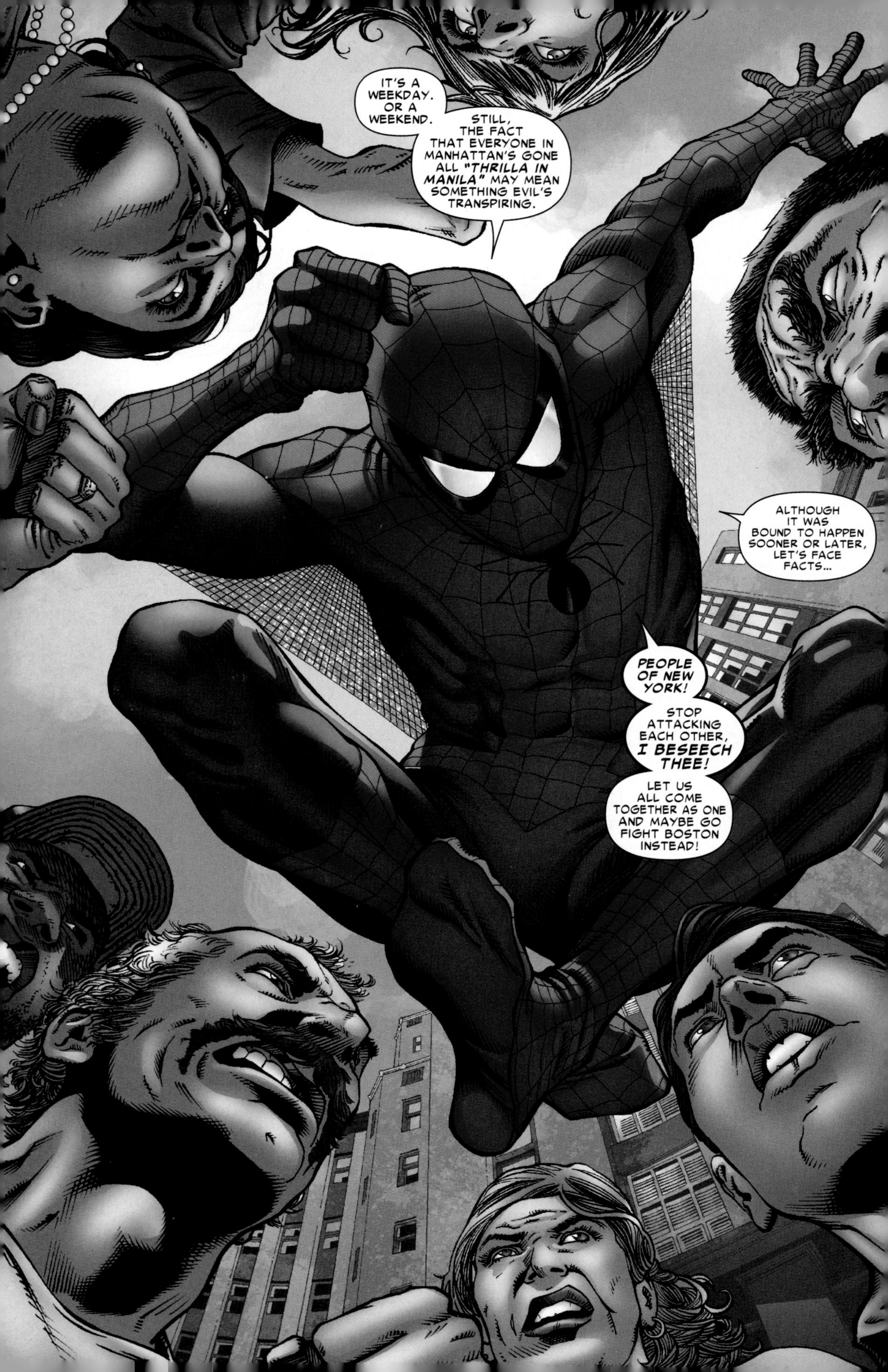
IT'S A WEEKDAY. OR A WEEKEND.
STILL, THE FACT THAT EVERYONE IN MANHATTAN'S GONE ALL "THRILLA IN MANILA" MAY MEAN SOMETHING EVIL'S TRANSPIRING.
ALTHOUGH IT WAS BOUND TO HAPPEN SOONER OR LATER, LET'S FACE FACTS...
PEOPLE OF NEW YORK!
STOP ATTACKING EACH OTHER, I BESEECH THEE!
LET US ALL COME TOGETHER AS ONE AND MAYBE GO FIGHT BOSTON INSTEAD!

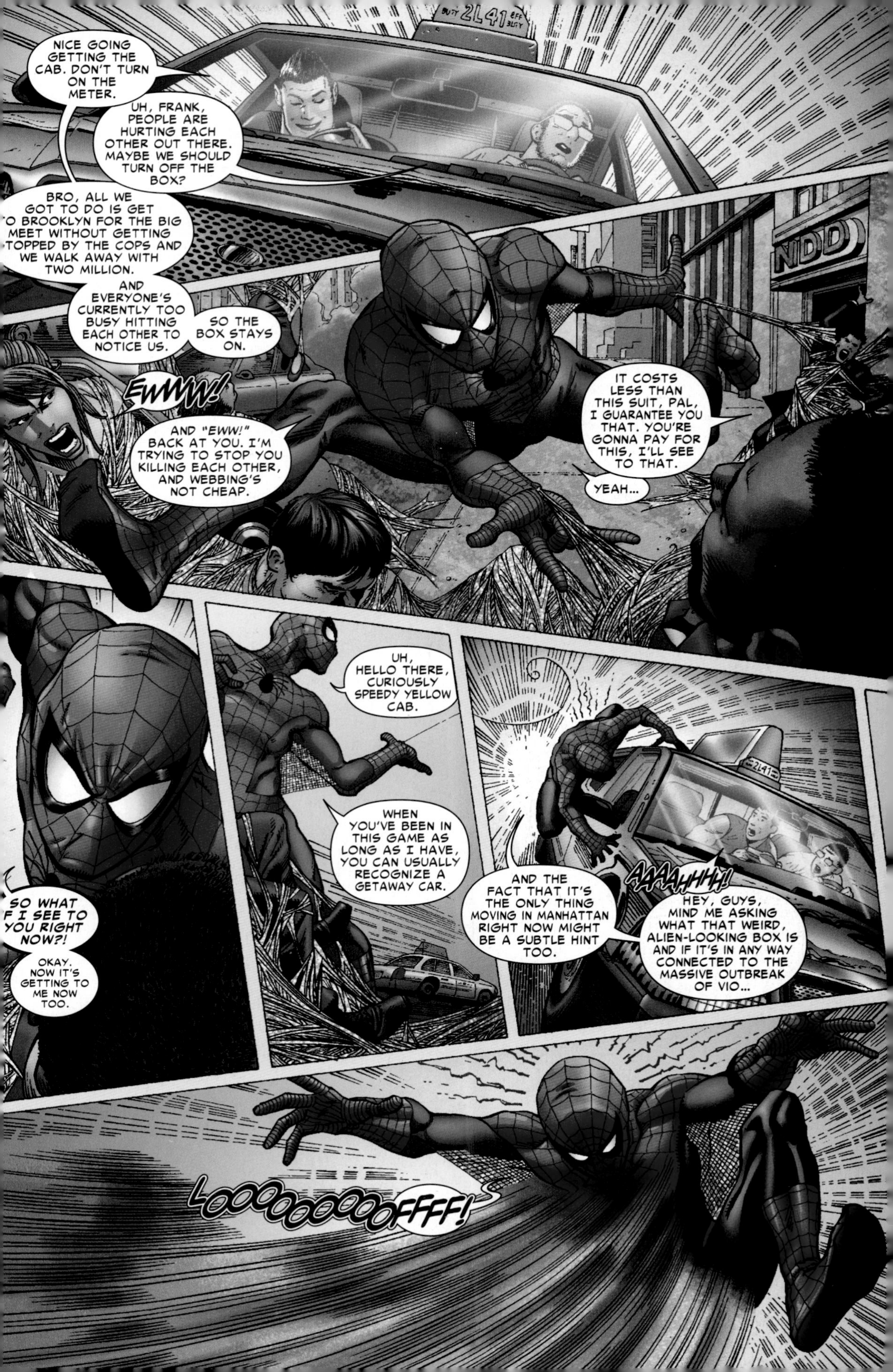

NICE GOING GETTING THE CAB. DON'T TURN ON THE METER.
UH, FRANK, PEOPLE ARE HURTING EACH OTHER OUT THERE. MAYBE WE SHOULD TURN OFF THE BOX?
BRO, ALL WE GOT TO DO IS GET TO BROOKLYN FOR THE BIG MEET WITHOUT GETTING STOPPED BY THE COPS AND WE WALK AWAY WITH TWO MILLION.
AND EVERYONE'S CURRENTLY TOO BUSY HITTING EACH OTHER TO NOTICE US.
SO THE BOX STAYS ON.
EWWW!
AND "EWW!" BACK AT YOU. I'M TRYING TO STOP YOU KILLING EACH OTHER, AND WEBBING'S NOT CHEAP.
IT COSTS LESS THAN THIS SUIT, PAL, I GUARANTEE YOU THAT. YOU'RE GONNA PAY FOR THIS, I'LL SEE TO THAT.
YEAH...
SO WHAT IF I SEE TO YOU RIGHT NOW?!
OKAY. NOW IT'S GETTING TO ME NOW TOO.
UH, HELLO THERE, CURIOUSLY SPEEDY YELLOW CAB.
WHEN YOU'VE BEEN IN THIS GAME AS LONG AS I HAVE, YOU CAN USUALLY RECOGNIZE A GETAWAY CAR.
AND THE FACT THAT IT'S THE ONLY THING MOVING IN MANHATTAN RIGHT NOW MIGHT BE A SUBTLE HINT TOO.
AAAAHHH!
HEY, GUYS, MIND ME ASKING WHAT THAT WEIRD, ALIEN-LOOKING BOX IS AND IF IT'S IN ANY WAY CONNECTED TO THE MASSIVE OUTBREAK OF VIO...
LOOOOOOOOOFFFF!

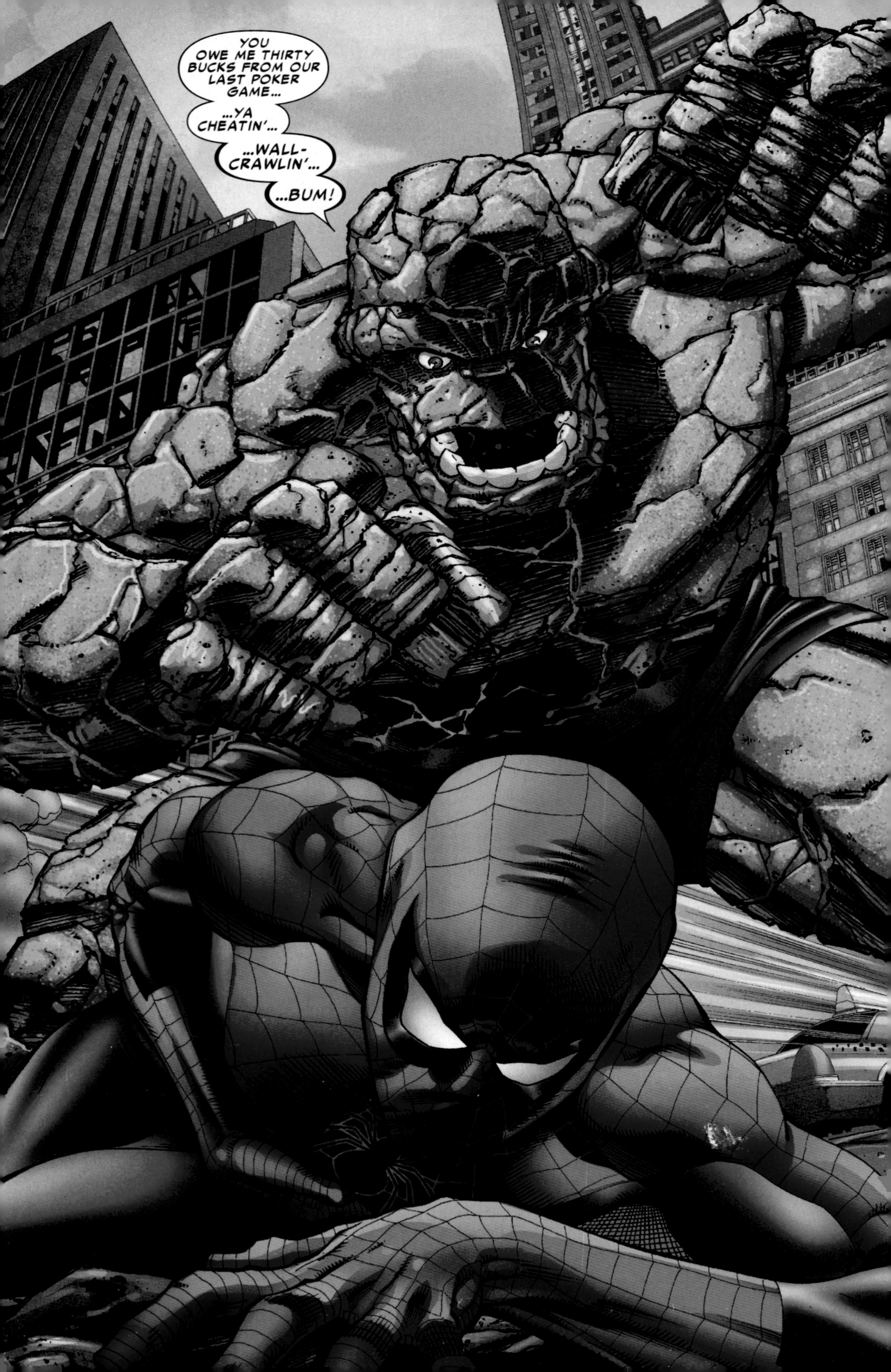
YOU OWE ME THIRTY BUCKS FROM OUR LAST POKER GAME...
...YA CHEATIN'...
...WALL-CRAWLIN'...
...BUM!

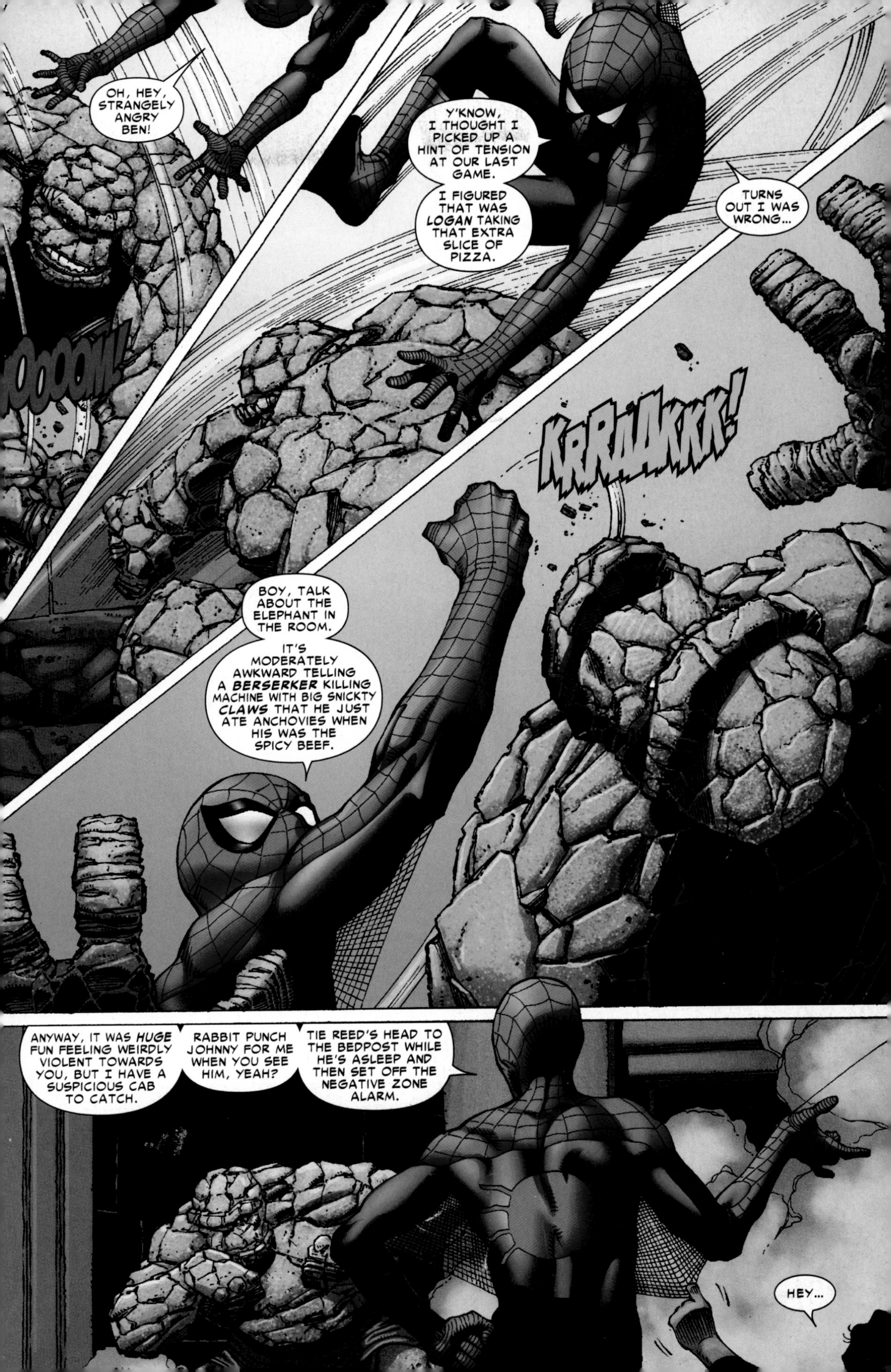
OH, HEY, STRANGELY ANGRY BEN!
Y'KNOW, I THOUGHT I PICKED UP A HINT OF TENSION AT OUR LAST GAME.
I FIGURED THAT WAS LOGAN TAKING THAT EXTRA SLICE OF PIZZA.
TURNS OUT I WAS WRONG...
OOOOM!!
KRRAAKKK!
BOY, TALK ABOUT THE ELEPHANT IN THE ROOM.
IT'S MODERATELY AWKWARD TELLING A BERSERKER KILLING MACHINE WITH BIG SNICKTY CLAWS THAT HE JUST ATE ANCHOVIES WHEN HIS WAS THE SPICY BEEF.
ANYWAY, IT WAS HUGE FUN FEELING WEIRDLY VIOLENT TOWARDS YOU, BUT I HAVE A SUSPICIOUS CAB TO CATCH.
RABBIT PUNCH JOHNNY FOR ME WHEN YOU SEE HIM, YEAH?
TIE REED'S HEAD TO THE BEDPOST WHILE HE'S ASLEEP AND THEN SET OFF THE NEGATIVE ZONE ALARM.
HEY...

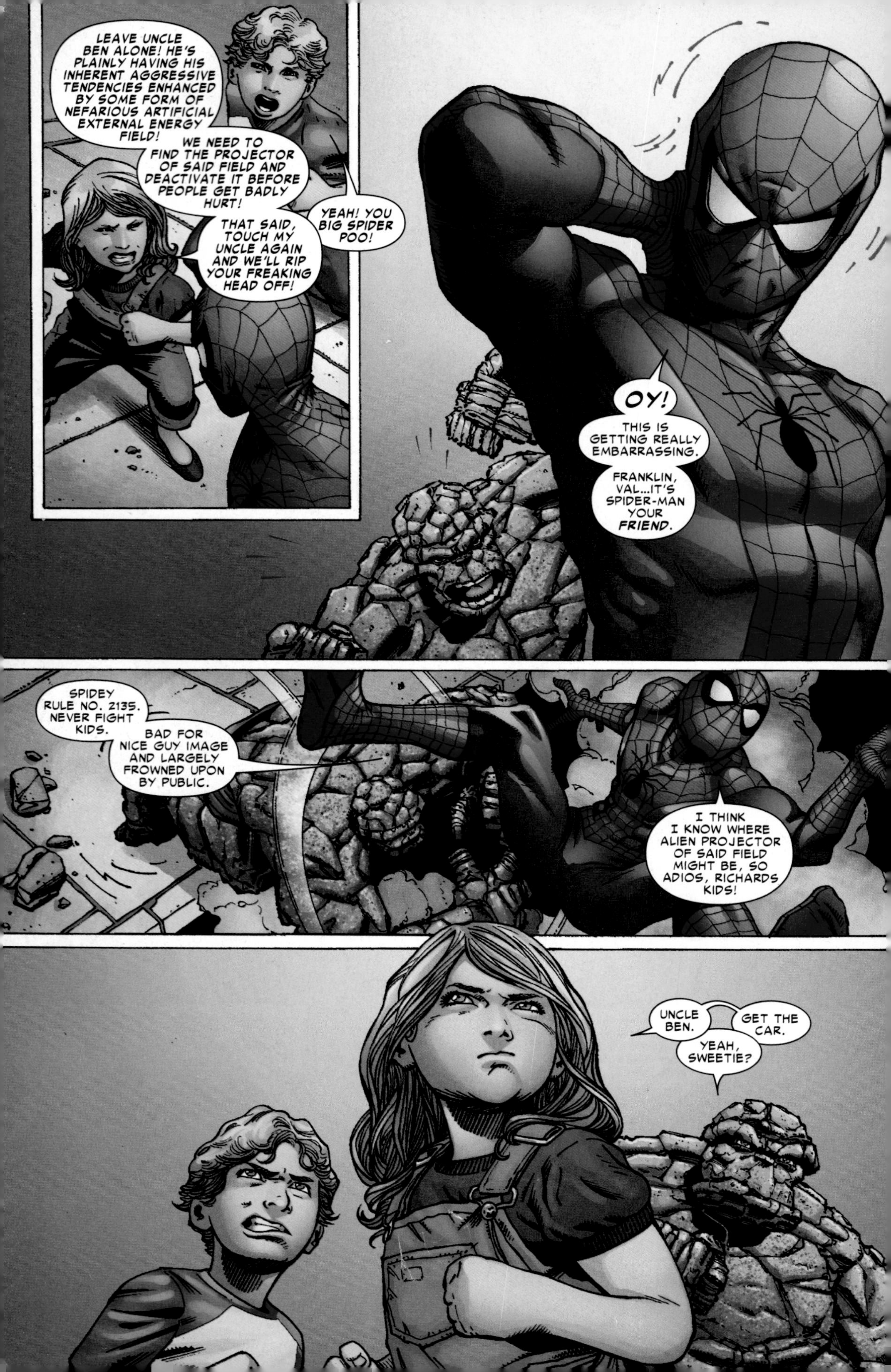
LEAVE UNCLE BEN ALONE! HE'S PLAINLY HAVING HIS INHERENT AGGRESSIVE TENDENCIES ENHANCED BY SOME FORM OF NEFARIOUS ARTIFICIAL EXTERNAL ENERGY FIELD!
WE NEED TO FIND THE PROJECTOR OF SAID FIELD AND DEACTIVATE IT BEFORE PEOPLE GET BADLY HURT!
YEAH! YOU BIG SPIDER POO!
THAT SAID, TOUCH MY UNCLE AGAIN AND WE'LL RIP YOUR FREAKING HEAD OFF!
OY!
THIS IS GETTING REALLY EMBARRASSING.
FRANKLIN, VAL...IT'S SPIDER-MAN YOUR FRIEND.
SPIDEY RULE NO. 2135. NEVER FIGHT KIDS.
BAD FOR NICE GUY IMAGE AND LARGELY FROWNED UPON BY PUBLIC.
I THINK I KNOW WHERE ALIEN PROJECTOR OF SAID FIELD MIGHT BE, SO ADIOS, RICHARDS KIDS!
UNCLE BEN.
YEAH, SWEETIE?
GET THE CAR.

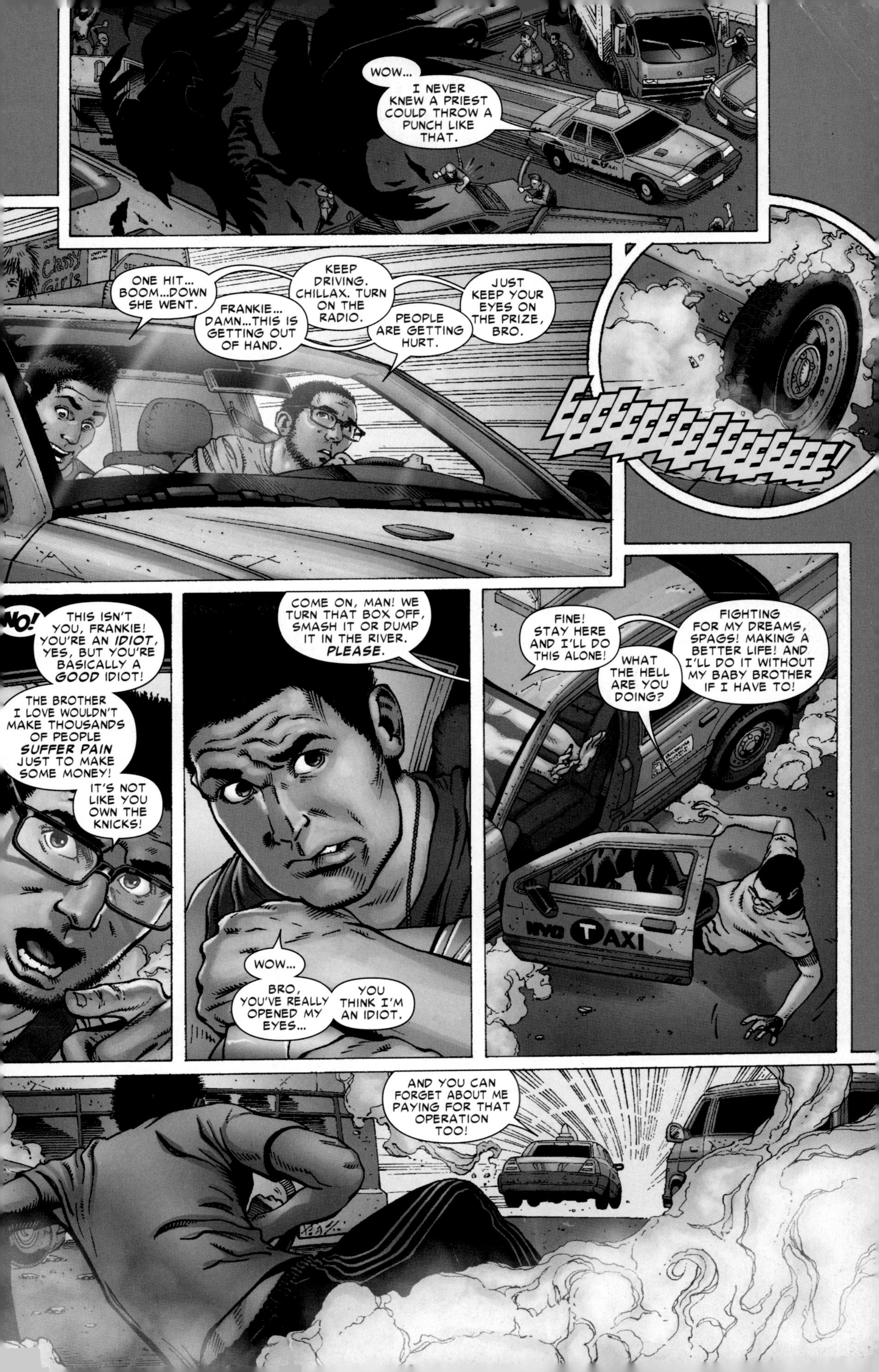
WOW... I NEVER KNEW A PRIEST COULD THROW A PUNCH LIKE THAT.
Classy Girls
ONE HIT... BOOM...DOWN SHE WENT.
FRANKIE... DAMN...THIS IS GETTING OUT OF HAND.
KEEP DRIVING. CHILLAX. TURN ON THE RADIO.
PEOPLE ARE GETTING HURT.
JUST KEEP YOUR EYES ON THE PRIZE, BRO.
EEEEEEEEEEEEEEEEEE!
NO!
THIS ISN'T YOU, FRANKIE! YOU'RE AN *IDIOT*, YES, BUT YOU'RE BASICALLY A *GOOD* IDIOT!
THE BROTHER I LOVE WOULDN'T MAKE THOUSANDS OF PEOPLE *SUFFER PAIN* JUST TO MAKE SOME MONEY!
IT'S NOT LIKE YOU OWN THE KNICKS!
COME ON, MAN! WE TURN THAT BOX OFF, SMASH IT OR DUMP IT IN THE RIVER. *PLEASE*.
WOW...
BRO, YOU'VE REALLY OPENED MY EYES...
YOU THINK I'M AN IDIOT.
FINE! STAY HERE AND I'LL DO THIS ALONE!
WHAT THE HELL ARE YOU DOING?
FIGHTING FOR MY DREAMS, SPAGS! MAKING A BETTER LIFE! AND I'LL DO IT WITHOUT MY BABY BROTHER IF I HAVE TO!
NYC TAXI
AND YOU CAN FORGET ABOUT ME PAYING FOR THAT OPERATION TOO!

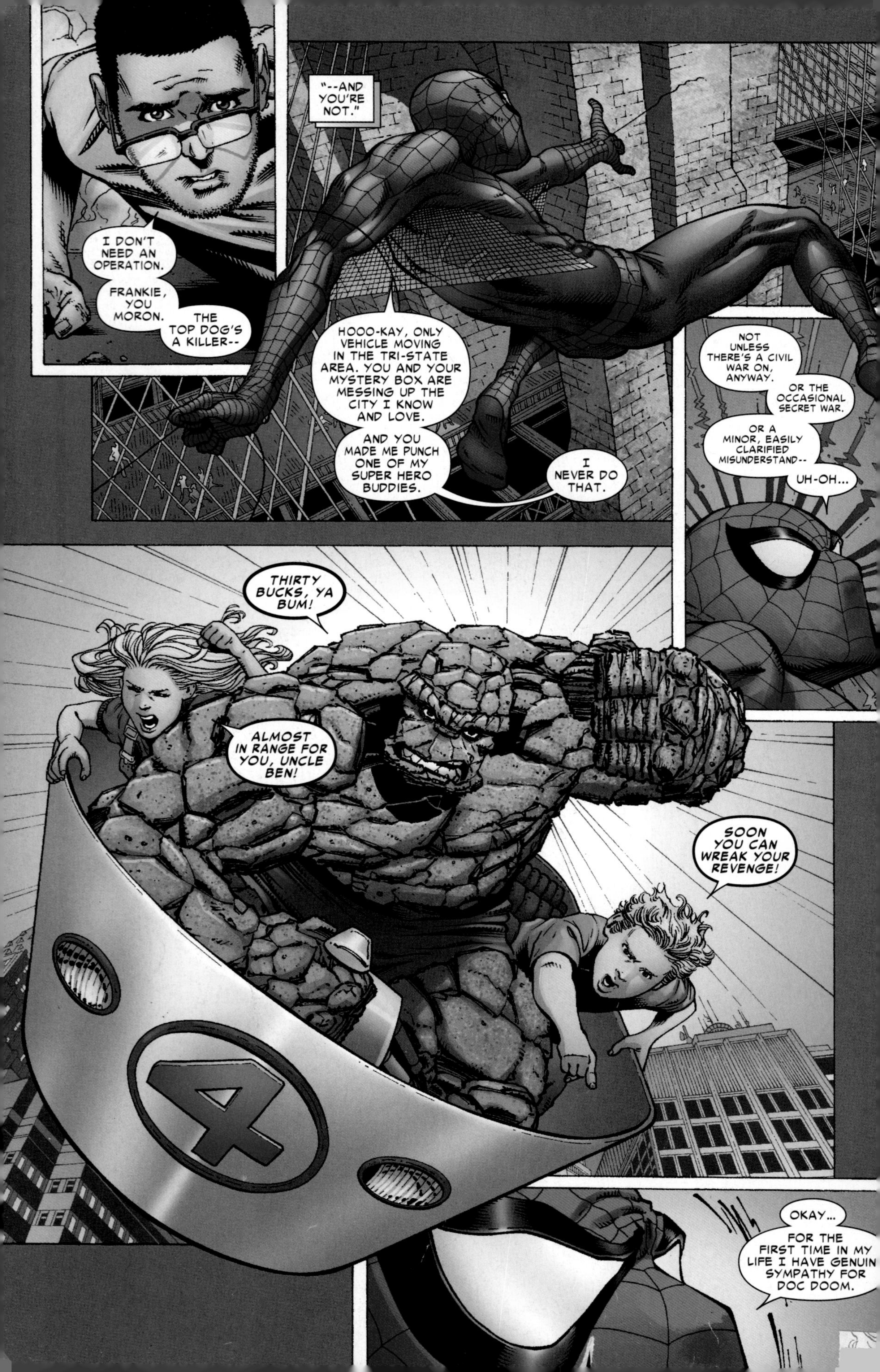

I DON'T NEED AN OPERATION.
FRANKIE, YOU MORON.
THE TOP DOG'S A KILLER--
"--AND YOU'RE NOT."
HOOO-KAY, ONLY VEHICLE MOVING IN THE TRI-STATE AREA. YOU AND YOUR MYSTERY BOX ARE MESSING UP THE CITY I KNOW AND LOVE.
AND YOU MADE ME PUNCH ONE OF MY SUPER HERO BUDDIES.
I NEVER DO THAT.
NOT UNLESS THERE'S A CIVIL WAR ON, ANYWAY.
OR THE OCCASIONAL SECRET WAR.
OR A MINOR, EASILY CLARIFIED MISUNDERSTAND--
UH-OH...
THIRTY BUCKS, YA BUM!
ALMOST IN RANGE FOR YOU, UNCLE BEN!
SOON YOU CAN WREAK YOUR REVENGE!
OKAY...
FOR THE FIRST TIME IN MY LIFE I HAVE GENUIN SYMPATHY FOR DOC DOOM.

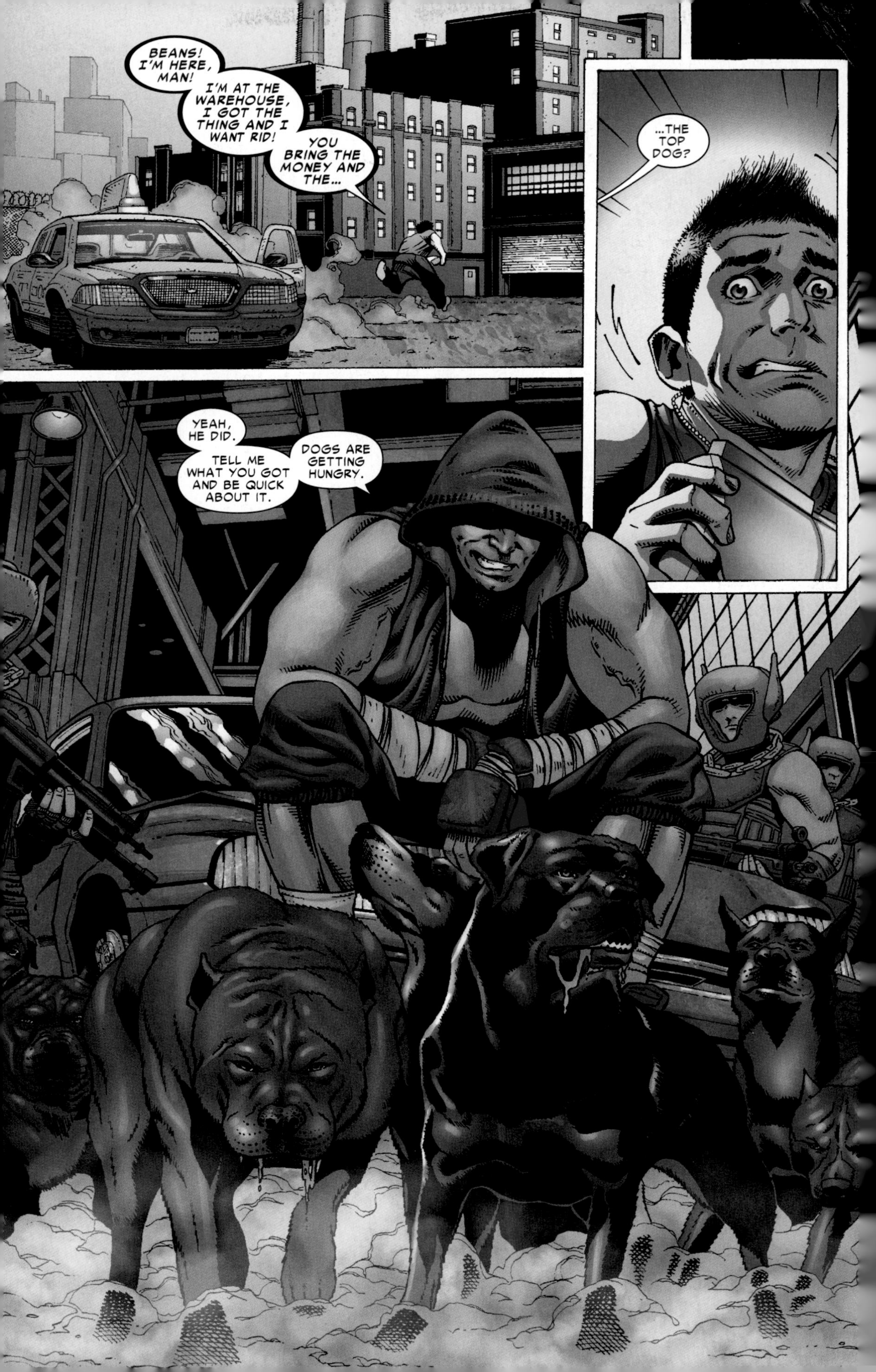

BEANS! I'M HERE, MAN!
I'M AT THE WAREHOUSE, I GOT THE THING AND I WANT RID!
YOU BRING THE MONEY AND THE...
...THE TOP DOG?
YEAH, HE DID.
TELL ME WHAT YOU GOT AND BE QUICK ABOUT IT.
DOGS ARE GETTING HUNGRY.

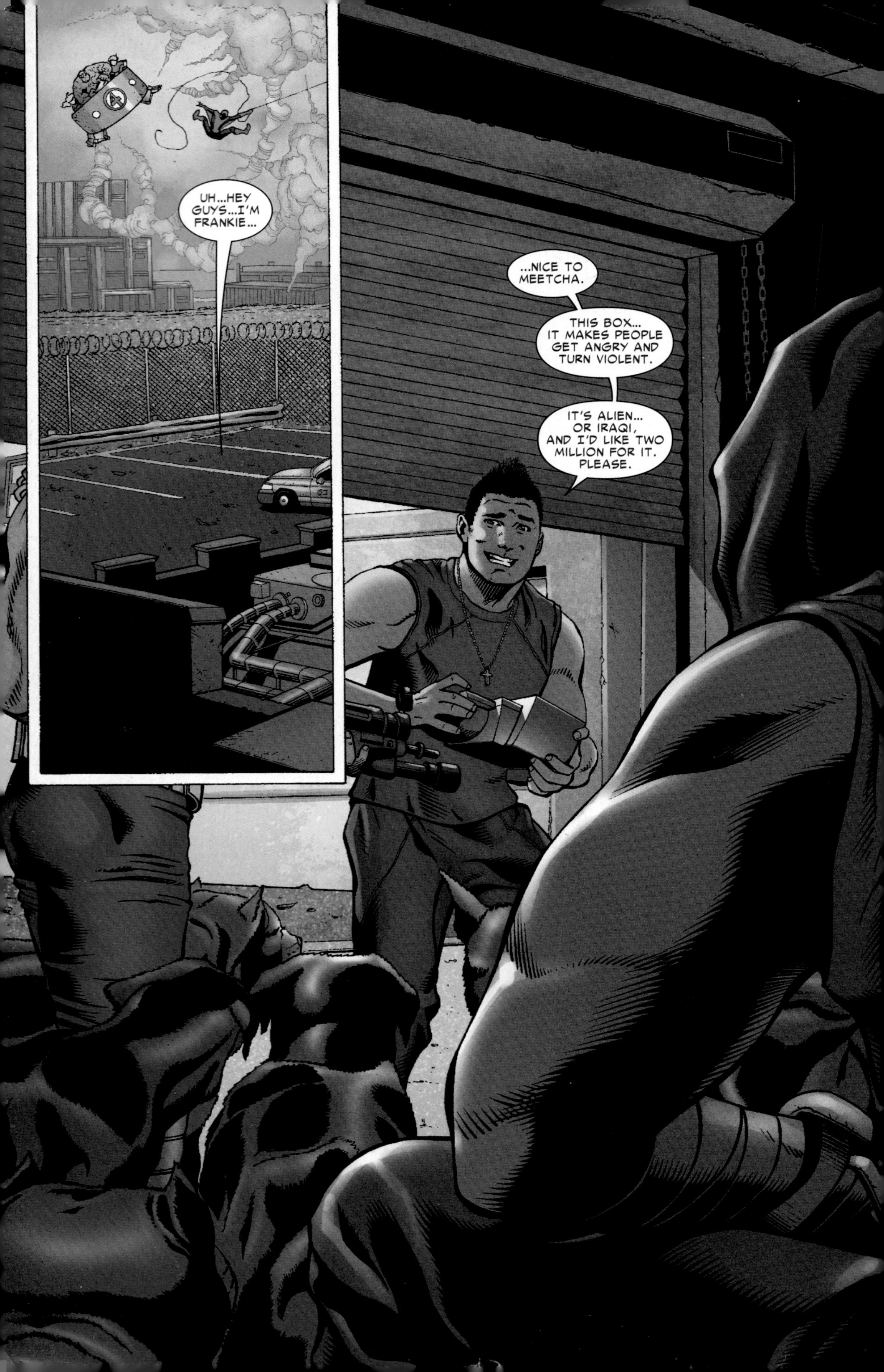
UH...HEY GUYS...I'M FRANKIE...
...NICE TO MEETCHA.
THIS BOX... IT MAKES PEOPLE GET ANGRY AND TURN VIOLENT.
IT'S ALIEN... OR IRAQI, AND I'D LIKE TWO MILLION FOR IT. PLEASE.

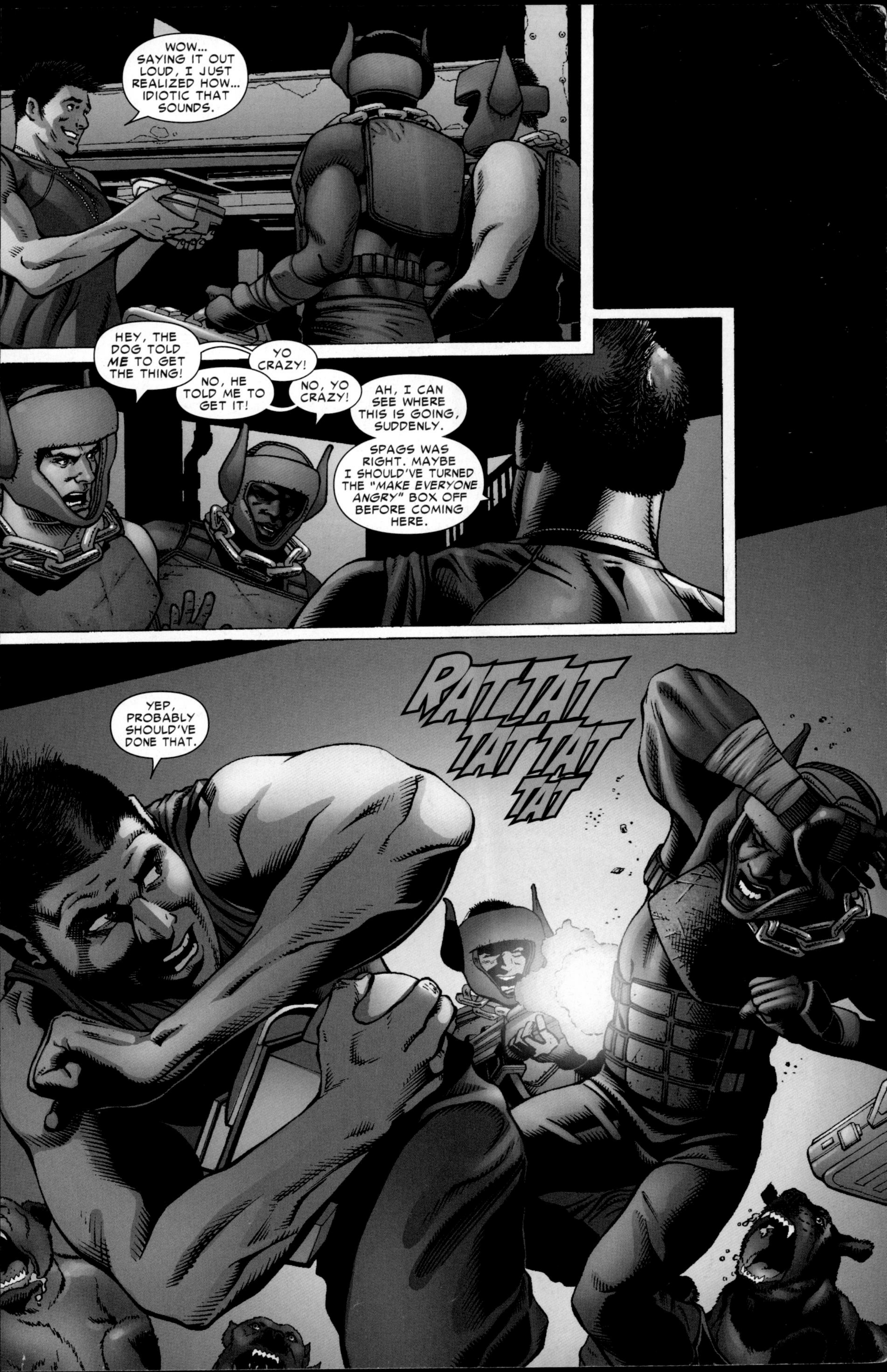
WOW... SAYING IT OUT LOUD, I JUST REALIZED HOW... IDIOTIC THAT SOUNDS.
HEY, THE DOG TOLD ME TO GET THE THING!
YO CRAZY!
NO, HE TOLD ME TO GET IT!
NO, YO CRAZY!
AH, I CAN SEE WHERE THIS IS GOING, SUDDENLY.
SPAGS WAS RIGHT. MAYBE I SHOULD'VE TURNED THE "MAKE EVERYONE ANGRY" BOX OFF BEFORE COMING HERE.
YEP, PROBABLY SHOULD'VE DONE THAT.
RAT-TAT TAT-TAT TAT

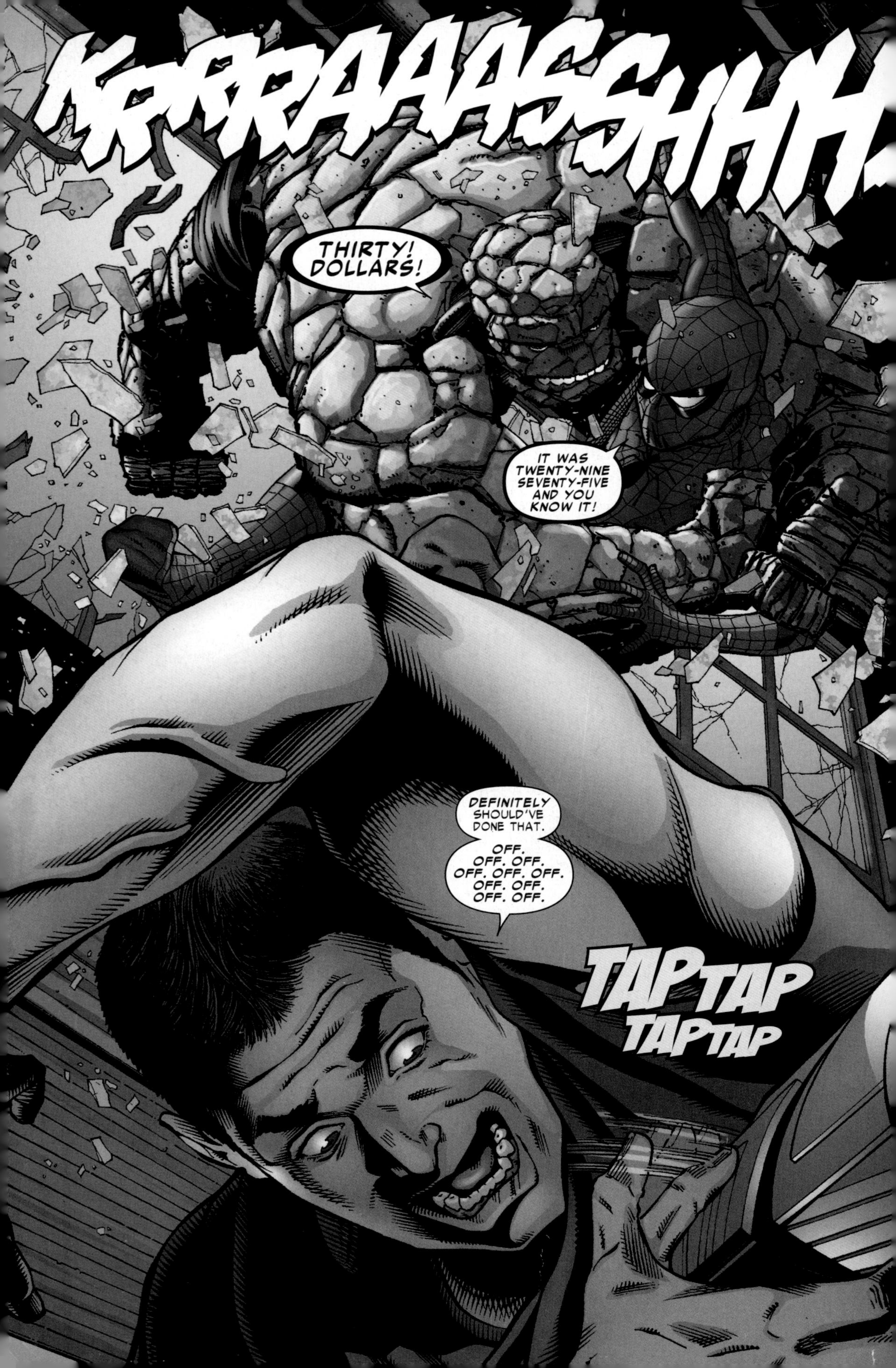
KRRRAAASSHHH!
THIRTY! DOLLARS!
IT WAS TWENTY-NINE SEVENTY-FIVE AND YOU KNOW IT!
DEFINITELY SHOULD'VE DONE THAT.
OFF. OFF. OFF. OFF. OFF. OFF. OFF. OFF. OFF. OFF.
TAPTAP TAPTAP

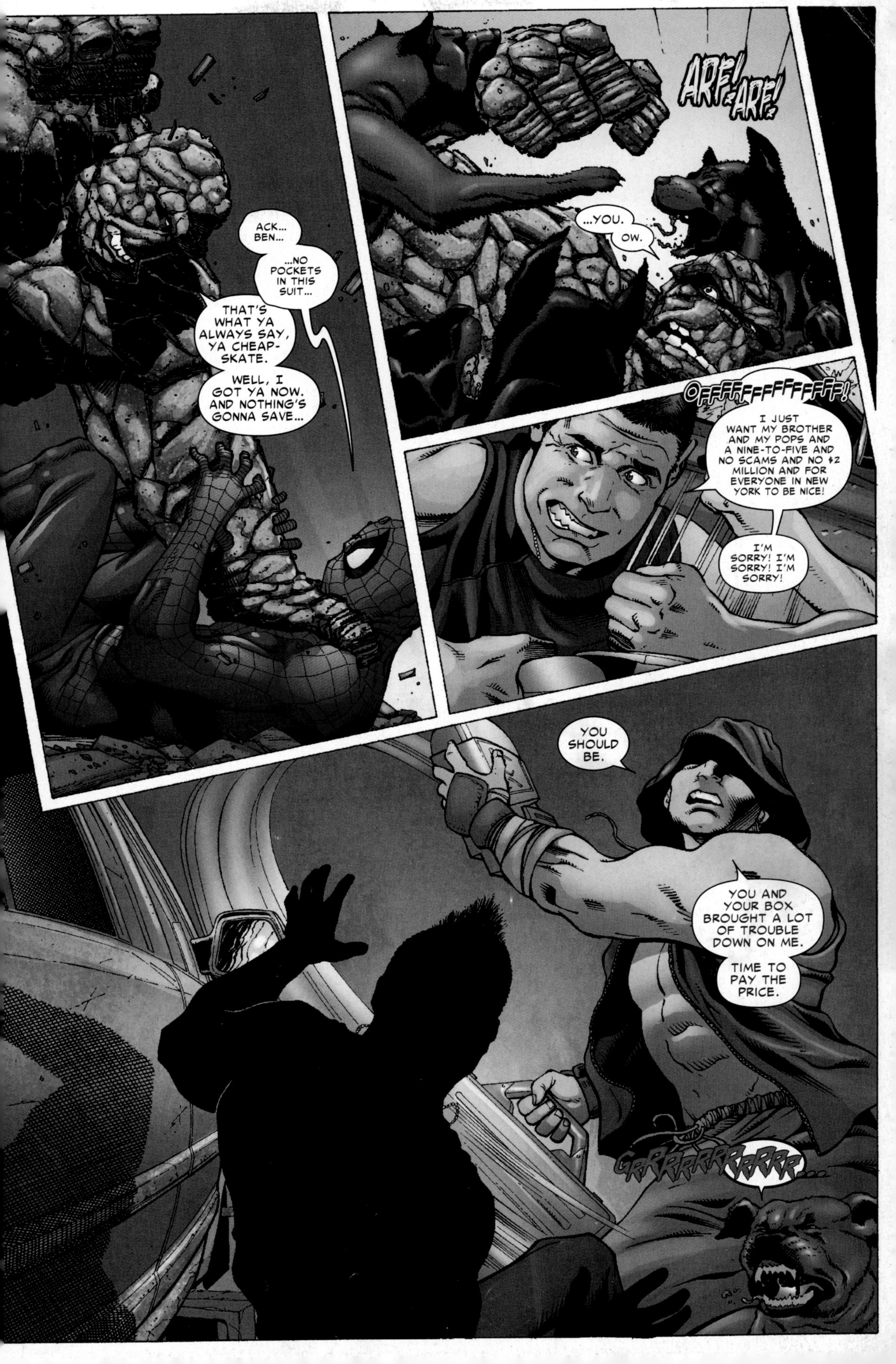
ACK... BEN...
...NO POCKETS IN THIS SUIT...
THAT'S WHAT YA ALWAYS SAY, YA CHEAP-SKATE.
WELL, I GOT YA NOW. AND NOTHING'S GONNA SAVE...
ARF! ARF!
...YOU. OW.
OFFFFFFFFFFFFFF!
I JUST WANT MY BROTHER AND MY POPS AND A NINE-TO-FIVE AND NO SCAMS AND NO $2 MILLION AND FOR EVERYONE IN NEW YORK TO BE NICE!
I'M SORRY! I'M SORRY! I'M SORRY!
YOU SHOULD BE.
YOU AND YOUR BOX BROUGHT A LOT OF TROUBLE DOWN ON ME.
TIME TO PAY THE PRICE.
GRRRRRRRRRRRR...

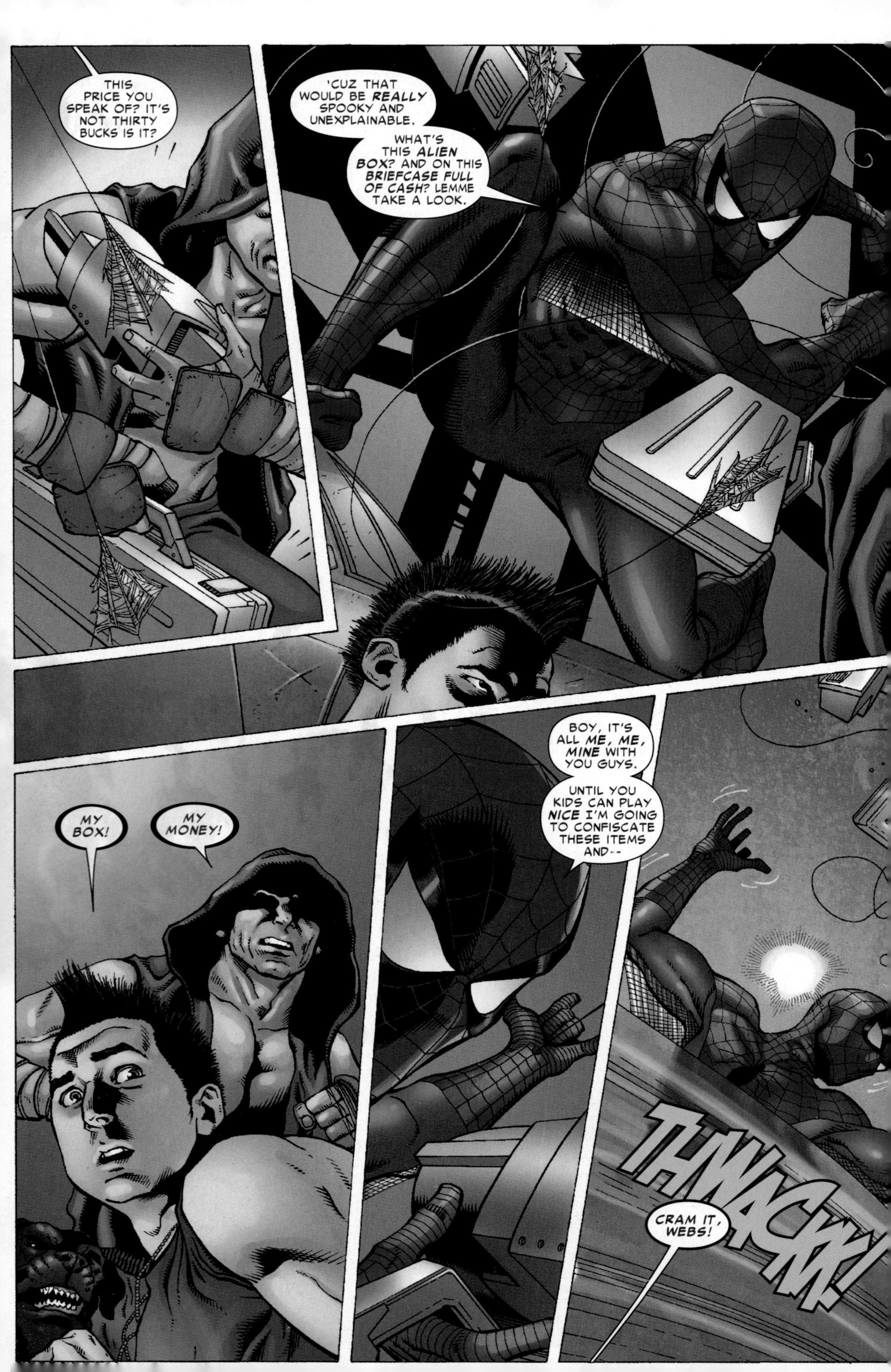

THIS PRICE YOU SPEAK OF? IT'S NOT THIRTY BUCKS IS IT?
'CUZ THAT WOULD BE REALLY SPOOKY AND UNEXPLAINABLE.
WHAT'S THIS ALIEN BOX? AND ON THIS BRIEFCASE FULL OF CASH? LEMME TAKE A LOOK.
MY BOX!
MY MONEY!
BOY, IT'S ALL ME, ME, MINE WITH YOU GUYS.
UNTIL YOU KIDS CAN PLAY NICE I'M GOING TO CONFISCATE THESE ITEMS AND--
THWACK!
CRAM IT, WEBS!

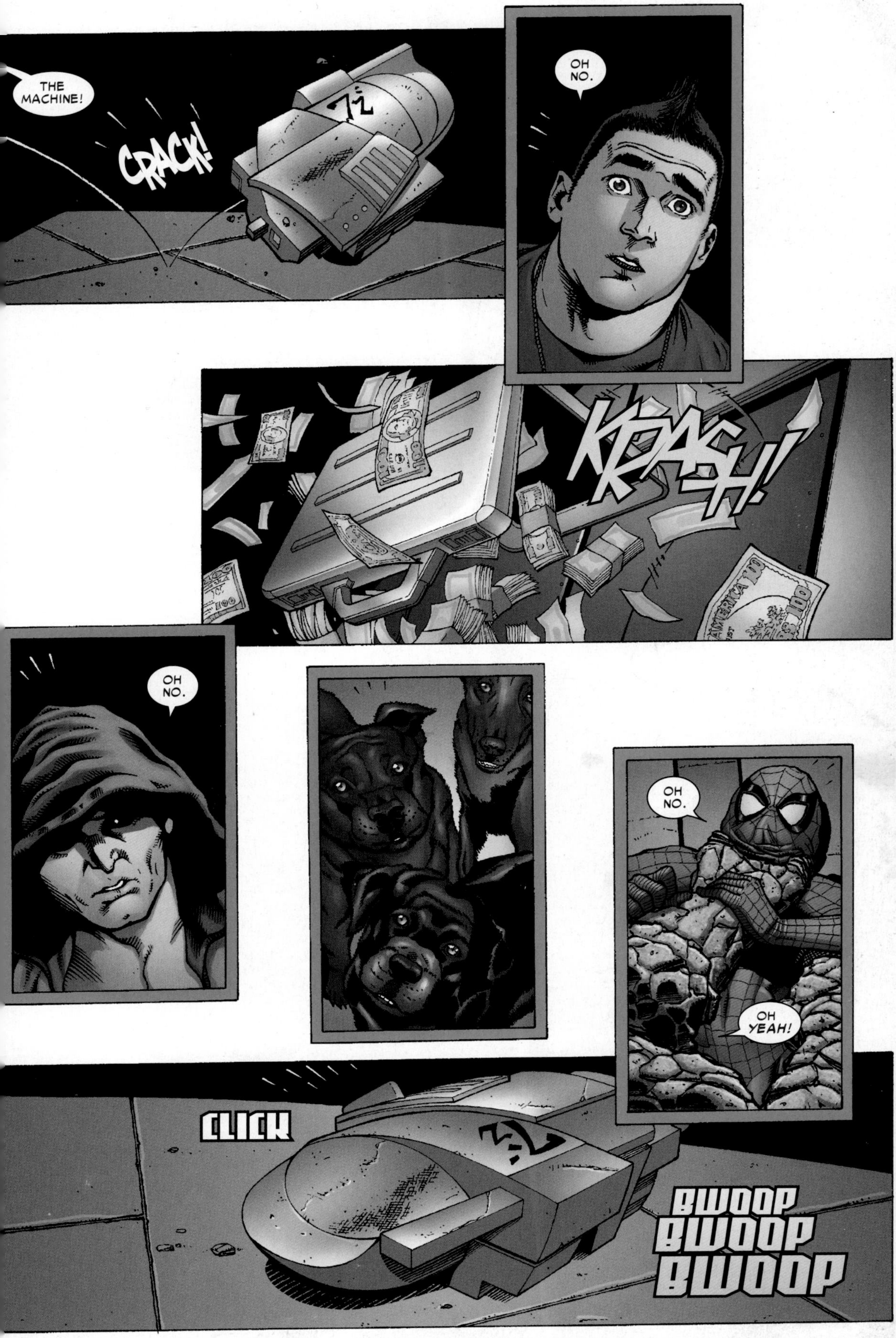
THE MACHINE!
CRACK!
OH NO.
KRASH!
OH NO.
OH NO.
OH YEAH!
CLICK
BWOOP
BWOOP
BWOOP

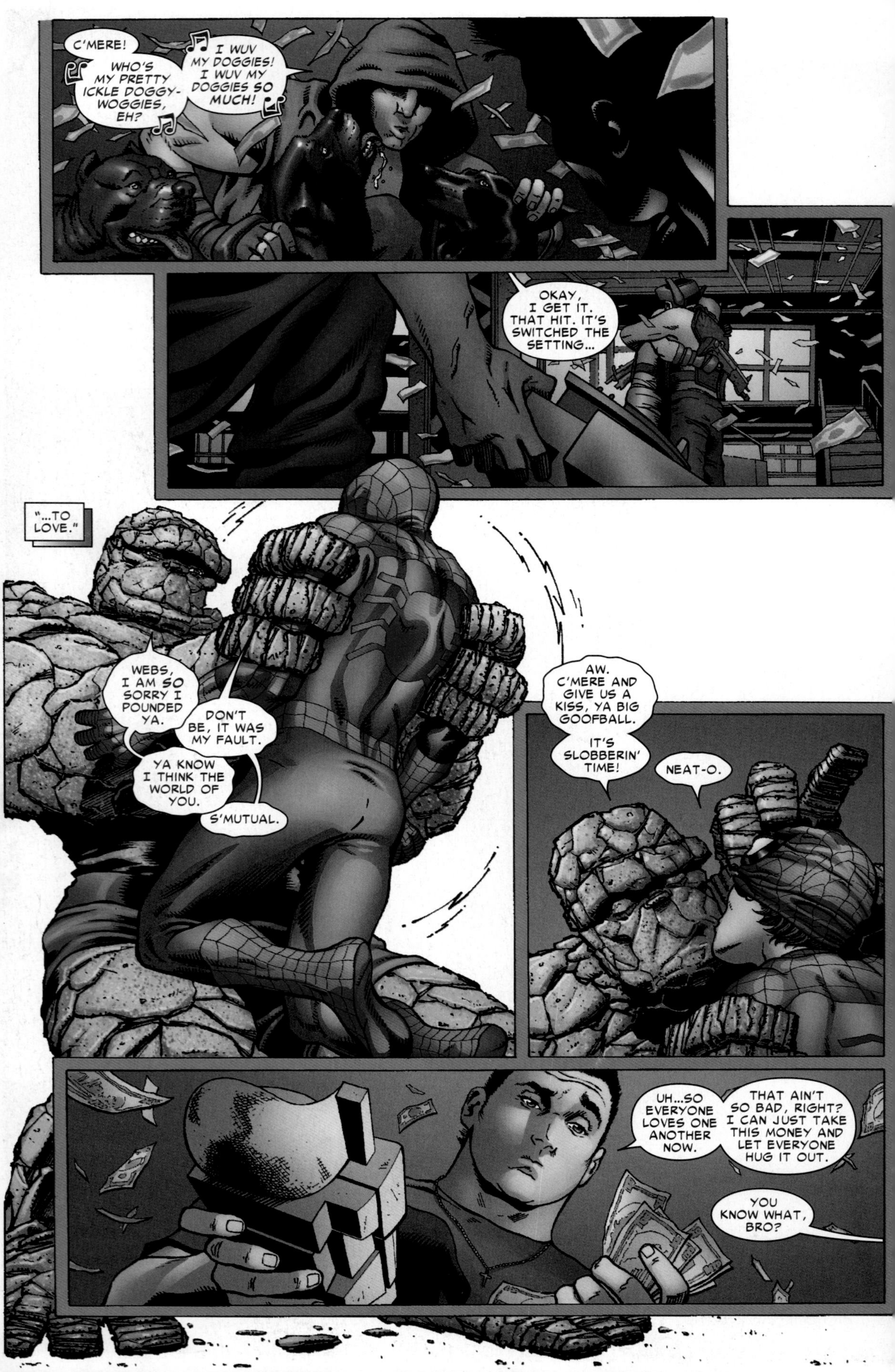
C'MERE!
WHO'S MY PRETTY ICKLE DOGGY-WOGGIES, EH?
I WUV MY DOGGIES! I WUV MY DOGGIES SO MUCH!
OKAY, I GET IT. THAT HIT. IT'S SWITCHED THE SETTING...
"...TO LOVE."
WEBS, I AM SO SORRY I POUNDED YA.
DON'T BE, IT WAS MY FAULT.
YA KNOW I THINK THE WORLD OF YOU.
S'MUTUAL.
AW. C'MERE AND GIVE US A KISS, YA BIG GOOFBALL.
IT'S SLOBBERIN' TIME!
NEAT-O.
UH...SO EVERYONE LOVES ONE ANOTHER NOW.
THAT AIN'T SO BAD, RIGHT? I CAN JUST TAKE THIS MONEY AND LET EVERYONE HUG IT OUT.
YOU KNOW WHAT, BRO?

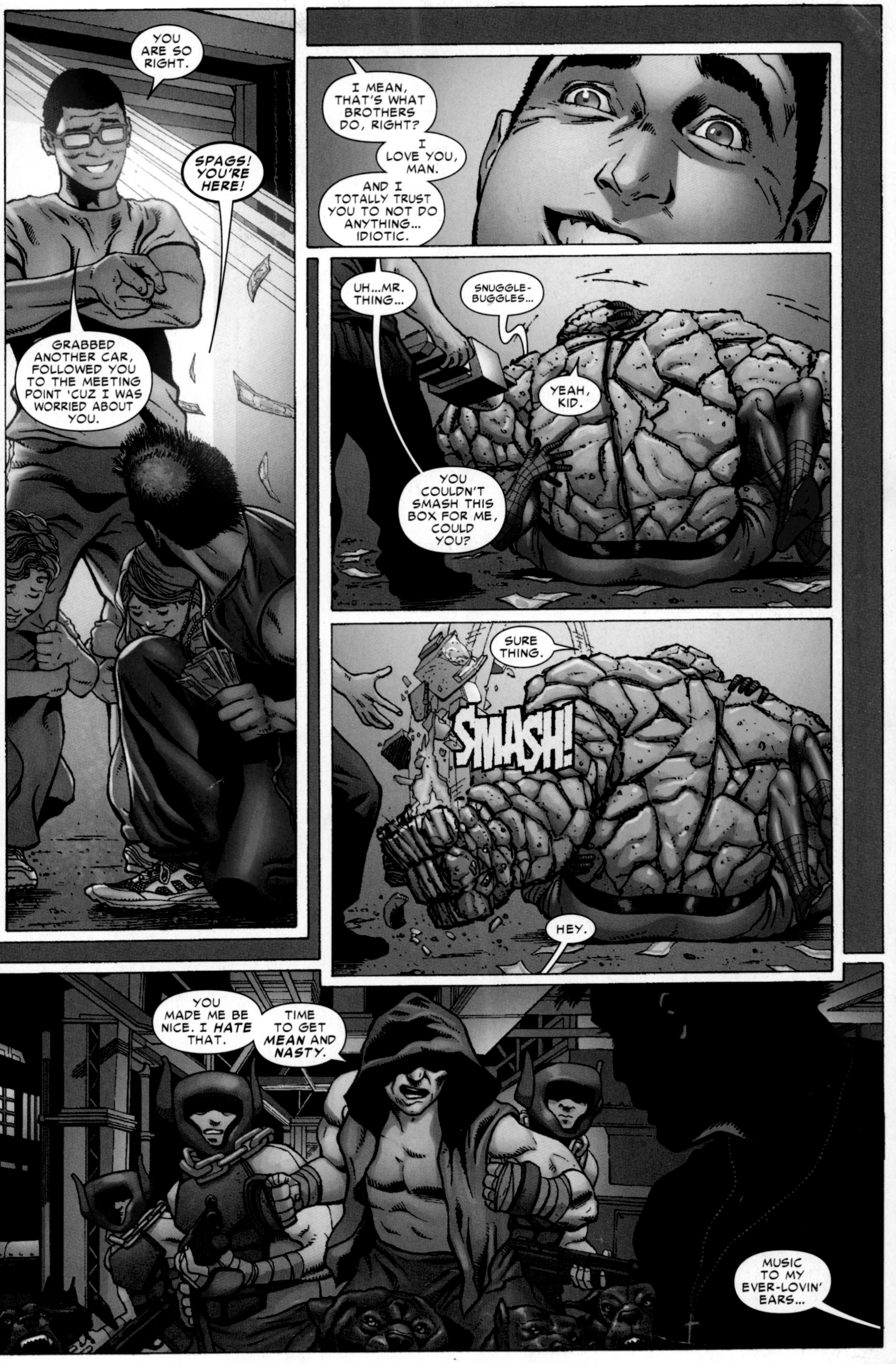
YOU ARE SO RIGHT.
SPAGS! YOU'RE HERE!
GRABBED ANOTHER CAR, FOLLOWED YOU TO THE MEETING POINT 'CUZ I WAS WORRIED ABOUT YOU.
I MEAN, THAT'S WHAT BROTHERS DO, RIGHT?
I LOVE YOU, MAN.
AND I TOTALLY TRUST YOU TO NOT DO ANYTHING... IDIOTIC.
UH...MR. THING...
SNUGGLE-BUGGLES...
YEAH, KID.
YOU COULDN'T SMASH THIS BOX FOR ME, COULD YOU?
SURE THING.
SMASH!
HEY.
YOU MADE ME BE NICE. I HATE THAT.
TIME TO GET MEAN AND NASTY.
MUSIC TO MY EVER-LOVIN' EARS...

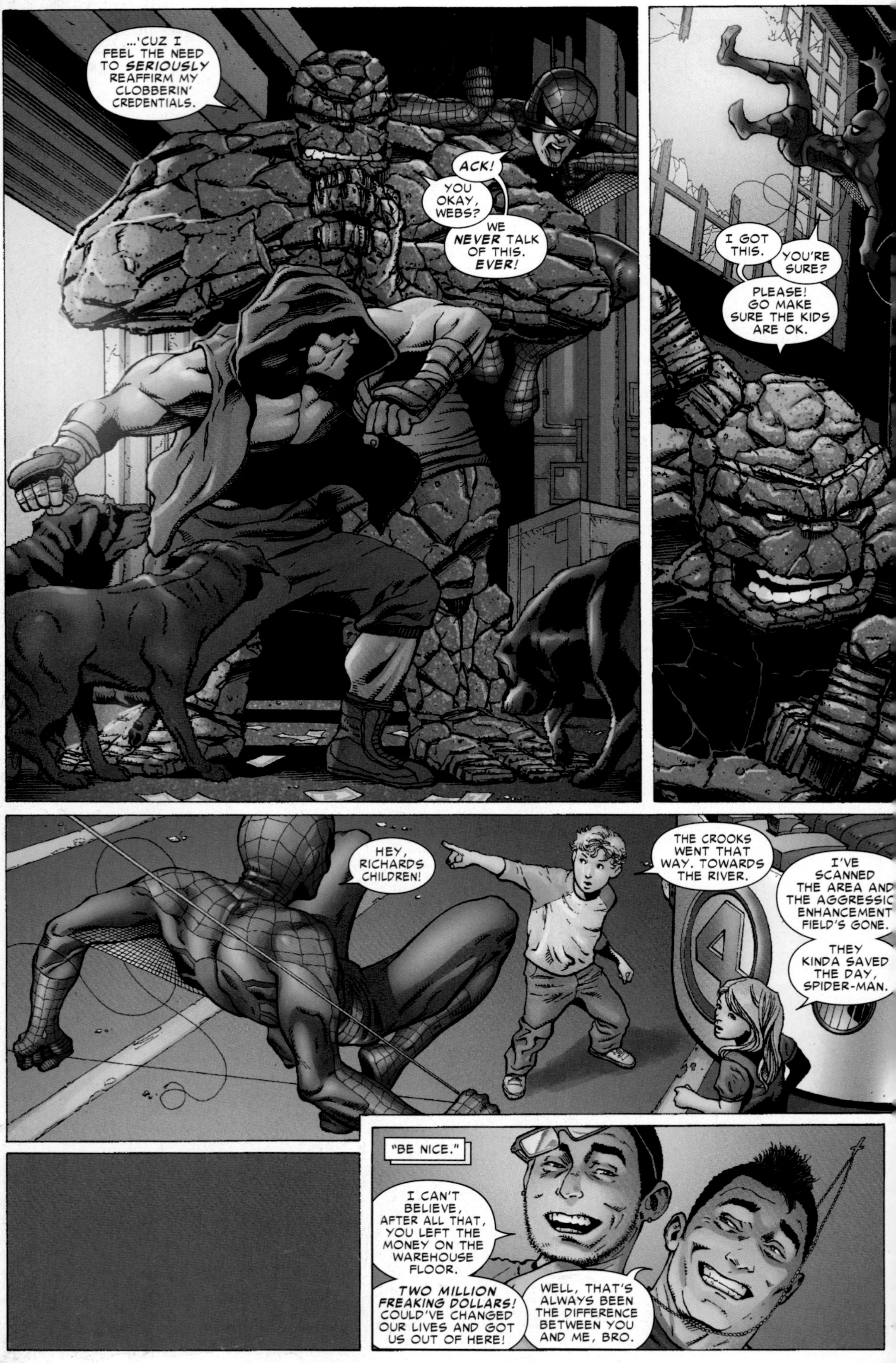
...'CUZ I FEEL THE NEED TO SERIOUSLY REAFFIRM MY CLOBBERIN' CREDENTIALS.
ACK!
YOU OKAY, WEBS?
WE NEVER TALK OF THIS. EVER!
I GOT THIS.
YOU'RE SURE?
PLEASE! GO MAKE SURE THE KIDS ARE OK.
HEY, RICHARDS CHILDREN!
THE CROOKS WENT THAT WAY. TOWARDS THE RIVER.
I'VE SCANNED THE AREA AND THE AGGRESSIC ENHANCEMENT FIELD'S GONE.
THEY KINDA SAVED THE DAY, SPIDER-MAN.
"BE NICE."
I CAN'T BELIEVE, AFTER ALL THAT, YOU LEFT THE MONEY ON THE WAREHOUSE FLOOR.
TWO MILLION FREAKING DOLLARS! COULD'VE CHANGED OUR LIVES AND GOT US OUT OF HERE!
WELL, THAT'S ALWAYS BEEN THE DIFFERENCE BETWEEN YOU AND ME, BRO.

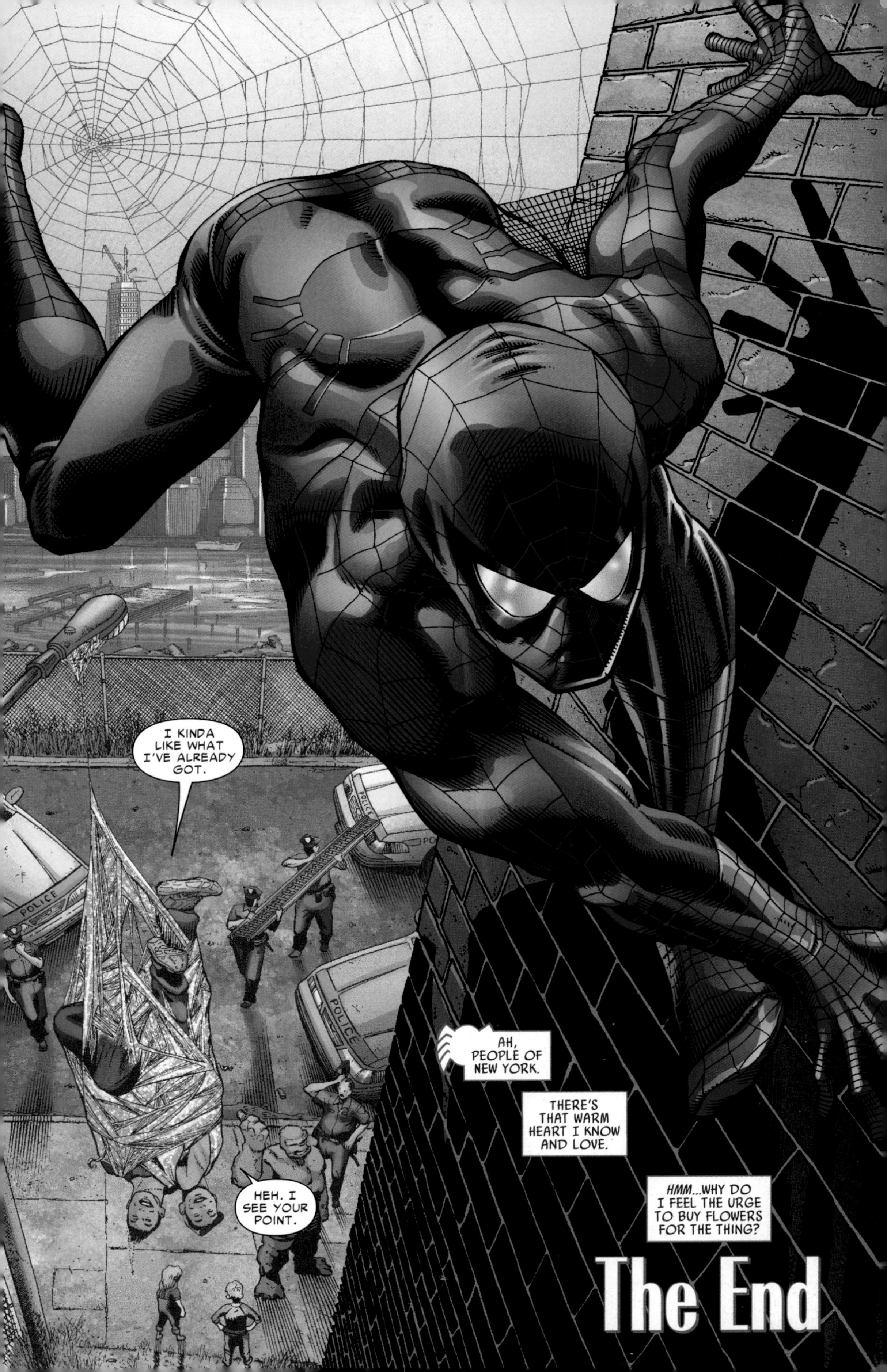
I KINDA LIKE WHAT I'VE ALREADY GOT.
AH, PEOPLE OF NEW YORK.
THERE'S THAT WARM HEART I KNOW AND LOVE.
HEH. I SEE YOUR POINT.
HMM...WHY DO I FEEL THE URGE TO BUY FLOWERS FOR THE THING?
The End

"We live in a cynical world, a cynical, cynical world, and we work in a business [of] tough competitors." That's what Tom Cruise said to Renee Zellweger in Jerry Magui[re] right before she told him to SHUT UP!

Everyone concentrates on Renee's "You had me at hello" part but check the scrip[t]. She rudely interrupts him with "shut up." Twice! When I heard that I knew deep in m[y] heart that here was a marriage that wouldn't last long.

A cynical world.

My son, Elliott, wears Spider-Man on his pyjamas. He's wearing them in bed rig[ht] now while I type this. He has several Spidey toys and, framed on his bedroom wall [is] a KILLER Stuart Immonen original page from Ultimate Spider-Man that shows Spid[ey] swinging past the Daily Bugle and cost more money than I care to recall. He likes oth[er] super heroes too. But he loves Spider-Man. Kids love Spider-Man. I love Spider-Ma[n] and I'm a jaded, cynical (that word again), bald, ruggedly handsome middle-aged ma[n]. The news is filled with horror on a nightly basis and I don't believe 95% of the wor[ds] that come out of our leaders' mouths. But I still love Spider-Man.

There's a million super heroes out there to chose from. A melange of costume[s] saving the day. So what makes Spidey stand out? It's the fact that he's always felt li[ke] one of us. Captain America, The Human Torch, Iron Man, they feel like they're the star[s]. They'd be on the red carpet, heading for the VIP room at the party. Spidey, you fee[l,] would be outside in the rain with you. And that's despite the fact that he's now save[d] the world a billion times, been an Avenger, invented his own web-shooters due to h[im] being a science genius etc. Personally, I'd rather Spidey not wear a suit of armour. H[is] heroism seems greater when he's wearing that thin cloth outfit. The one he stitch[ed] together himself...it's a testament to all the great writers Spidey's had over the yea[rs] that he remains grounded despite his extraordinary exploits. It's inherent in Stan Le[e] and Steve Ditko's brilliant original concept.

And he always tries to do good. I genuinely take a lot of heart from the fact tha[t] when you study the tricks of writing and you're trying to learn how to make reade[rs] like a character, the answer is a remarkably simple one – have them do a kindness [to] someone. Spidey does this more than any super hero character I can think of, usual[ly] to the cost of his own personal life. And that's why he's so beloved, I think. He does th[is] when he's an ordinary guy.

Turn on the news and you're besieged by war, greed and appalling crimes. It ca[n] make you give up on humanity. And then you realise that, on an intrinsic level, there[']s nothing that human beings respond to more than kindness and sacrifice.

It's not such a cynical world when Spider-Man's around.

Rob Williams, Oct. 201[2]

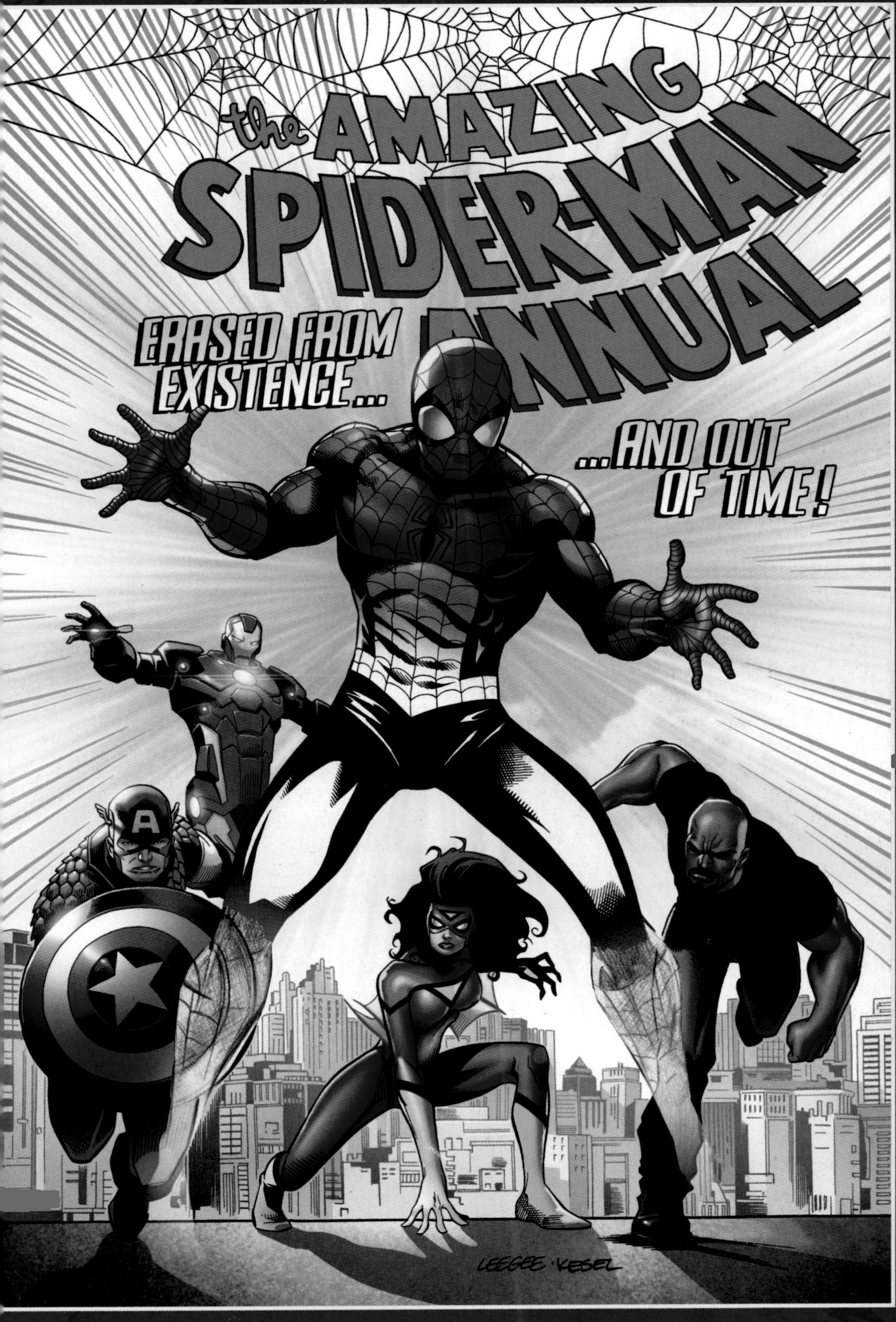
the AMAZING SPIDER-MAN ANNUAL
ERASED FROM EXISTENCE...
...AND OUT OF TIME!
LEEGEE · KESEL

AMAZING SPIDER-MAN ANNUAL #39

While attending a demonstration in radiology, high school science student Peter Parker was bitten by a spider that had accidentally been exposed to radioactive rays. Through a miracle of science, Peter soon found that he had gained the spider's powers...and had, in effect, become a human spider! After the tragic death of his Uncle Ben at the hands of a robber he let escape, Peter Parker learned that with great power must also come great responsibility. Today, Peter works as a top researcher at Horizon Labs, but he still finds time to save the world as a member of the Avengers and as...

the AMAZING SPIDER-MAN

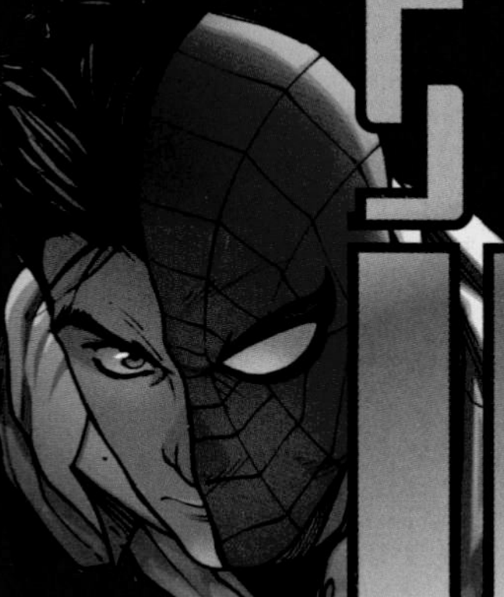

SPIDER WHO?

BRIAN REED writer

LEE GARBETT pencils

JOHN LUCAS inks

ANTONIO FABELA color art

VC'S JOE CARAMAGNA letters

LEE GARBETT, KARL KESEL and WIL QUINTANA cover

ELLIE PYLE editor

STEPHEN WACKER senior editor

AXEL ALONSO editor in chief

JOE QUESADA chief creative officer

DAN BUCKLEY publisher

ALAN FINE executive producer

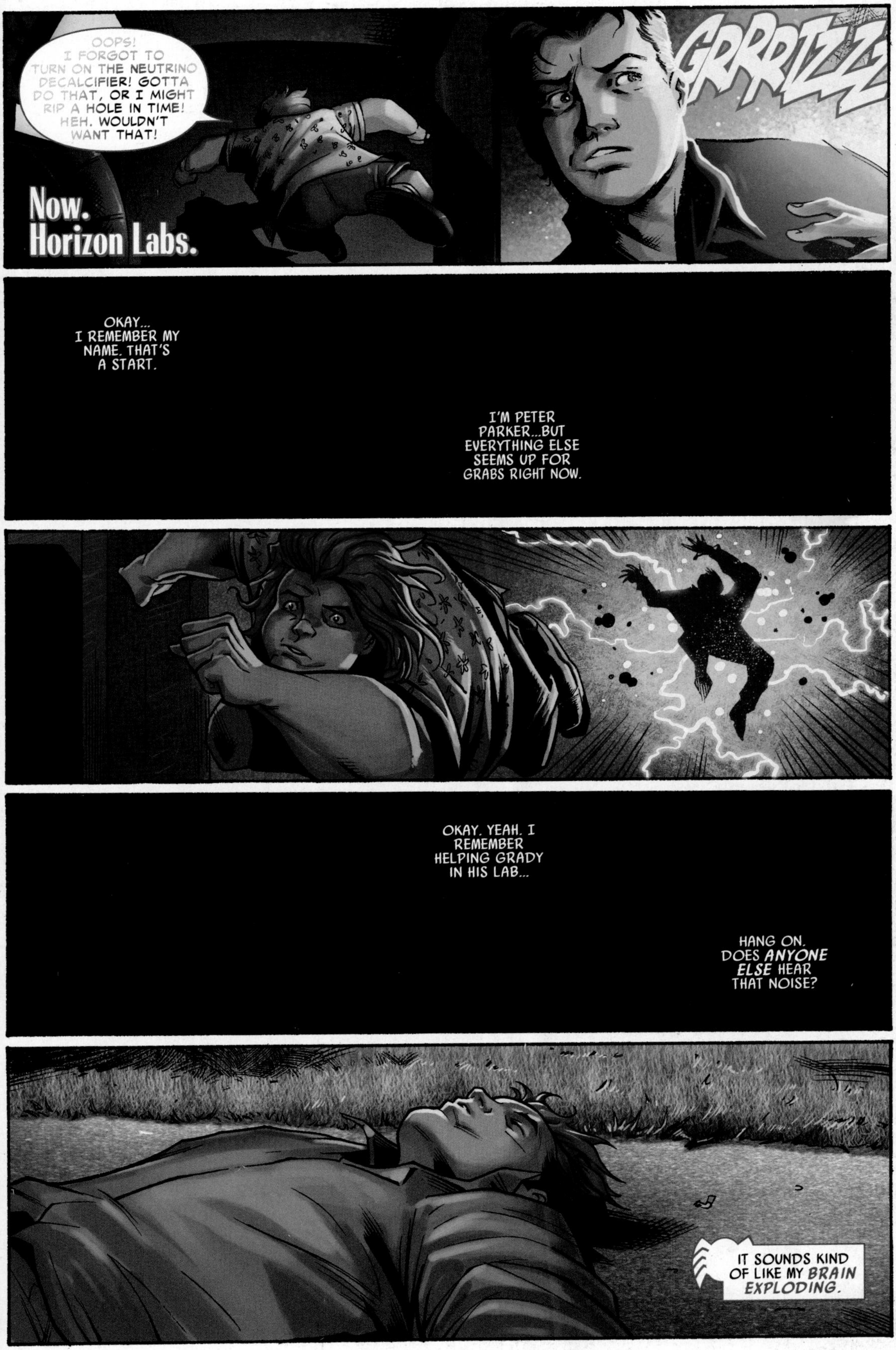
OOPS! I FORGOT TO TURN ON THE NEUTRINO DECALCIFIER! GOTTA DO THAT, OR I MIGHT RIP A HOLE IN TIME! HEH. WOULDN'T WANT THAT!
Now. Horizon Labs.
GRRRIZZ
OKAY... I REMEMBER MY NAME. THAT'S A START.
I'M PETER PARKER...BUT EVERYTHING ELSE SEEMS UP FOR GRABS RIGHT NOW.
OKAY. YEAH. I REMEMBER HELPING GRADY IN HIS LAB...
HANG ON. DOES ANYONE ELSE HEAR THAT NOISE?
IT SOUNDS KIND OF LIKE MY BRAIN EXPLODING.

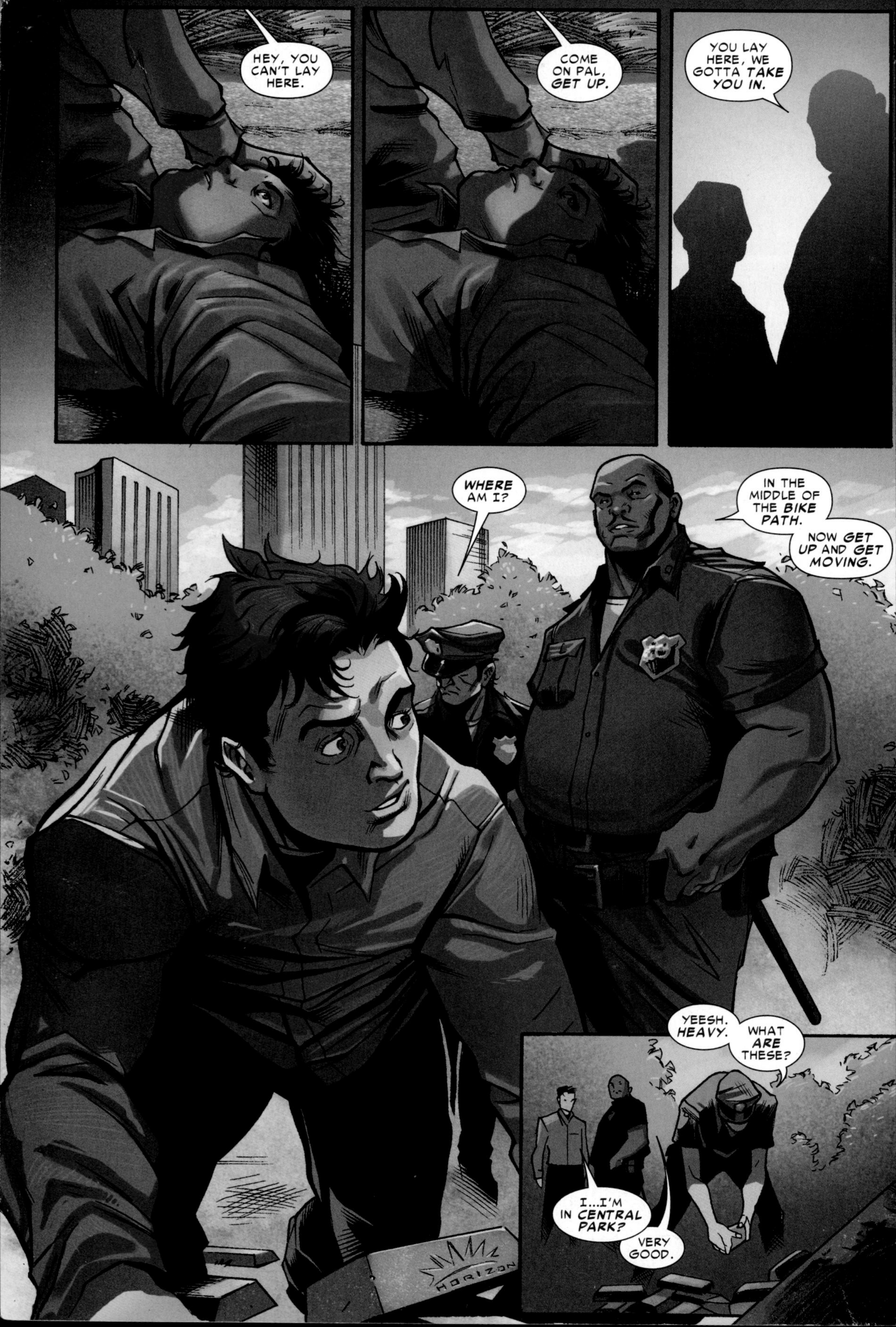
HEY, YOU CAN'T LAY HERE.
COME ON PAL, GET UP.
YOU LAY HERE, WE GOTTA TAKE YOU IN.
WHERE AM I?
IN THE MIDDLE OF THE BIKE PATH.
NOW GET UP AND GET MOVING.
YEESH. HEAVY.
WHAT ARE THESE?
I...I'M IN CENTRAL PARK?
VERY GOOD.
HORIZON

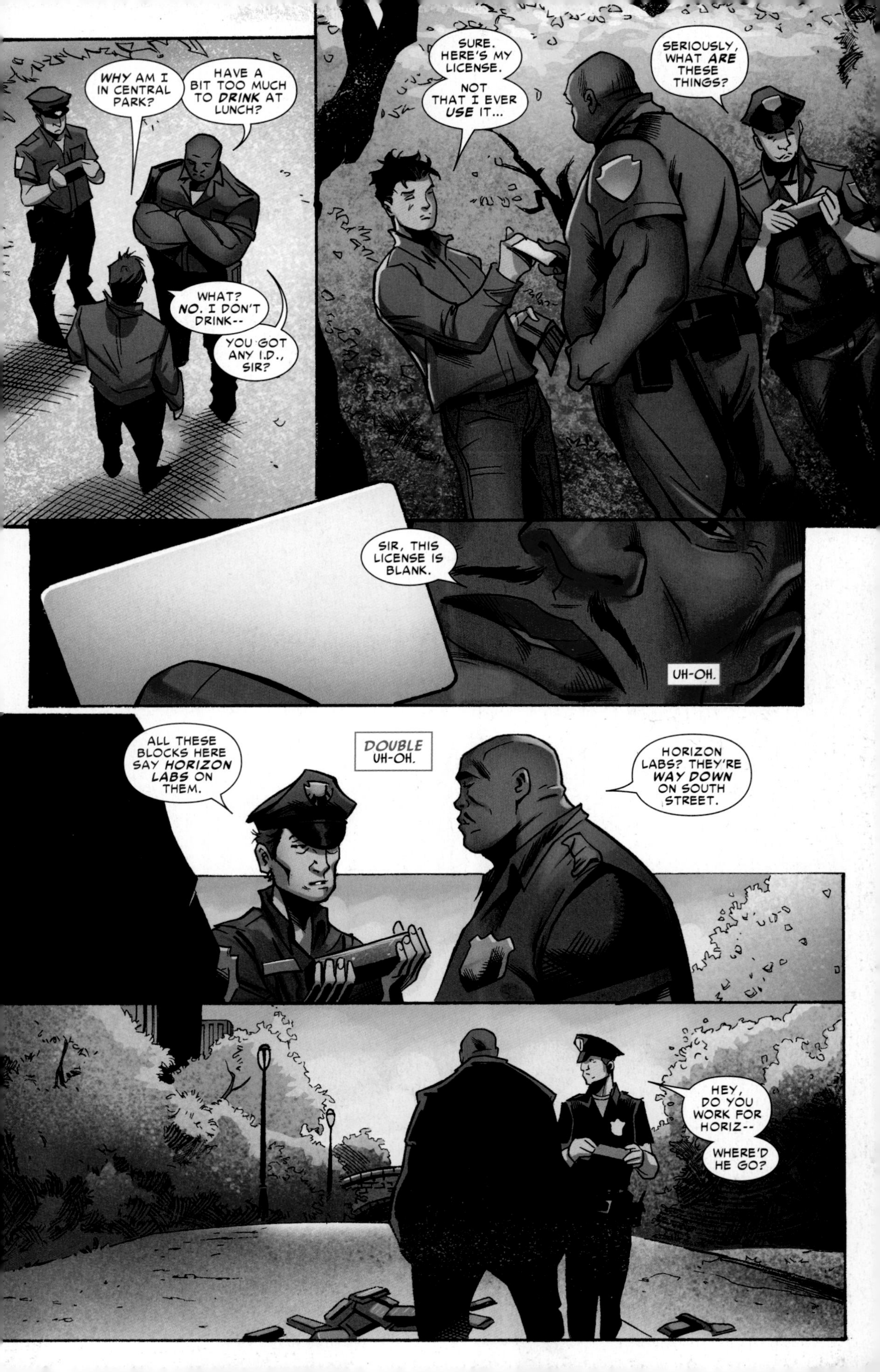
WHY AM I IN CENTRAL PARK?
HAVE A BIT TOO MUCH TO DRINK AT LUNCH?
WHAT? NO. I DON'T DRINK--
YOU GOT ANY I.D., SIR?
SURE. HERE'S MY LICENSE.
NOT THAT I EVER USE IT...
SERIOUSLY, WHAT ARE THESE THINGS?
SIR, THIS LICENSE IS BLANK.
UH-OH.
ALL THESE BLOCKS HERE SAY HORIZON LABS ON THEM.
DOUBLE UH-OH.
HORIZON LABS? THEY'RE WAY DOWN ON SOUTH STREET.
HEY, DO YOU WORK FOR HORIZ--
WHERE'D HE GO?

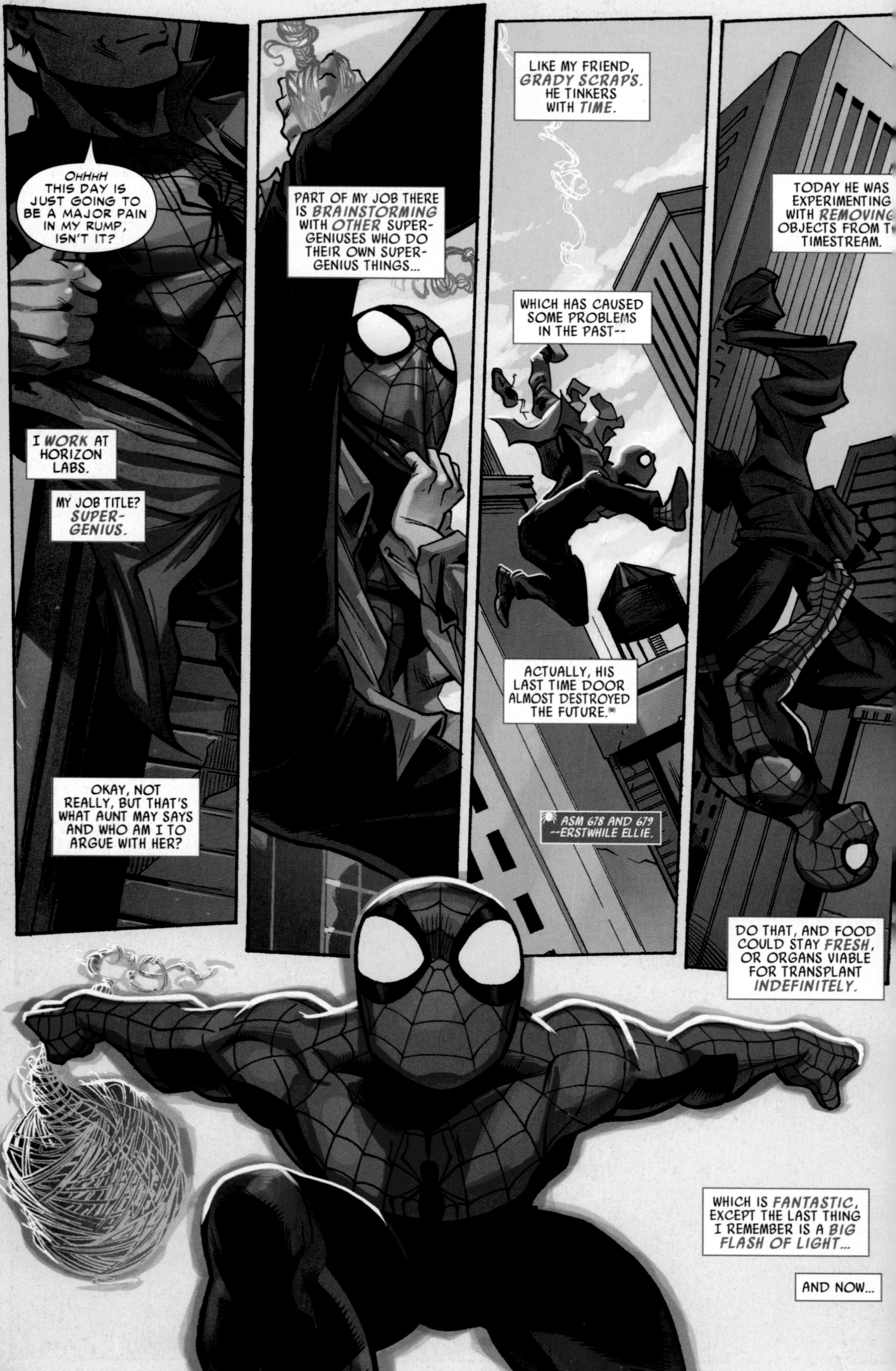

OHHHH THIS DAY IS JUST GOING TO BE A MAJOR PAIN IN MY RUMP, ISN'T IT?
I WORK AT HORIZON LABS.
MY JOB TITLE? SUPER-GENIUS.
OKAY, NOT REALLY, BUT THAT'S WHAT AUNT MAY SAYS AND WHO AM I TO ARGUE WITH HER?
PART OF MY JOB THERE IS BRAINSTORMING WITH OTHER SUPER-GENIUSES WHO DO THEIR OWN SUPER-GENIUS THINGS...
LIKE MY FRIEND, GRADY SCRAPS. HE TINKERS WITH TIME.
WHICH HAS CAUSED SOME PROBLEMS IN THE PAST--
ACTUALLY, HIS LAST TIME DOOR ALMOST DESTROYED THE FUTURE.*
*ASM 678 AND 679 --ERSTWHILE ELLIE.
TODAY HE WAS EXPERIMENTING WITH REMOVING OBJECTS FROM T
TIMESTREAM.
DO THAT, AND FOOD COULD STAY FRESH, OR ORGANS VIABLE FOR TRANSPLANT INDEFINITELY.
WHICH IS FANTASTIC, EXCEPT THE LAST THING I REMEMBER IS A BIG FLASH OF LIGHT...
AND NOW...

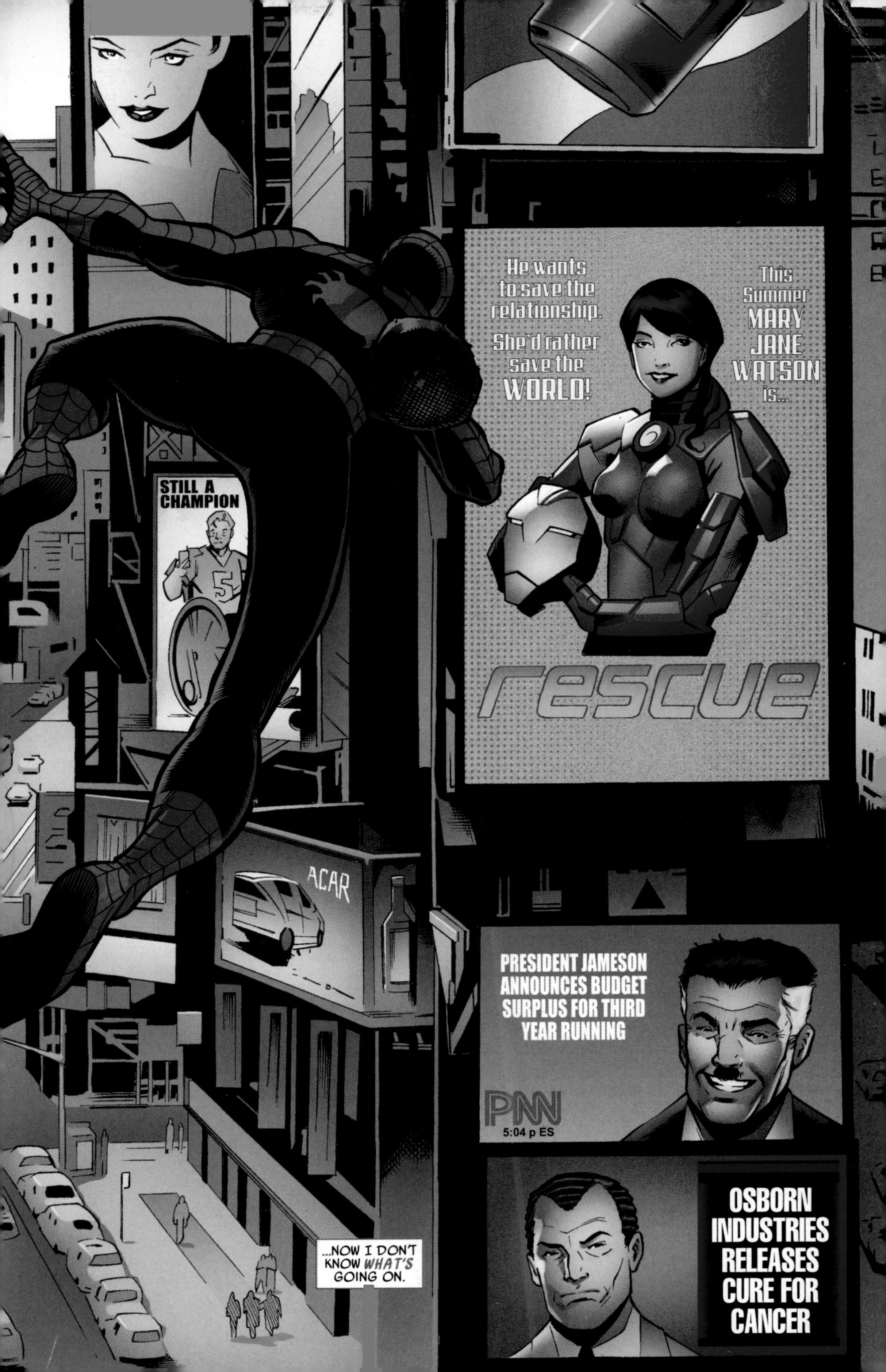
STILL A CHAMPION
He wants to save the relationship.
She'd rather save the WORLD!
This Summer MARY JANE WATSON is...
rescue
ACAR
PRESIDENT JAMESON ANNOUNCES BUDGET SURPLUS FOR THIRD YEAR RUNNING
PNN
5:04 p ES
OSBORN INDUSTRIES RELEASES CURE FOR CANCER
...NOW I DON'T KNOW WHAT'S GOING ON.

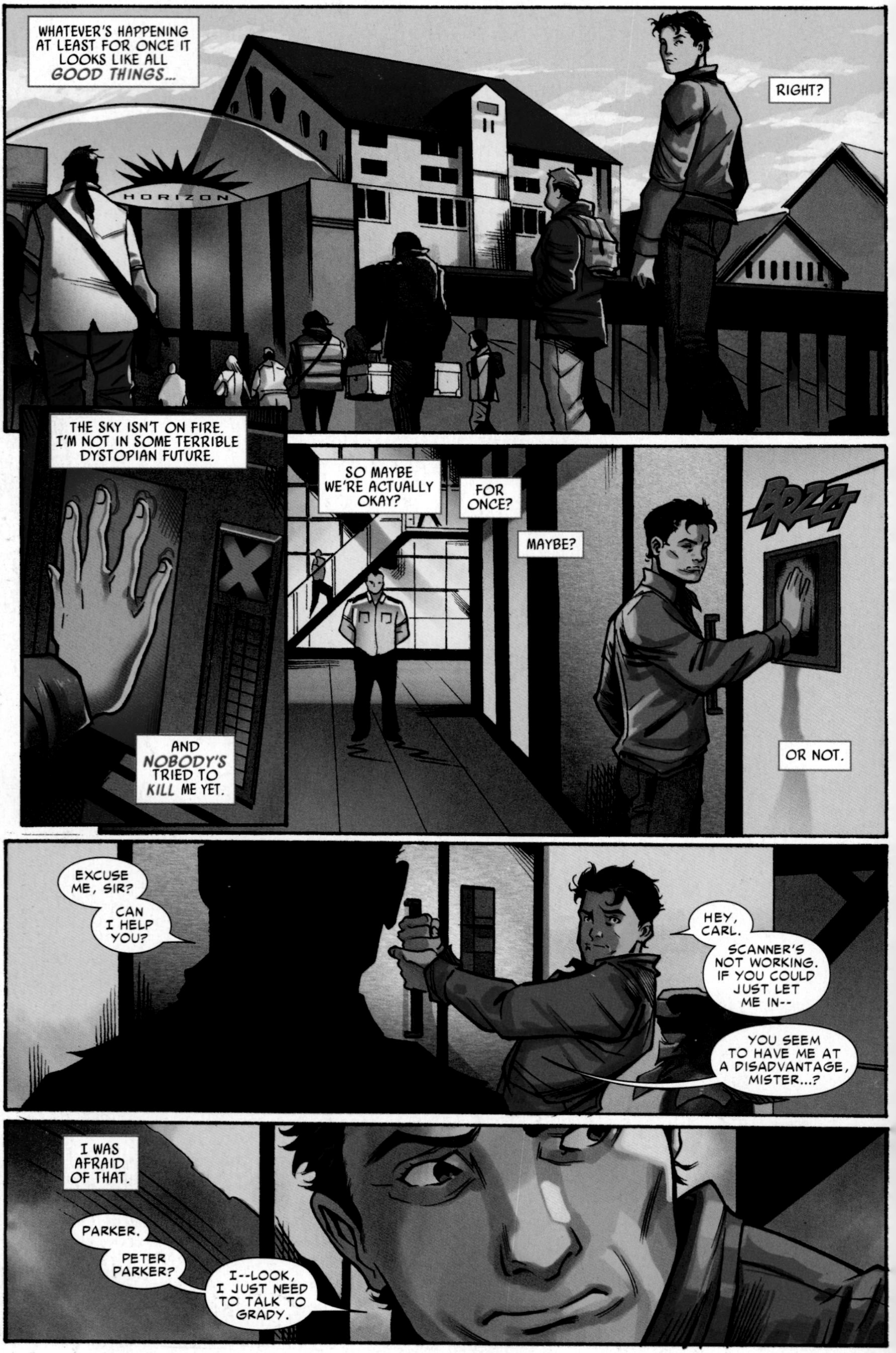
WHATEVER'S HAPPENING AT LEAST FOR ONCE IT LOOKS LIKE ALL GOOD THINGS...
HORIZON
RIGHT?
THE SKY ISN'T ON FIRE. I'M NOT IN SOME TERRIBLE DYSTOPIAN FUTURE.
AND NOBODY'S TRIED TO KILL ME YET.
SO MAYBE WE'RE ACTUALLY OKAY?
FOR ONCE?
MAYBE?
BRZZT
OR NOT.
EXCUSE ME, SIR?
CAN I HELP YOU?
HEY, CARL.
SCANNER'S NOT WORKING. IF YOU COULD JUST LET ME IN--
YOU SEEM TO HAVE ME AT A DISADVANTAGE, MISTER...?
I WAS AFRAID OF THAT.
PARKER.
PETER PARKER?
I--LOOK, I JUST NEED TO TALK TO GRADY.

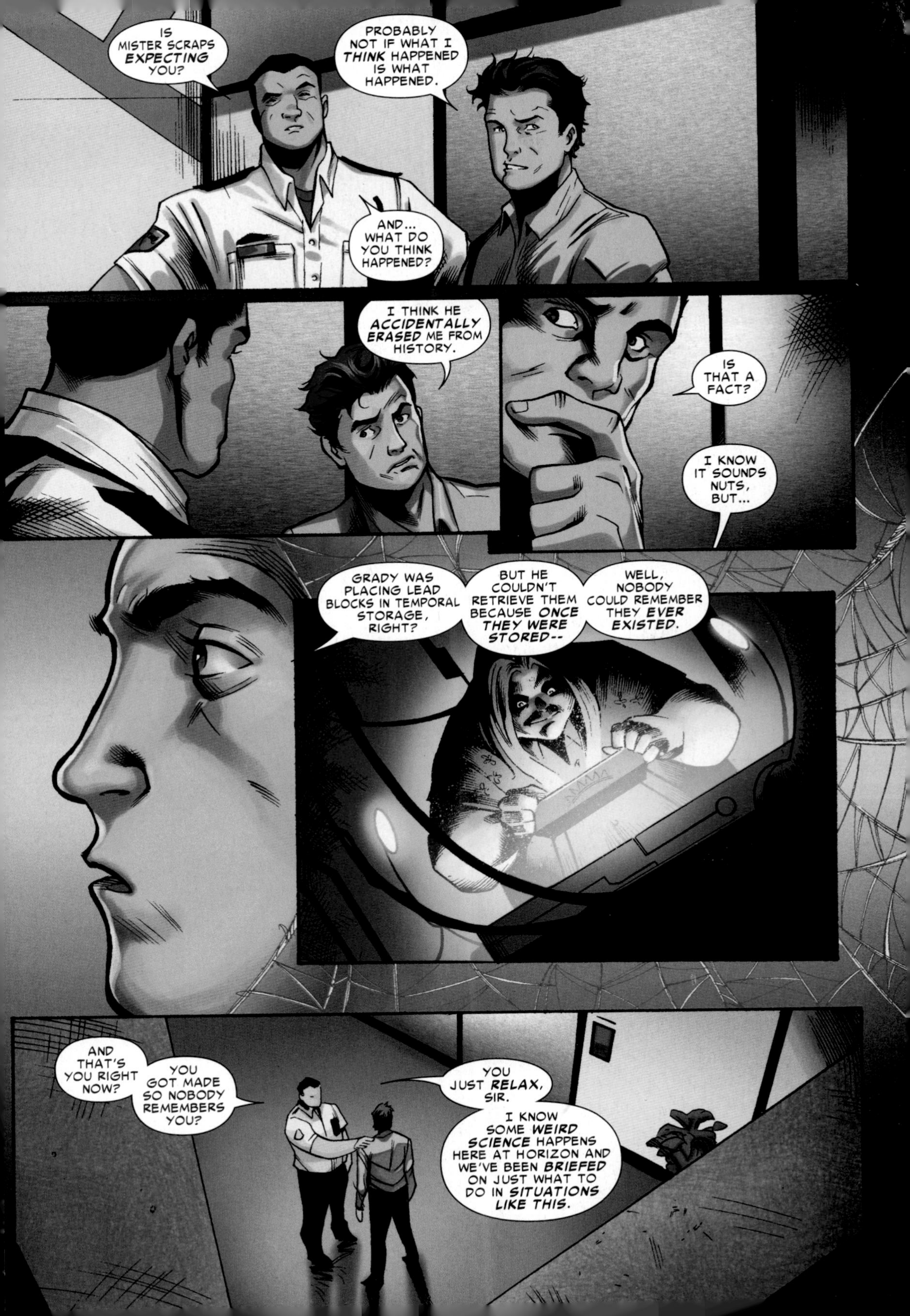
IS MISTER SCRAPS EXPECTING YOU?
PROBABLY NOT IF WHAT I THINK HAPPENED IS WHAT HAPPENED.
AND... WHAT DO YOU THINK HAPPENED?
I THINK HE ACCIDENTALLY ERASED ME FROM HISTORY.
IS THAT A FACT?
I KNOW IT SOUNDS NUTS, BUT...
GRADY WAS PLACING LEAD BLOCKS IN TEMPORAL STORAGE, RIGHT?
BUT HE COULDN'T RETRIEVE THEM BECAUSE ONCE THEY WERE STORED--
WELL, NOBODY COULD REMEMBER THEY EVER EXISTED.
AND THAT'S YOU RIGHT NOW?
YOU GOT MADE SO NOBODY REMEMBERS YOU?
YOU JUST RELAX, SIR.
I KNOW SOME WEIRD SCIENCE HAPPENS HERE AT HORIZON AND WE'VE BEEN BRIEFED ON JUST WHAT TO DO IN SITUATIONS LIKE THIS.

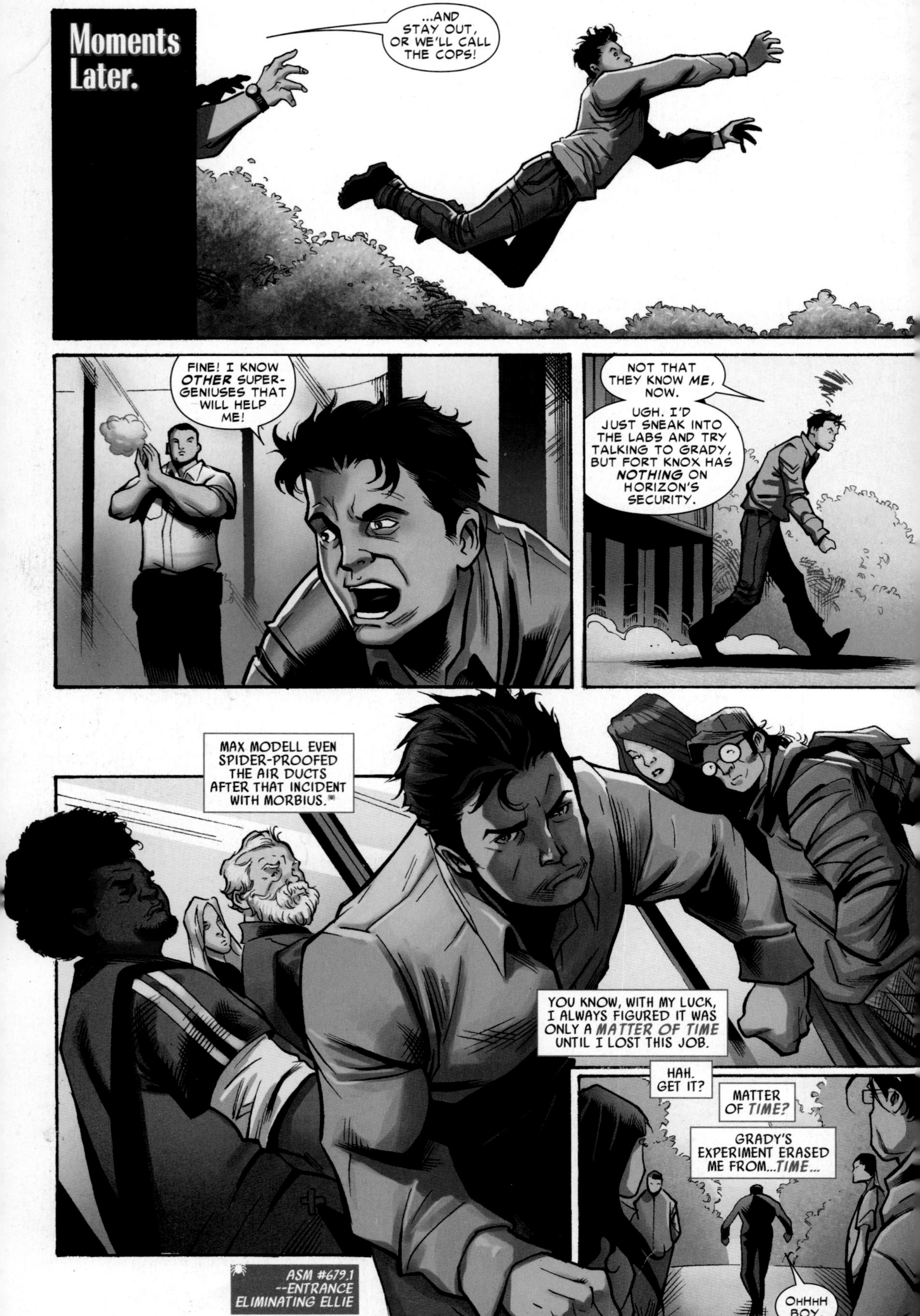
Moments Later.
...AND STAY OUT, OR WE'LL CALL THE COPS!
FINE! I KNOW OTHER SUPER-GENIUSES THAT WILL HELP ME!
NOT THAT THEY KNOW ME, NOW.
UGH. I'D JUST SNEAK INTO THE LABS AND TRY TALKING TO GRADY, BUT FORT KNOX HAS NOTHING ON HORIZON'S SECURITY.
MAX MODELL EVEN SPIDER-PROOFED THE AIR DUCTS AFTER THAT INCIDENT WITH MORBIUS.*
YOU KNOW, WITH MY LUCK, I ALWAYS FIGURED IT WAS ONLY A MATTER OF TIME UNTIL I LOST THIS JOB.
HAH. GET IT?
MATTER OF TIME?
GRADY'S EXPERIMENT ERASED ME FROM...TIME...
OHHHH BOY.
ASM #679.1 --ENTRANCE ELIMINATING ELLIE

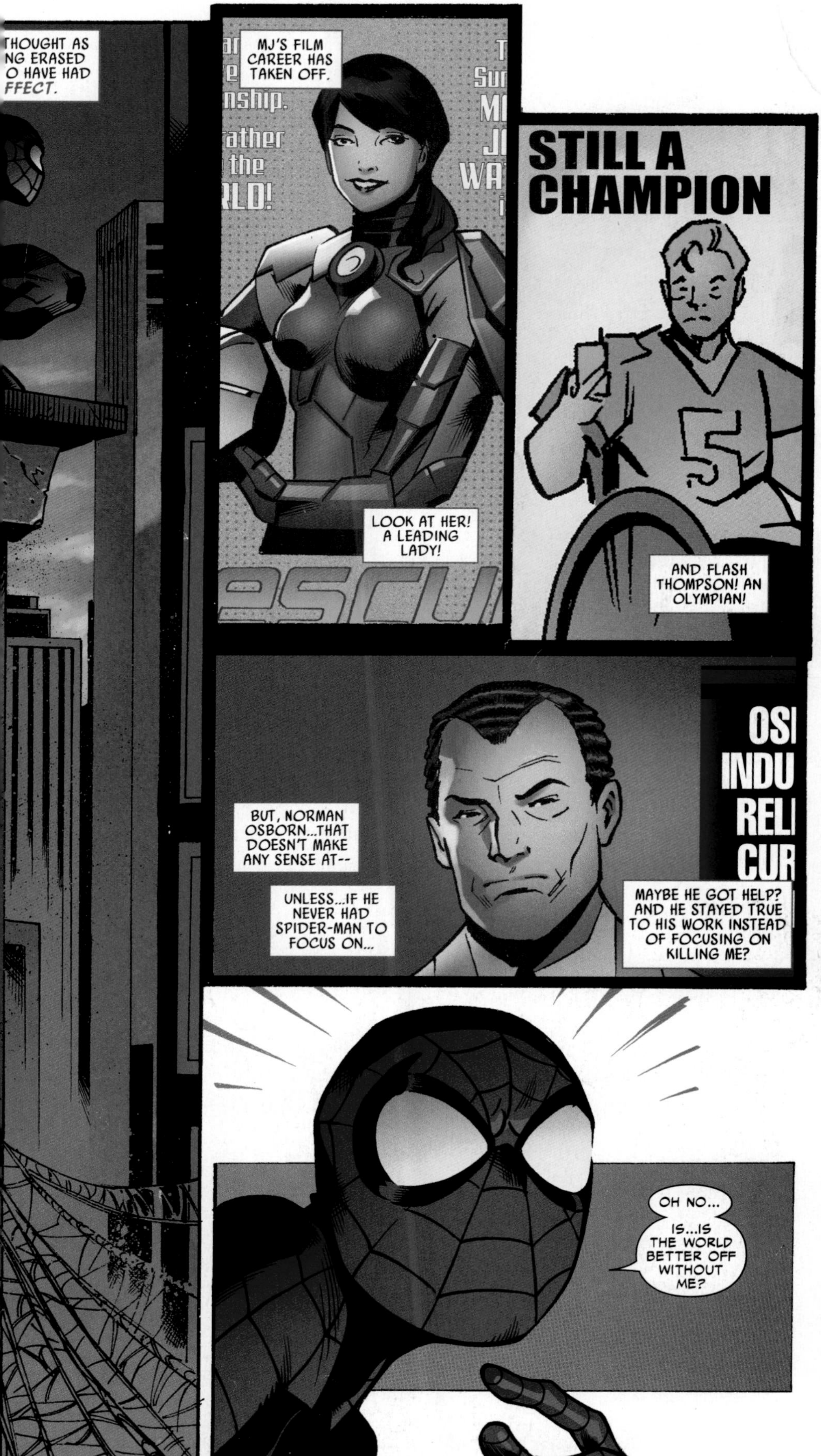
THOUGHT AS
NG ERASED
O HAVE HAD
FFECT.
MJ'S FILM CAREER HAS TAKEN OFF.
LOOK AT HER! A LEADING LADY!
STILL A CHAMPION
AND FLASH THOMPSON! AN OLYMPIAN!
BUT, NORMAN OSBORN...THAT DOESN'T MAKE ANY SENSE AT--
UNLESS...IF HE NEVER HAD SPIDER-MAN TO FOCUS ON...
MAYBE HE GOT HELP? AND HE STAYED TRUE TO HIS WORK INSTEAD OF FOCUSING ON KILLING ME?
OH NO...
IS...IS THE WORLD BETTER OFF WITHOUT ME?

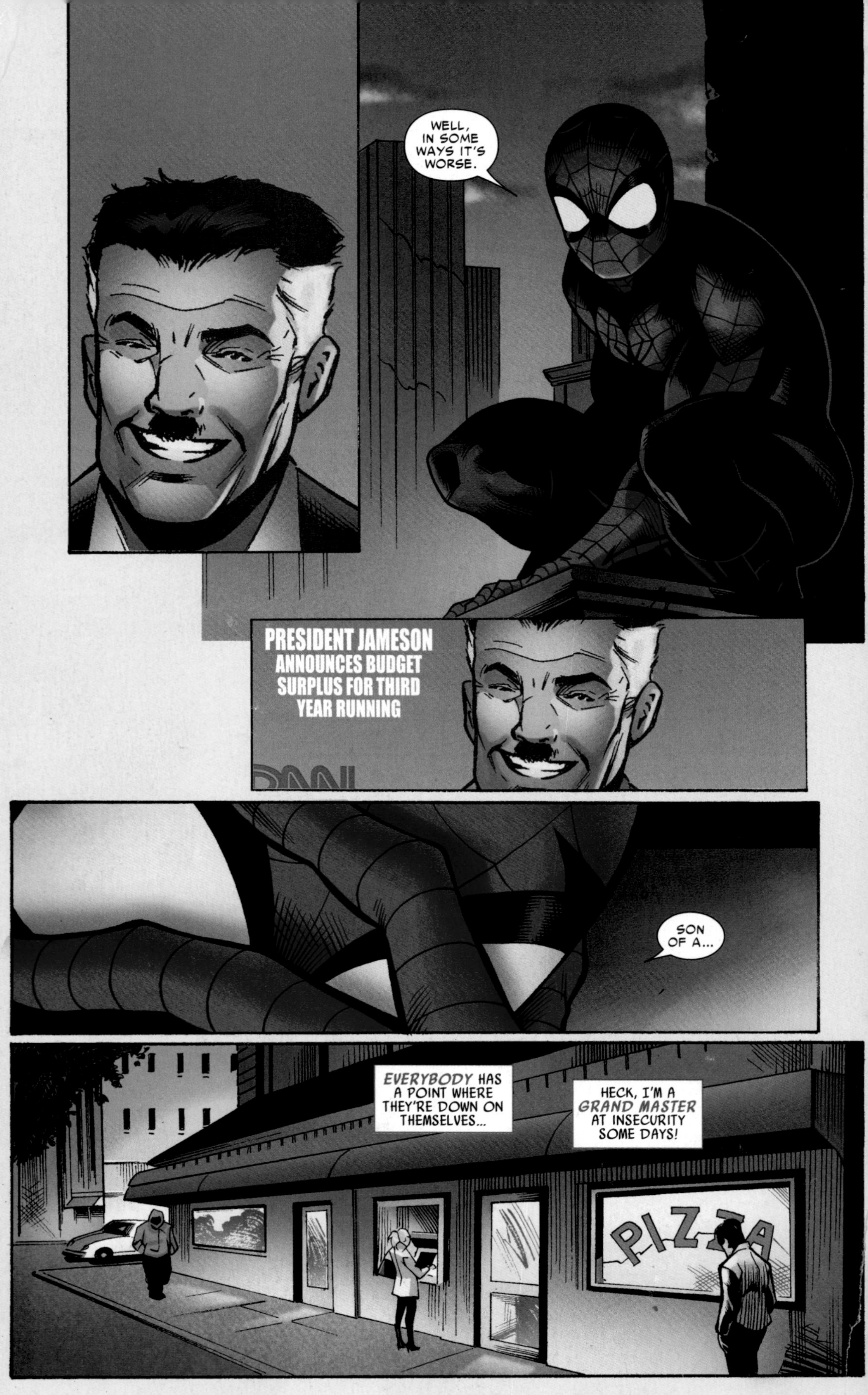
WELL, IN SOME WAYS IT'S WORSE.
PRESIDENT JAMESON ANNOUNCES BUDGET SURPLUS FOR THIRD YEAR RUNNING
SON OF A...
EVERYBODY HAS A POINT WHERE THEY'RE DOWN ON THEMSELVES...
HECK, I'M A GRAND MASTER AT INSECURITY SOME DAYS!
PIZZA

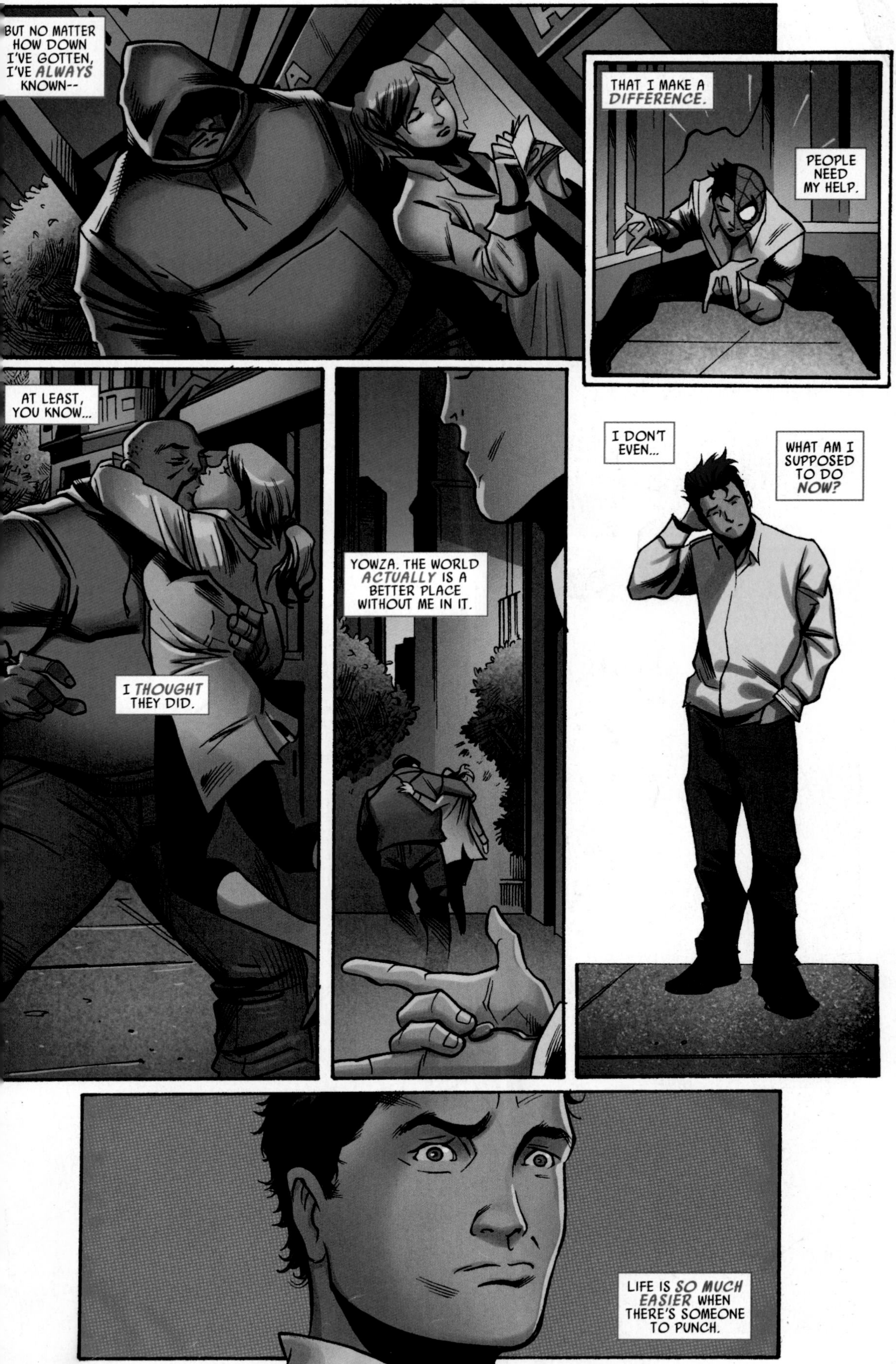
BUT NO MATTER HOW DOWN I'VE GOTTEN, I'VE ALWAYS KNOWN--
THAT I MAKE A DIFFERENCE.
PEOPLE NEED MY HELP.
AT LEAST, YOU KNOW...
I THOUGHT THEY DID.
YOWZA. THE WORLD ACTUALLY IS A BETTER PLACE WITHOUT ME IN IT.
I DON'T EVEN...
WHAT AM I SUPPOSED TO DO NOW?
LIFE IS SO MUCH EASIER WHEN THERE'S SOMEONE TO PUNCH.

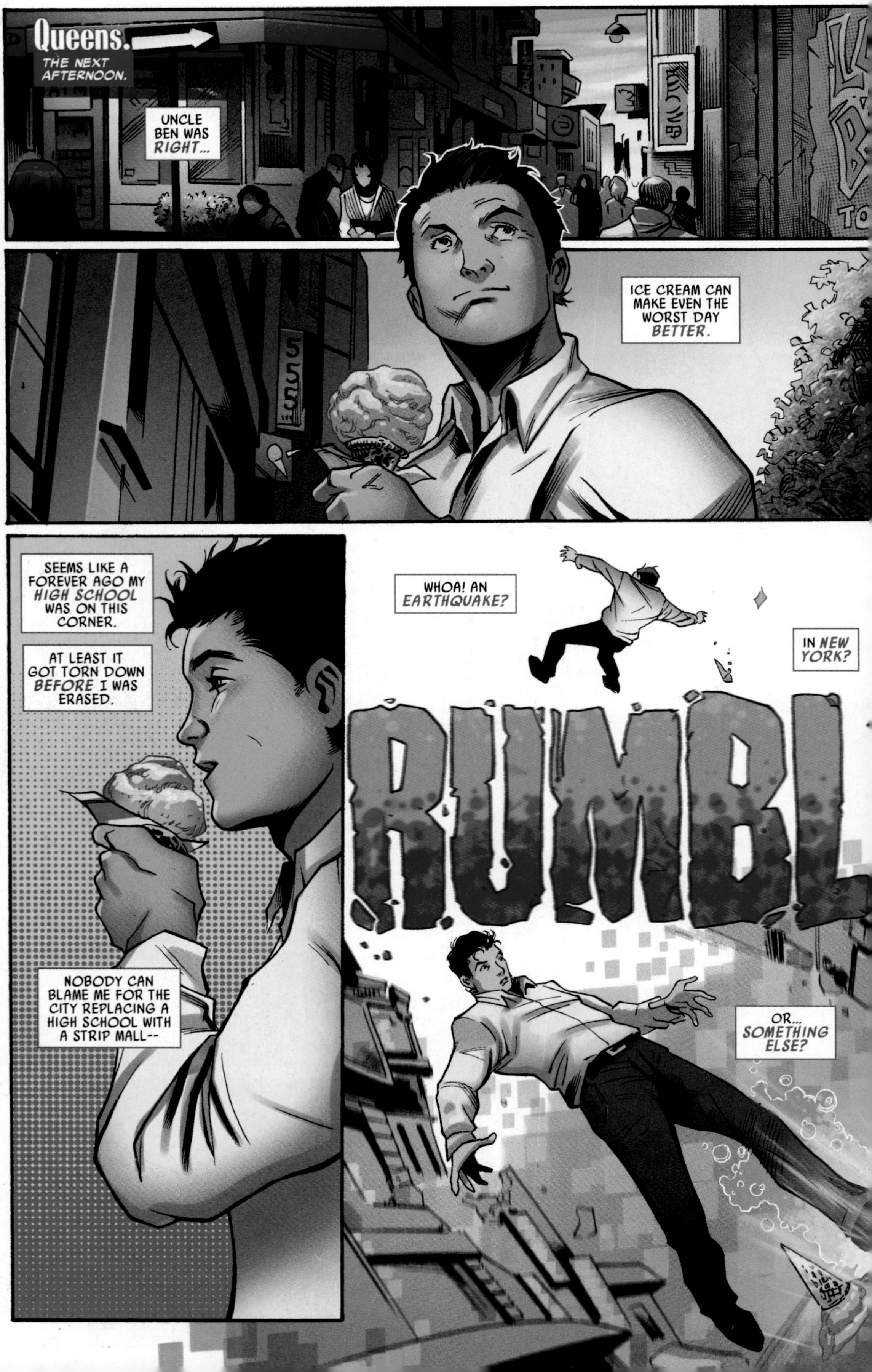
Queens.
THE NEXT AFTERNOON.
UNCLE BEN WAS RIGHT...
ICE CREAM CAN MAKE EVEN THE WORST DAY BETTER.
SEEMS LIKE A FOREVER AGO MY HIGH SCHOOL WAS ON THIS CORNER.
AT LEAST IT GOT TORN DOWN BEFORE I WAS ERASED.
NOBODY CAN BLAME ME FOR THE CITY REPLACING A HIGH SCHOOL WITH A STRIP MALL--
WHOA! AN EARTHQUAKE?
IN NEW YORK?
RUMBL
OR... SOMETHING ELSE?

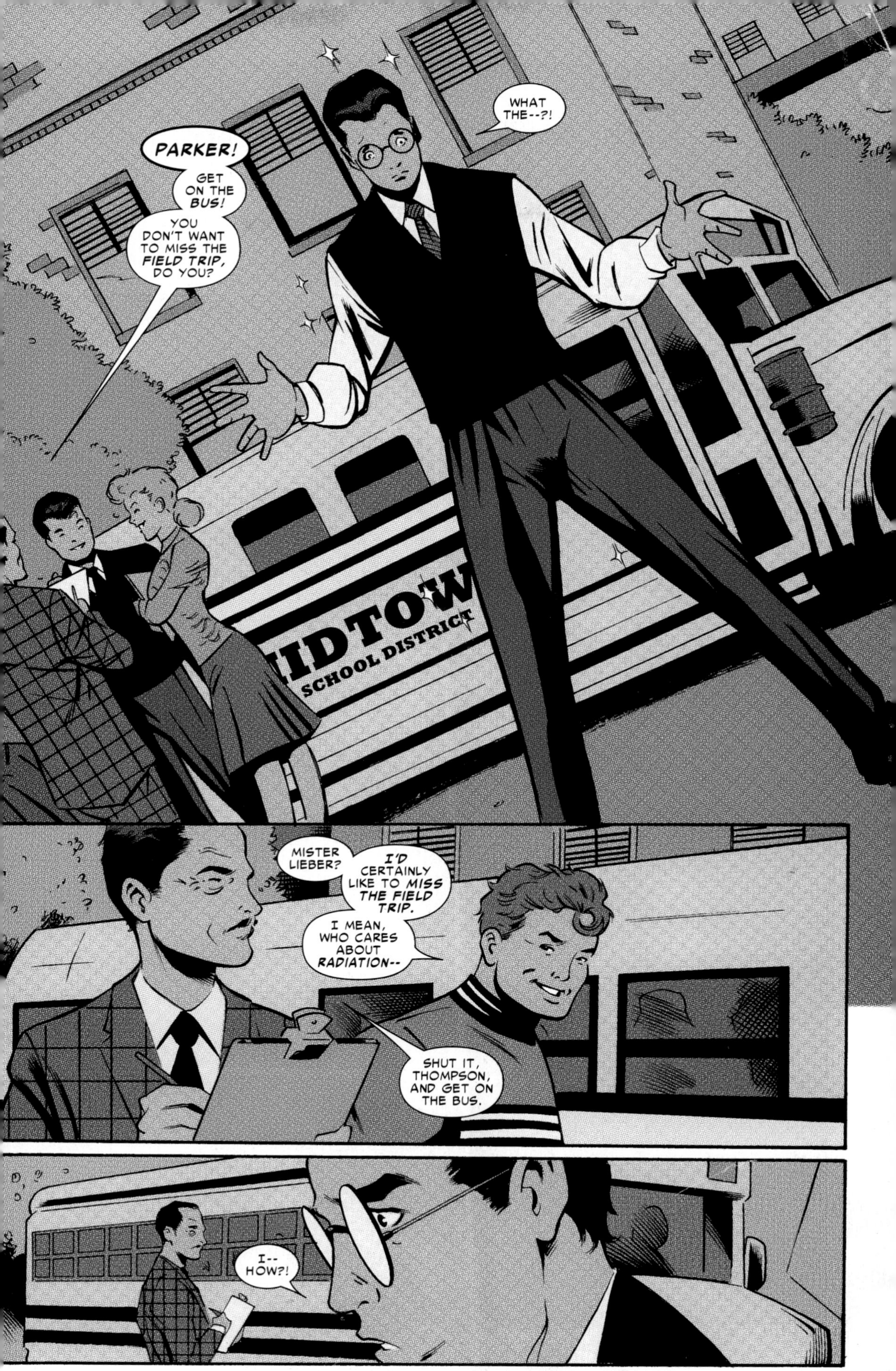
PARKER!
GET ON THE BUS!
YOU DON'T WANT TO MISS THE FIELD TRIP, DO YOU?
WHAT THE--?!
MIDTOWN
SCHOOL DISTRICT
MISTER LIEBER?
I'D CERTAINLY LIKE TO MISS THE FIELD TRIP.
I MEAN, WHO CARES ABOUT RADIATION--
SHUT IT, THOMPSON, AND GET ON THE BUS.
I-- HOW?!

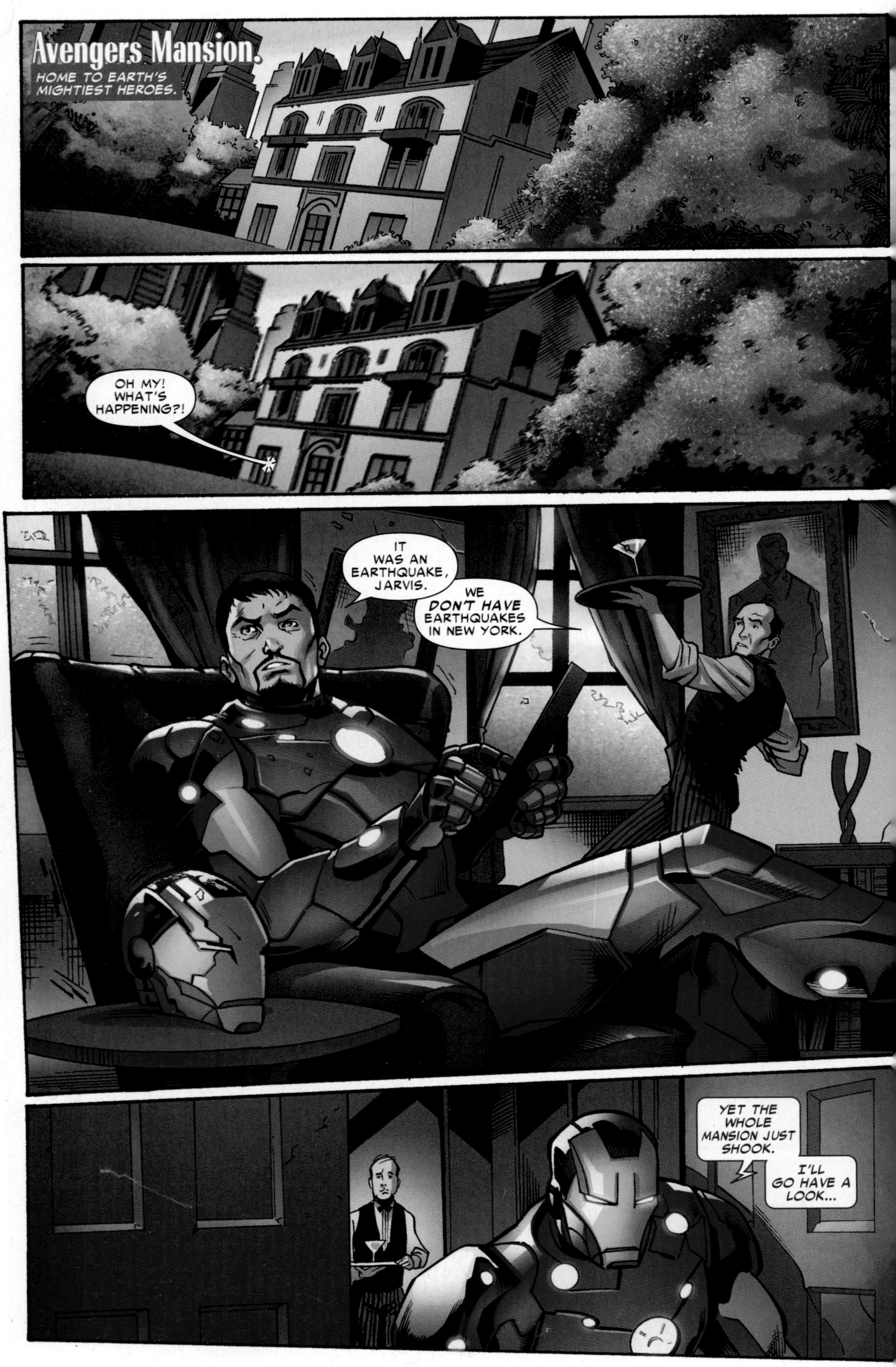
Avengers Mansion.
HOME TO EARTH'S MIGHTIEST HEROES.
OH MY! WHAT'S HAPPENING?!
IT WAS AN EARTHQUAKE, JARVIS.
WE DON'T HAVE EARTHQUAKES IN NEW YORK.
YET THE WHOLE MANSION JUST SHOOK.
I'LL GO HAVE A LOOK...

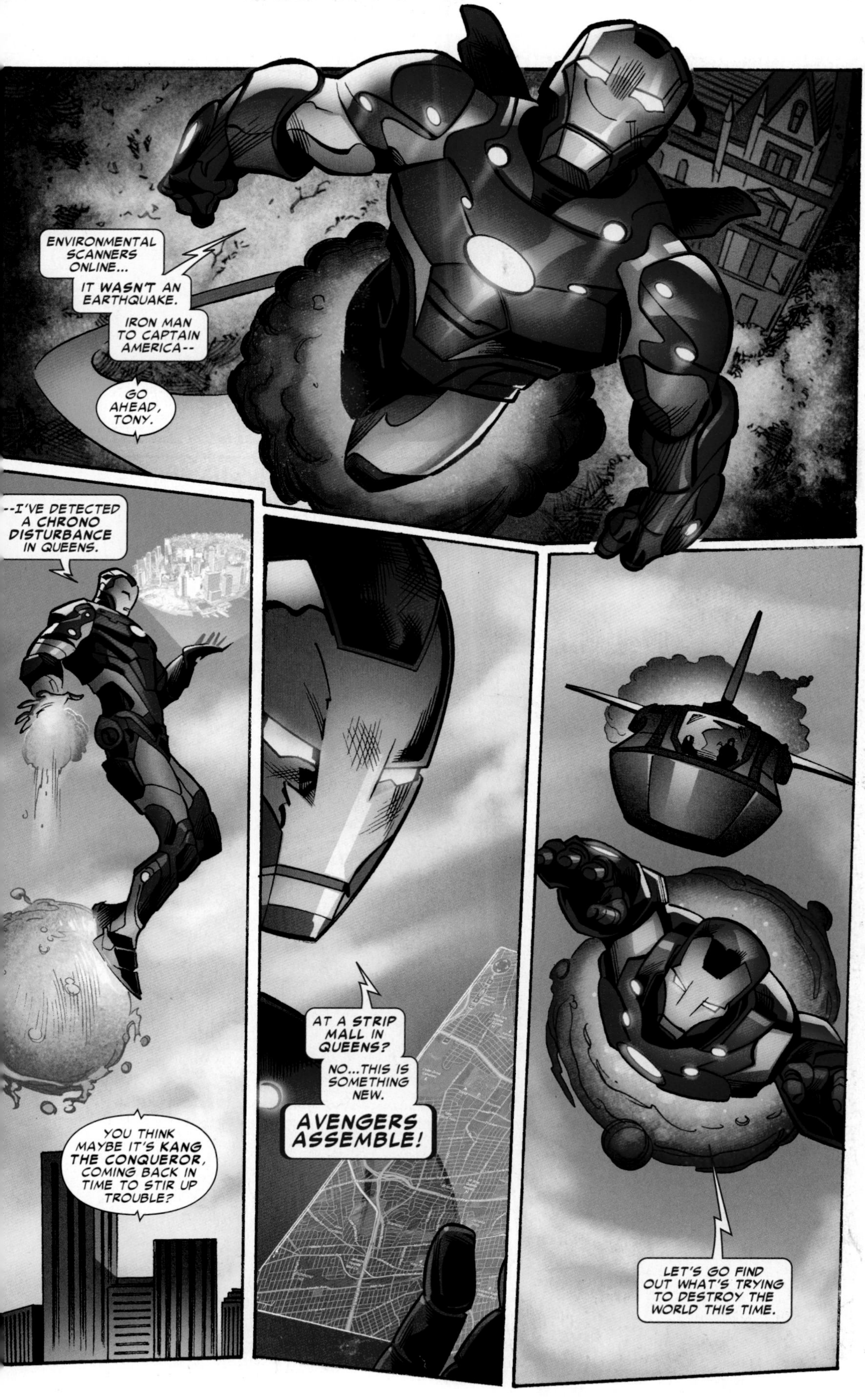
ENVIRONMENTAL SCANNERS ONLINE...
IT WASN'T AN EARTHQUAKE.
IRON MAN TO CAPTAIN AMERICA--
GO AHEAD, TONY.
--I'VE DETECTED A CHRONO DISTURBANCE IN QUEENS.
YOU THINK MAYBE IT'S KANG THE CONQUEROR, COMING BACK IN TIME TO STIR UP TROUBLE?
AT A STRIP MALL IN QUEENS?
NO...THIS IS SOMETHING NEW.
AVENGERS ASSEMBLE!
LET'S GO FIND OUT WHAT'S TRYING TO DESTROY THE WORLD THIS TIME.

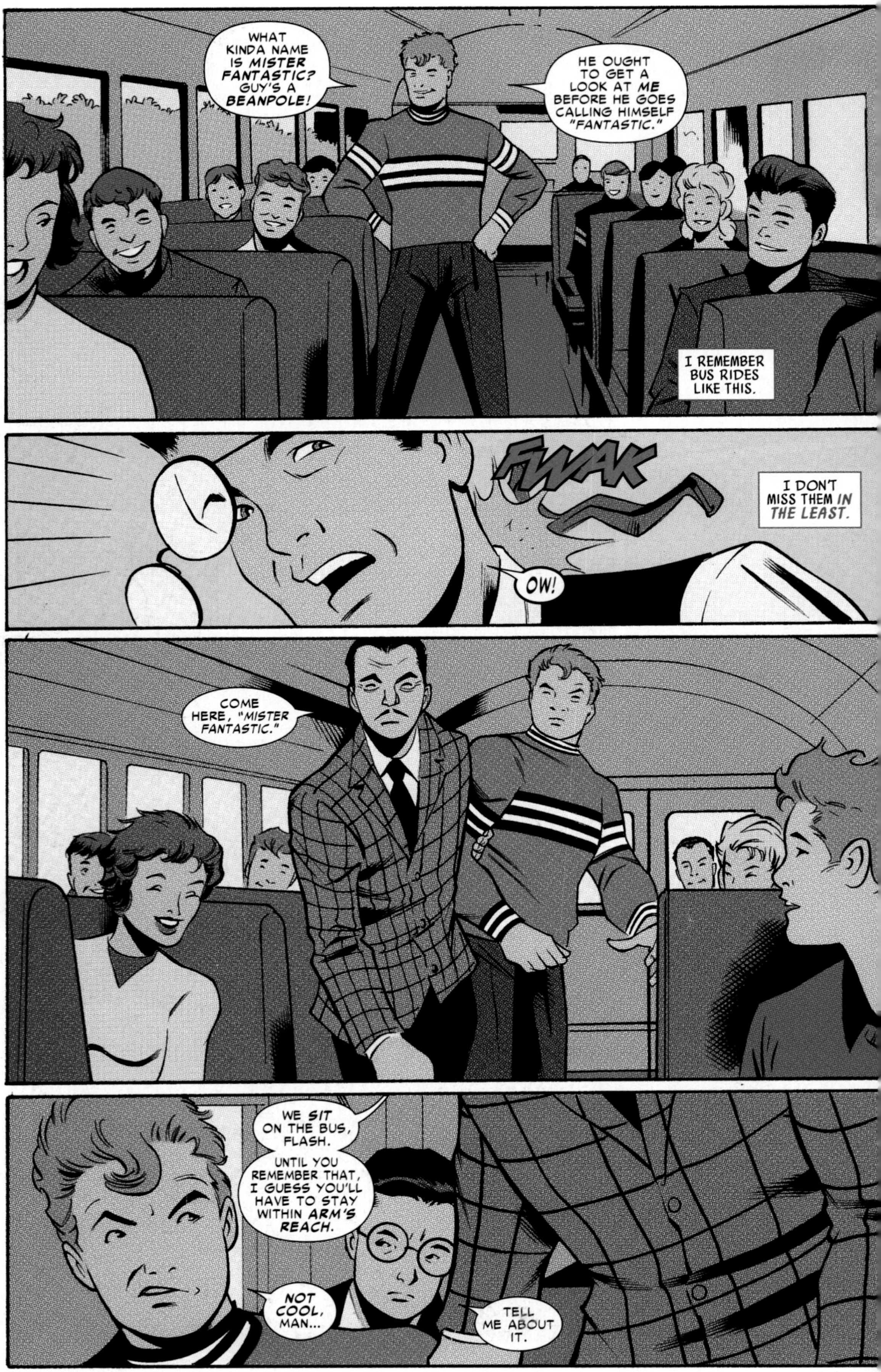
WHAT KINDA NAME IS MISTER FANTASTIC? GUY'S A BEANPOLE!
HE OUGHT TO GET A LOOK AT ME BEFORE HE GOES CALLING HIMSELF "FANTASTIC."
I REMEMBER BUS RIDES LIKE THIS.
FWAK
I DON'T MISS THEM IN THE LEAST.
OW!
COME HERE, "MISTER FANTASTIC."
WE SIT ON THE BUS, FLASH.
UNTIL YOU REMEMBER THAT, I GUESS YOU'LL HAVE TO STAY WITHIN ARM'S REACH.
NOT COOL, MAN...
TELL ME ABOUT IT.

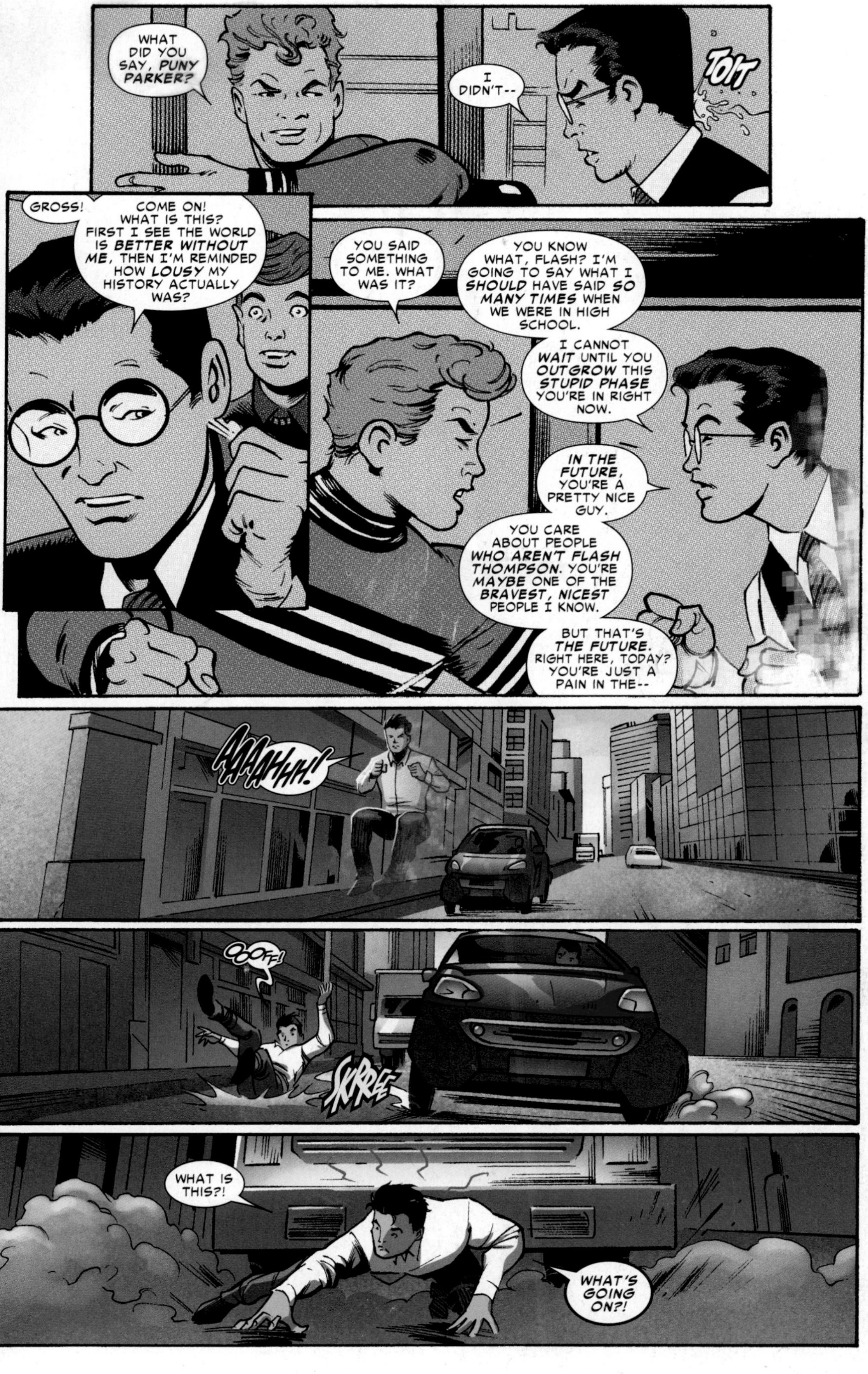

WHAT DID YOU SAY, PUNY PARKER?
I DIDN'T--
TOIT
GROSS!
COME ON! WHAT IS THIS? FIRST I SEE THE WORLD IS BETTER WITHOUT ME, THEN I'M REMINDED HOW LOUSY MY HISTORY ACTUALLY WAS?
YOU SAID SOMETHING TO ME. WHAT WAS IT?
YOU KNOW WHAT, FLASH? I'M GOING TO SAY WHAT I SHOULD HAVE SAID SO MANY TIMES WHEN WE WERE IN HIGH SCHOOL.
I CANNOT WAIT UNTIL YOU OUTGROW THIS STUPID PHASE YOU'RE IN RIGHT NOW.
IN THE FUTURE, YOU'RE A PRETTY NICE GUY.
YOU CARE ABOUT PEOPLE WHO AREN'T FLASH THOMPSON. YOU'RE MAYBE ONE OF THE BRAVEST, NICEST PEOPLE I KNOW.
BUT THAT'S THE FUTURE. RIGHT HERE, TODAY? YOU'RE JUST A PAIN IN THE--
AAAAHHH!
OOOFF!
SKRREE
WHAT IS THIS?!
WHAT'S GOING ON?!

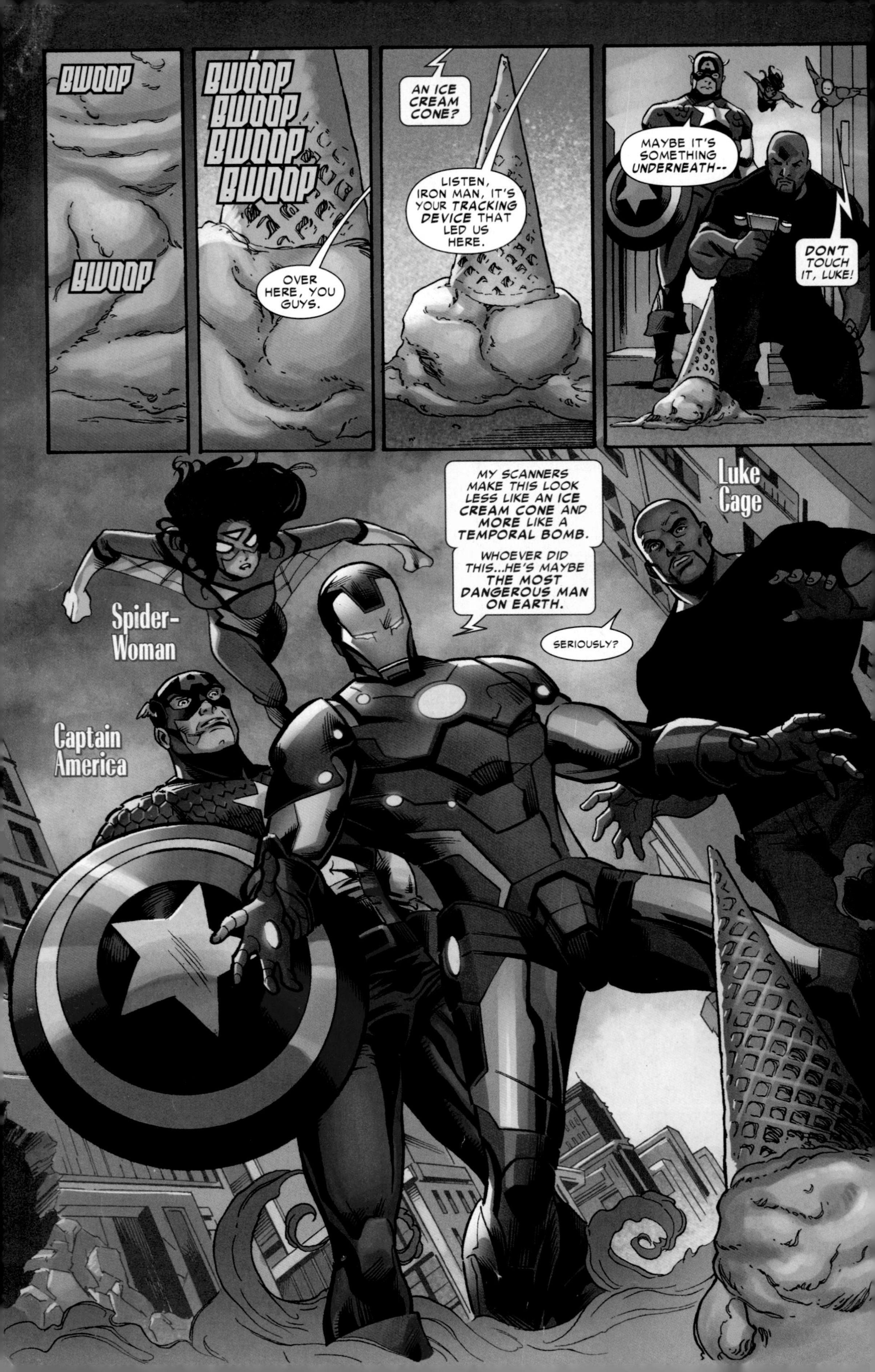
BWOOP
BWOOP
BWOOP BWOOP BWOOP BWOOP
OVER HERE, YOU GUYS.
AN ICE CREAM CONE?
LISTEN, IRON MAN, IT'S YOUR TRACKING DEVICE THAT LED US HERE.
MAYBE IT'S SOMETHING UNDERNEATH--
DON'T TOUCH IT, LUKE!
MY SCANNERS MAKE THIS LOOK LESS LIKE AN ICE CREAM CONE AND MORE LIKE A TEMPORAL BOMB.
WHOEVER DID THIS...HE'S MAYBE THE MOST DANGEROUS MAN ON EARTH.
SERIOUSLY?
Luke Cage
Spider-Woman
Captain America

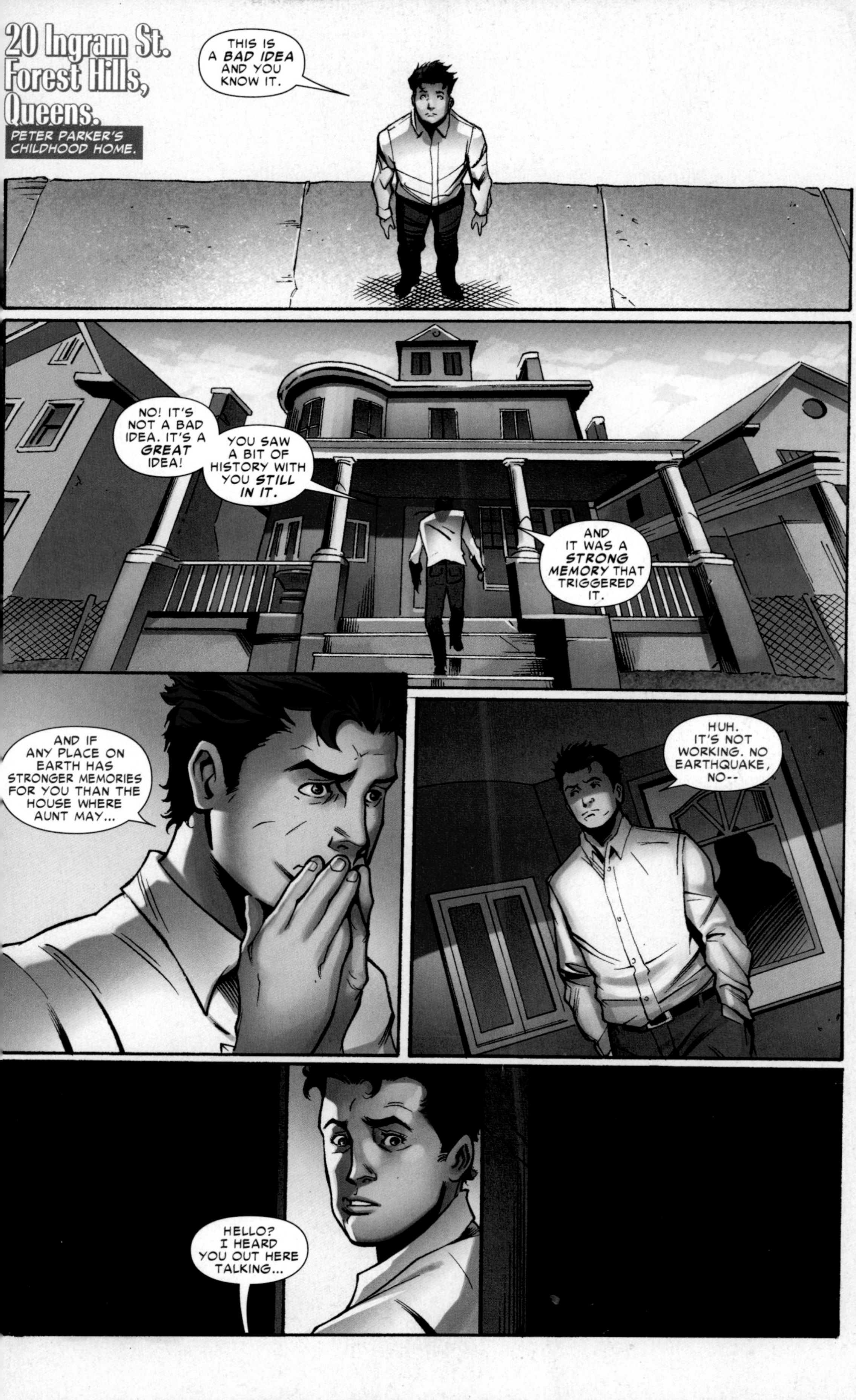
20 Ingram St. Forest Hills, Queens.
PETER PARKER'S CHILDHOOD HOME.
THIS IS A BAD IDEA AND YOU KNOW IT.
NO! IT'S NOT A BAD IDEA. IT'S A GREAT IDEA!
YOU SAW A BIT OF HISTORY WITH YOU STILL IN IT.
AND IT WAS A STRONG MEMORY THAT TRIGGERED IT.
AND IF ANY PLACE ON EARTH HAS STRONGER MEMORIES FOR YOU THAN THE HOUSE WHERE AUNT MAY...
HUH. IT'S NOT WORKING. NO EARTHQUAKE, NO--
HELLO? I HEARD YOU OUT HERE TALKING...

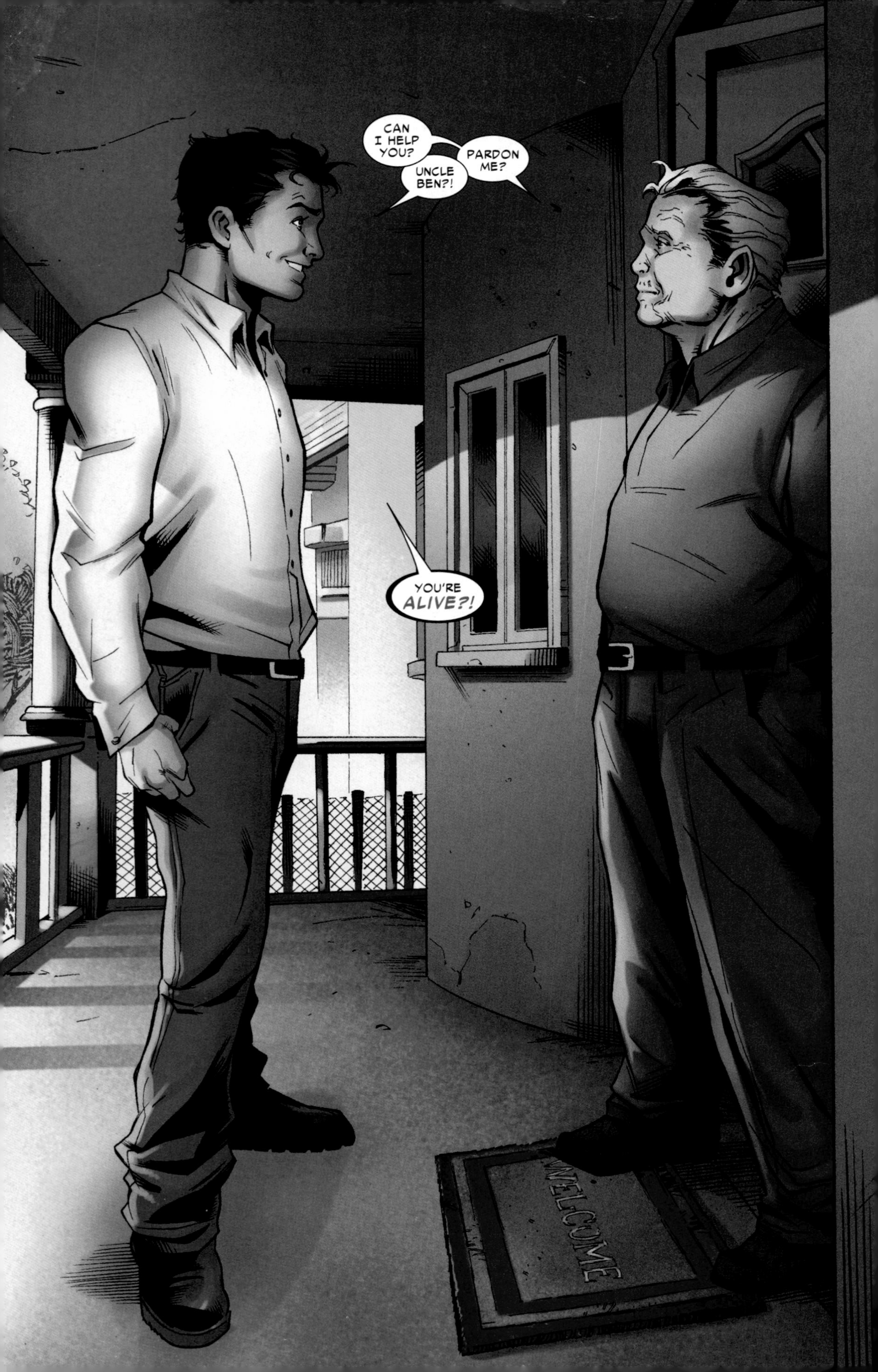
CAN I HELP YOU?
UNCLE BEN?!
PARDON ME?
YOU'RE ALIVE?!
WELCOME

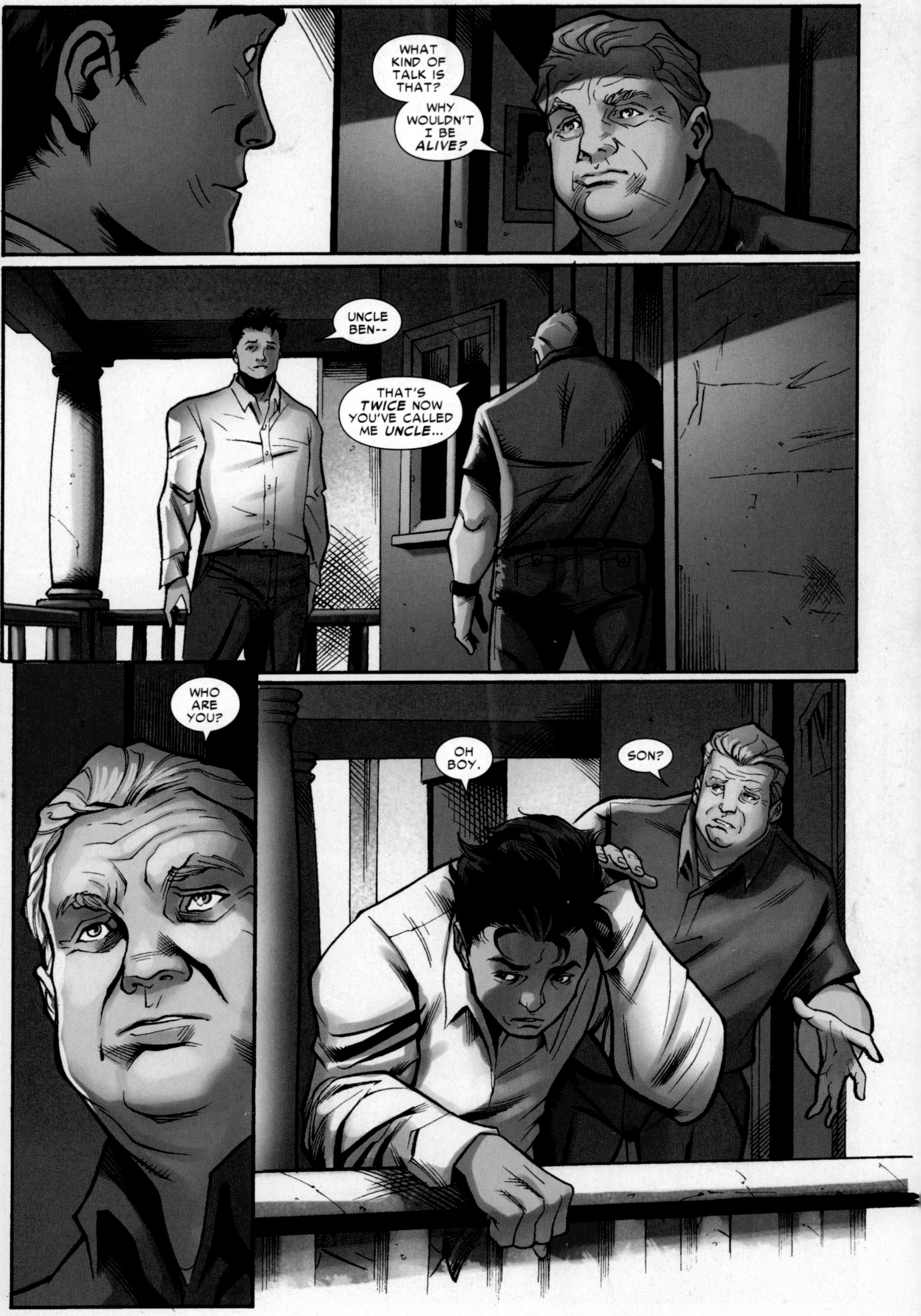
WHAT KIND OF TALK IS THAT?
WHY WOULDN'T I BE *ALIVE?*
UNCLE BEN--
THAT'S *TWICE* NOW YOU'VE CALLED ME *UNCLE*...
WHO ARE YOU?
OH BOY.
SON?

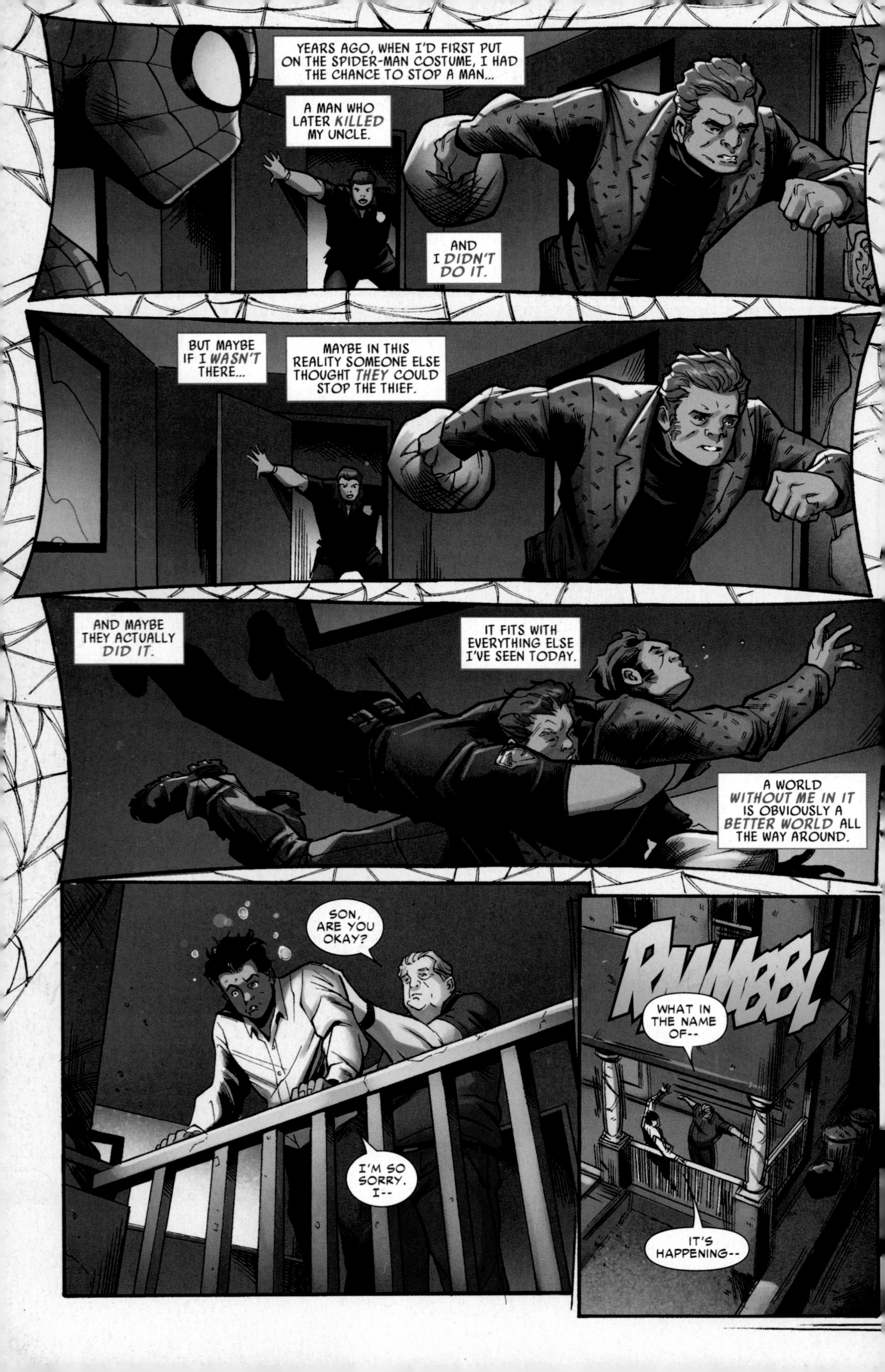
YEARS AGO, WHEN I'D FIRST PUT ON THE SPIDER-MAN COSTUME, I HAD THE CHANCE TO STOP A MAN...
A MAN WHO LATER KILLED MY UNCLE.
AND I DIDN'T DO IT.
BUT MAYBE IF I WASN'T THERE...
MAYBE IN THIS REALITY SOMEONE ELSE THOUGHT THEY COULD STOP THE THIEF.
AND MAYBE THEY ACTUALLY DID IT.
IT FITS WITH EVERYTHING ELSE I'VE SEEN TODAY.
A WORLD WITHOUT ME IN IT IS OBVIOUSLY A BETTER WORLD ALL THE WAY AROUND.
SON, ARE YOU OKAY?
I'M SO SORRY. I--
RUMBBL
WHAT IN THE NAME OF--
IT'S HAPPENING--

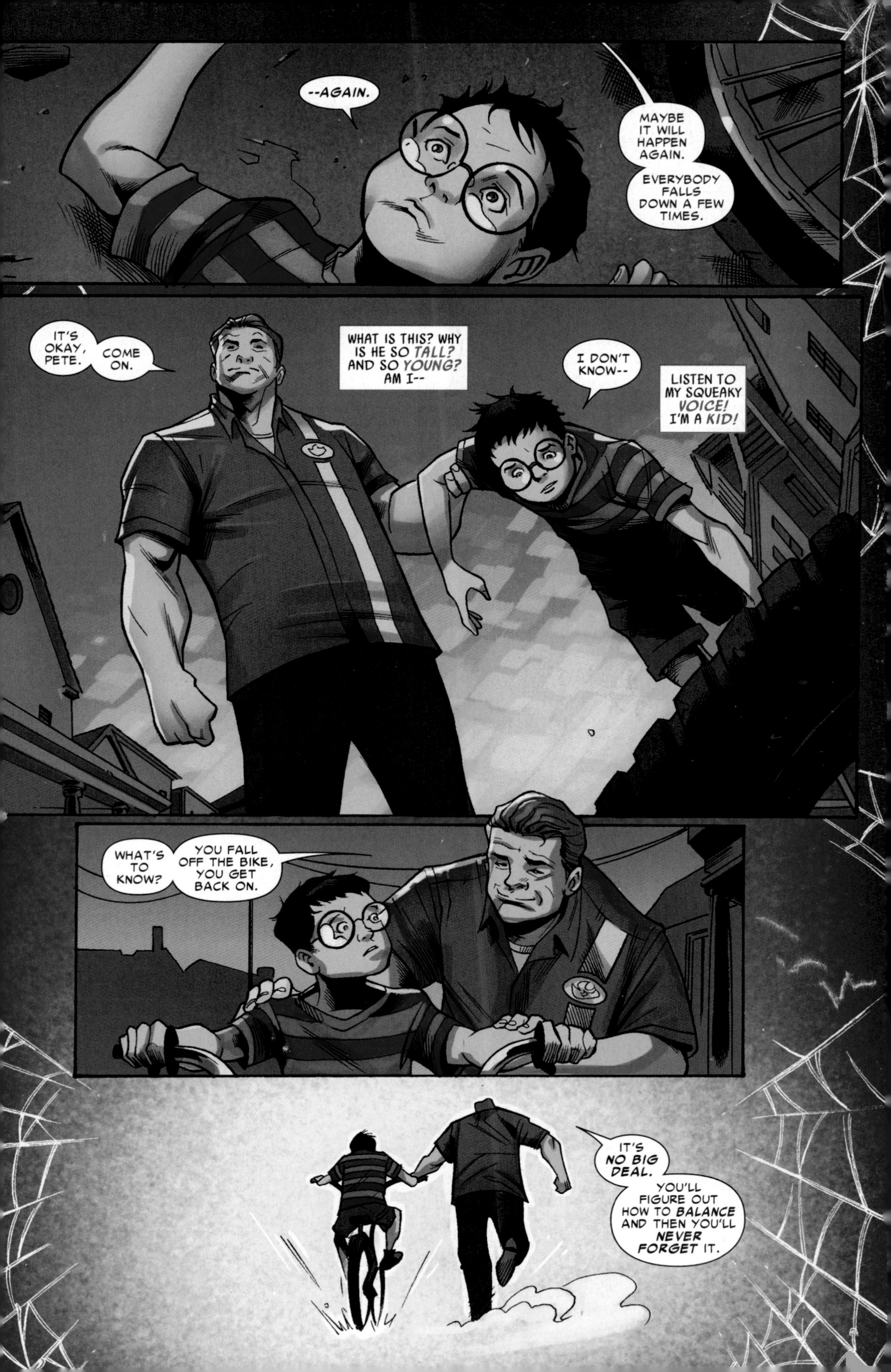
--AGAIN.
MAYBE IT WILL HAPPEN AGAIN.
EVERYBODY FALLS DOWN A FEW TIMES.
IT'S OKAY, PETE.
COME ON.
WHAT IS THIS? WHY IS HE SO TALL? AND SO YOUNG? AM I--
I DON'T KNOW--
LISTEN TO MY SQUEAKY VOICE! I'M A KID!
WHAT'S TO KNOW?
YOU FALL OFF THE BIKE, YOU GET BACK ON.
IT'S NO BIG DEAL.
YOU'LL FIGURE OUT HOW TO BALANCE AND THEN YOU'LL NEVER FORGET IT.

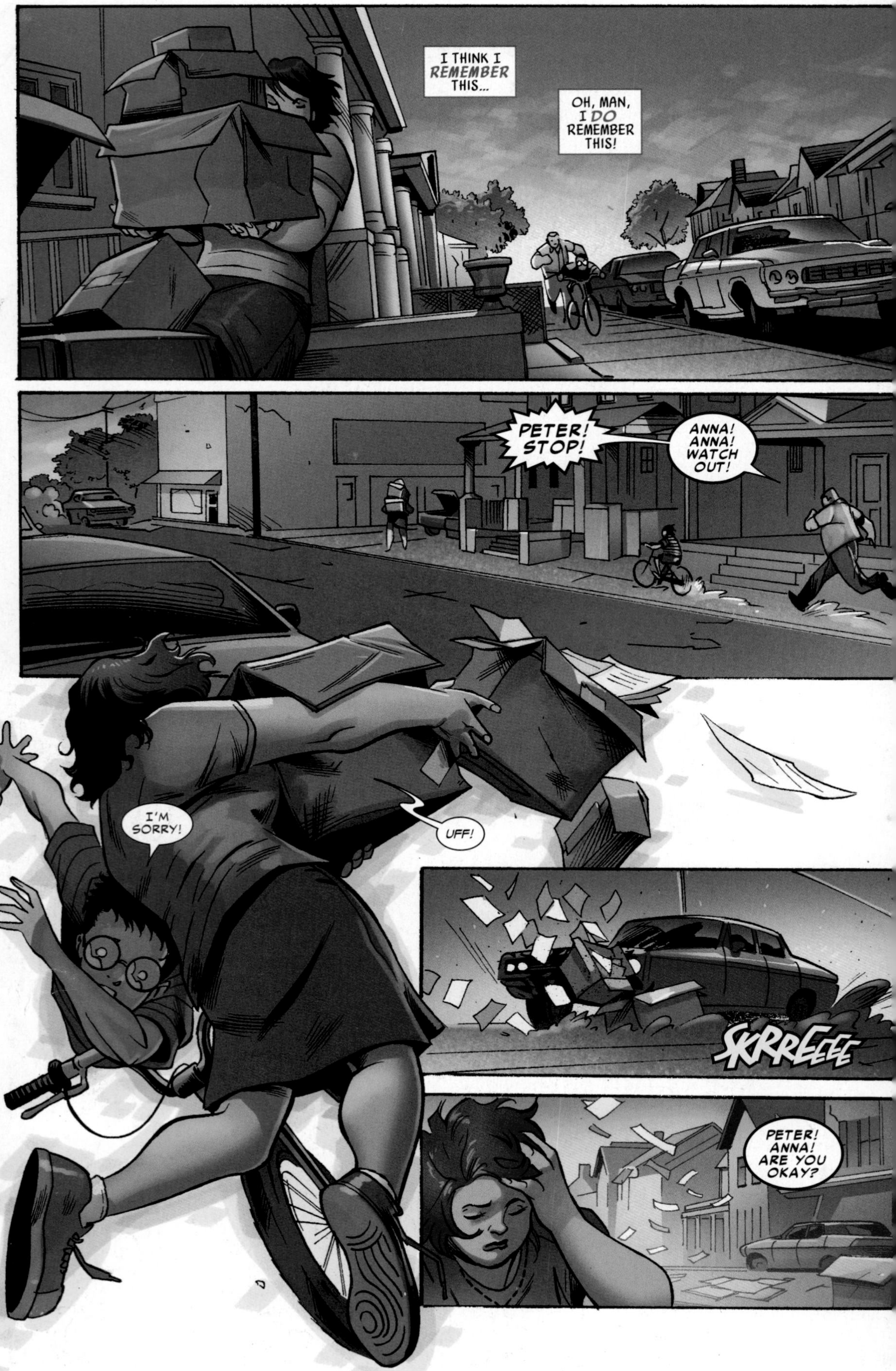
I THINK I REMEMBER THIS...
OH, MAN, I DO REMEMBER THIS!
PETER! STOP!
ANNA! ANNA! WATCH OUT!
I'M SORRY!
UFF!
SKRREEEEE
PETER! ANNA! ARE YOU OKAY?

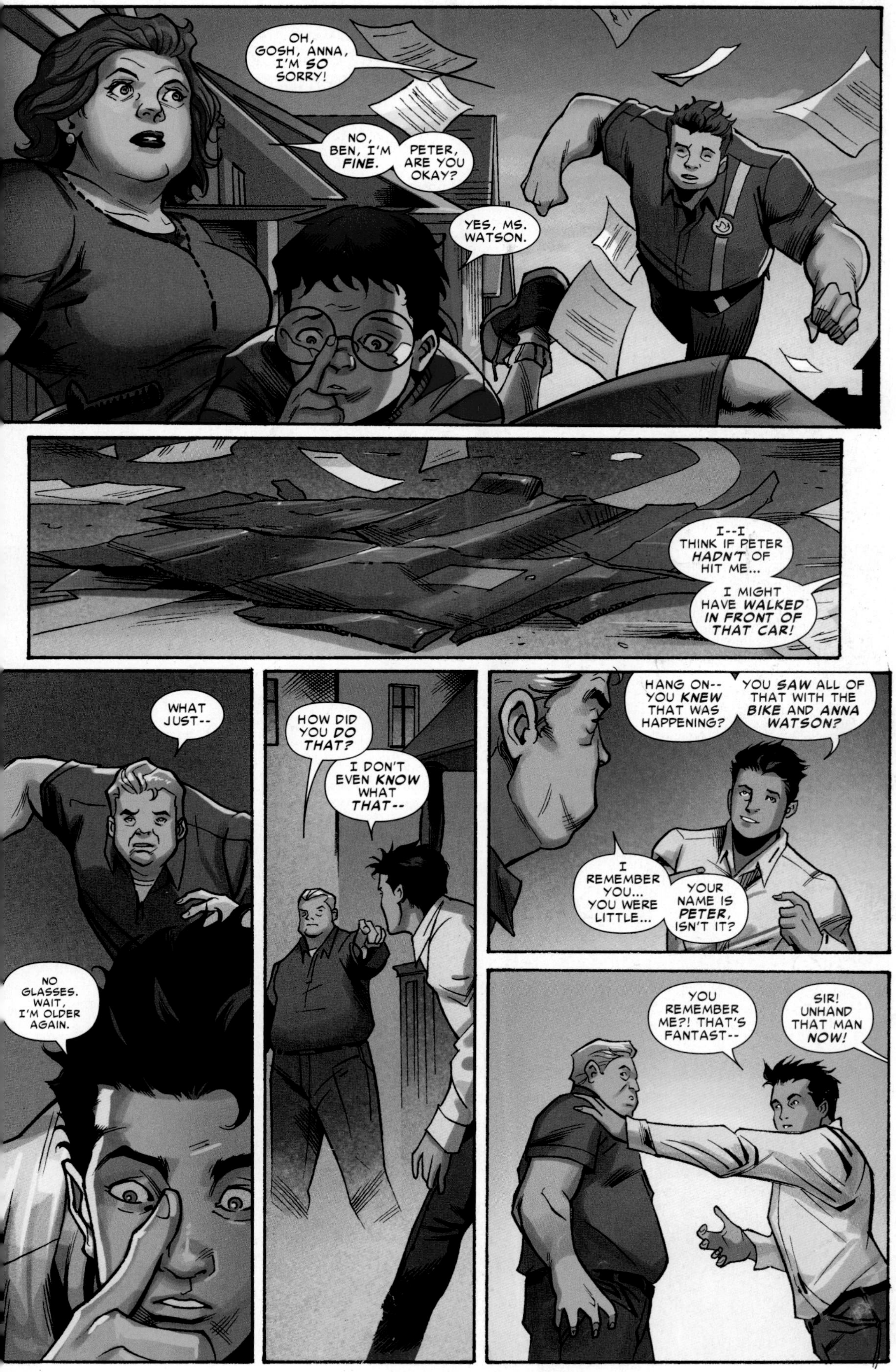
OH, GOSH, ANNA, I'M SO SORRY!
NO, BEN, I'M FINE.
PETER, ARE YOU OKAY?
YES, MS. WATSON.
I--I THINK IF PETER HADN'T OF HIT ME...
I MIGHT HAVE WALKED IN FRONT OF THAT CAR!
WHAT JUST--
NO GLASSES. WAIT, I'M OLDER AGAIN.
HOW DID YOU DO THAT?
I DON'T EVEN KNOW WHAT THAT--
HANG ON-- YOU KNEW THAT WAS HAPPENING?
YOU SAW ALL OF THAT WITH THE BIKE AND ANNA WATSON?
I REMEMBER YOU... YOU WERE LITTLE...
YOUR NAME IS PETER, ISN'T IT?
YOU REMEMBER ME?! THAT'S FANTAST--
SIR! UNHAND THAT MAN NOW!

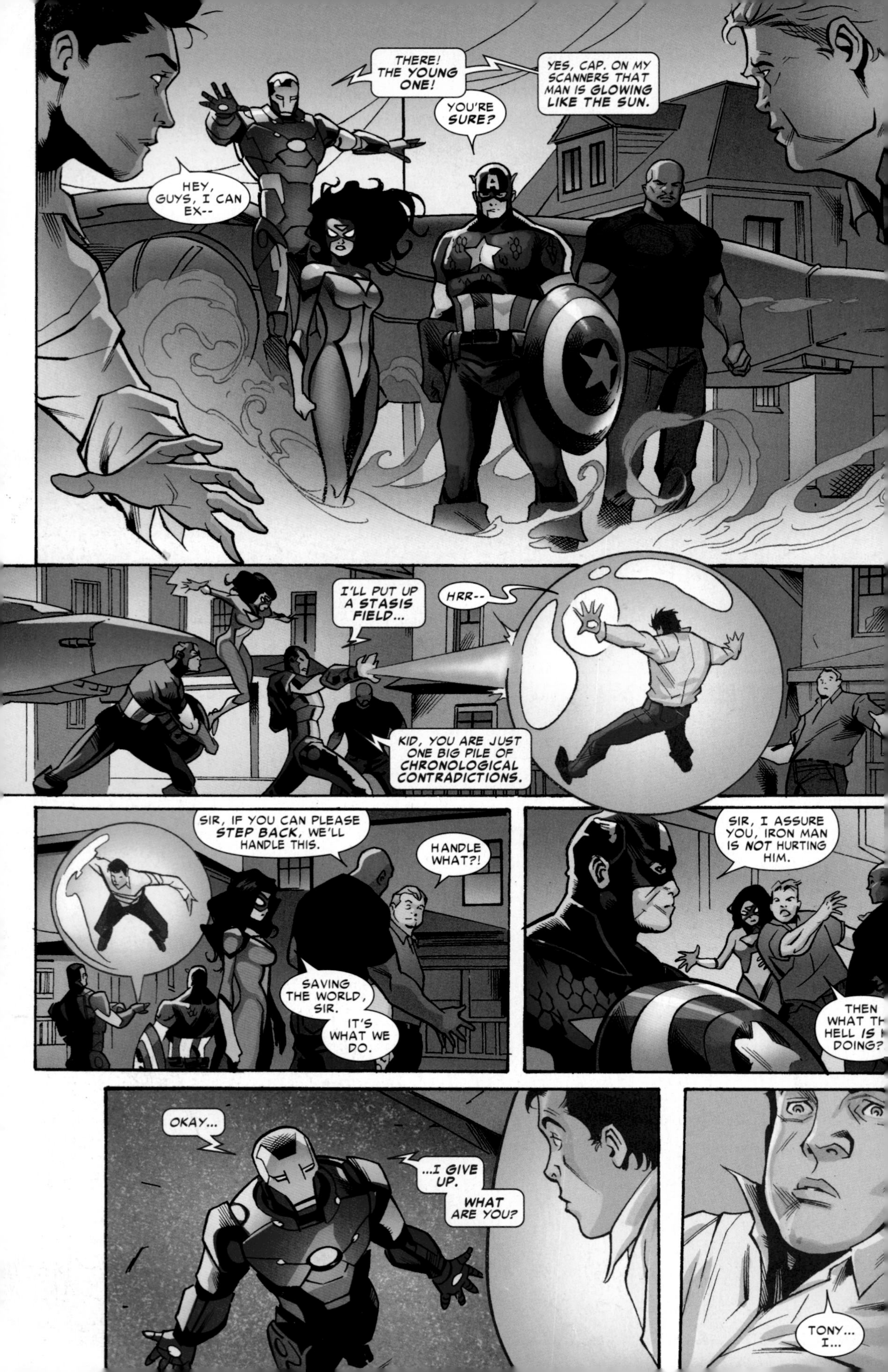
HEY, GUYS, I CAN EX--
THERE! THE YOUNG ONE!
YOU'RE SURE?
YES, CAP. ON MY SCANNERS THAT MAN IS GLOWING LIKE THE SUN.
I'LL PUT UP A STASIS FIELD...
HRR--
KID, YOU ARE JUST ONE BIG PILE OF CHRONOLOGICAL CONTRADICTIONS.
SIR, IF YOU CAN PLEASE STEP BACK, WE'LL HANDLE THIS.
HANDLE WHAT?!
SAVING THE WORLD, SIR.
IT'S WHAT WE DO.
SIR, I ASSURE YOU, IRON MAN IS NOT HURTING HIM.
OKAY...
...I GIVE UP.
WHAT ARE YOU?
TONY... I...

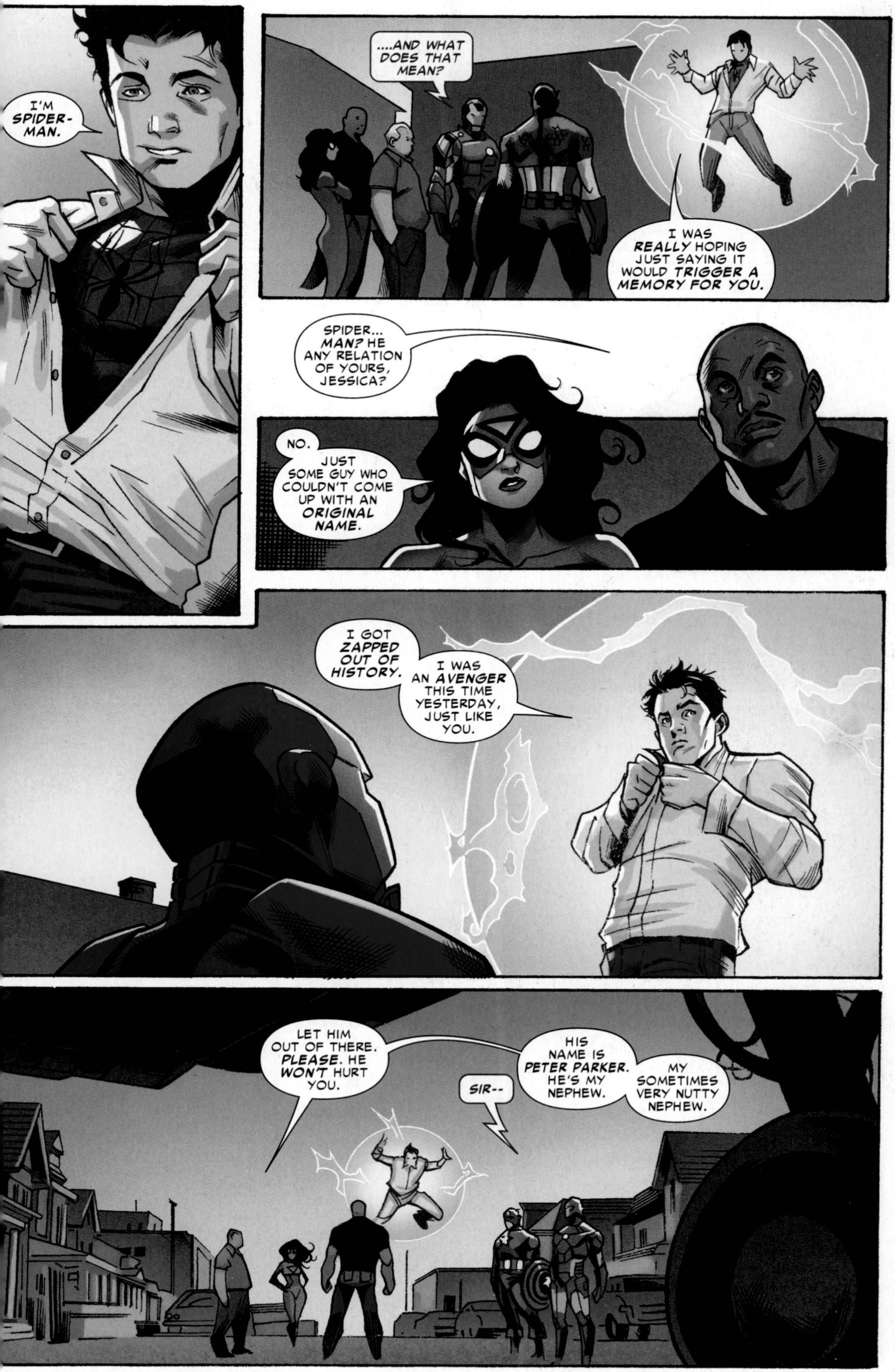
I'M SPIDER-MAN.
....AND WHAT DOES THAT MEAN?
I WAS REALLY HOPING JUST SAYING IT WOULD TRIGGER A MEMORY FOR YOU.
SPIDER... MAN? HE ANY RELATION OF YOURS, JESSICA?
NO.
JUST SOME GUY WHO COULDN'T COME UP WITH AN ORIGINAL NAME.
I GOT ZAPPED OUT OF HISTORY.
I WAS AN AVENGER THIS TIME YESTERDAY, JUST LIKE YOU.
LET HIM OUT OF THERE. PLEASE. HE WON'T HURT YOU.
SIR--
HIS NAME IS PETER PARKER. HE'S MY NEPHEW.
MY SOMETIMES VERY NUTTY NEPHEW.

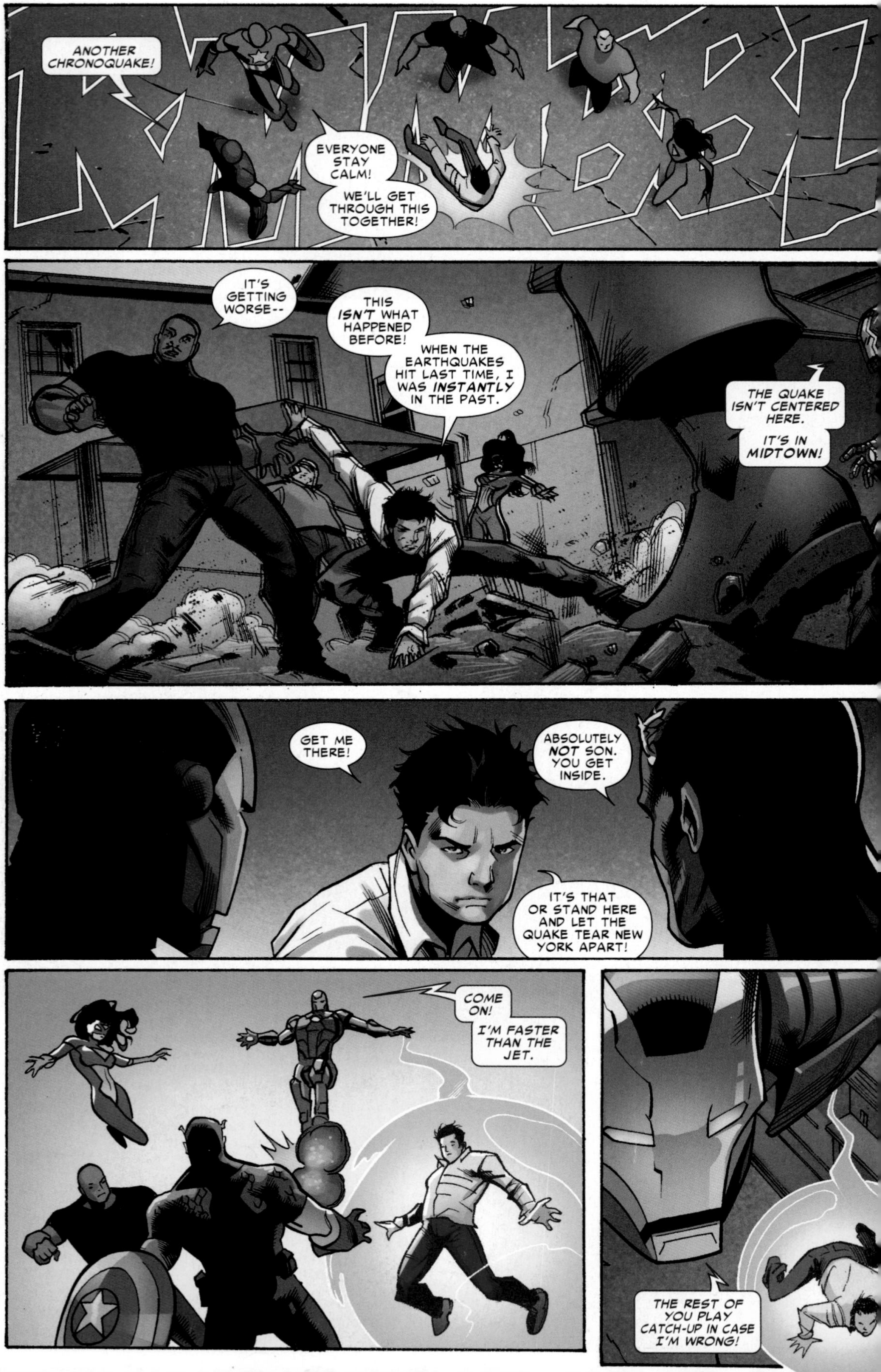

ANOTHER CHRONOQUAKE!
EVERYONE STAY CALM!
WE'LL GET THROUGH THIS TOGETHER!
IT'S GETTING WORSE--
THIS ISN'T WHAT HAPPENED BEFORE!
WHEN THE EARTHQUAKES HIT LAST TIME, I WAS INSTANTLY IN THE PAST.
THE QUAKE ISN'T CENTERED HERE.
IT'S IN MIDTOWN!
GET ME THERE!
ABSOLUTELY NOT SON. YOU GET INSIDE.
IT'S THAT OR STAND HERE AND LET THE QUAKE TEAR NEW YORK APART!
COME ON!
I'M FASTER THAN THE JET.
THE REST OF YOU PLAY CATCH-UP IN CASE I'M WRONG!

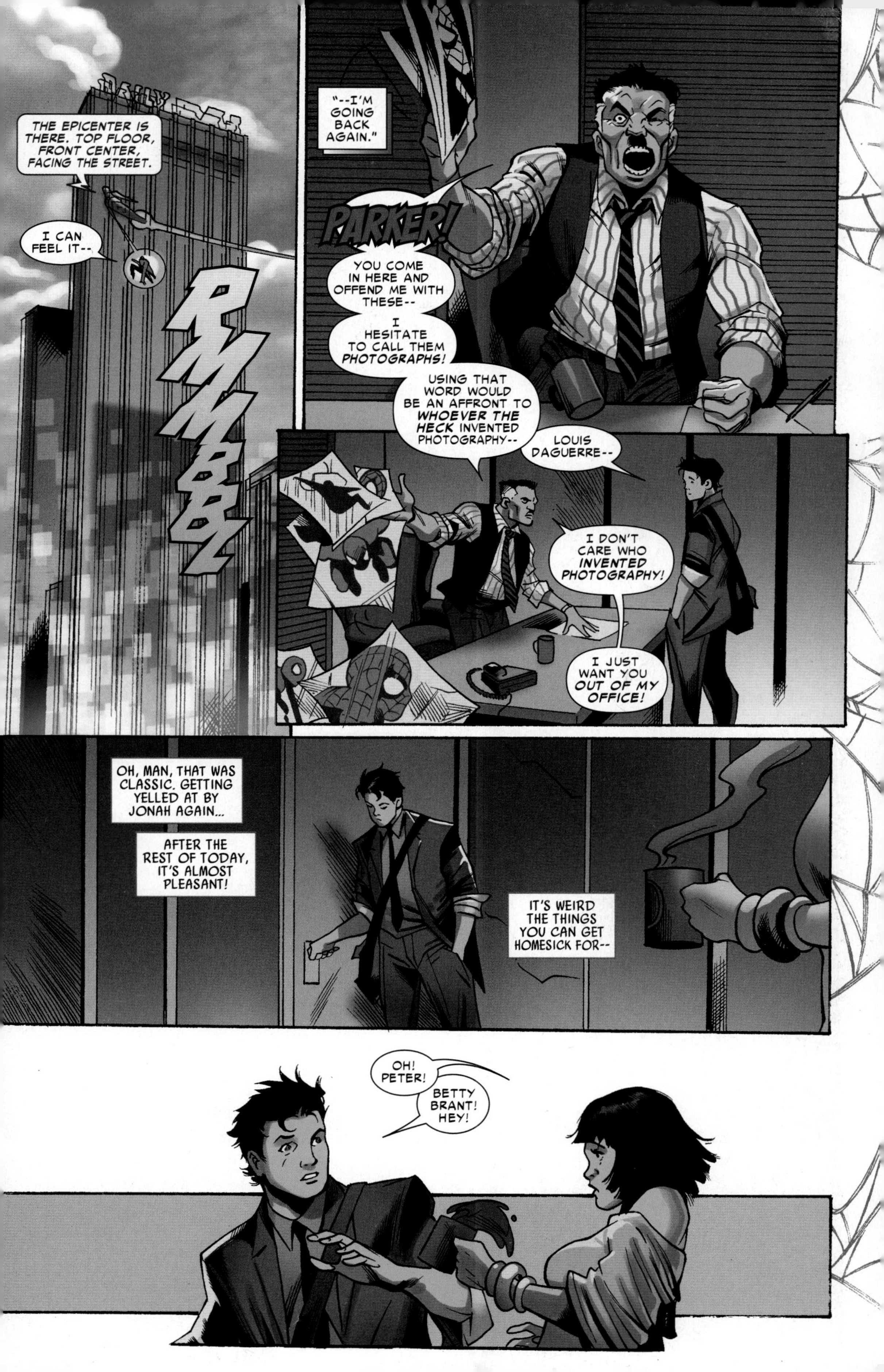
THE EPICENTER IS THERE. TOP FLOOR, FRONT CENTER, FACING THE STREET.
I CAN FEEL IT--
RMMBBL
"--I'M GOING BACK AGAIN."
PARKER!
YOU COME IN HERE AND OFFEND ME WITH THESE--
I HESITATE TO CALL THEM PHOTOGRAPHS!
USING THAT WORD WOULD BE AN AFFRONT TO WHOEVER THE HECK INVENTED PHOTOGRAPHY--
LOUIS DAGUERRE--
I DON'T CARE WHO INVENTED PHOTOGRAPHY!
I JUST WANT YOU OUT OF MY OFFICE!
OH, MAN, THAT WAS CLASSIC. GETTING YELLED AT BY JONAH AGAIN...
AFTER THE REST OF TODAY, IT'S ALMOST PLEASANT!
IT'S WEIRD THE THINGS YOU CAN GET HOMESICK FOR--
OH! PETER!
BETTY BRANT! HEY!

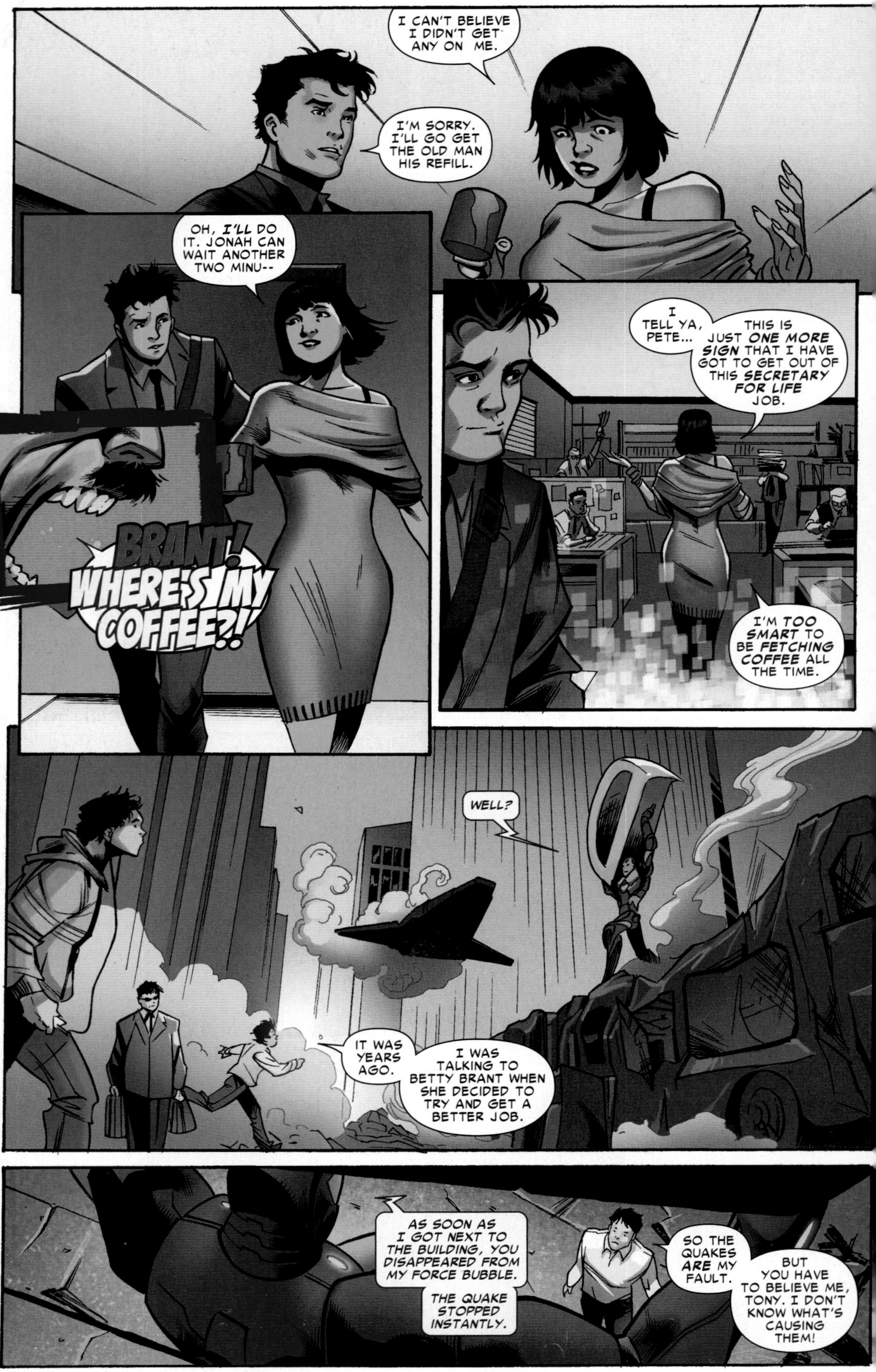
I CAN'T BELIEVE I DIDN'T GET ANY ON ME.
I'M SORRY. I'LL GO GET THE OLD MAN HIS REFILL.
OH, I'LL DO IT. JONAH CAN WAIT ANOTHER TWO MINU--
BRANT! WHERE'S MY COFFEE?!
I TELL YA, PETE...
THIS IS JUST ONE MORE SIGN THAT I HAVE GOT TO GET OUT OF THIS SECRETARY FOR LIFE JOB.
I'M TOO SMART TO BE FETCHING COFFEE ALL THE TIME.
WELL?
IT WAS YEARS AGO.
I WAS TALKING TO BETTY BRANT WHEN SHE DECIDED TO TRY AND GET A BETTER JOB.
AS SOON AS I GOT NEXT TO THE BUILDING, YOU DISAPPEARED FROM MY FORCE BUBBLE.
THE QUAKE STOPPED INSTANTLY.
SO THE QUAKES ARE MY FAULT.
BUT YOU HAVE TO BELIEVE ME, TONY. I DON'T KNOW WHAT'S CAUSING THEM!

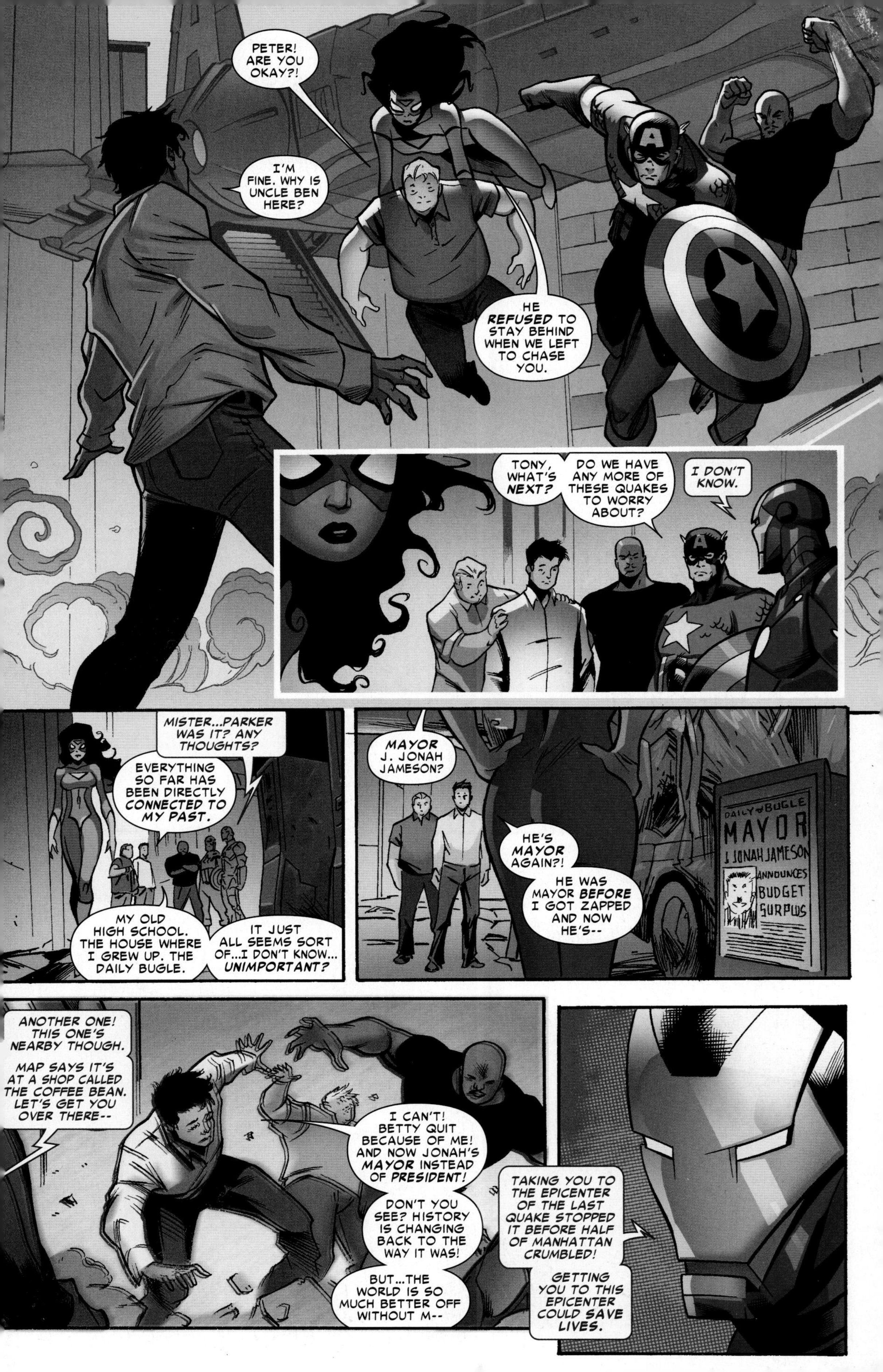
PETER! ARE YOU OKAY?!
I'M FINE. WHY IS UNCLE BEN HERE?
HE REFUSED TO STAY BEHIND WHEN WE LEFT TO CHASE YOU.
TONY, WHAT'S NEXT?
DO WE HAVE ANY MORE OF THESE QUAKES TO WORRY ABOUT?
I DON'T KNOW.
MISTER...PARKER WAS IT? ANY THOUGHTS?
EVERYTHING SO FAR HAS BEEN DIRECTLY CONNECTED TO MY PAST.
MY OLD HIGH SCHOOL. THE HOUSE WHERE I GREW UP. THE DAILY BUGLE.
IT JUST ALL SEEMS SORT OF...I DON'T KNOW... UNIMPORTANT?
MAYOR J. JONAH JAMESON?
DAILY BUGLE
MAYOR
J. JONAH JAMESON
ANNOUNCES BUDGET SURPLUS
HE'S MAYOR AGAIN?!
HE WAS MAYOR BEFORE I GOT ZAPPED AND NOW HE'S--
ANOTHER ONE! THIS ONE'S NEARBY THOUGH.
MAP SAYS IT'S AT A SHOP CALLED THE COFFEE BEAN. LET'S GET YOU OVER THERE--
I CAN'T! BETTY QUIT BECAUSE OF ME! AND NOW JONAH'S MAYOR INSTEAD OF PRESIDENT!
DON'T YOU SEE? HISTORY IS CHANGING BACK TO THE WAY IT WAS!
BUT...THE WORLD IS SO MUCH BETTER OFF WITHOUT M--
TAKING YOU TO THE EPICENTER OF THE LAST QUAKE STOPPED IT BEFORE HALF OF MANHATTAN CRUMBLED!
GETTING YOU TO THIS EPICENTER COULD SAVE LIVES.

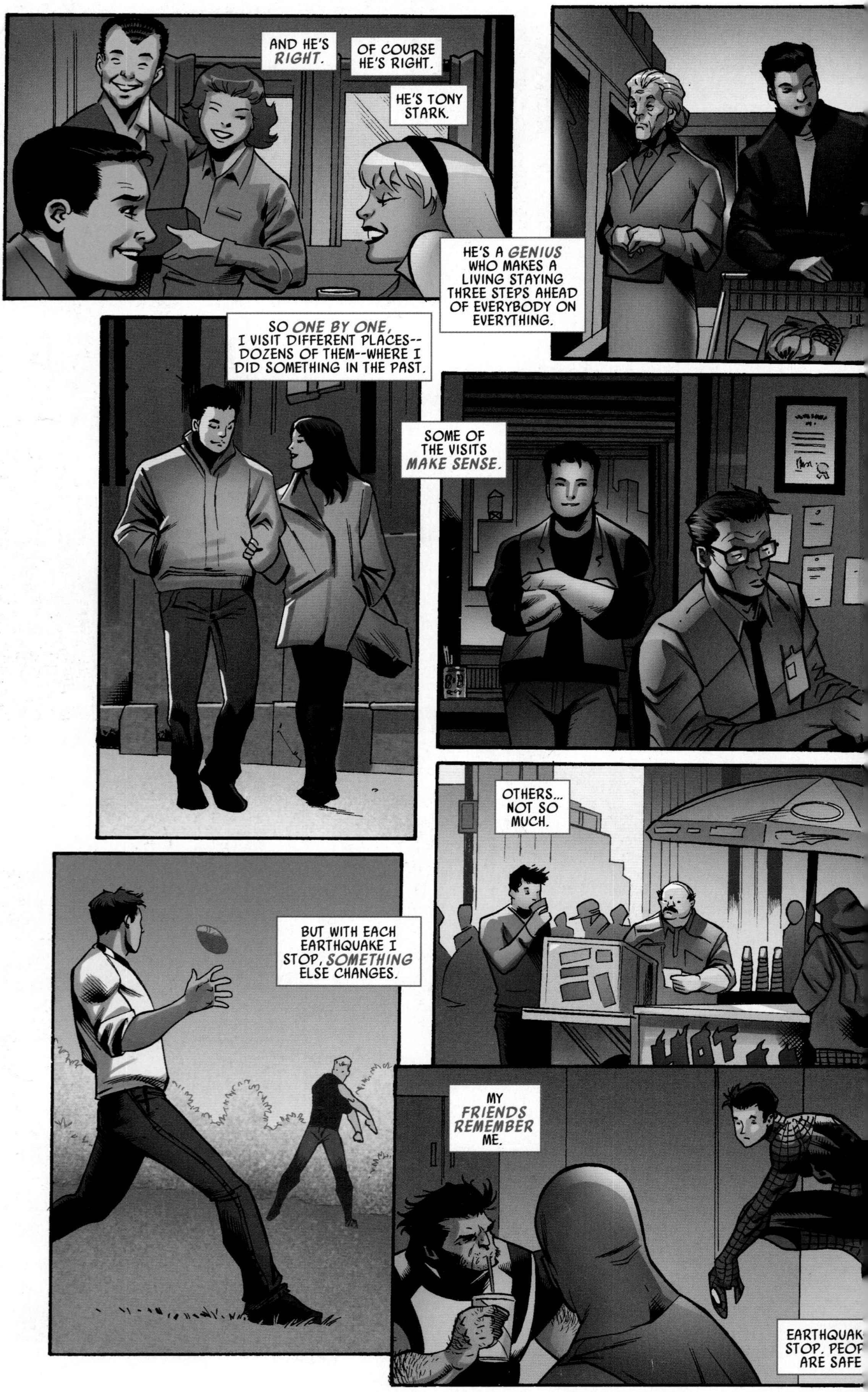
AND HE'S RIGHT.
OF COURSE HE'S RIGHT.
HE'S TONY STARK.
HE'S A GENIUS WHO MAKES A LIVING STAYING THREE STEPS AHEAD OF EVERYBODY ON EVERYTHING.
SO ONE BY ONE, I VISIT DIFFERENT PLACES--DOZENS OF THEM--WHERE I DID SOMETHING IN THE PAST.
SOME OF THE VISITS MAKE SENSE.
OTHERS... NOT SO MUCH.
BUT WITH EACH EARTHQUAKE I STOP, SOMETHING ELSE CHANGES.
MY FRIENDS REMEMBER ME.
EARTHQUAK
STOP. PEOP
ARE SAFE

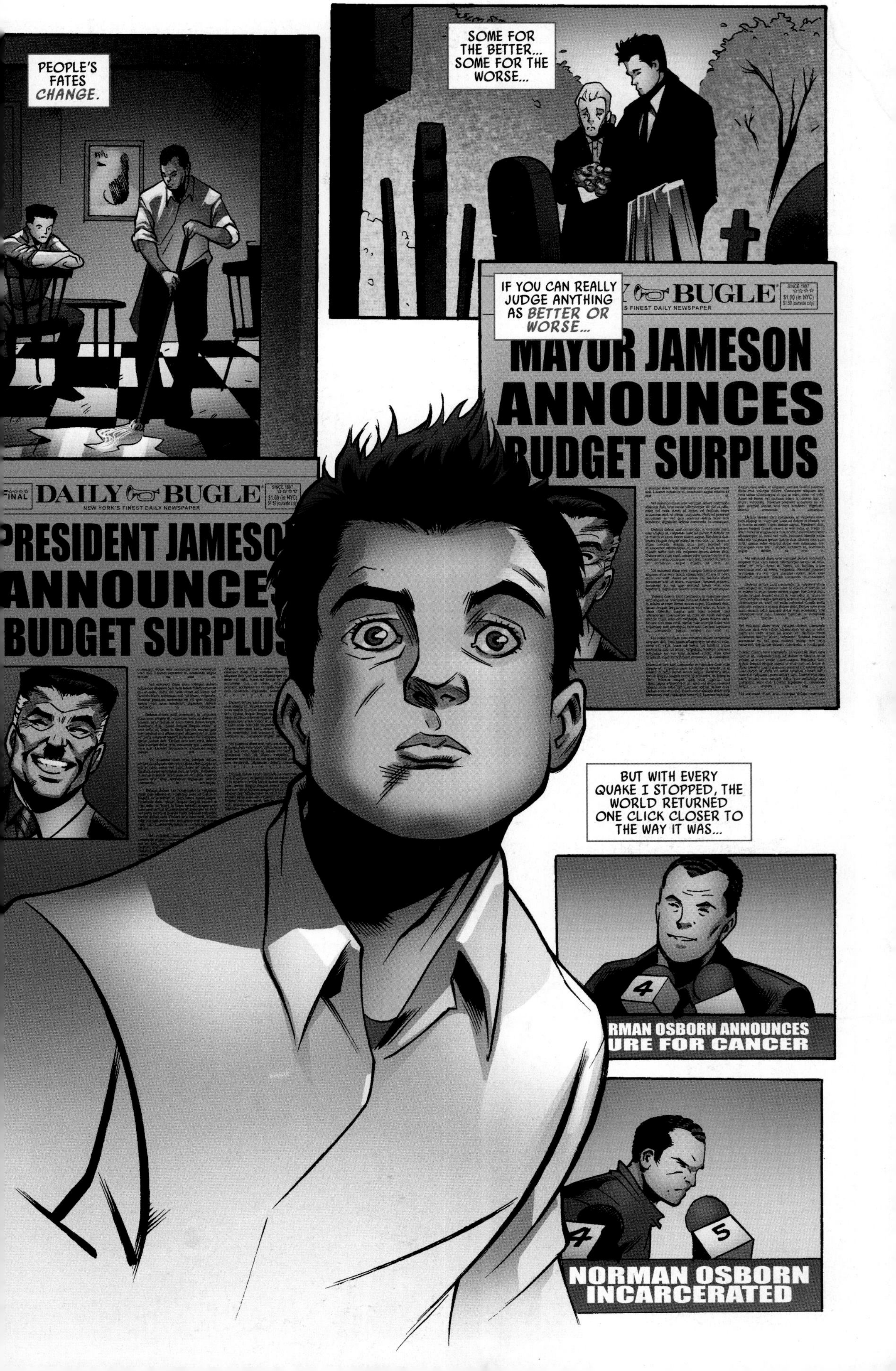

PEOPLE'S FATES CHANGE.
SOME FOR THE BETTER... SOME FOR THE WORSE...
IF YOU CAN REALLY JUDGE ANYTHING AS BETTER OR WORSE...
BUGLE
MAYOR JAMESON ANNOUNCES BUDGET SURPLUS
FINAL DAILY BUGLE
NEW YORK'S FINEST DAILY NEWSPAPER
PRESIDENT JAMESON ANNOUNCES BUDGET SURPLUS
BUT WITH EVERY QUAKE I STOPPED, THE WORLD RETURNED ONE CLICK CLOSER TO THE WAY IT WAS...
RMAN OSBORN ANNOUNCES URE FOR CANCER
NORMAN OSBORN INCARCERATED

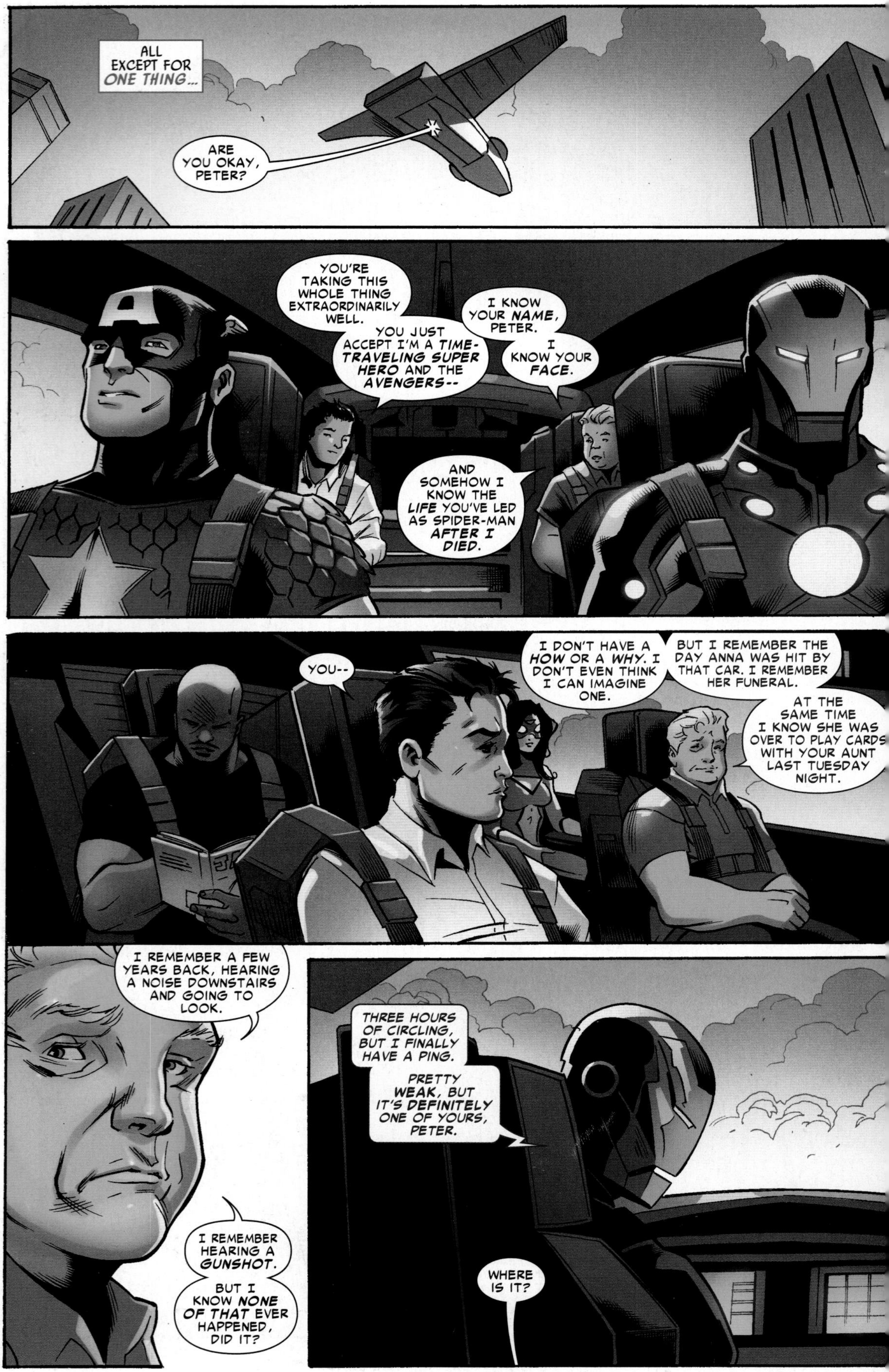
ALL EXCEPT FOR ONE THING...
ARE YOU OKAY, PETER?
YOU'RE TAKING THIS WHOLE THING EXTRAORDINARILY WELL.
YOU JUST ACCEPT I'M A TIME-TRAVELING SUPER HERO AND THE AVENGERS--
I KNOW YOUR NAME, PETER.
I KNOW YOUR FACE.
AND SOMEHOW I KNOW THE LIFE YOU'VE LED AS SPIDER-MAN AFTER I DIED.
YOU--
I DON'T HAVE A HOW OR A WHY. I DON'T EVEN THINK I CAN IMAGINE ONE.
BUT I REMEMBER THE DAY ANNA WAS HIT BY THAT CAR. I REMEMBER HER FUNERAL.
AT THE SAME TIME I KNOW SHE WAS OVER TO PLAY CARDS WITH YOUR AUNT LAST TUESDAY NIGHT.
I REMEMBER A FEW YEARS BACK, HEARING A NOISE DOWNSTAIRS AND GOING TO LOOK.
I REMEMBER HEARING A GUNSHOT.
BUT I KNOW NONE OF THAT EVER HAPPENED, DID IT?
THREE HOURS OF CIRCLING, BUT I FINALLY HAVE A PING.
PRETTY WEAK, BUT IT'S DEFINITELY ONE OF YOURS, PETER.
WHERE IS IT?

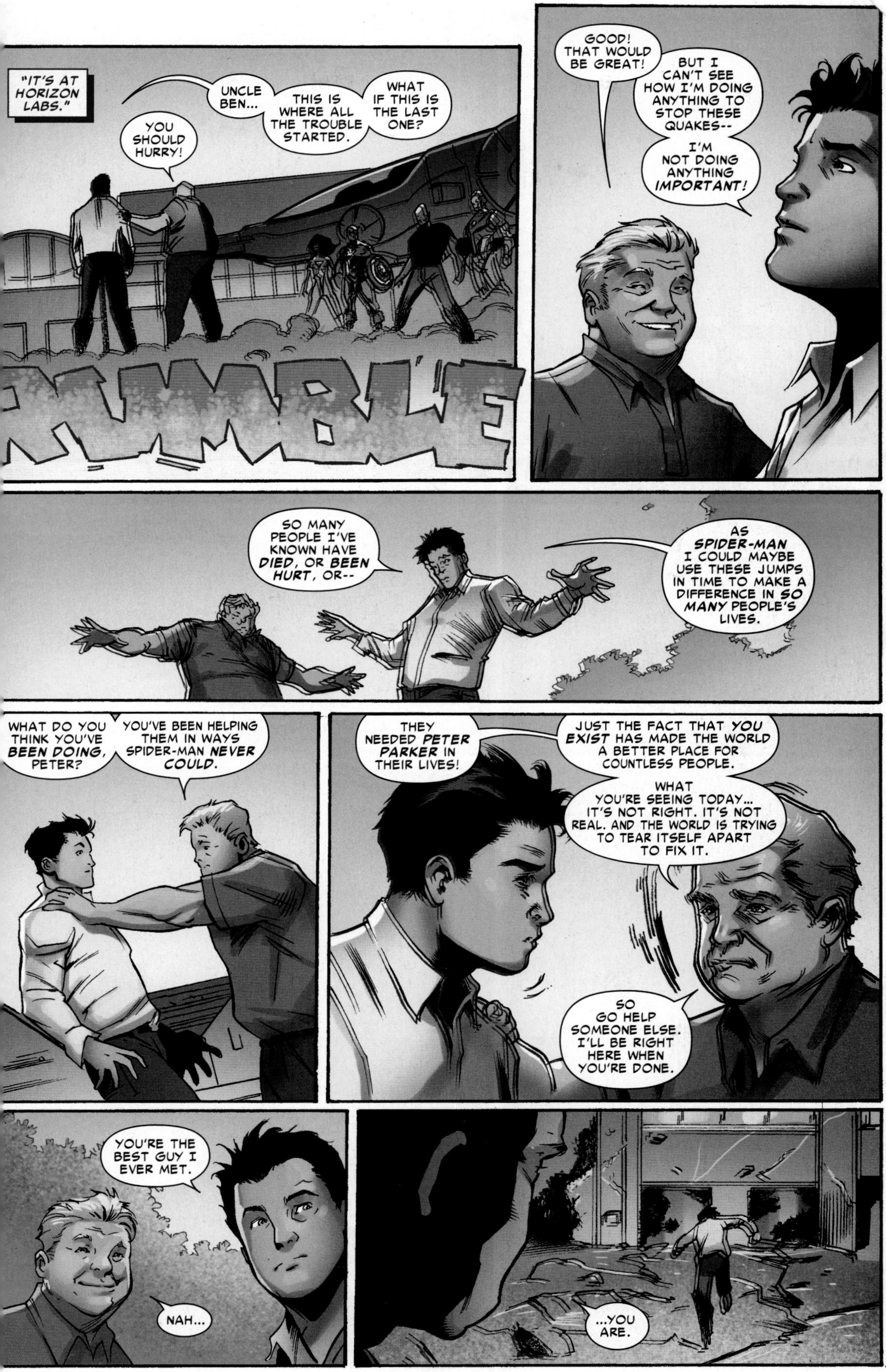
"IT'S AT HORIZON LABS."
UNCLE BEN...
THIS IS WHERE ALL THE TROUBLE STARTED.
WHAT IF THIS IS THE LAST ONE?
YOU SHOULD HURRY!
RUMBLE
GOOD! THAT WOULD BE GREAT!
BUT I CAN'T SEE HOW I'M DOING ANYTHING TO STOP THESE QUAKES--
I'M NOT DOING ANYTHING IMPORTANT!
SO MANY PEOPLE I'VE KNOWN HAVE DIED, OR BEEN HURT, OR--
AS SPIDER-MAN I COULD MAYBE USE THESE JUMPS IN TIME TO MAKE A DIFFERENCE IN SO MANY PEOPLE'S LIVES.
WHAT DO YOU THINK YOU'VE BEEN DOING, PETER?
YOU'VE BEEN HELPING THEM IN WAYS SPIDER-MAN NEVER COULD.
THEY NEEDED PETER PARKER IN THEIR LIVES!
JUST THE FACT THAT YOU EXIST HAS MADE THE WORLD A BETTER PLACE FOR COUNTLESS PEOPLE.
WHAT YOU'RE SEEING TODAY... IT'S NOT RIGHT. IT'S NOT REAL. AND THE WORLD IS TRYING TO TEAR ITSELF APART TO FIX IT.
SO GO HELP SOMEONE ELSE. I'LL BE RIGHT HERE WHEN YOU'RE DONE.
YOU'RE THE BEST GUY I EVER MET.
NAH...
...YOU ARE.

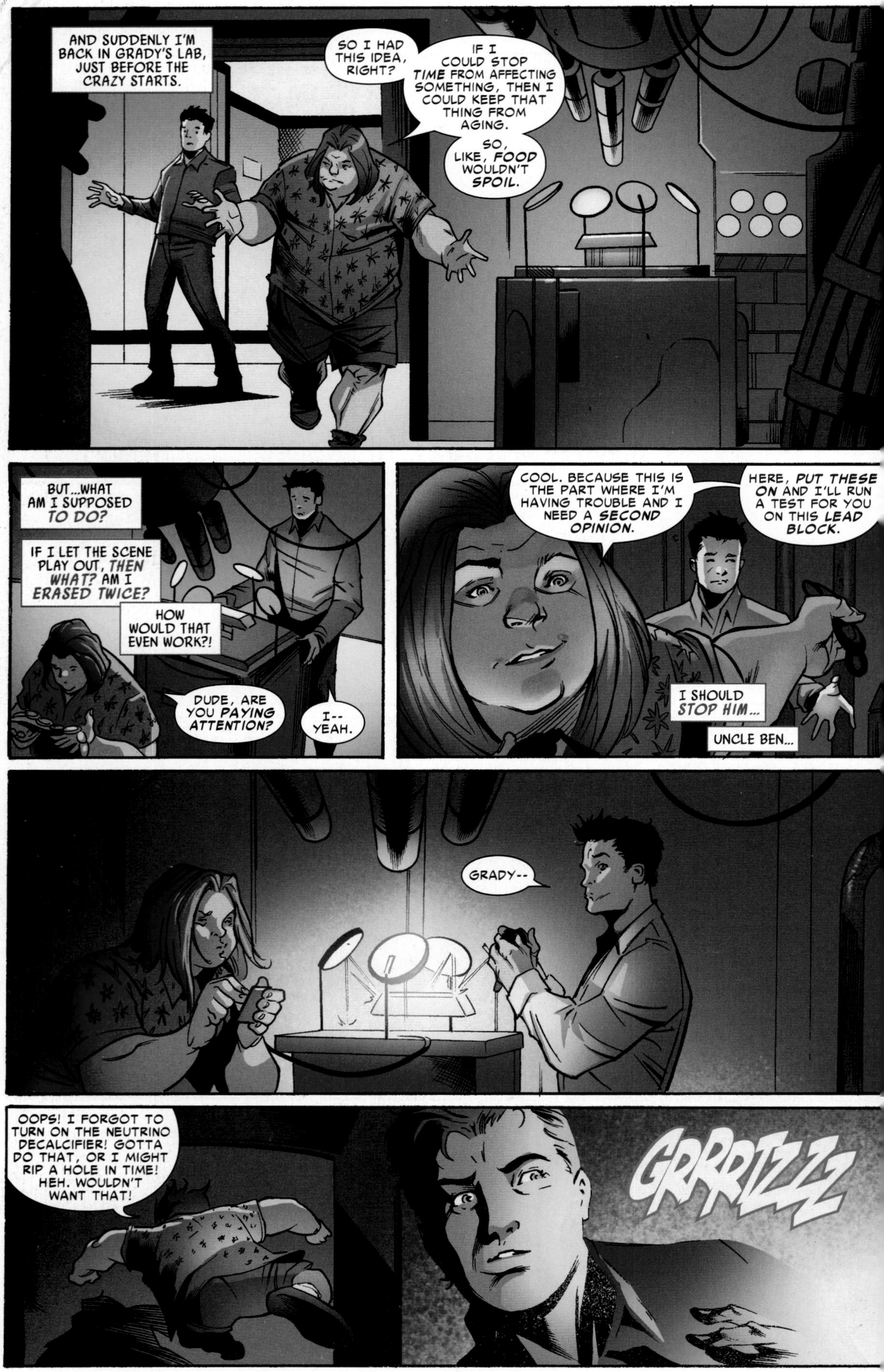
AND SUDDENLY I'M BACK IN GRADY'S LAB, JUST BEFORE THE CRAZY STARTS.
SO I HAD THIS IDEA, RIGHT?
IF I COULD STOP TIME FROM AFFECTING SOMETHING, THEN I COULD KEEP THAT THING FROM AGING.
SO, LIKE, FOOD WOULDN'T SPOIL.
BUT...WHAT AM I SUPPOSED TO DO?
IF I LET THE SCENE PLAY OUT, THEN WHAT? AM I ERASED TWICE?
HOW WOULD THAT EVEN WORK?!
DUDE, ARE YOU PAYING ATTENTION?
I-- YEAH.
COOL. BECAUSE THIS IS THE PART WHERE I'M HAVING TROUBLE AND I NEED A SECOND OPINION.
HERE, PUT THESE ON AND I'LL RUN A TEST FOR YOU ON THIS LEAD BLOCK.
I SHOULD STOP HIM...
UNCLE BEN...
GRADY--
OOPS! I FORGOT TO TURN ON THE NEUTRINO DECALCIFIER! GOTTA DO THAT, OR I MIGHT RIP A HOLE IN TIME! HEH. WOULDN'T WANT THAT!
GRRRIZZZ

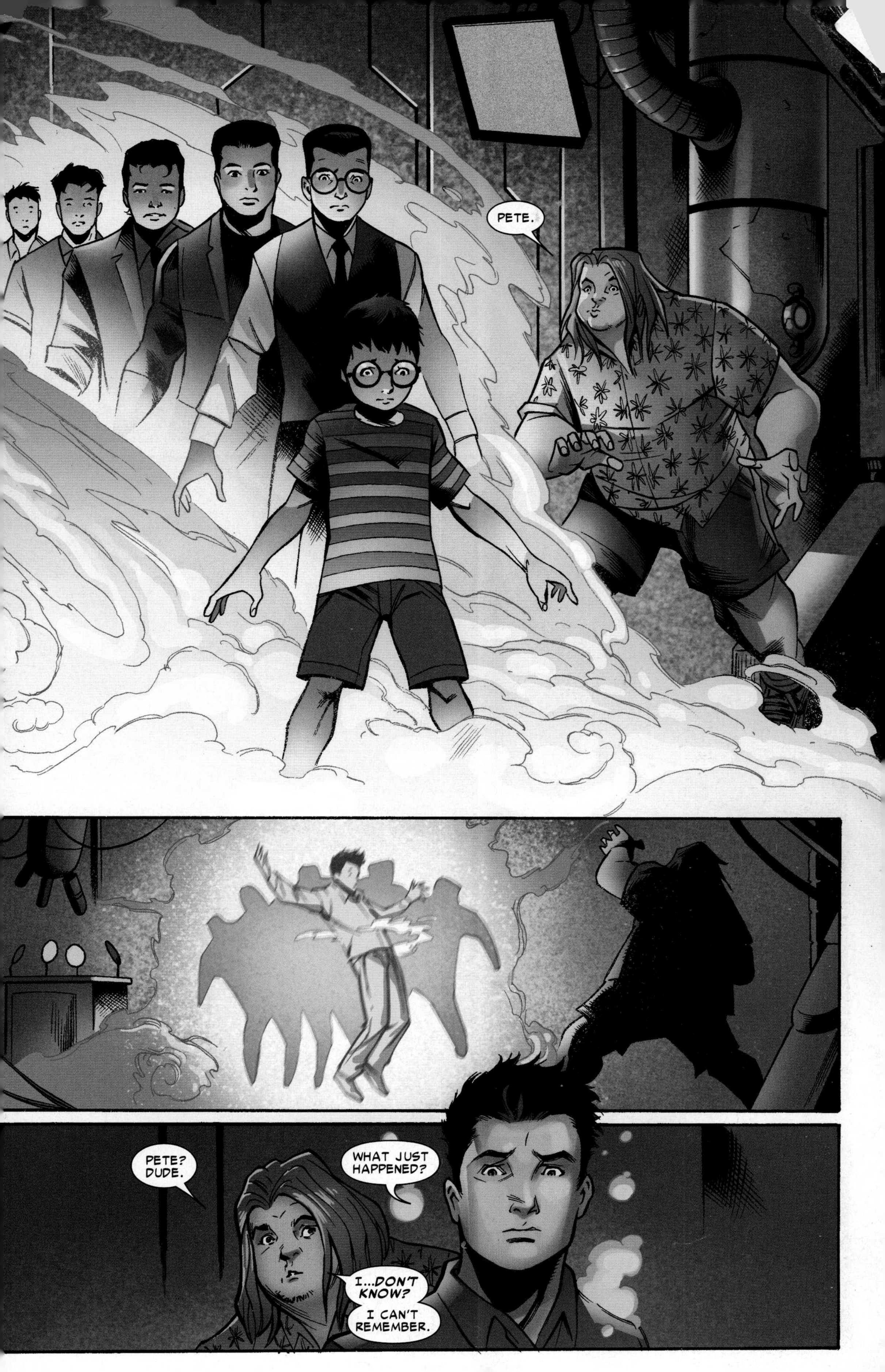
PETE.
PETE? DUDE.
WHAT JUST HAPPENED?
I...DON'T KNOW?
I CAN'T REMEMBER.

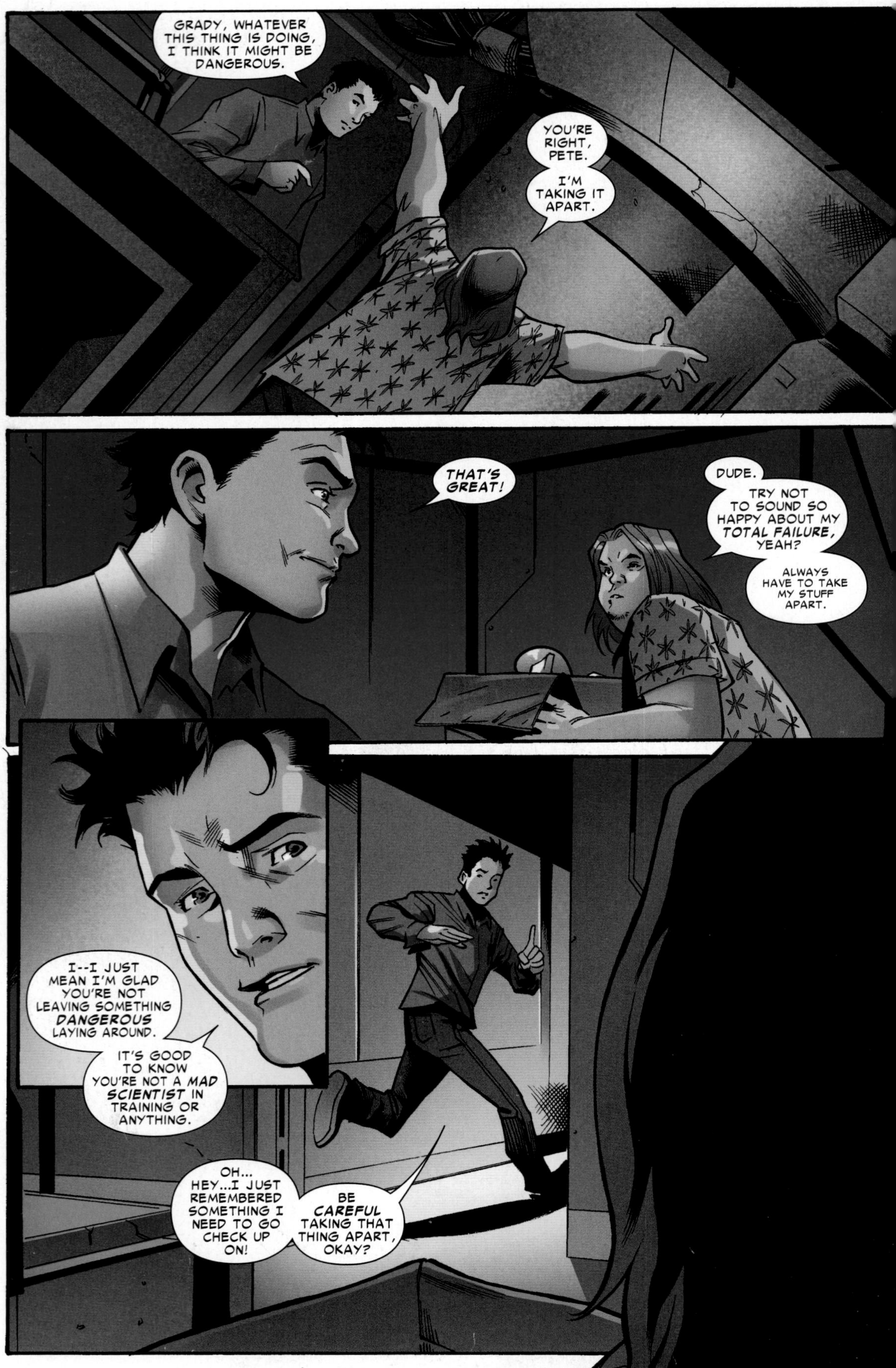
GRADY, WHATEVER THIS THING IS DOING, I THINK IT MIGHT BE DANGEROUS.
YOU'RE RIGHT, PETE.
I'M TAKING IT APART.
THAT'S GREAT!
DUDE.
TRY NOT TO SOUND SO HAPPY ABOUT MY TOTAL FAILURE, YEAH?
ALWAYS HAVE TO TAKE MY STUFF APART.
I--I JUST MEAN I'M GLAD YOU'RE NOT LEAVING SOMETHING DANGEROUS LAYING AROUND.
IT'S GOOD TO KNOW YOU'RE NOT A MAD SCIENTIST IN TRAINING OR ANYTHING.
OH... HEY...I JUST REMEMBERED SOMETHING I NEED TO GO CHECK UP ON!
BE CAREFUL TAKING THAT THING APART, OKAY?

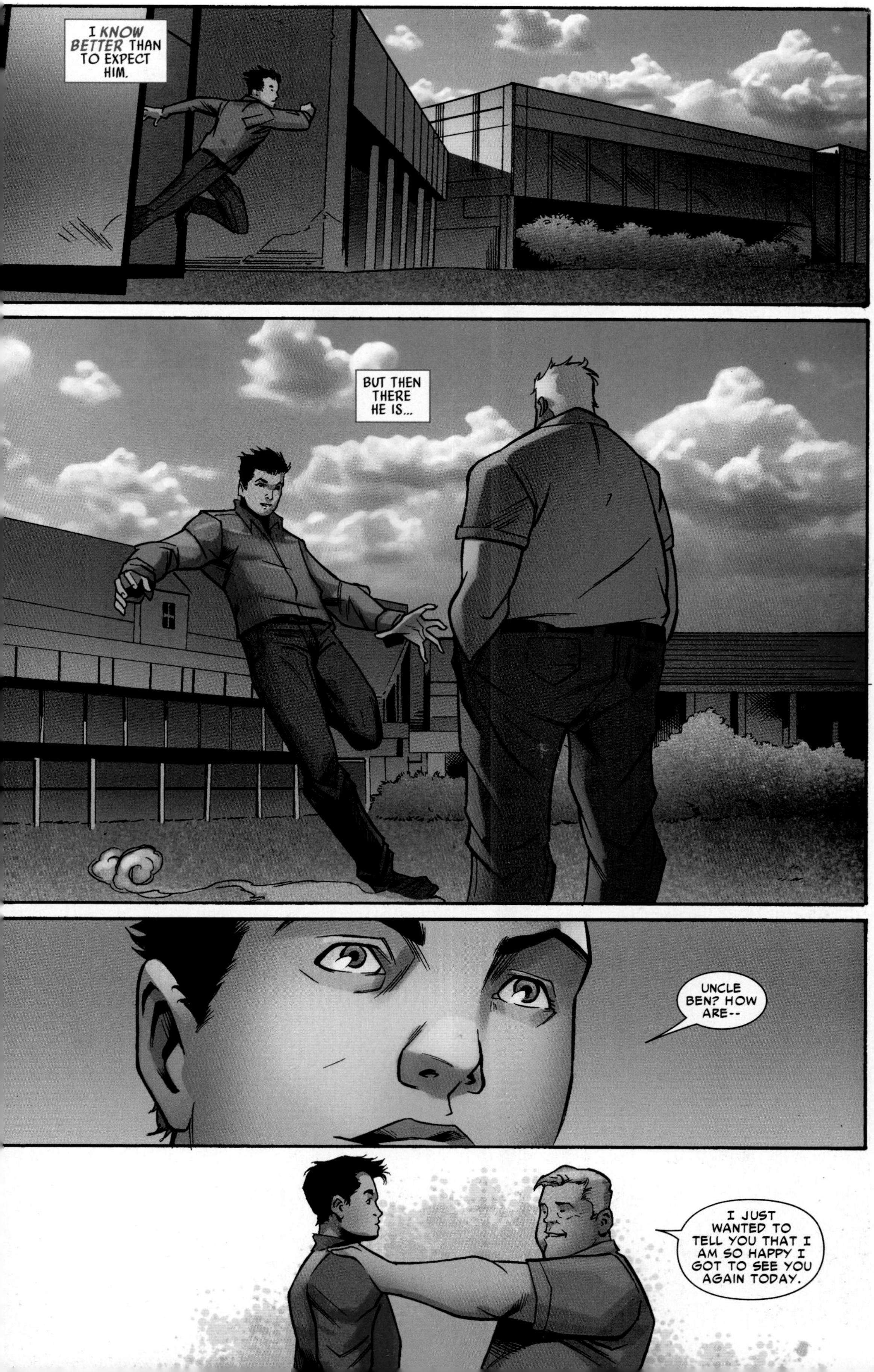

I *KNOW BETTER* THAN TO EXPECT HIM.
BUT THEN THERE HE IS...
UNCLE BEN? HOW ARE--
I JUST WANTED TO TELL YOU THAT I AM SO HAPPY I GOT TO SEE YOU AGAIN TODAY.

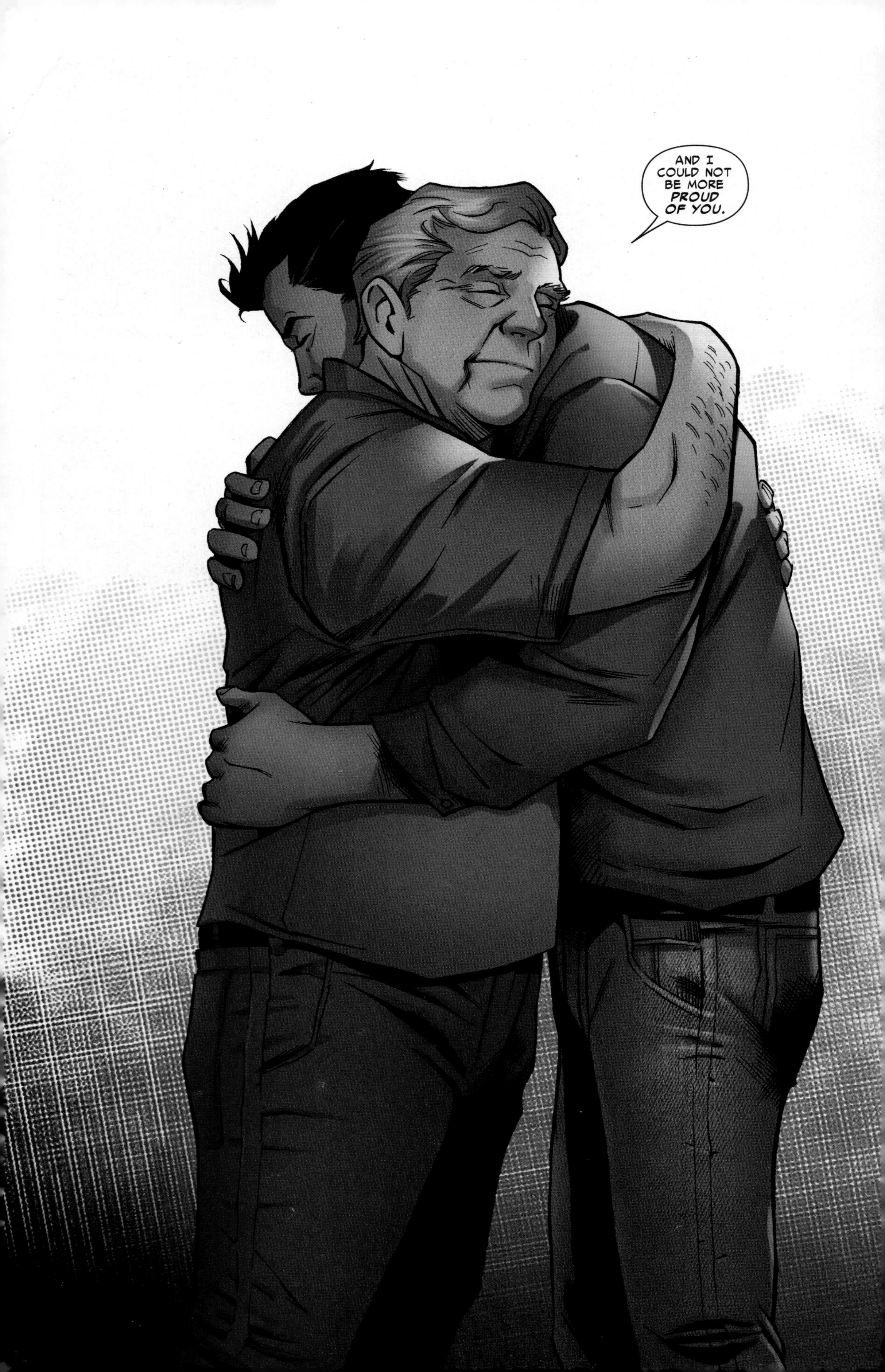
AND I COULD NOT BE MORE PROUD OF YOU.

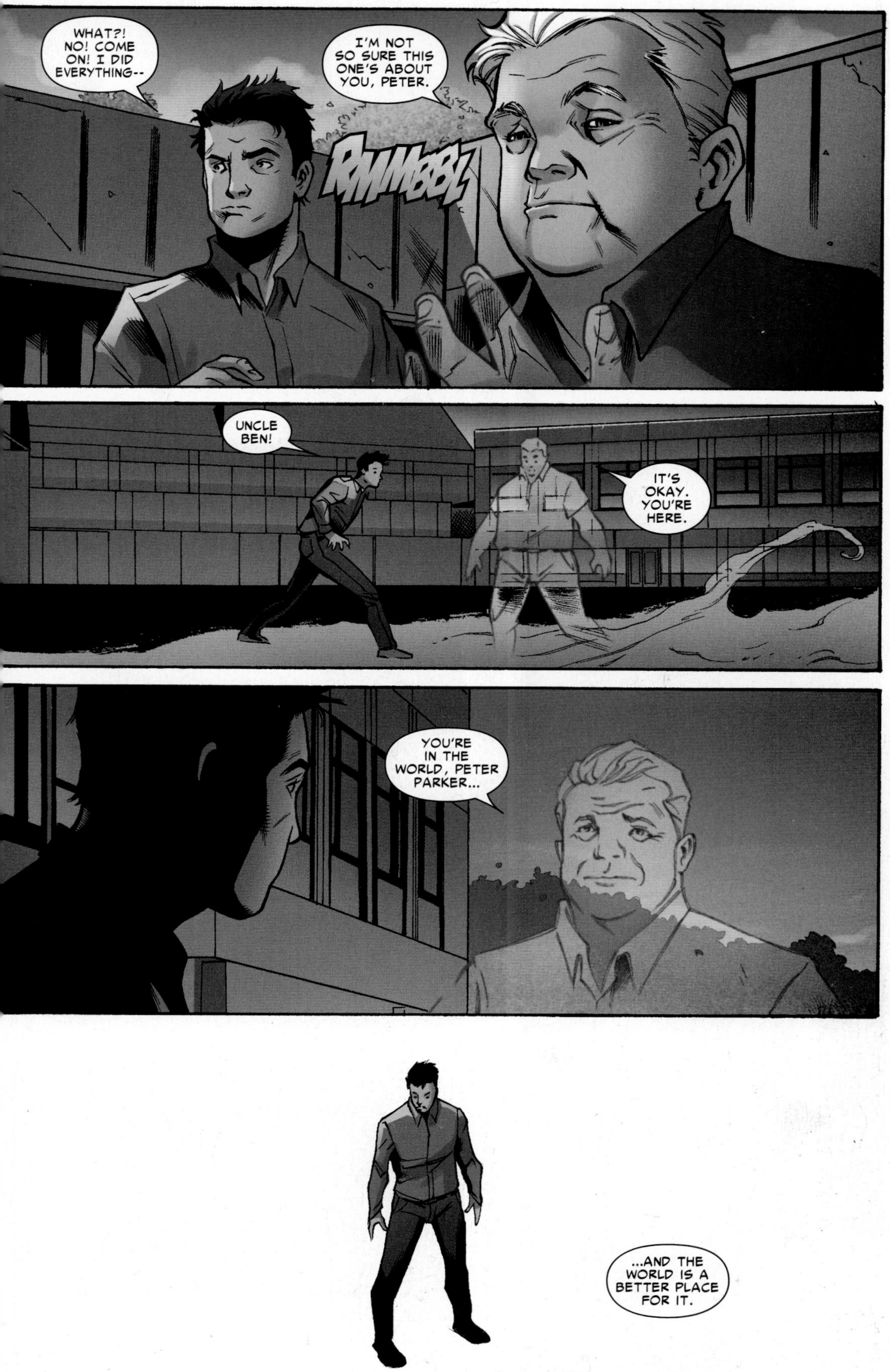
WHAT?! NO! COME ON! I DID EVERYTHING--
I'M NOT SO SURE THIS ONE'S ABOUT YOU, PETER.
RMMBBL
UNCLE BEN!
IT'S OKAY. YOU'RE HERE.
YOU'RE IN THE WORLD, PETER PARKER...
...AND THE WORLD IS A BETTER PLACE FOR IT.

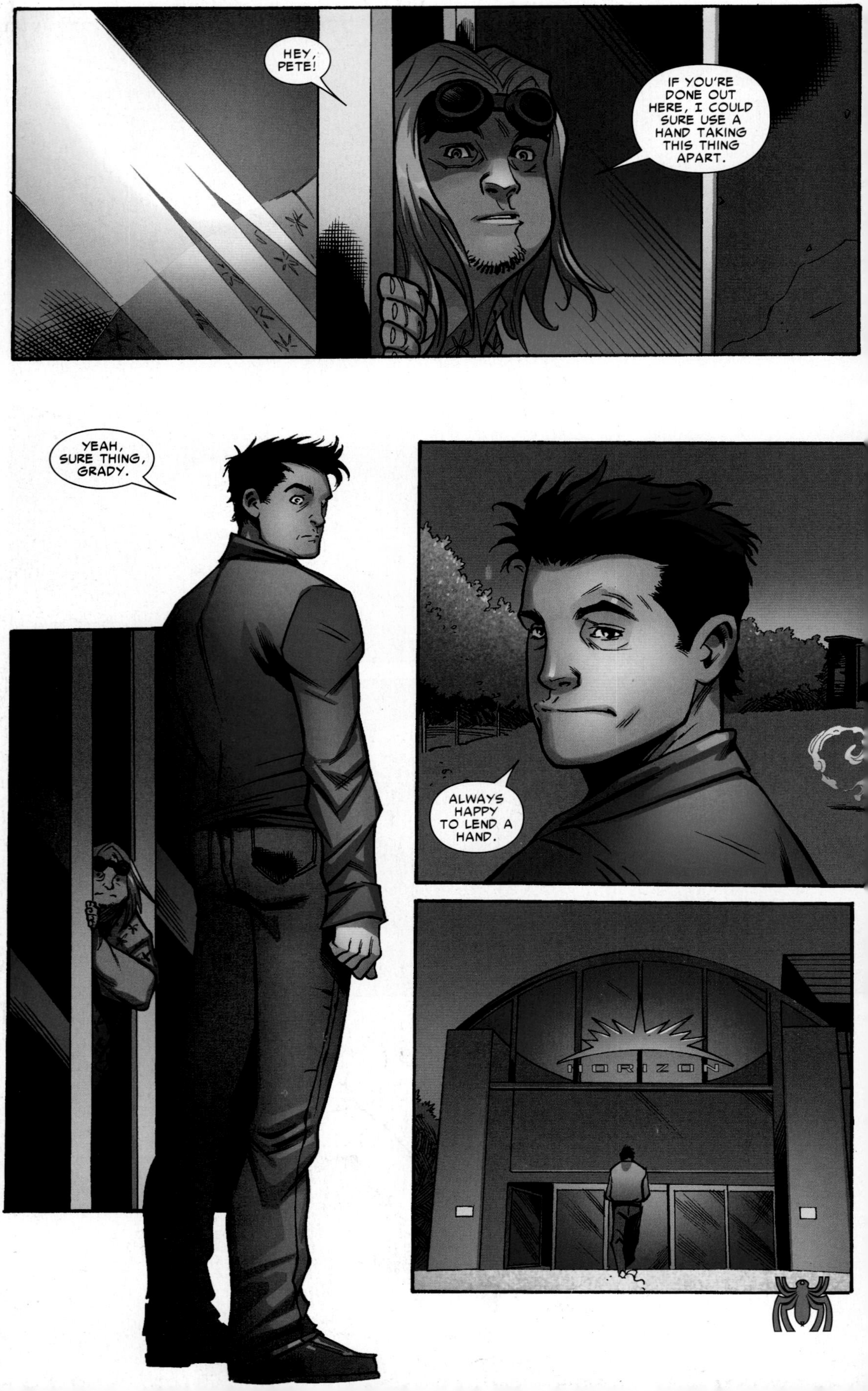
HEY, PETE!
IF YOU'RE DONE OUT HERE, I COULD SURE USE A HAND TAKING THIS THING APART.
YEAH, SURE THING, GRADY.
ALWAYS HAPPY TO LEND A HAND.
HORIZON

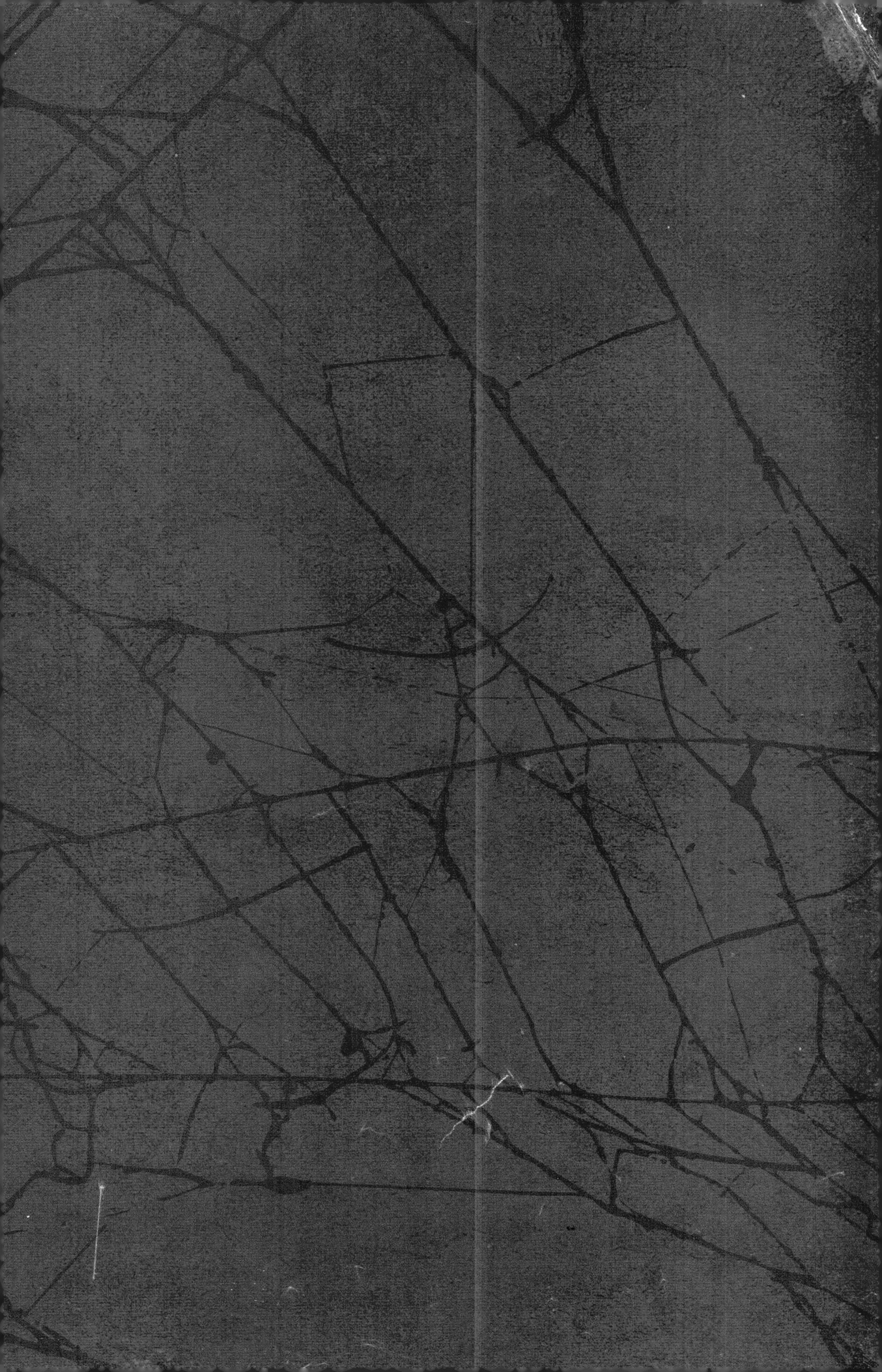

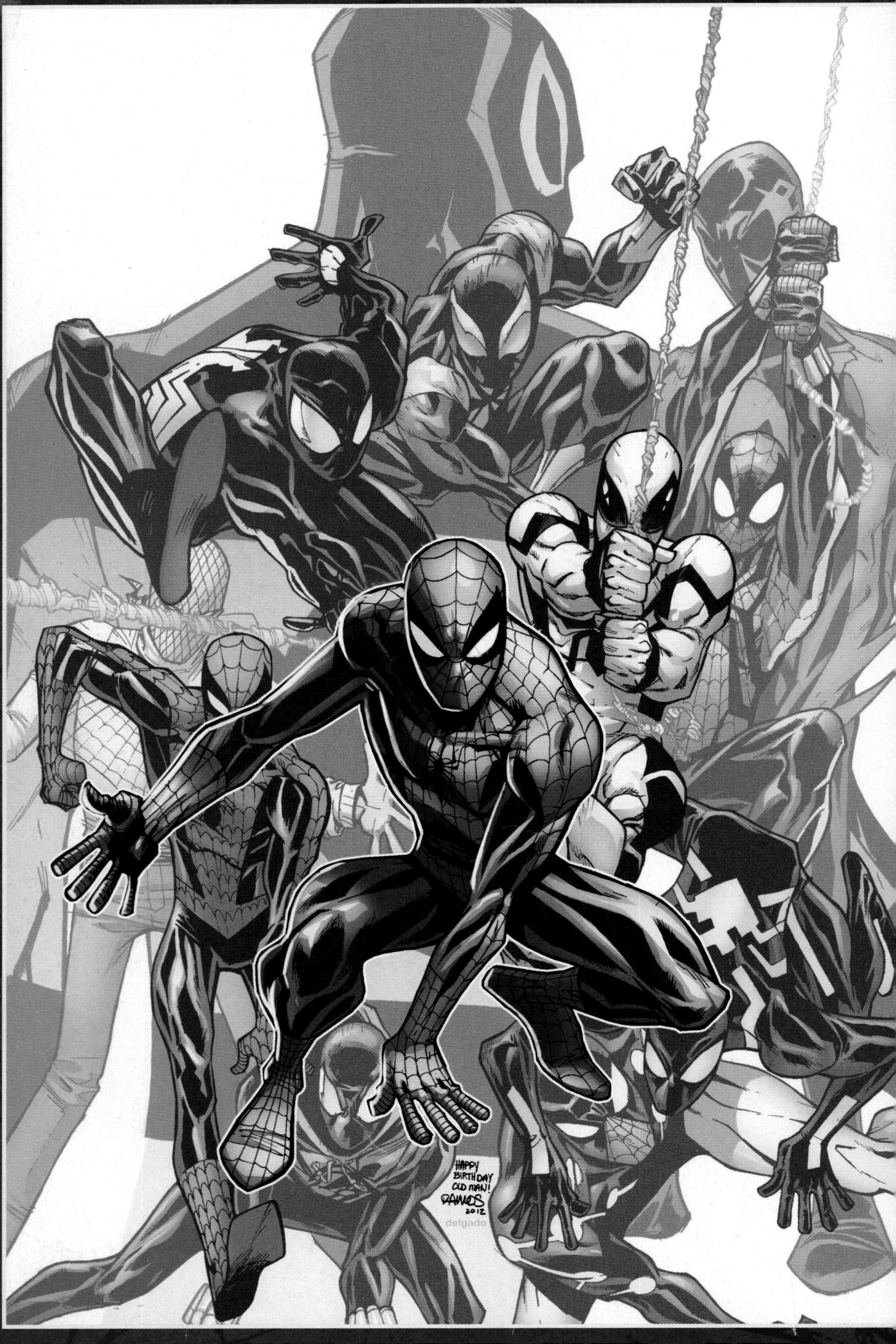
HAPPY BIRTHDAY OLD MAN!
RAMOS 2012
delgado

AMAZING SPIDER-MAN #692

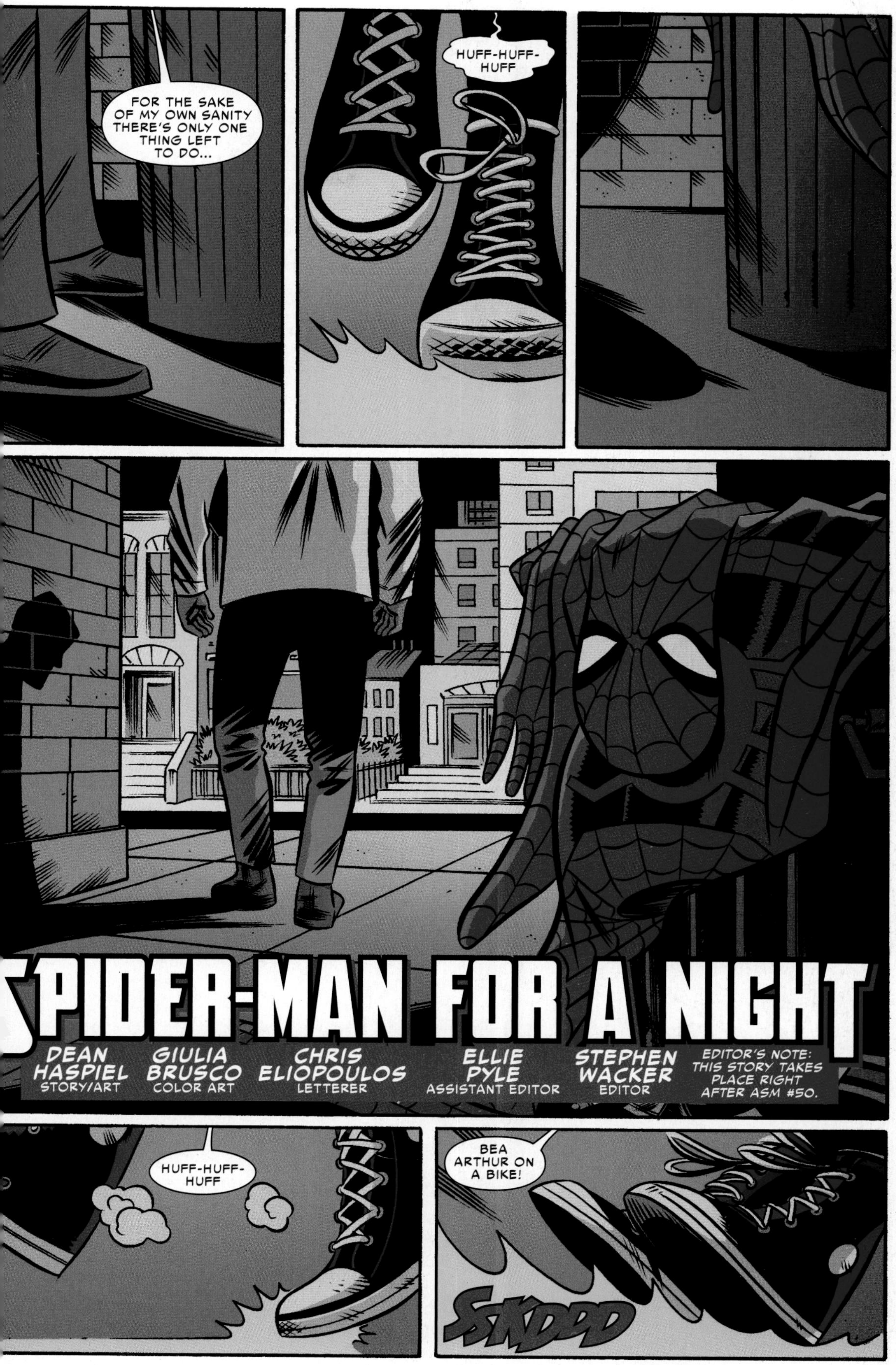
FOR THE SAKE OF MY OWN SANITY THERE'S ONLY ONE THING LEFT TO DO...
HUFF-HUFF-HUFF
SPIDER-MAN FOR A NIGHT
DEAN HASPIEL STORY/ART
GIULIA BRUSCO COLOR ART
CHRIS ELIOPOULOS LETTERER
ELLIE PYLE ASSISTANT EDITOR
STEPHEN WACKER EDITOR
EDITOR'S NOTE: THIS STORY TAKES PLACE RIGHT AFTER ASM #50.
HUFF-HUFF-HUFF
BEA ARTHUR ON A BIKE!
SSKDDD

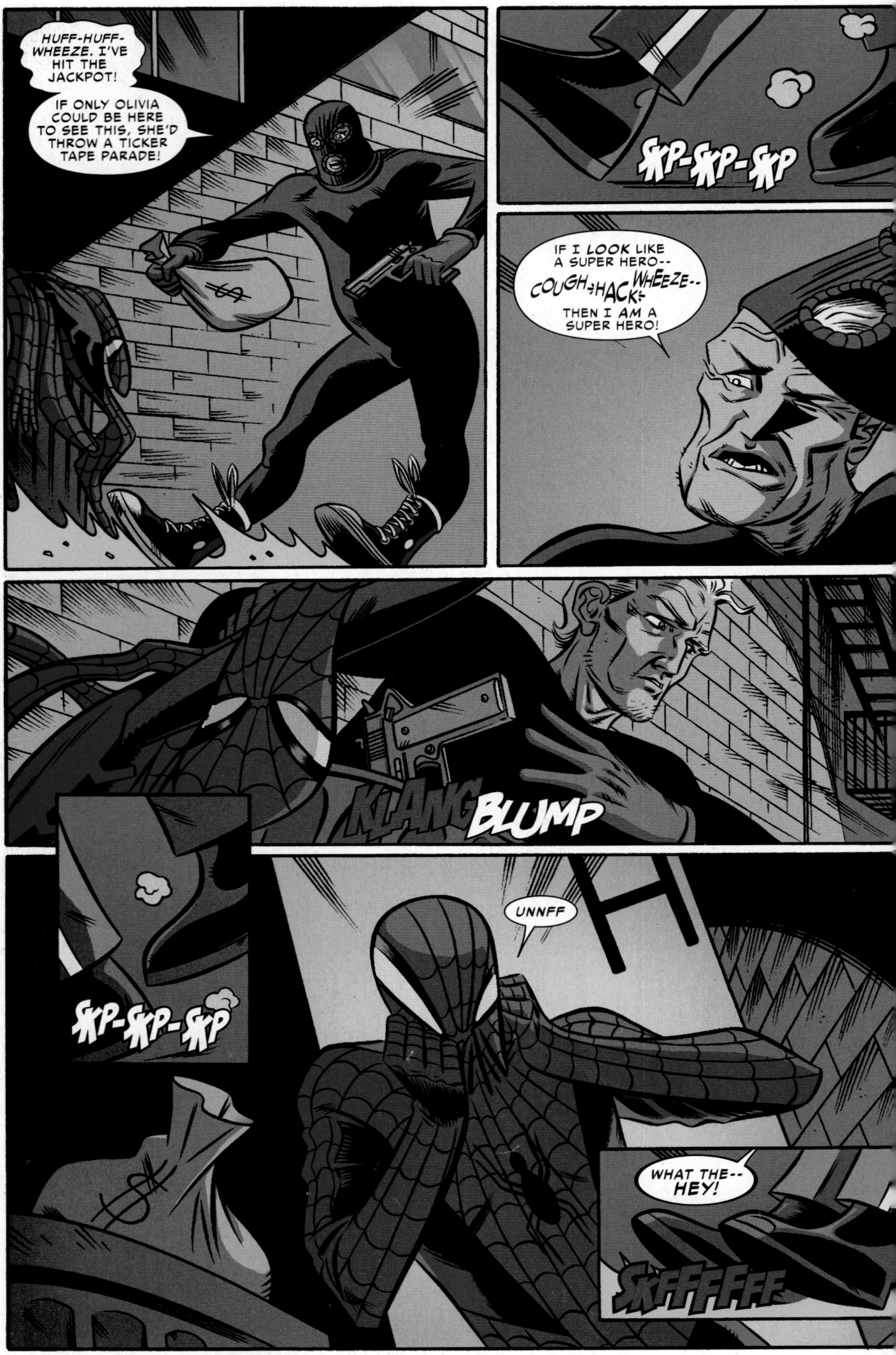

HUFF-HUFF-WHEEZE. I'VE HIT THE JACKPOT!
IF ONLY OLIVIA COULD BE HERE TO SEE THIS, SHE'D THROW A TICKER TAPE PARADE!
SKP-SKP-SKP
IF I LOOK LIKE A SUPER HERO-- COUGH HACK WHEEZE-- THEN I AM A SUPER HERO!
KLANG
BLUMP
SKP-SKP-SKP
UNNFF
WHAT THE-- HEY!
SKFFFFFF

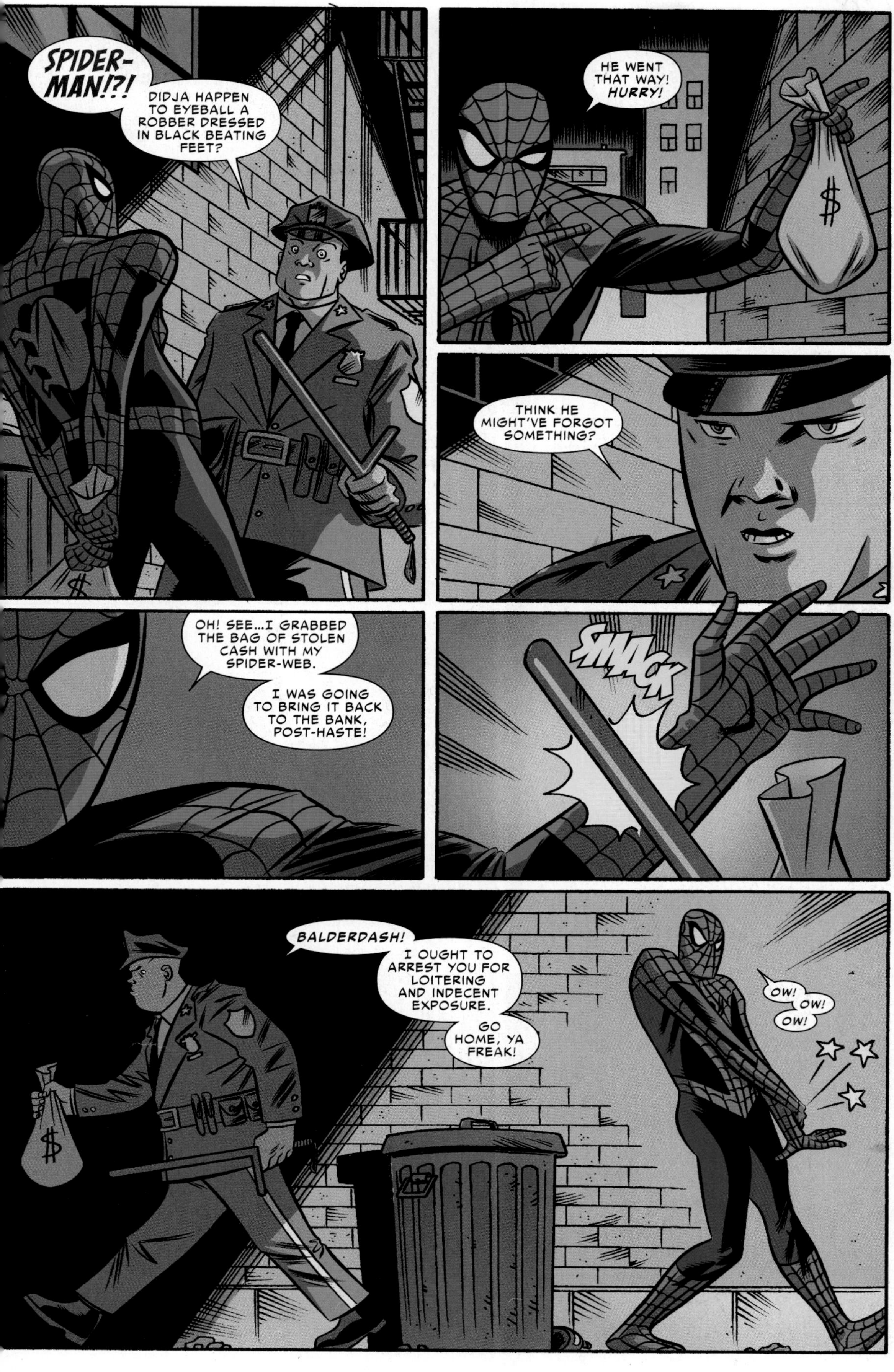
SPIDER-MAN!?!
DIDJA HAPPEN TO EYEBALL A ROBBER DRESSED IN BLACK BEATING FEET?
HE WENT THAT WAY! HURRY!
THINK HE MIGHT'VE FORGOT SOMETHING?
OH! SEE...I GRABBED THE BAG OF STOLEN CASH WITH MY SPIDER-WEB.
I WAS GOING TO BRING IT BACK TO THE BANK, POST-HASTE!
SMACK
BALDERDASH!
I OUGHT TO ARREST YOU FOR LOITERING AND INDECENT EXPOSURE.
GO HOME, YA FREAK!
OW! OW! OW!

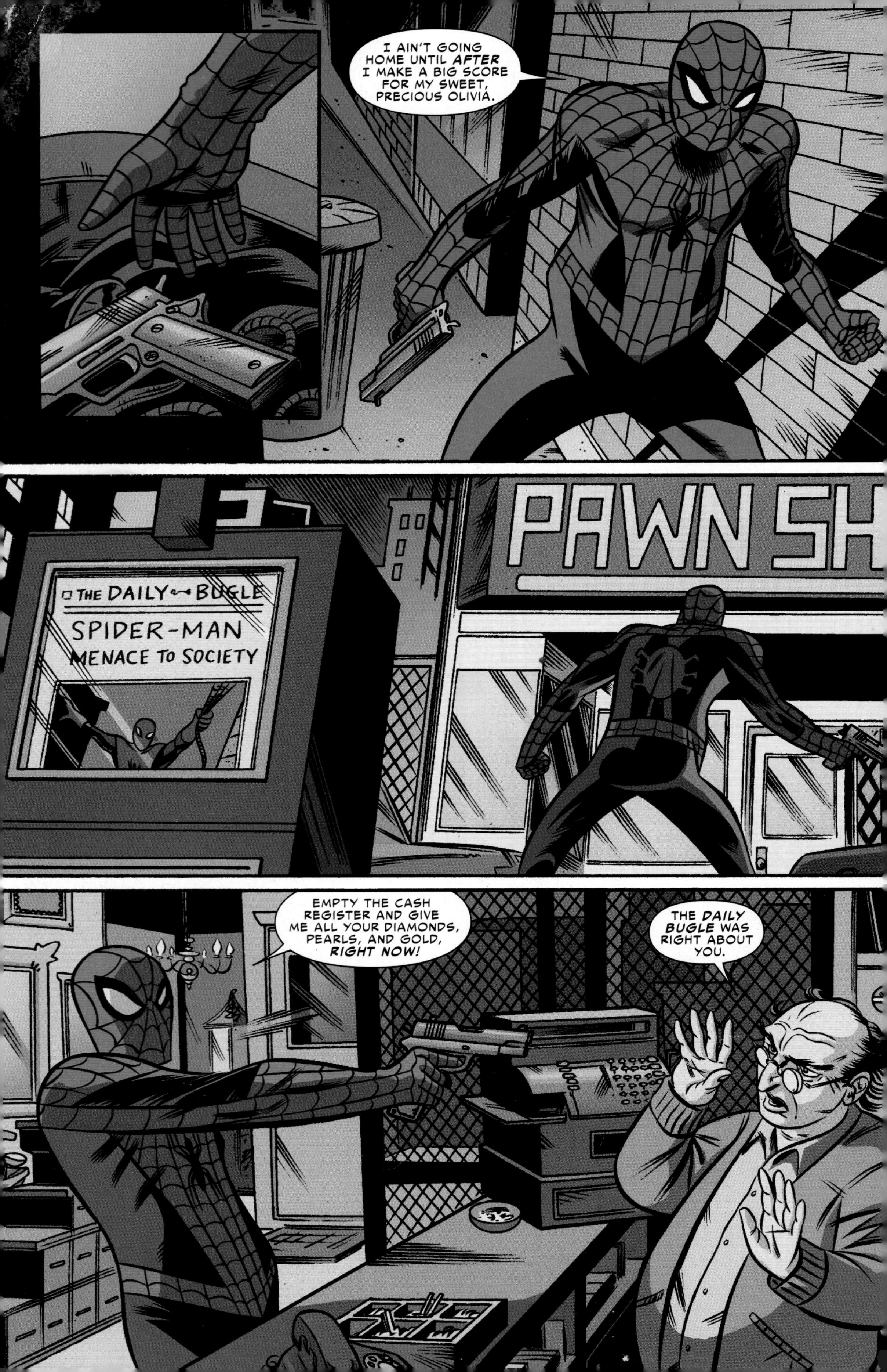
I AIN'T GOING HOME UNTIL *AFTER* I MAKE A BIG SCORE FOR MY SWEET, PRECIOUS OLIVIA.
PAWN SH
THE DAILY BUGLE
SPIDER-MAN
MENACE TO SOCIETY
EMPTY THE CASH REGISTER AND GIVE ME ALL YOUR DIAMONDS, PEARLS, AND GOLD, *RIGHT NOW!*
THE *DAILY BUGLE* WAS RIGHT ABOUT YOU.

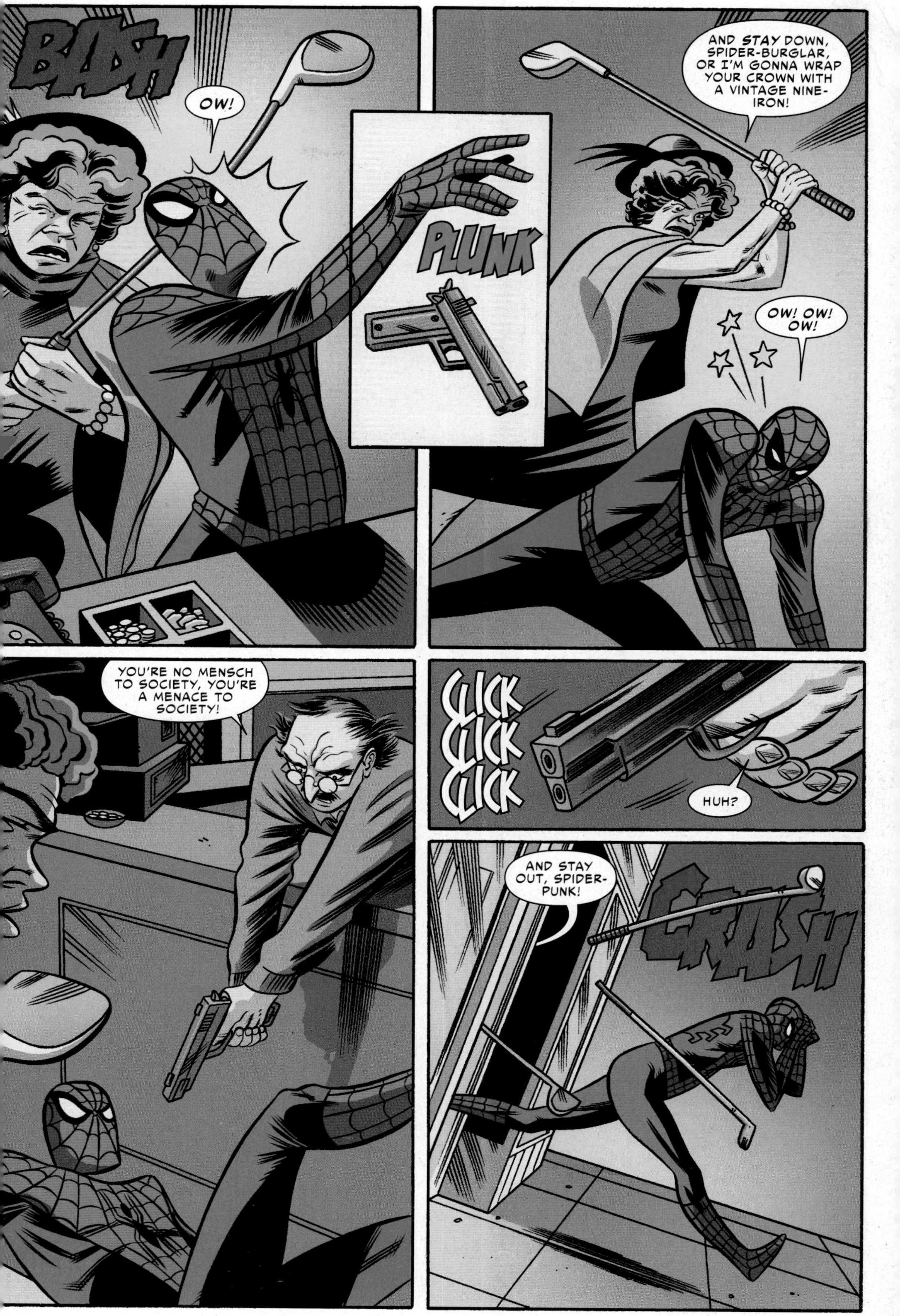
BASH
OW!
PLUNK
AND STAY DOWN, SPIDER-BURGLAR, OR I'M GONNA WRAP YOUR CROWN WITH A VINTAGE NINE-IRON!
OW! OW! OW!
YOU'RE NO MENSCH TO SOCIETY, YOU'RE A MENACE TO SOCIETY!
CLICK CLICK CLICK
HUH?
AND STAY OUT, SPIDER-PUNK!
CRASH

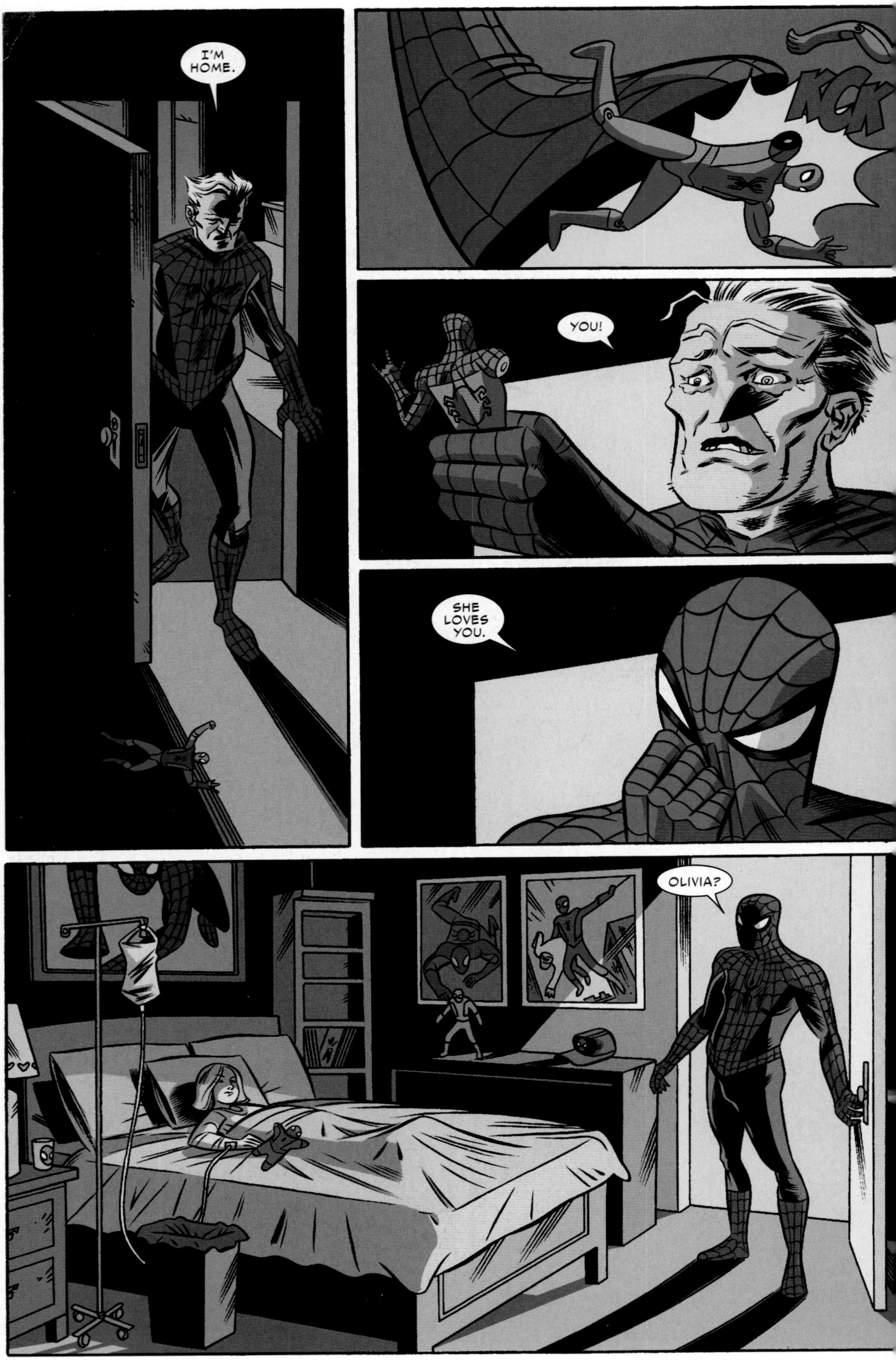
I'M HOME.
KCK
YOU!
SHE LOVES YOU.
OLIVIA?

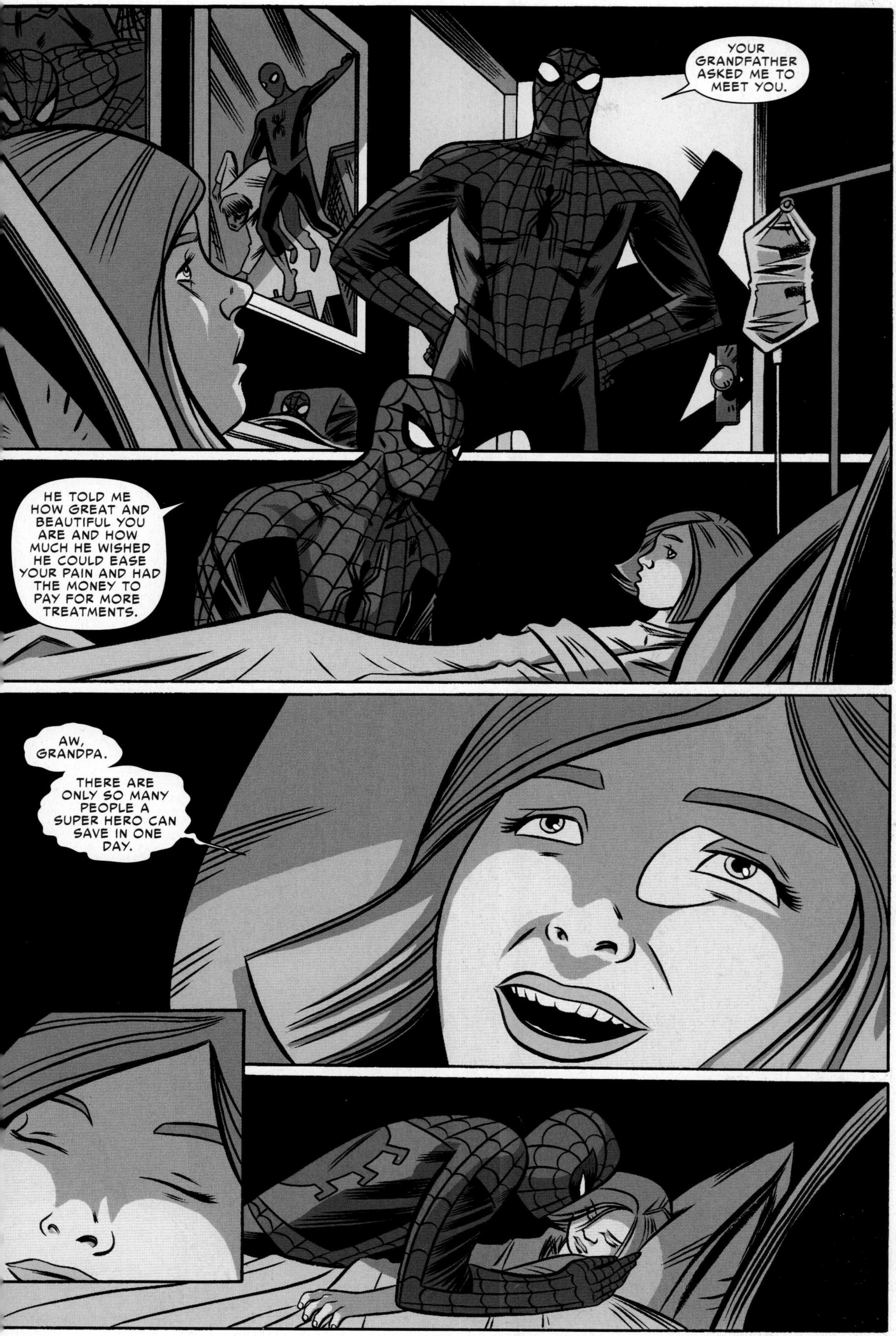
YOUR GRANDFATHER ASKED ME TO MEET YOU.
HE TOLD ME HOW GREAT AND BEAUTIFUL YOU ARE AND HOW MUCH HE WISHED HE COULD EASE YOUR PAIN AND HAD THE MONEY TO PAY FOR MORE TREATMENTS.
AW, GRANDPA.
THERE ARE ONLY SO MANY PEOPLE A SUPER HERO CAN SAVE IN ONE DAY.

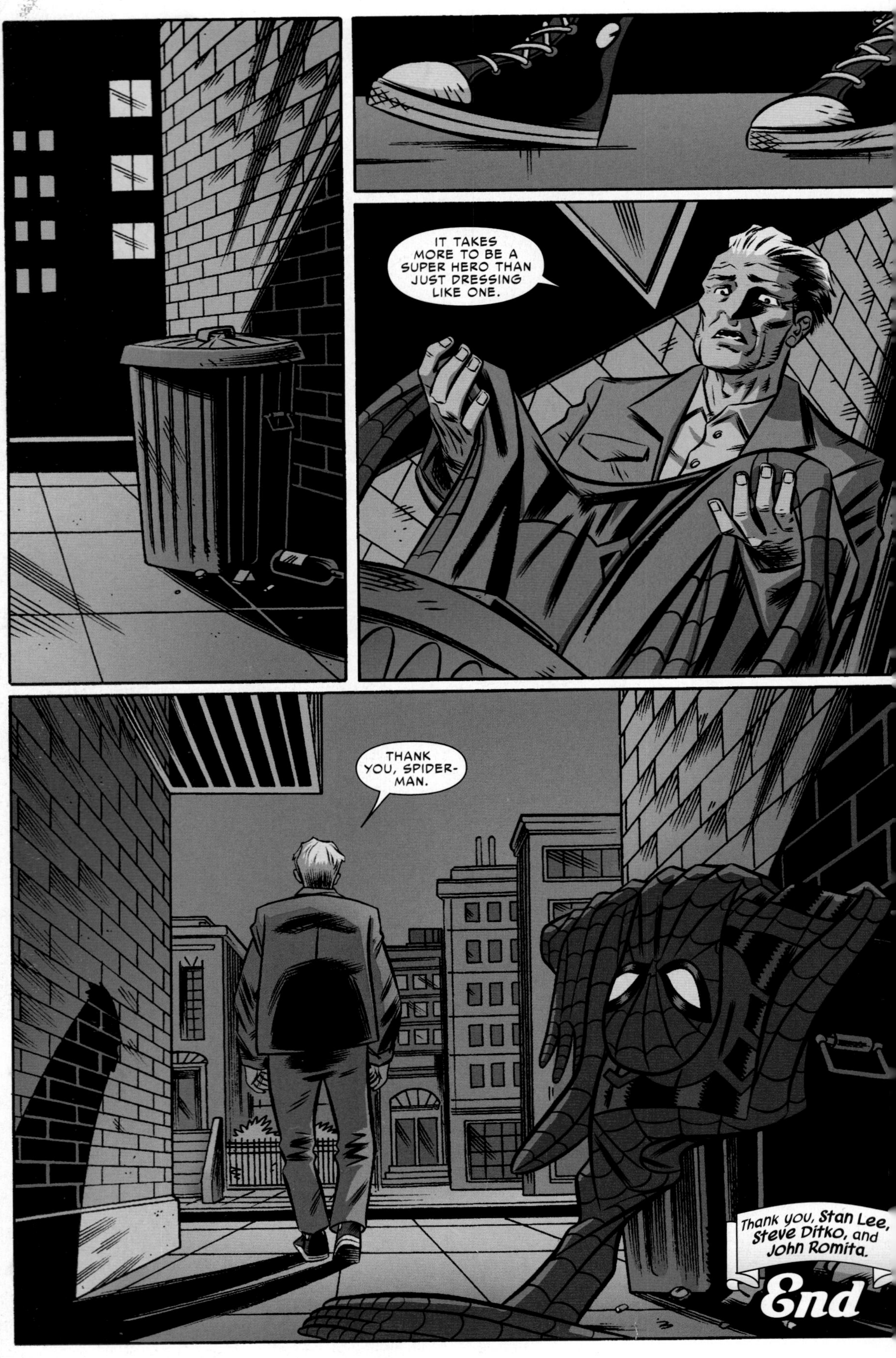
IT TAKES MORE TO BE A SUPER HERO THAN JUST DRESSING LIKE ONE.
THANK YOU, SPIDER-MAN.
Thank you, Stan Lee, Steve Ditko, and John Romita.
End

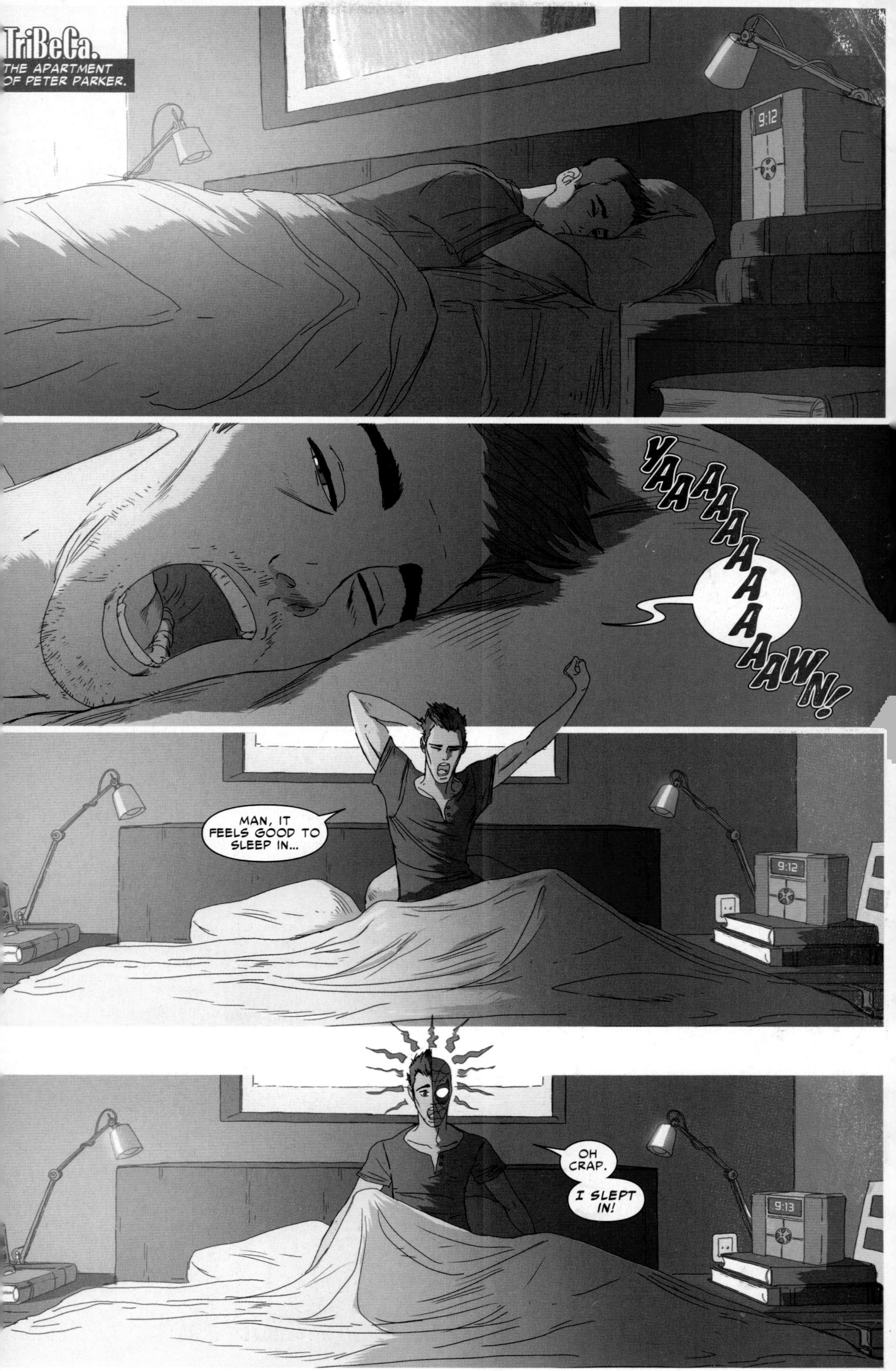
TriBeCa.
THE APARTMENT OF PETER PARKER.
9:12
YAAAAAAAAAAWN!
MAN, IT FEELS GOOD TO SLEEP IN...
9:12
OH CRAP.
I SLEPT IN!
9:13

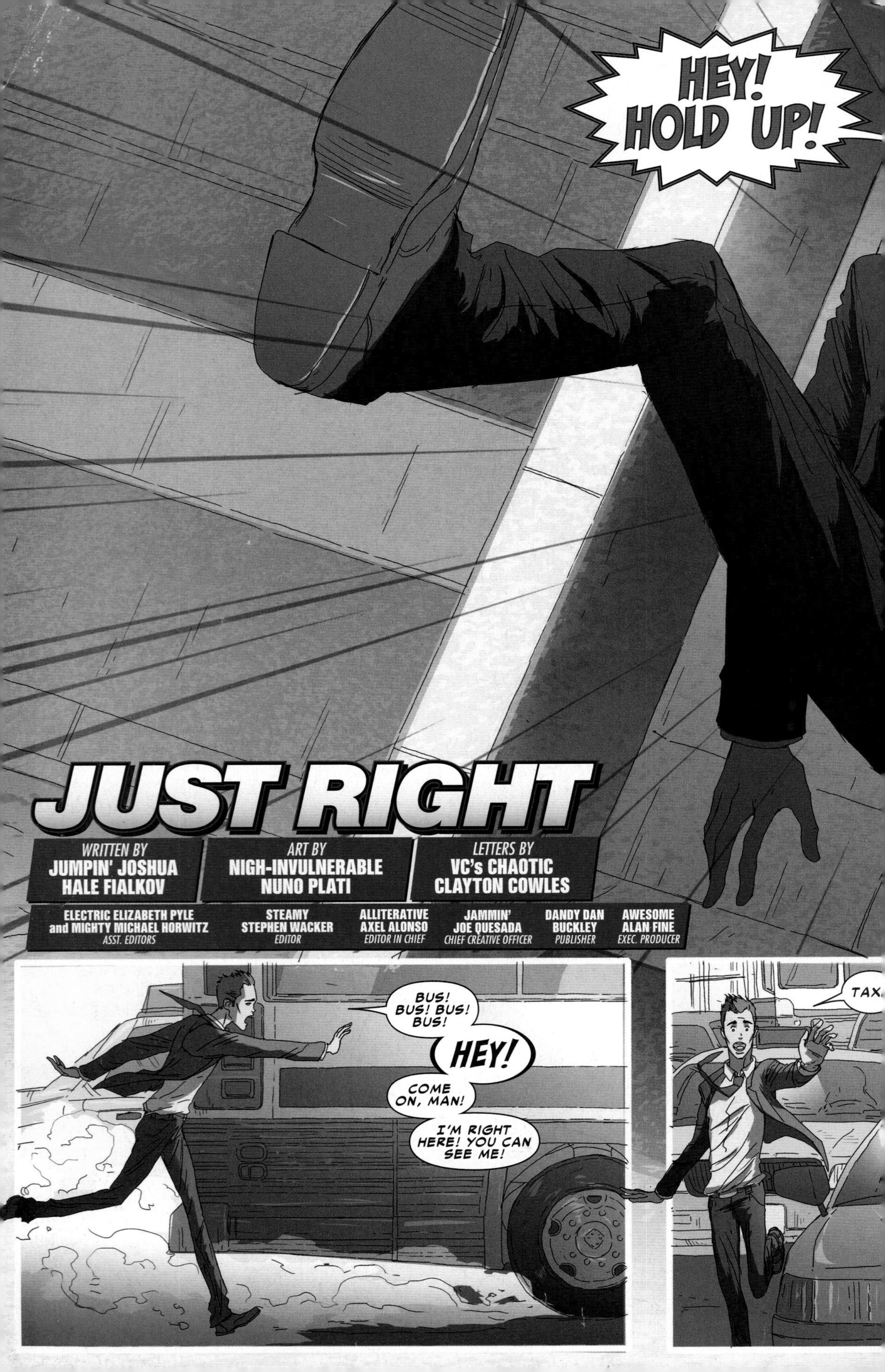

HEY! HOLD UP!
JUST RIGHT
WRITTEN BY JUMPIN' JOSHUA HALE FIALKOV
ART BY NIGH-INVULNERABLE NUNO PLATI
LETTERS BY VC's CHAOTIC CLAYTON COWLES
ELECTRIC ELIZABETH PYLE and MIGHTY MICHAEL HORWITZ ASST. EDITORS
STEAMY STEPHEN WACKER EDITOR
ALLITERATIVE AXEL ALONSO EDITOR IN CHIEF
JAMMIN' JOE QUESADA CHIEF CREATIVE OFFICER
DANDY DAN BUCKLEY PUBLISHER
AWESOME ALAN FINE EXEC. PRODUCER
BUS! BUS! BUS! BUS!
HEY!
COME ON, MAN!
I'M RIGHT HERE! YOU CAN SEE ME!
TAX

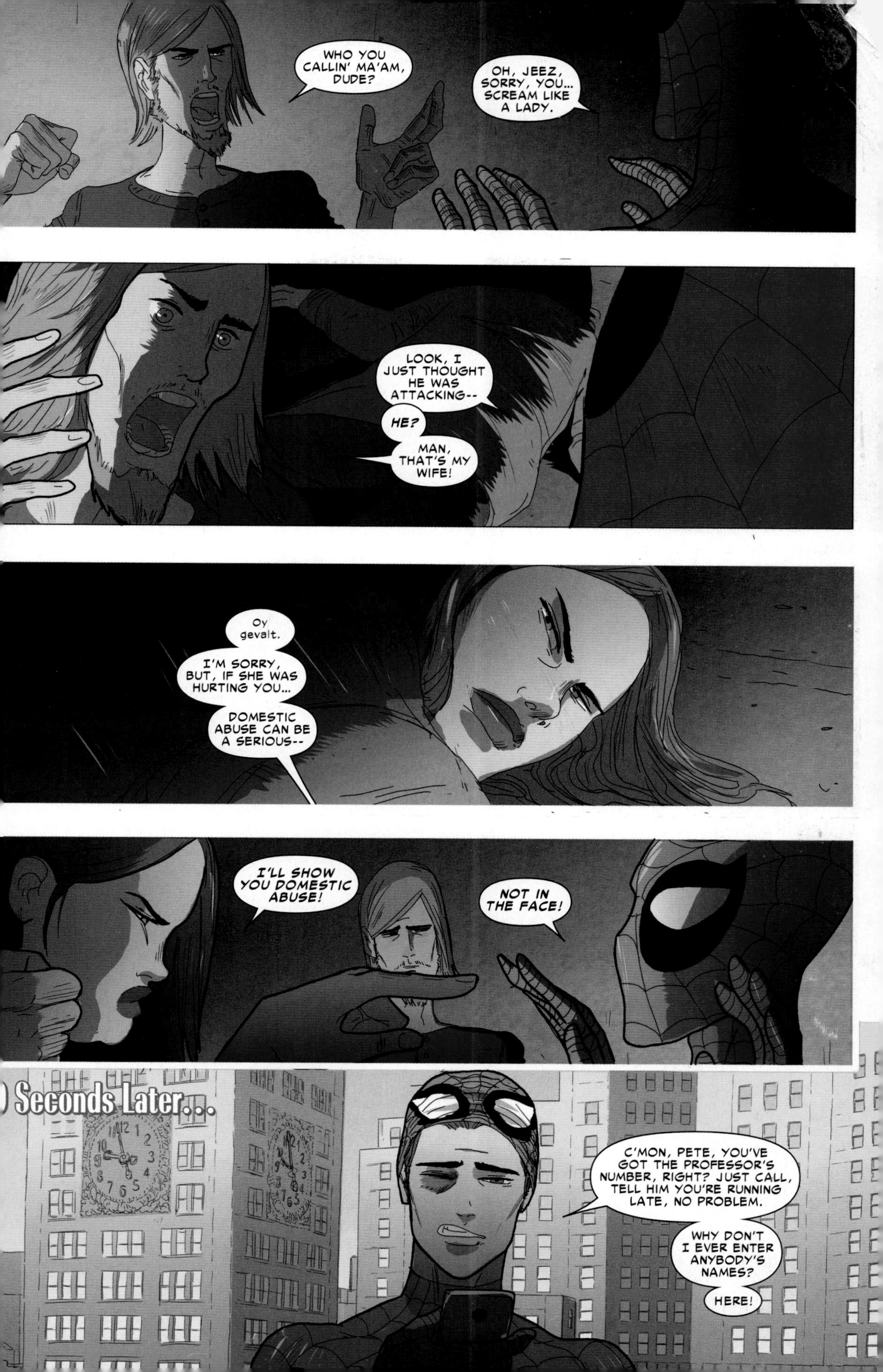
WHO YOU CALLIN' MA'AM, DUDE?
OH, JEEZ, SORRY, YOU... SCREAM LIKE A LADY.
LOOK, I JUST THOUGHT HE WAS ATTACKING--
HE?
MAN, THAT'S MY WIFE!
Oy gevalt.
I'M SORRY, BUT, IF SHE WAS HURTING YOU...
DOMESTIC ABUSE CAN BE A SERIOUS--
I'LL SHOW YOU DOMESTIC ABUSE!
NOT IN THE FACE!
Seconds Later...
C'MON, PETE, YOU'VE GOT THE PROFESSOR'S NUMBER, RIGHT? JUST CALL, TELL HIM YOU'RE RUNNING LATE, NO PROBLEM.
WHY DON'T I EVER ENTER ANYBODY'S NAMES?
HERE!

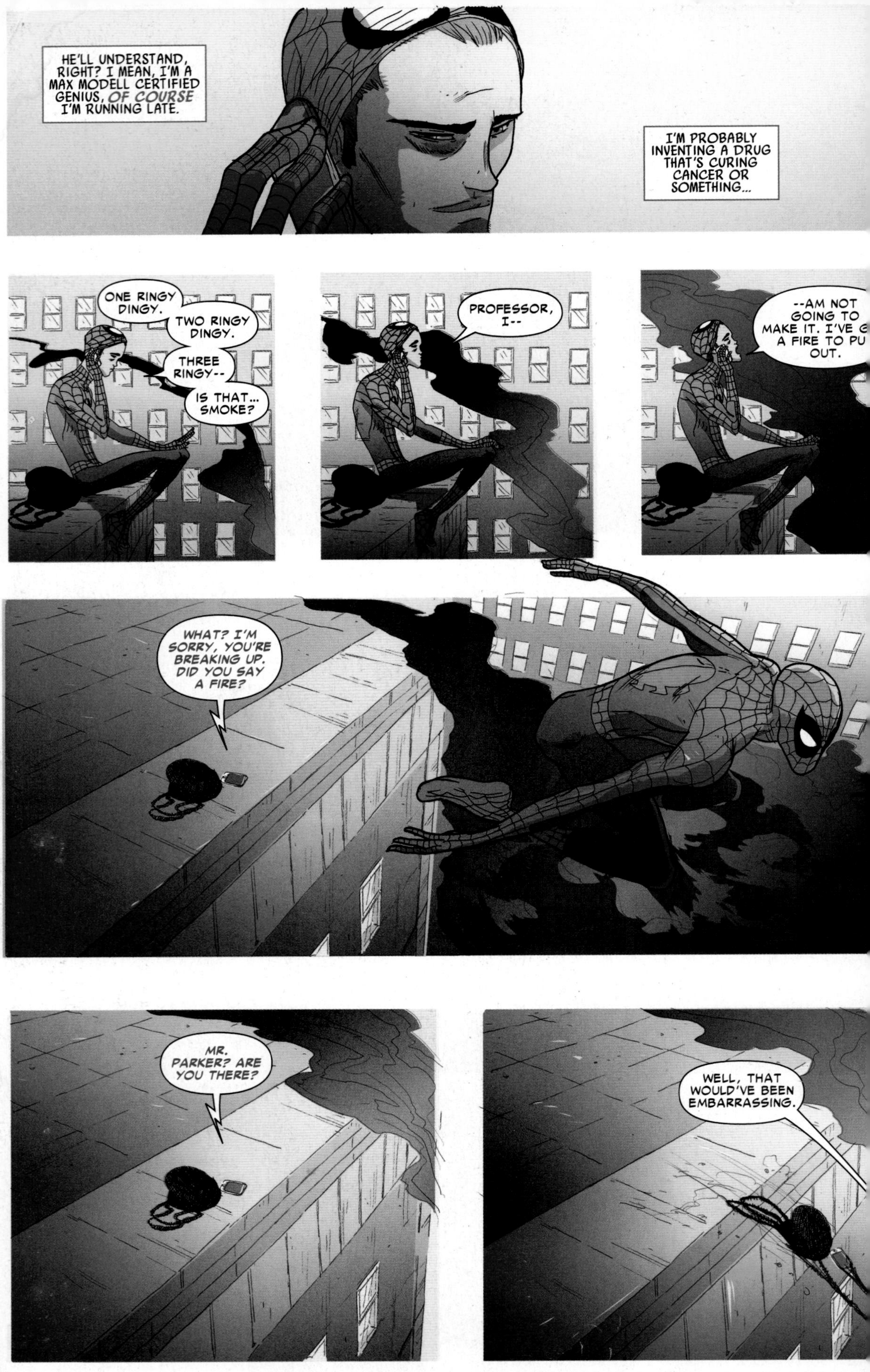
HE'LL UNDERSTAND, RIGHT? I MEAN, I'M A MAX MODELL CERTIFIED GENIUS, OF COURSE I'M RUNNING LATE.
I'M PROBABLY INVENTING A DRUG THAT'S CURING CANCER OR SOMETHING...
ONE RINGY DINGY.
TWO RINGY DINGY.
THREE RINGY--
IS THAT... SMOKE?
PROFESSOR, I--
--AM NOT GOING TO MAKE IT. I'VE G A FIRE TO PU OUT.
WHAT? I'M SORRY, YOU'RE BREAKING UP. DID YOU SAY A FIRE?
MR. PARKER? ARE YOU THERE?
WELL, THAT WOULD'VE BEEN EMBARRASSING.

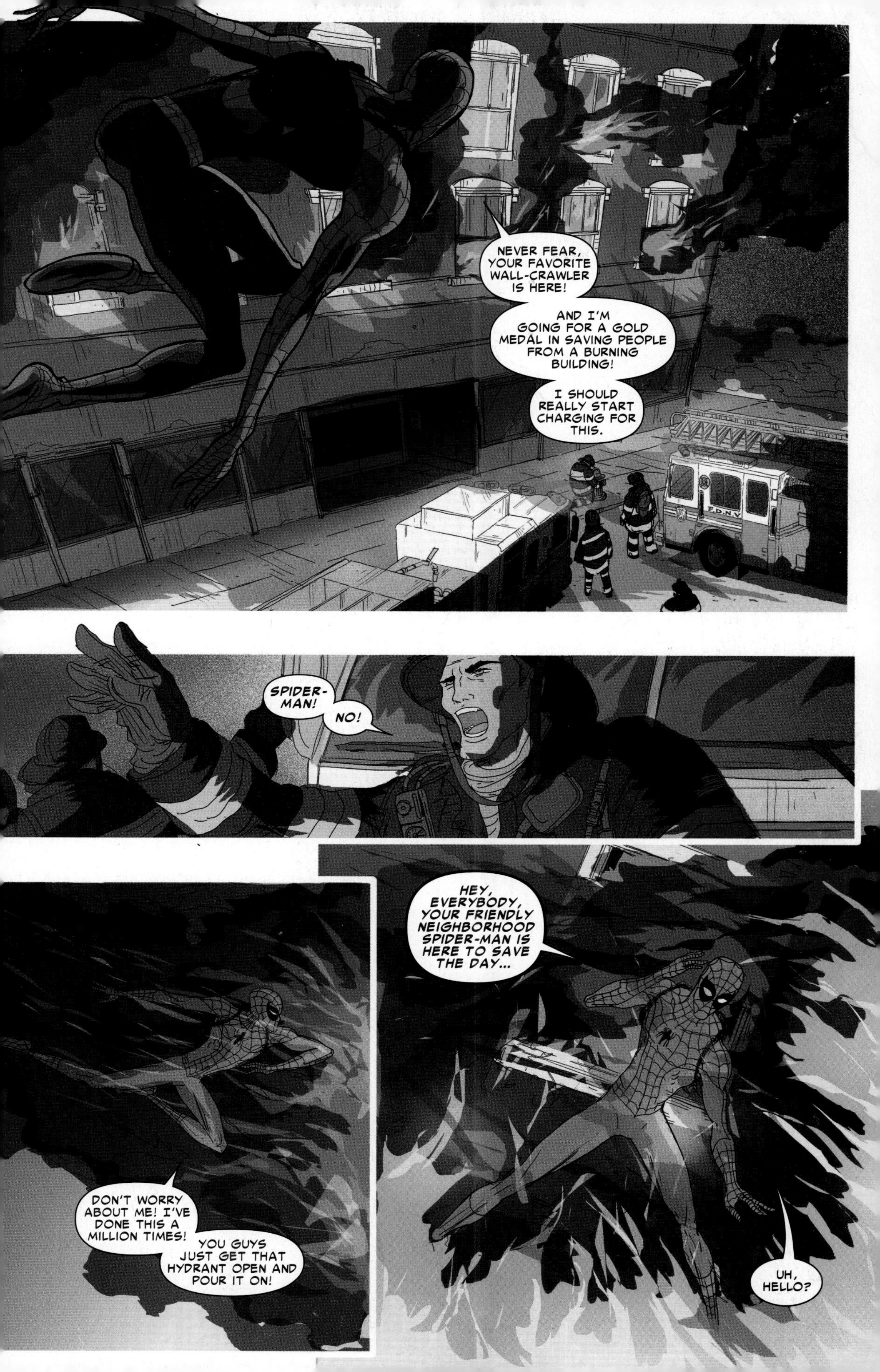
NEVER FEAR, YOUR FAVORITE WALL-CRAWLER IS HERE!
AND I'M GOING FOR A GOLD MEDAL IN SAVING PEOPLE FROM A BURNING BUILDING!
I SHOULD REALLY START CHARGING FOR THIS.
F.D.N.Y.
SPIDER-MAN!
NO!
DON'T WORRY ABOUT ME! I'VE DONE THIS A MILLION TIMES!
YOU GUYS JUST GET THAT HYDRANT OPEN AND POUR IT ON!
HEY, EVERYBODY, YOUR FRIENDLY NEIGHBORHOOD SPIDER-MAN IS HERE TO SAVE THE DAY...
UH, HELLO?

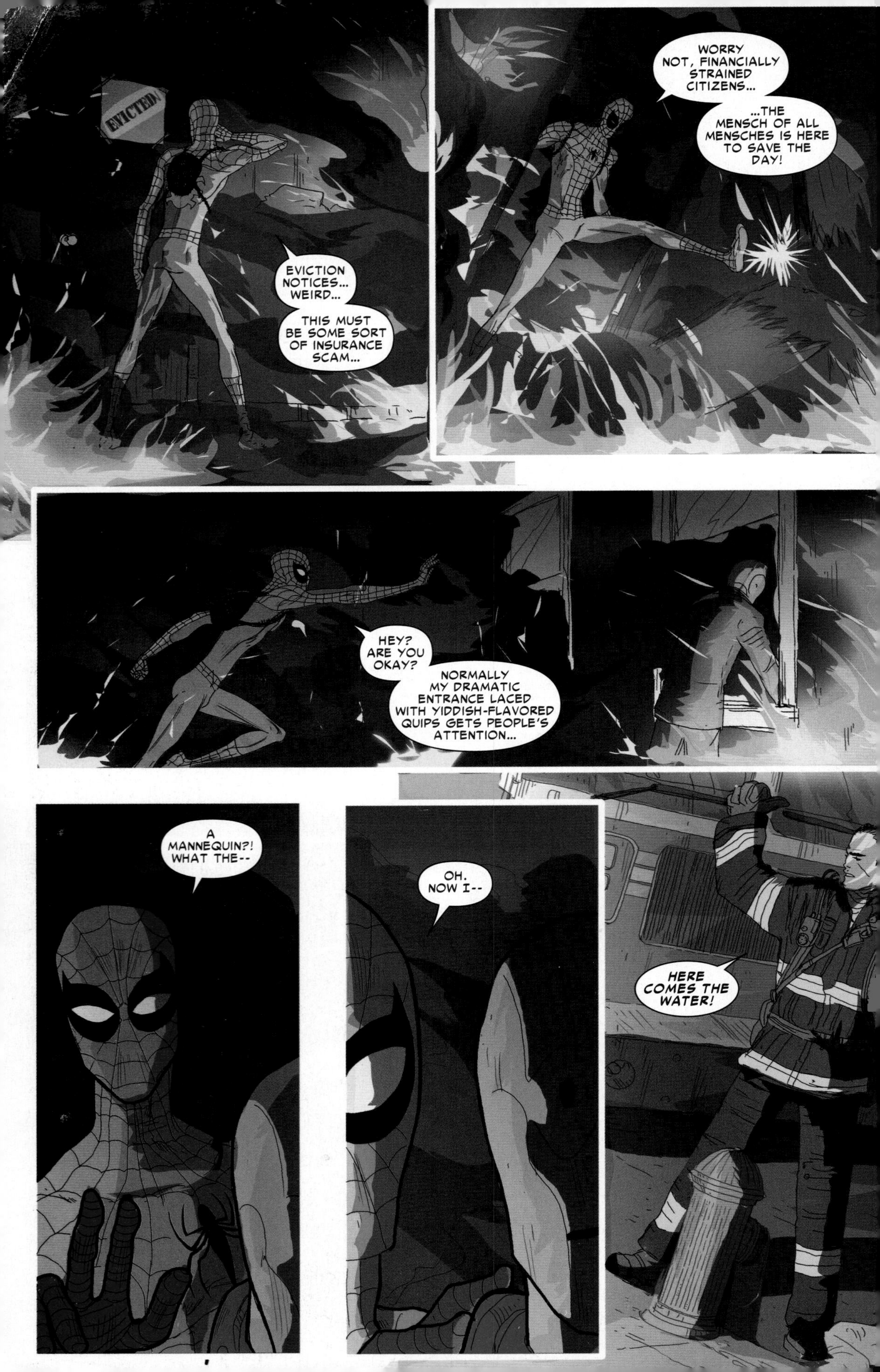
EVICTED
EVICTION NOTICES... WEIRD...
THIS MUST BE SOME SORT OF INSURANCE SCAM...
WORRY NOT, FINANCIALLY STRAINED CITIZENS...
...THE MENSCH OF ALL MENSCHES IS HERE TO SAVE THE DAY!
HEY? ARE YOU OKAY?
NORMALLY MY DRAMATIC ENTRANCE LACED WITH YIDDISH-FLAVORED QUIPS GETS PEOPLE'S ATTENTION...
A MANNEQUIN?! WHAT THE--
OH. NOW I--
HERE COMES THE WATER!

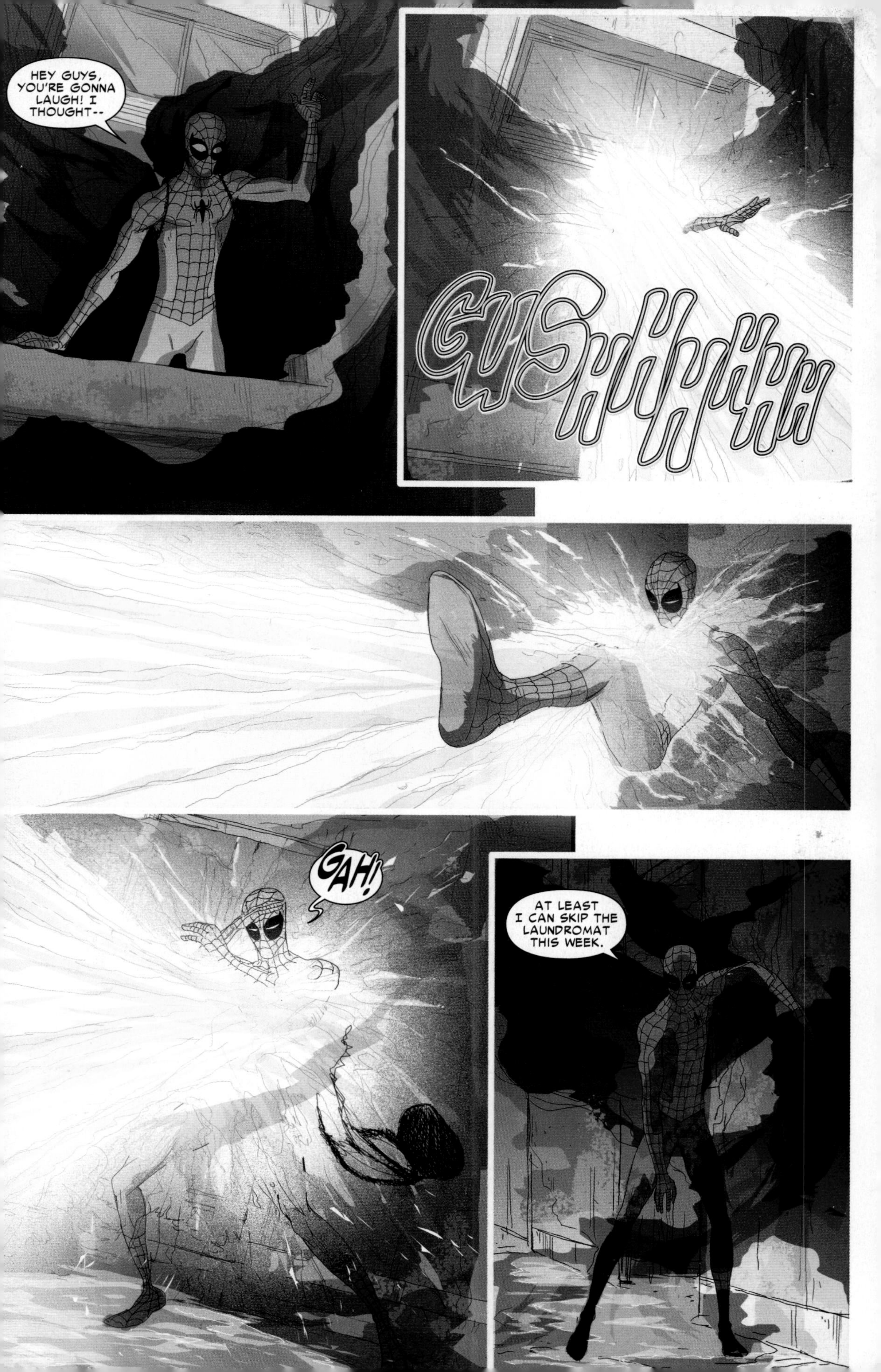
HEY GUYS, YOU'RE GONNA LAUGH! I THOUGHT--
GUSHHHHH
GAH!
AT LEAST I CAN SKIP THE LAUNDROMAT THIS WEEK.

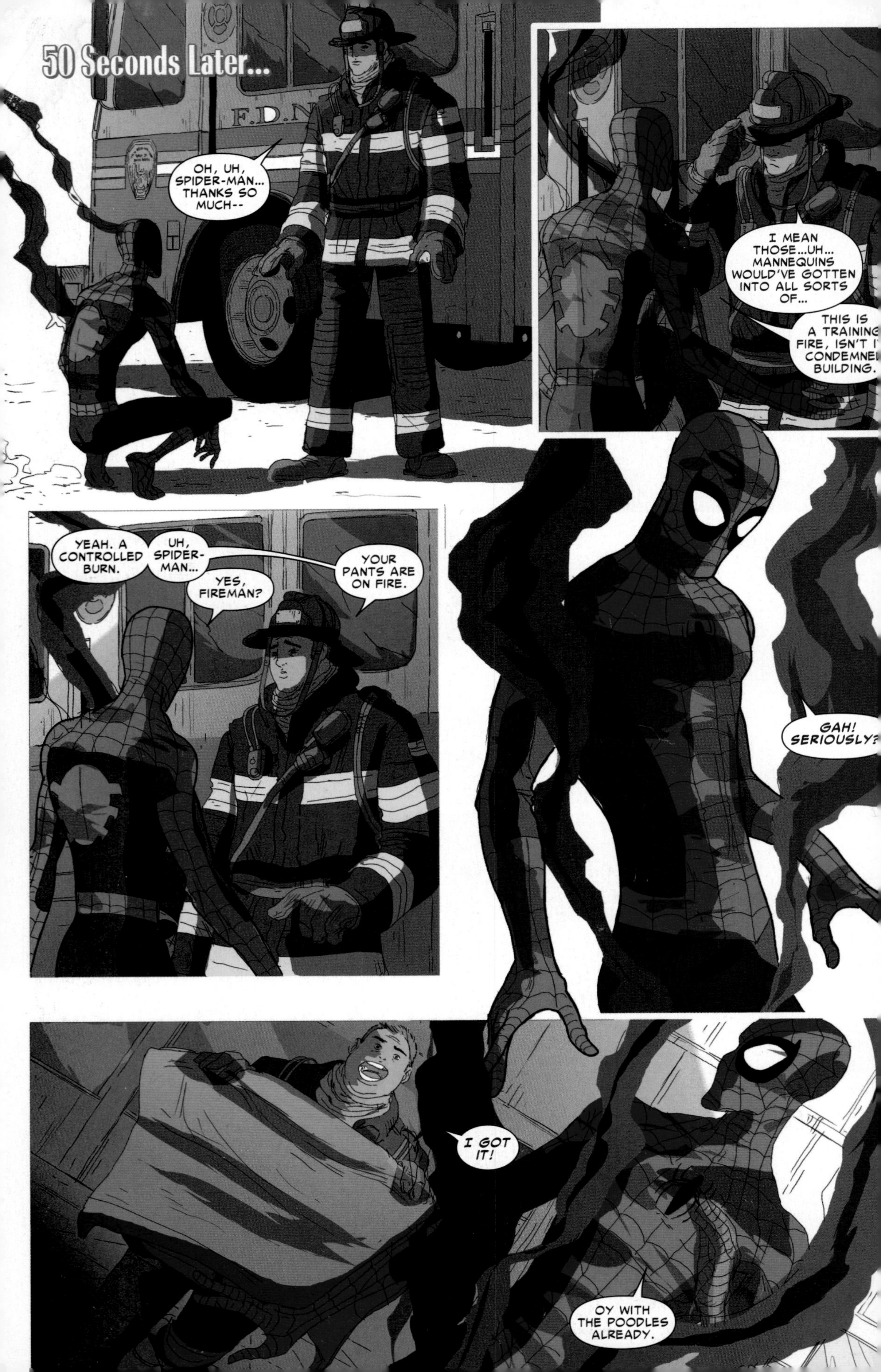
50 Seconds Later...
F.D.N
OH, UH, SPIDER-MAN... THANKS SO MUCH--
I MEAN THOSE...UH... MANNEQUINS WOULD'VE GOTTEN INTO ALL SORTS OF...
THIS IS A TRAINING FIRE, ISN'T IT? CONDEMNED BUILDING.
YEAH. A CONTROLLED BURN.
UH, SPIDER-MAN...
YES, FIREMAN?
YOUR PANTS ARE ON FIRE.
GAH! SERIOUSLY?
I GOT IT!
OY WITH THE POODLES ALREADY.

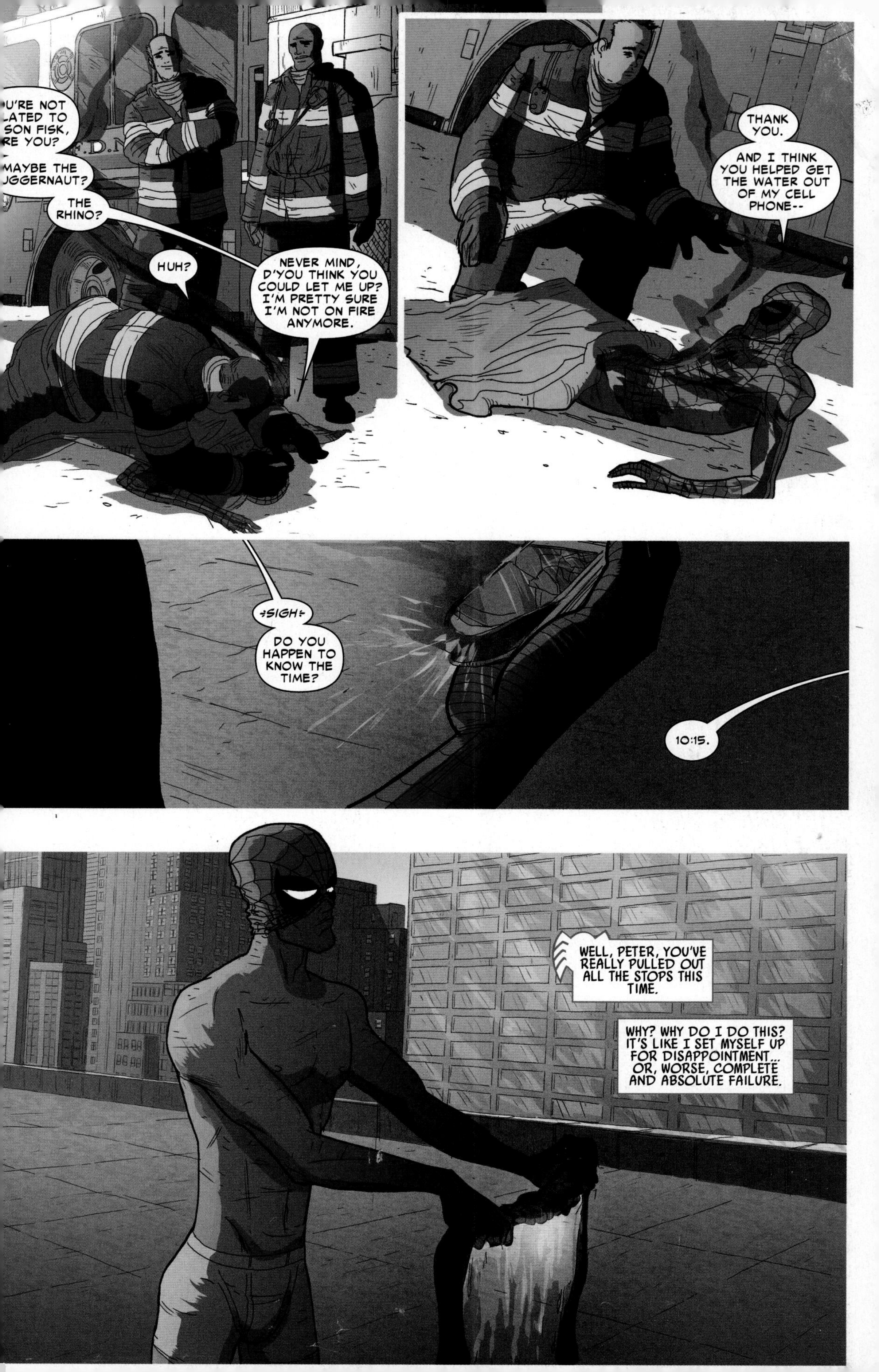
U'RE NOT
LATED TO
SON FISK,
RE YOU?
MAYBE THE
UGGERNAUT?
THE RHINO?
HUH?
NEVER MIND, D'YOU THINK YOU COULD LET ME UP? I'M PRETTY SURE I'M NOT ON FIRE ANYMORE.
THANK YOU.
AND I THINK YOU HELPED GET THE WATER OUT OF MY CELL PHONE--
-SIGH-
DO YOU HAPPEN TO KNOW THE TIME?
10:15.
WELL, PETER, YOU'VE REALLY PULLED OUT ALL THE STOPS THIS TIME.
WHY? WHY DO I DO THIS? IT'S LIKE I SET MYSELF UP FOR DISAPPOINTMENT... OR, WORSE, COMPLETE AND ABSOLUTE FAILURE.

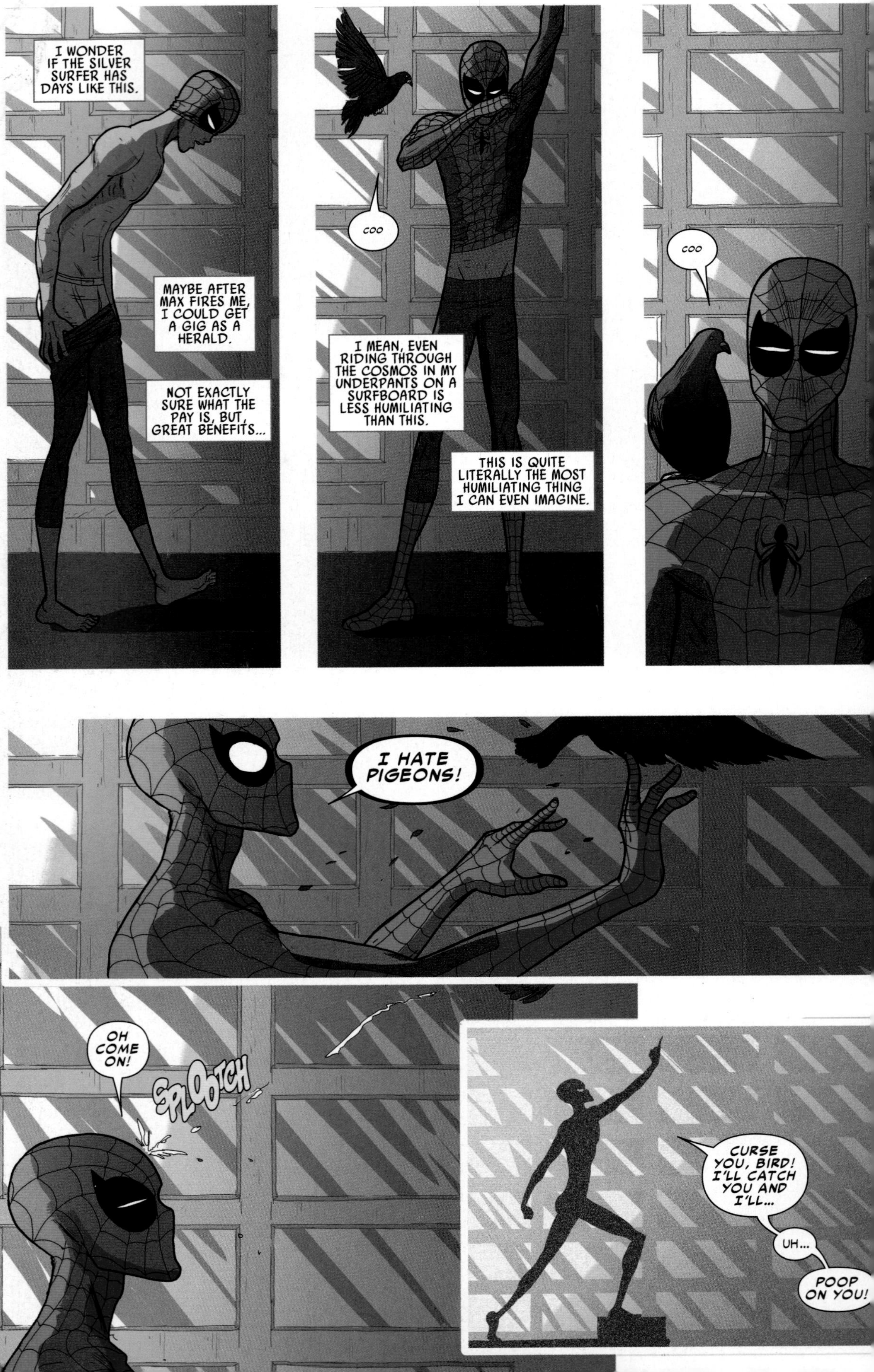
I WONDER IF THE SILVER SURFER HAS DAYS LIKE THIS.
MAYBE AFTER MAX FIRES ME, I COULD GET A GIG AS A HERALD.
NOT EXACTLY SURE WHAT THE PAY IS, BUT, GREAT BENEFITS...
COO
I MEAN, EVEN RIDING THROUGH THE COSMOS IN MY UNDERPANTS ON A SURFBOARD IS LESS HUMILIATING THAN THIS.
THIS IS QUITE LITERALLY THE MOST HUMILIATING THING I CAN EVEN IMAGINE.
COO
I HATE PIGEONS!
OH COME ON!
SPLOOTCH
CURSE YOU, BIRD! I'LL CATCH YOU AND I'LL...
UH...
POOP ON YOU!

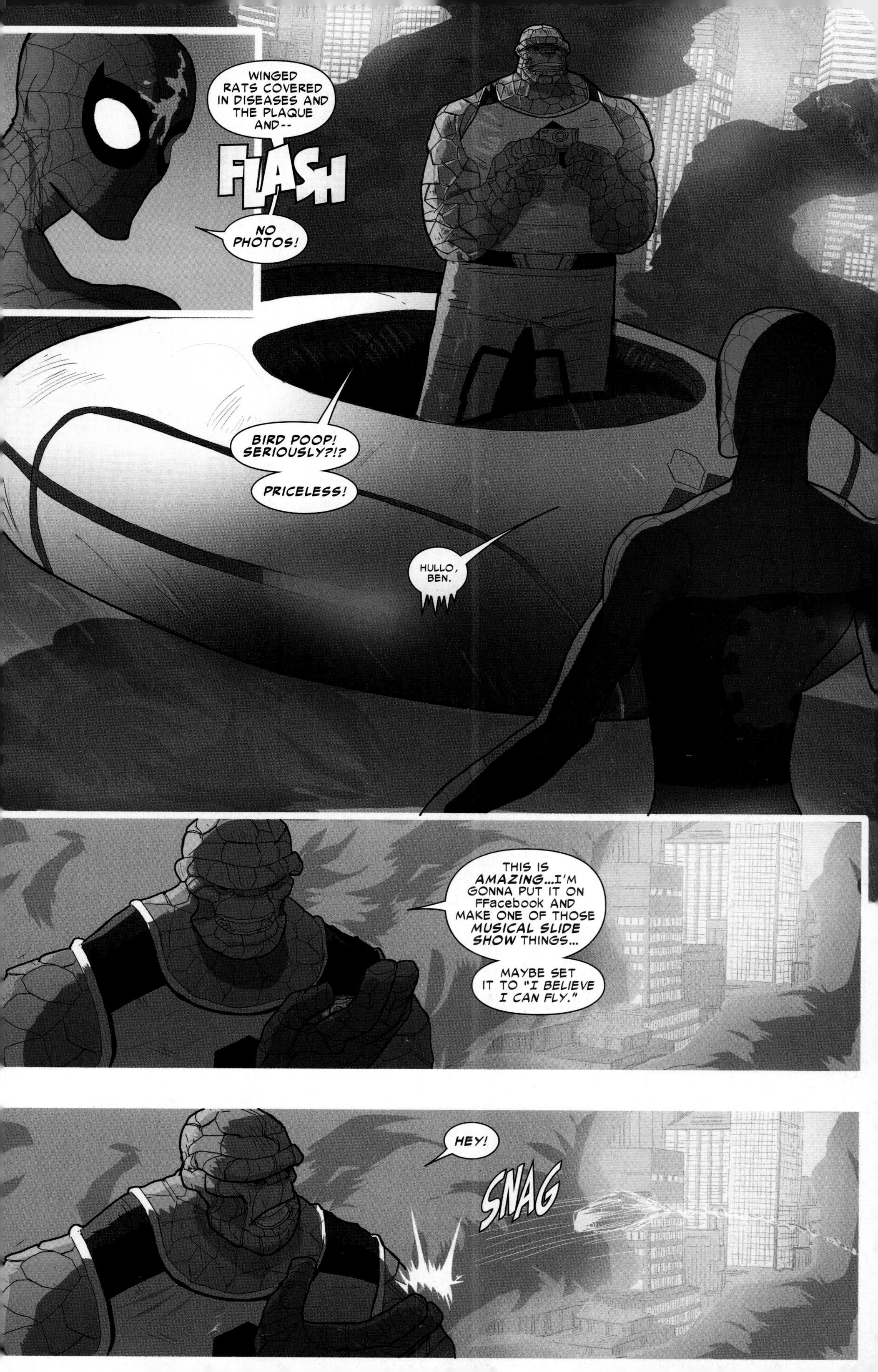
WINGED RATS COVERED IN DISEASES AND THE PLAQUE AND--
FLASH
NO PHOTOS!
BIRD POOP! SERIOUSLY?!?
PRICELESS!
HULLO, BEN.
THIS IS AMAZING...I'M GONNA PUT IT ON FFacebook AND MAKE ONE OF THOSE MUSICAL SLIDE SHOW THINGS...
MAYBE SET IT TO "I BELIEVE I CAN FLY."
HEY!
SNAG

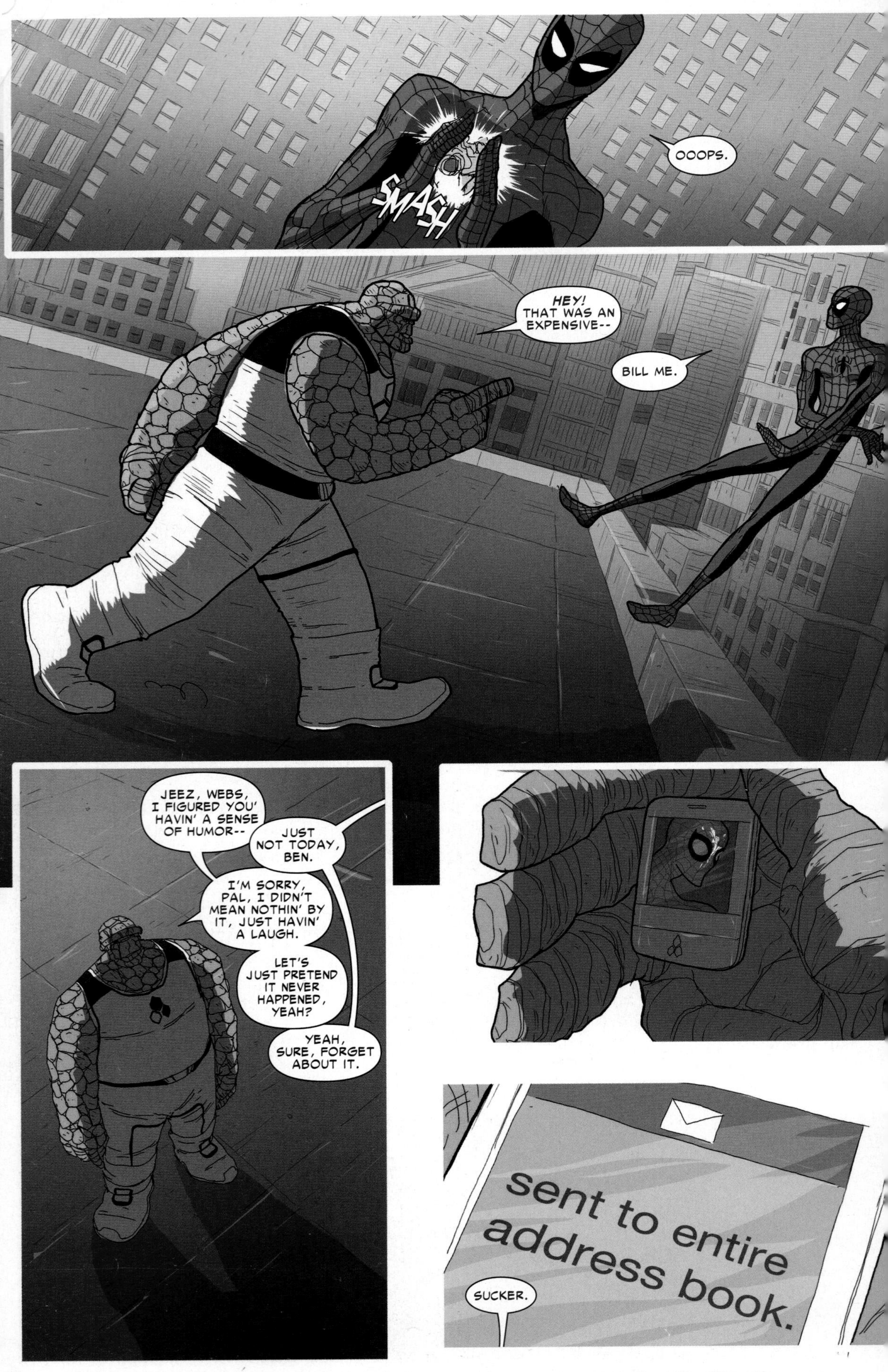

OOOPS.
SMASH
HEY! THAT WAS AN EXPENSIVE--
BILL ME.
JEEZ, WEBS, I FIGURED YOU' HAVIN' A SENSE OF HUMOR--
JUST NOT TODAY, BEN.
I'M SORRY, PAL, I DIDN'T MEAN NOTHIN' BY IT, JUST HAVIN' A LAUGH.
LET'S JUST PRETEND IT NEVER HAPPENED, YEAH?
YEAH, SURE, FORGET ABOUT IT.
sent to entire address book.
SUCKER.

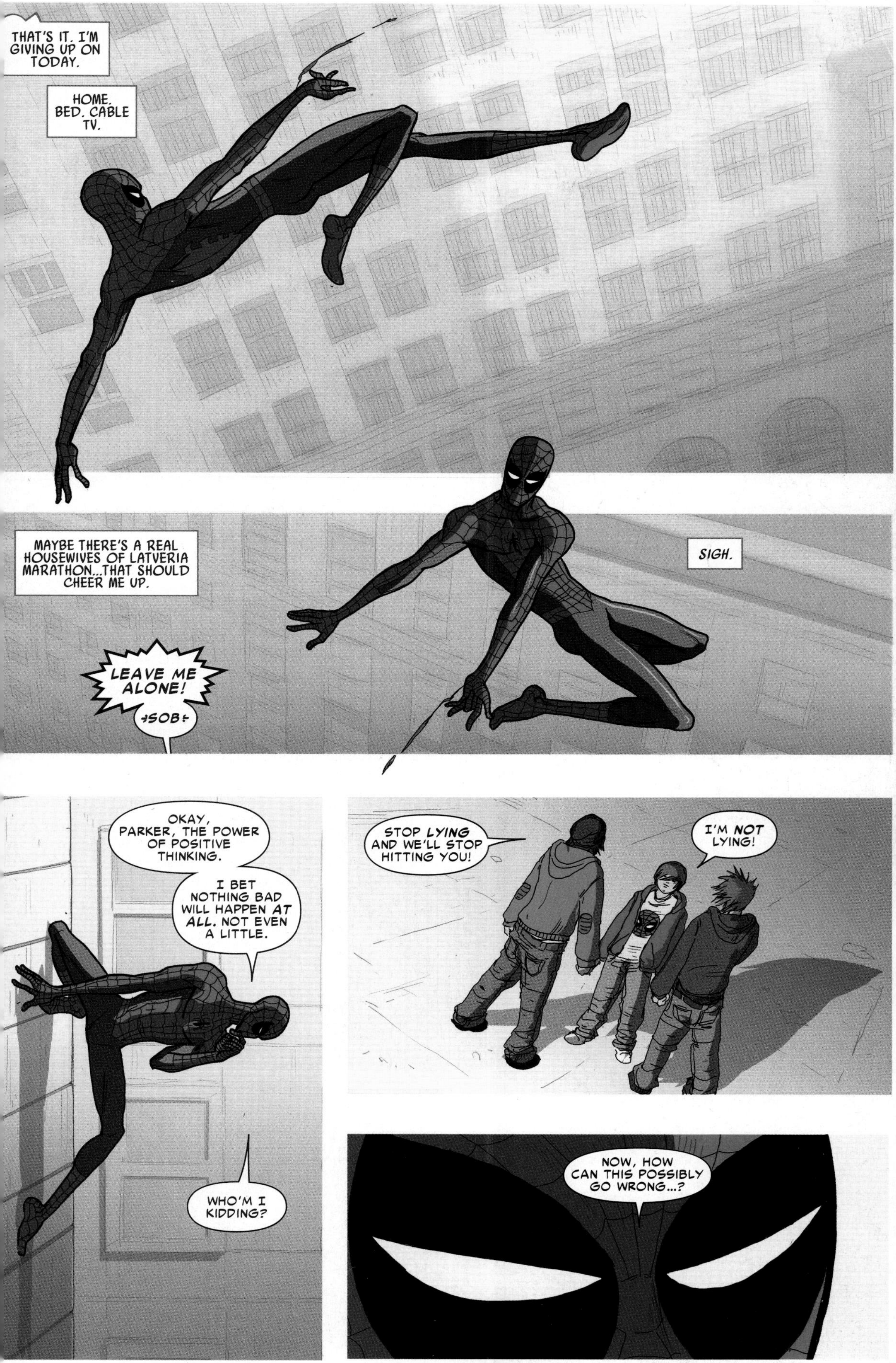
THAT'S IT. I'M GIVING UP ON TODAY.
HOME. BED. CABLE TV.
MAYBE THERE'S A REAL HOUSEWIVES OF LATVERIA MARATHON...THAT SHOULD CHEER ME UP.
SIGH.
LEAVE ME ALONE!
SOB
OKAY, PARKER, THE POWER OF POSITIVE THINKING.
I BET NOTHING BAD WILL HAPPEN AT ALL. NOT EVEN A LITTLE.
WHO'M I KIDDING?
STOP LYING AND WE'LL STOP HITTING YOU!
I'M NOT LYING!
NOW, HOW CAN THIS POSSIBLY GO WRONG...?

OH YEAH? YOU KNOW SPIDER-MAN? THEN WHY AIN'T HE HERE TO HELP YOU?

WHA?!

HEY!

LOOK, YOU'RE PROBABLY GOING TO TURN OUT TO BE REHEARSING FOR A *PLAY* OR SOME SORT OF MYSTERIO-MADE HOLOGRAM *USED TO TRAP ME*, OR, I DON'T KNOW, THE *EVIL POWER PACK* OR SOMETHING, *BUT*, ON THE OFF-CHANCE THAT YOU REALLY ARE WHAT I THINK YOU ARE...

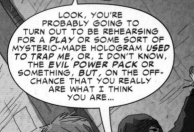

LEAVE THE KID ALONE, JERKS.

GAAAH!

YOU OKAY, KID?

SPIDER-MAN?!

GET THIS CRUD OFFA ME!

I CAN'T BELIEVE YOU'RE REALLY HERE.

C'MON! WE WERE JUST PLAYING AROUND!

I'M HERE WHENEVER INNOCENCE IS THREATENED, KID.

YOU WANT TO GET OUT [OF] HERE? GO SOM[E] PLACE AND TALK?

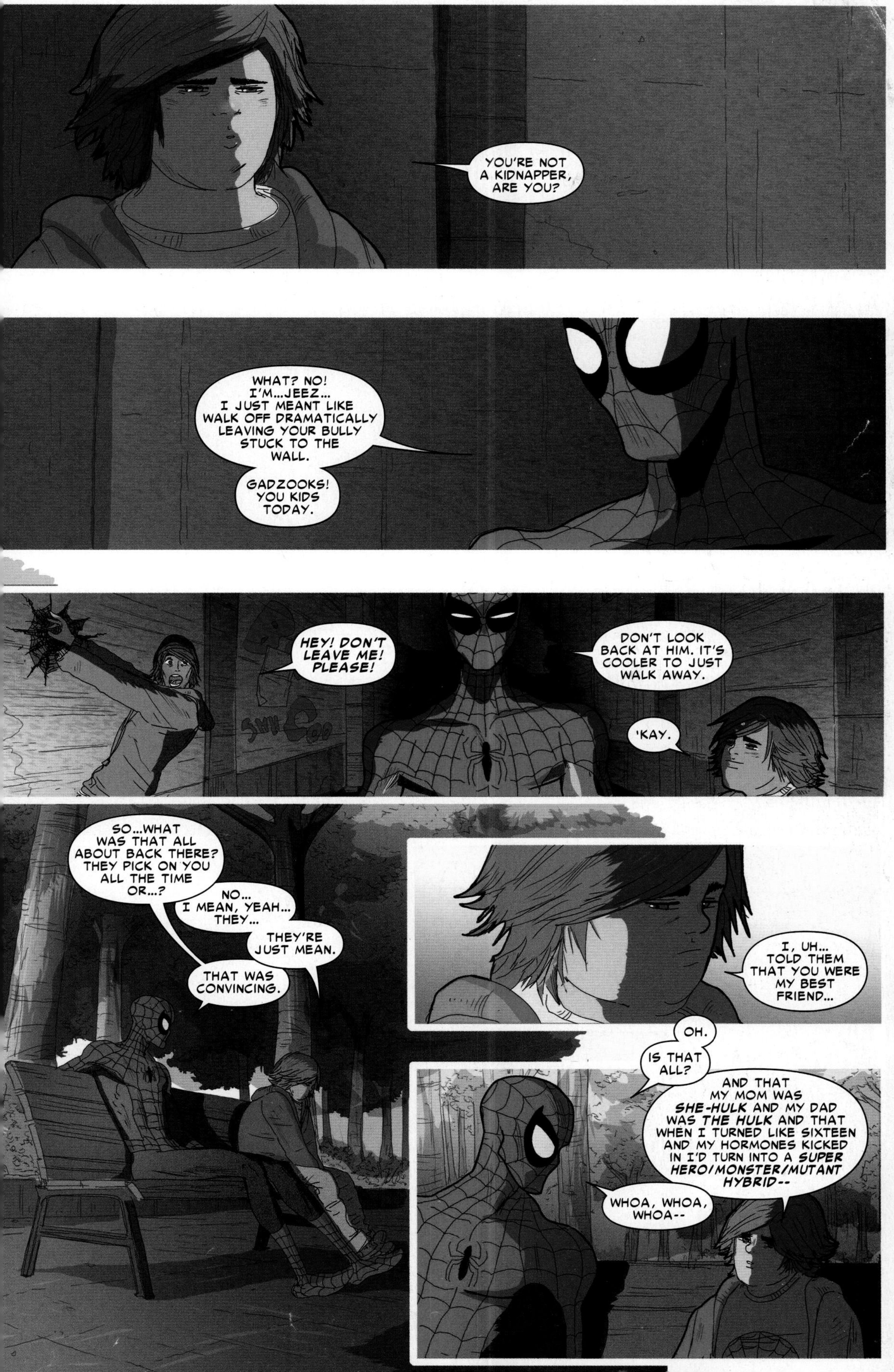

YOU'RE NOT A KIDNAPPER, ARE YOU?
WHAT? NO! I'M...JEEZ... I JUST MEANT LIKE WALK OFF DRAMATICALLY LEAVING YOUR BULLY STUCK TO THE WALL.
GADZOOKS! YOU KIDS TODAY.
HEY! DON'T LEAVE ME! PLEASE!
DON'T LOOK BACK AT HIM. IT'S COOLER TO JUST WALK AWAY.
'KAY.
SO...WHAT WAS THAT ALL ABOUT BACK THERE? THEY PICK ON YOU ALL THE TIME OR...?
NO... I MEAN, YEAH... THEY...
THEY'RE JUST MEAN.
THAT WAS CONVINCING.
I, UH... TOLD THEM THAT YOU WERE MY BEST FRIEND...
OH.
IS THAT ALL?
AND THAT MY MOM WAS SHE-HULK AND MY DAD WAS THE HULK AND THAT WHEN I TURNED LIKE SIXTEEN AND MY HORMONES KICKED IN I'D TURN INTO A SUPER HERO/MONSTER/MUTANT HYBRID--
WHOA, WHOA, WHOA--

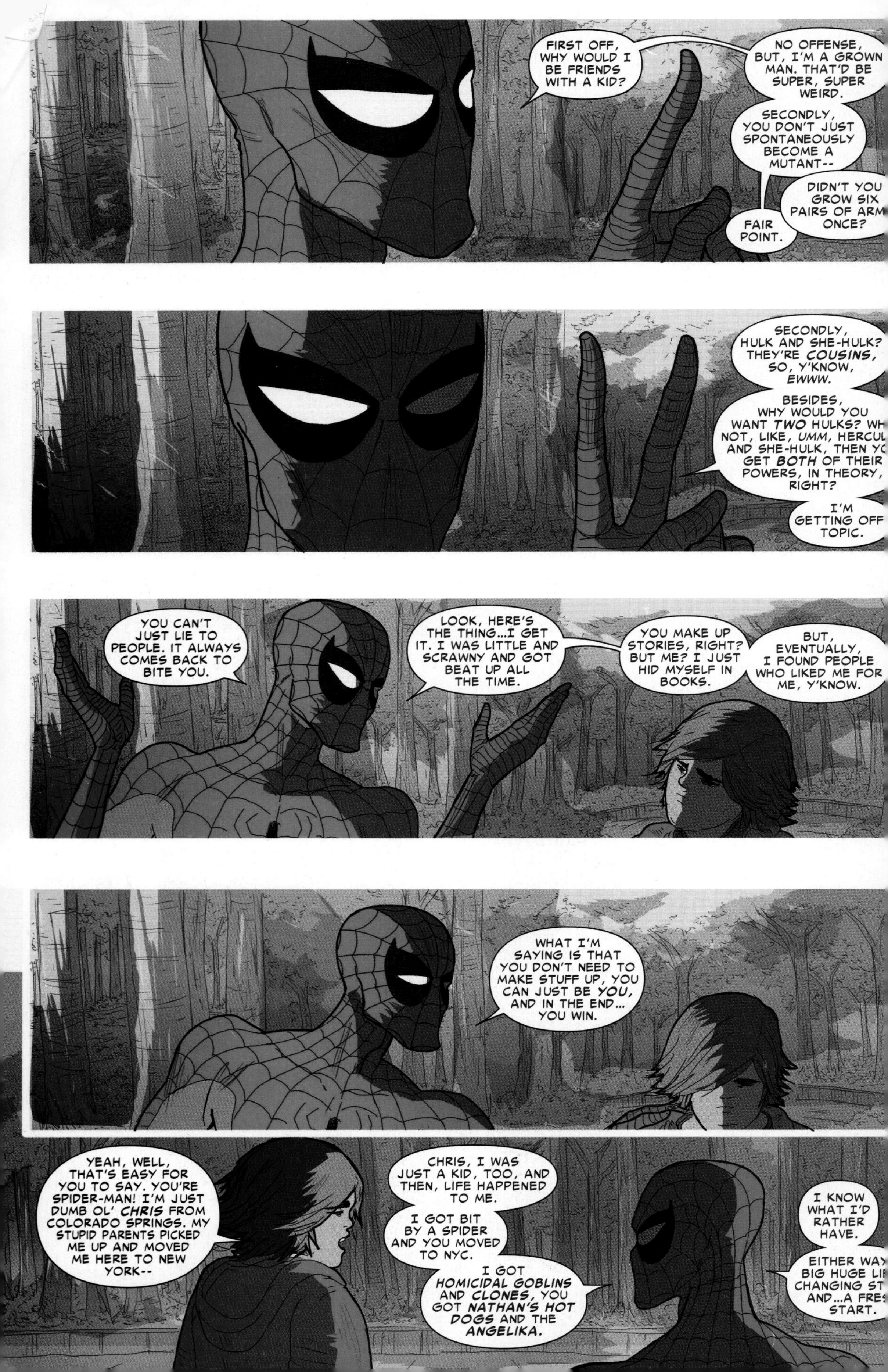
FIRST OFF, WHY WOULD I BE FRIENDS WITH A KID?
NO OFFENSE, BUT, I'M A GROWN MAN. THAT'D BE SUPER, SUPER WEIRD.
SECONDLY, YOU DON'T JUST SPONTANEOUSLY BECOME A MUTANT--
DIDN'T YOU GROW SIX PAIRS OF ARM ONCE?
FAIR POINT.
SECONDLY, HULK AND SHE-HULK? THEY'RE *COUSINS*, SO, Y'KNOW, *EWWW.*
BESIDES, WHY WOULD YOU WANT *TWO* HULKS? WH NOT, LIKE, *UMM*, HERCUL AND SHE-HULK, THEN YO GET *BOTH* OF THEIR POWERS, IN THEORY, RIGHT?
I'M GETTING OFF TOPIC.
YOU CAN'T JUST LIE TO PEOPLE. IT ALWAYS COMES BACK TO BITE YOU.
LOOK, HERE'S THE THING...I GET IT. I WAS LITTLE AND SCRAWNY AND GOT BEAT UP ALL THE TIME.
YOU MAKE UP STORIES, RIGHT? BUT ME? I JUST HID MYSELF IN BOOKS.
BUT, EVENTUALLY, I FOUND PEOPLE WHO LIKED ME FOR ME, Y'KNOW.
WHAT I'M SAYING IS THAT YOU DON'T NEED TO MAKE STUFF UP, YOU CAN JUST BE *YOU*, AND IN THE END... YOU WIN.
YEAH, WELL, THAT'S EASY FOR YOU TO SAY. YOU'RE SPIDER-MAN! I'M JUST DUMB OL' *CHRIS* FROM COLORADO SPRINGS. MY STUPID PARENTS PICKED ME UP AND MOVED ME HERE TO NEW YORK--
CHRIS, I WAS JUST A KID, TOO, AND THEN, LIFE HAPPENED TO ME.
I GOT BIT BY A SPIDER AND YOU MOVED TO NYC.
I GOT *HOMICIDAL GOBLINS* AND *CLONES*, YOU GOT *NATHAN'S HOT DOGS* AND THE *ANGELIKA*.
I KNOW WHAT I'D RATHER HAVE.
EITHER WAY BIG HUGE LI CHANGING ST AND...A FRES START.

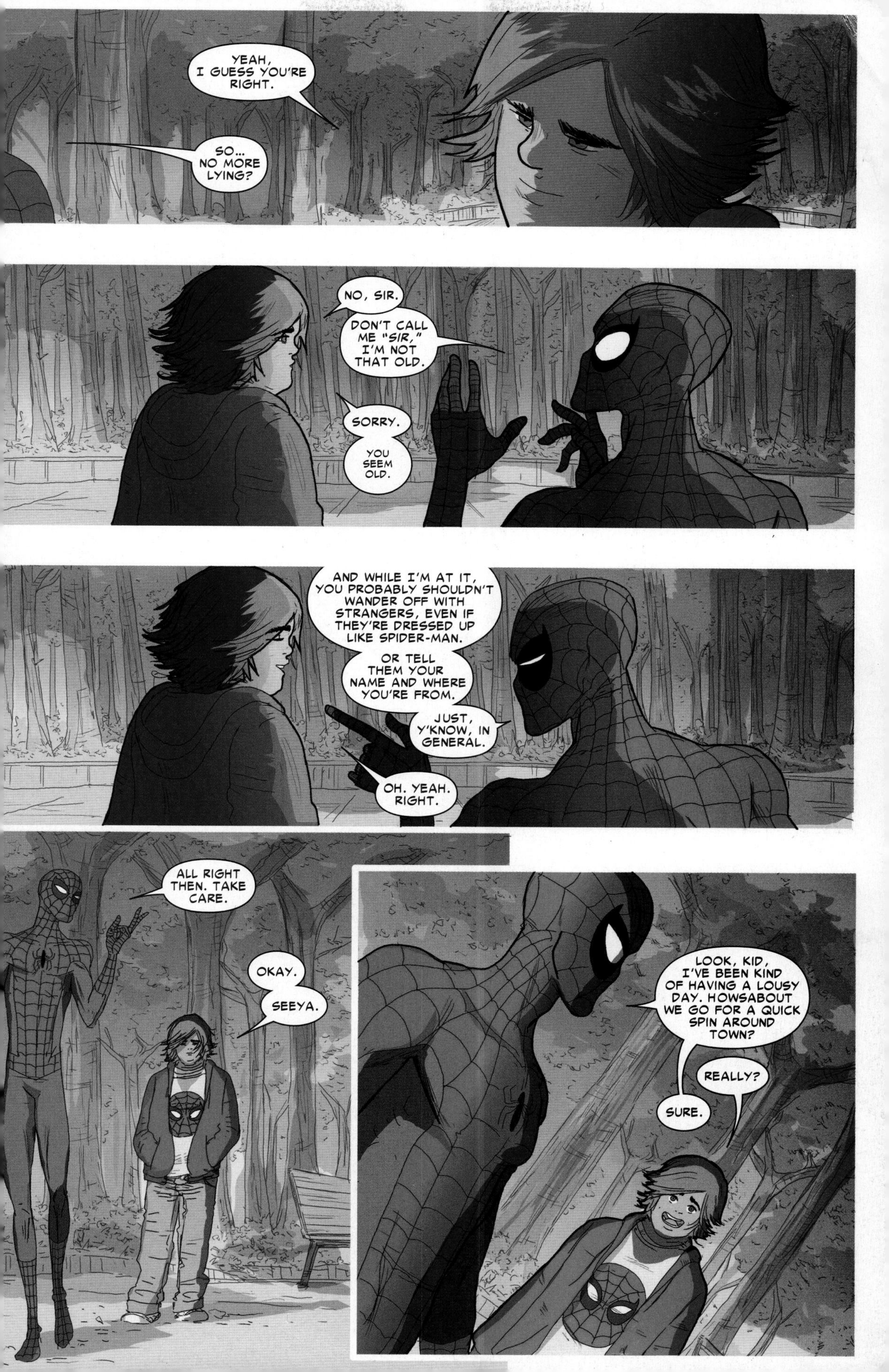
YEAH, I GUESS YOU'RE RIGHT.
SO... NO MORE LYING?
NO, SIR.
DON'T CALL ME "SIR," I'M NOT THAT OLD.
SORRY.
YOU SEEM OLD.
AND WHILE I'M AT IT, YOU PROBABLY SHOULDN'T WANDER OFF WITH STRANGERS, EVEN IF THEY'RE DRESSED UP LIKE SPIDER-MAN.
OR TELL THEM YOUR NAME AND WHERE YOU'RE FROM.
JUST, Y'KNOW, IN GENERAL.
OH. YEAH. RIGHT.
ALL RIGHT THEN. TAKE CARE.
OKAY.
SEEYA.
LOOK, KID, I'VE BEEN KIND OF HAVING A LOUSY DAY. HOWSABOUT WE GO FOR A QUICK SPIN AROUND TOWN?
REALLY?
SURE.

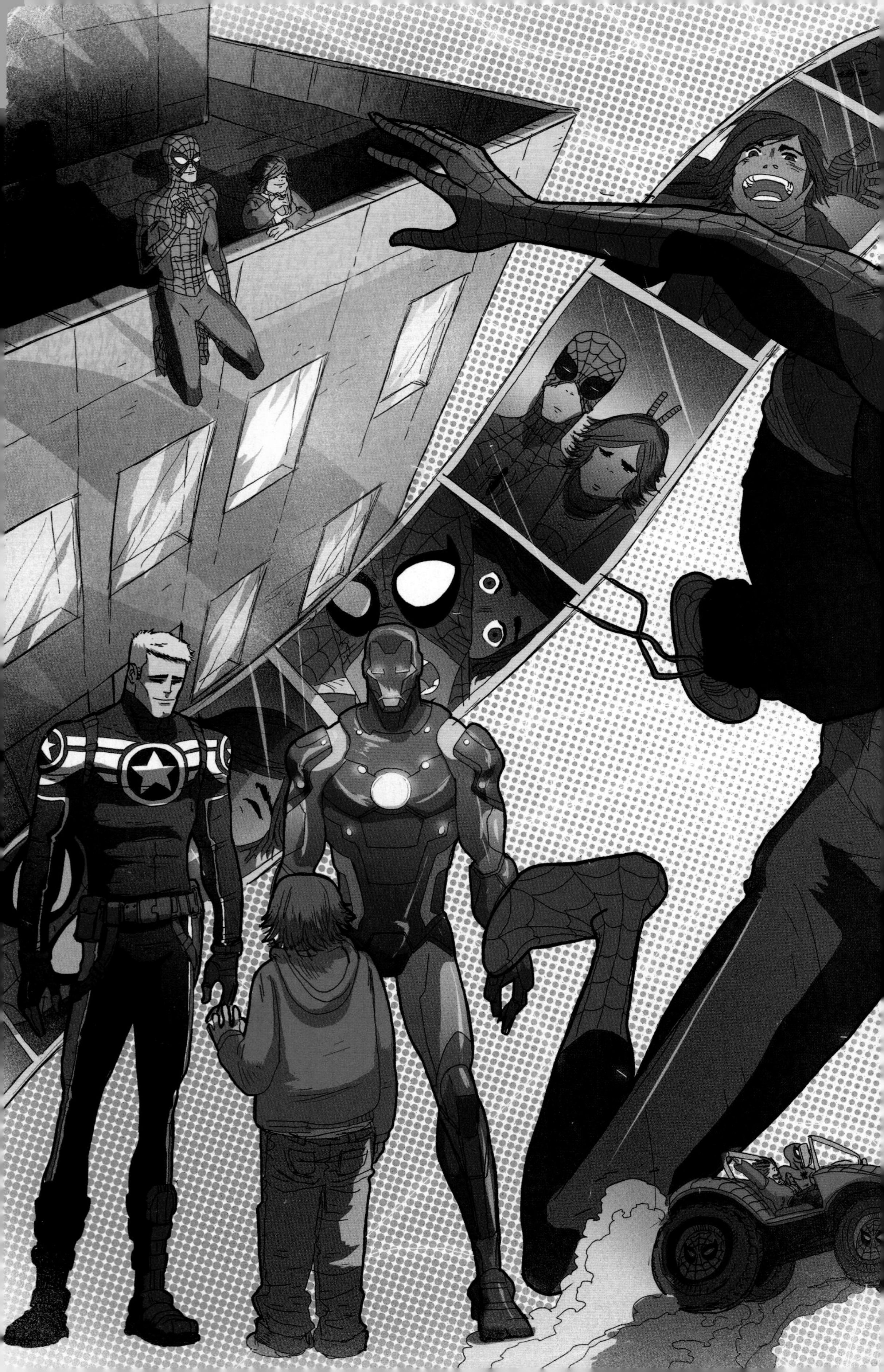

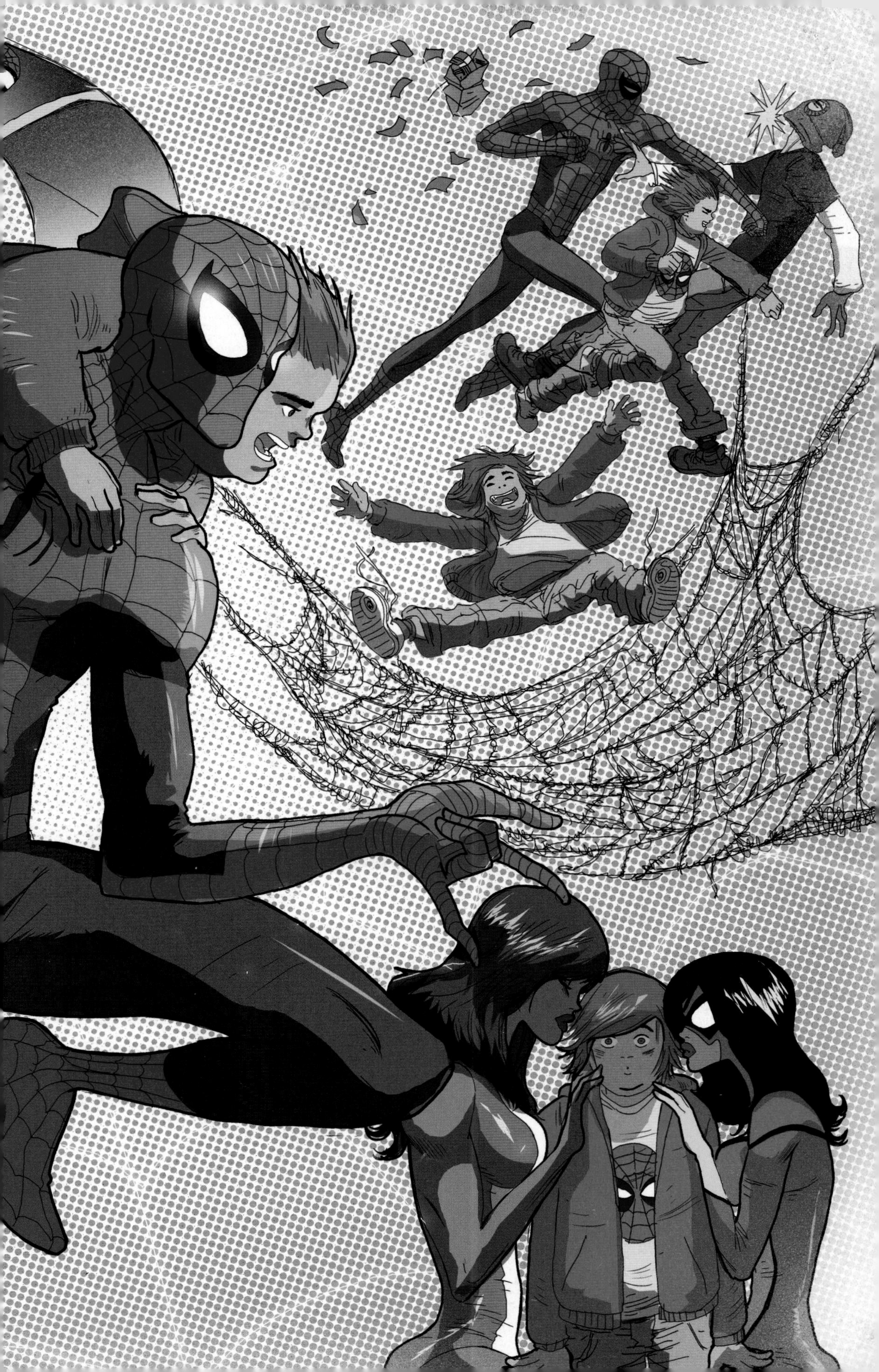

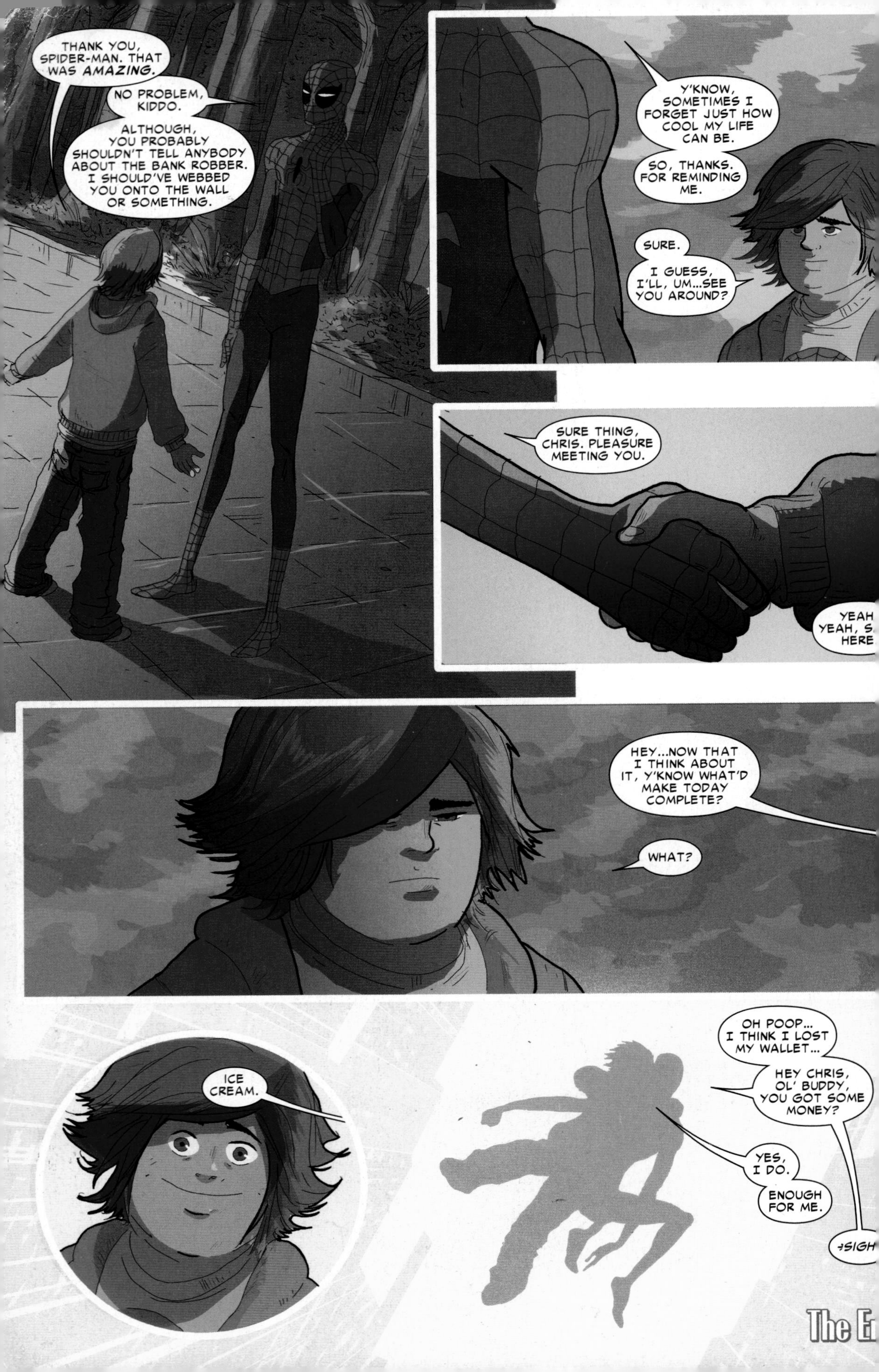
THANK YOU, SPIDER-MAN. THAT WAS AMAZING.
NO PROBLEM, KIDDO.
ALTHOUGH, YOU PROBABLY SHOULDN'T TELL ANYBODY ABOUT THE BANK ROBBER. I SHOULD'VE WEBBED YOU ONTO THE WALL OR SOMETHING.
Y'KNOW, SOMETIMES I FORGET JUST HOW COOL MY LIFE CAN BE.
SO, THANKS. FOR REMINDING ME.
SURE.
I GUESS, I'LL, UM...SEE YOU AROUND?
SURE THING, CHRIS. PLEASURE MEETING YOU.
YEAH
YEAH, S
HERE
HEY...NOW THAT I THINK ABOUT IT, Y'KNOW WHAT'D MAKE TODAY COMPLETE?
WHAT?
ICE CREAM.
OH POOP... I THINK I LOST MY WALLET...
HEY CHRIS, OL' BUDDY, YOU GOT SOME MONEY?
YES, I DO.
ENOUGH FOR ME.
SIGH
The E

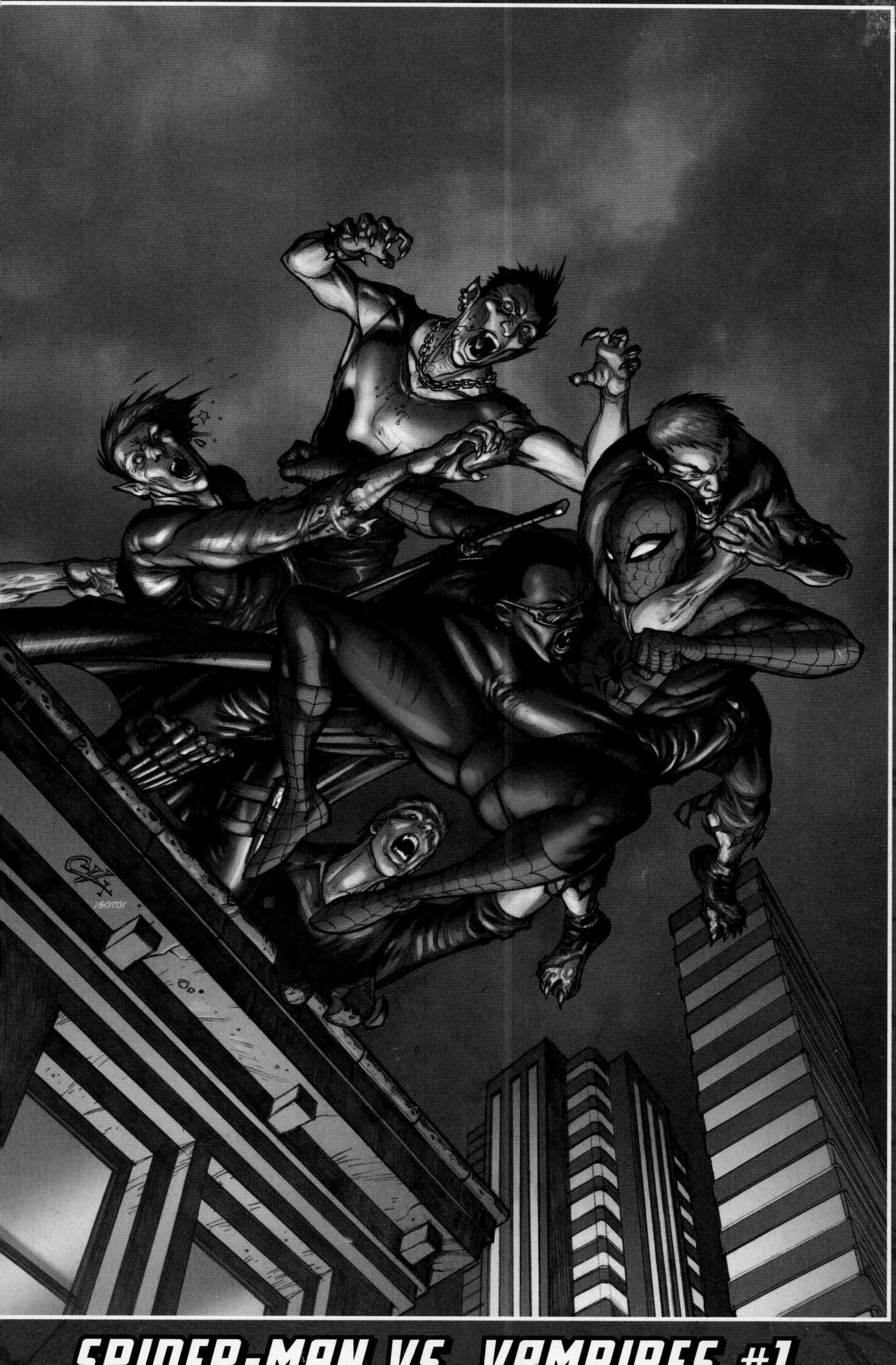

SPIDER-MAN VS. VAMPIRES #1

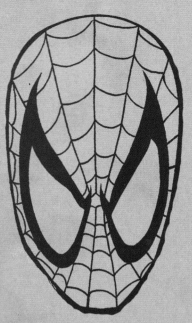

While attending a demonstration in radiology, high school student Peter Parker was bitten by a spider which had accidentally been exposed to radioactive rays. Through a miracle of science, Peter soon found that he had gained the Spider's powers and had, in effect, become a human arachnid! From that day on he was THE AMAZING SPIDER-MAN!

BLADE! VAMPIRE HUNTER! Born in the slums of London, his mother was feasted on by a vampire before his birth and her infected blood gave him the superhuman powers of the vampire race while keeping him a human capable of living in the daylight. Now he uses his powers to hunt the undead and protect the living!

THE SPIDER & THE SWORD

WRITTEN BY KEVIN GREVIOUX

PENCILS BY ROBERTO CASTRO

INKS BY WALDEN WONG & SANDU FLOREA

COLORS BY SOTOCOLOR, KALISZ, FABELA & MOSSA

LETTERS BY DAVE SHARPE

PRODUCTION RANDALL MILLER

EDITOR TOM BRENNAN

EDITOR-IN-CHIEF JOE QUESADA

PUBLISHER DAN BUCKLEY

EXECUTIVE PRODUCER ALAN FINE

DIGITAL PRODUCTION MANAGER TIM SMITH 3   DIGITAL COORDINATOR HARRY GO

VP DIGITAL CONTENT MANAGER JOHN CERILLI

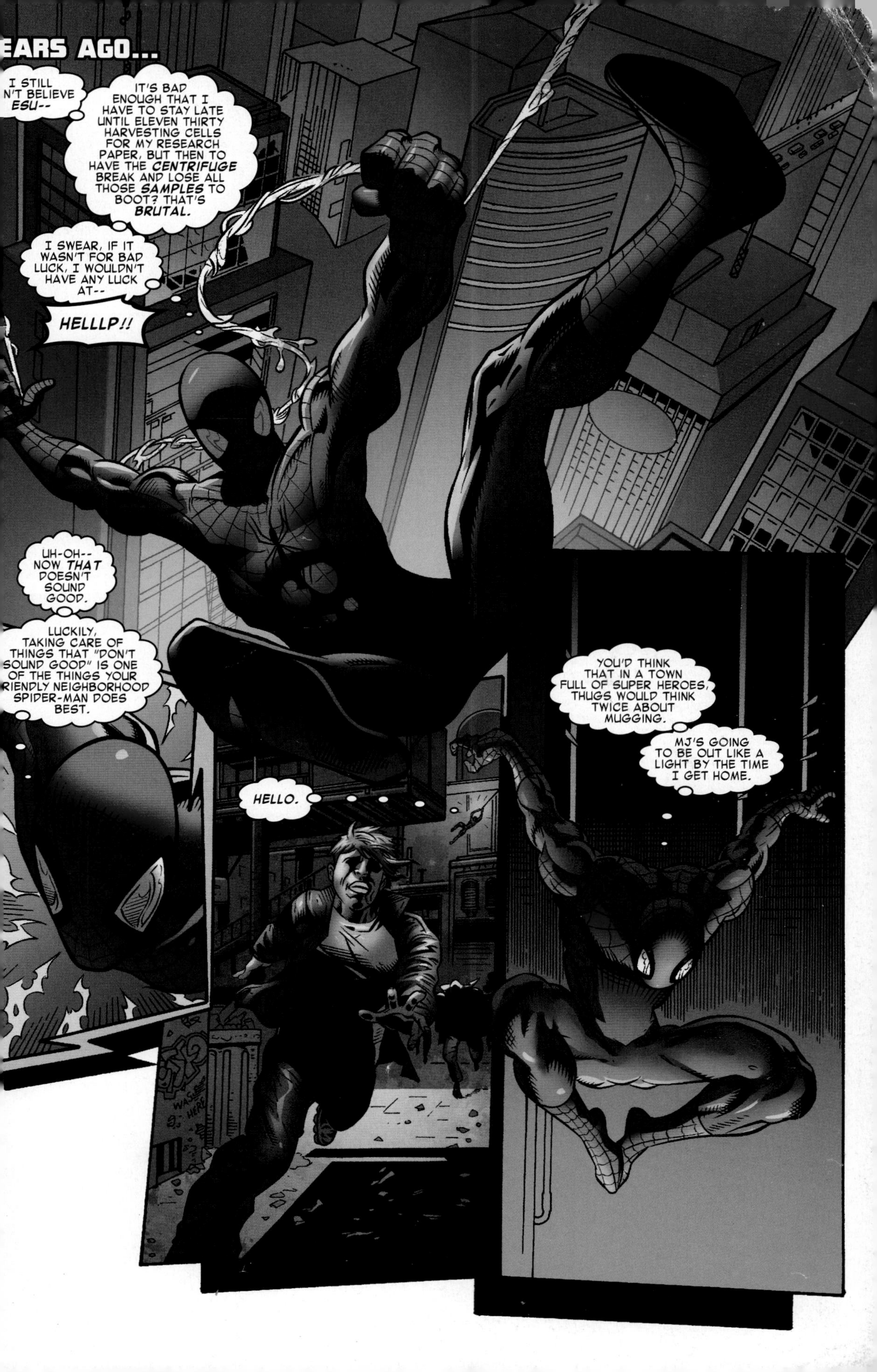

EARS AGO...
I STILL N'T BELIEVE ESU--
IT'S BAD ENOUGH THAT I HAVE TO STAY LATE UNTIL ELEVEN THIRTY HARVESTING CELLS FOR MY RESEARCH PAPER, BUT THEN TO HAVE THE CENTRIFUGE BREAK AND LOSE ALL THOSE SAMPLES TO BOOT? THAT'S BRUTAL.
I SWEAR, IF IT WASN'T FOR BAD LUCK, I WOULDN'T HAVE ANY LUCK AT--
HELLLP!!
UH-OH-- NOW THAT DOESN'T SOUND GOOD.
LUCKILY, TAKING CARE OF THINGS THAT "DON'T SOUND GOOD" IS ONE OF THE THINGS YOUR RIENDLY NEIGHBORHOOD SPIDER-MAN DOES BEST.
HELLO.
YOU'D THINK THAT IN A TOWN FULL OF SUPER HEROES, THUGS WOULD THINK TWICE ABOUT MUGGING.
MJ'S GOING TO BE OUT LIKE A LIGHT BY THE TIME I GET HOME.

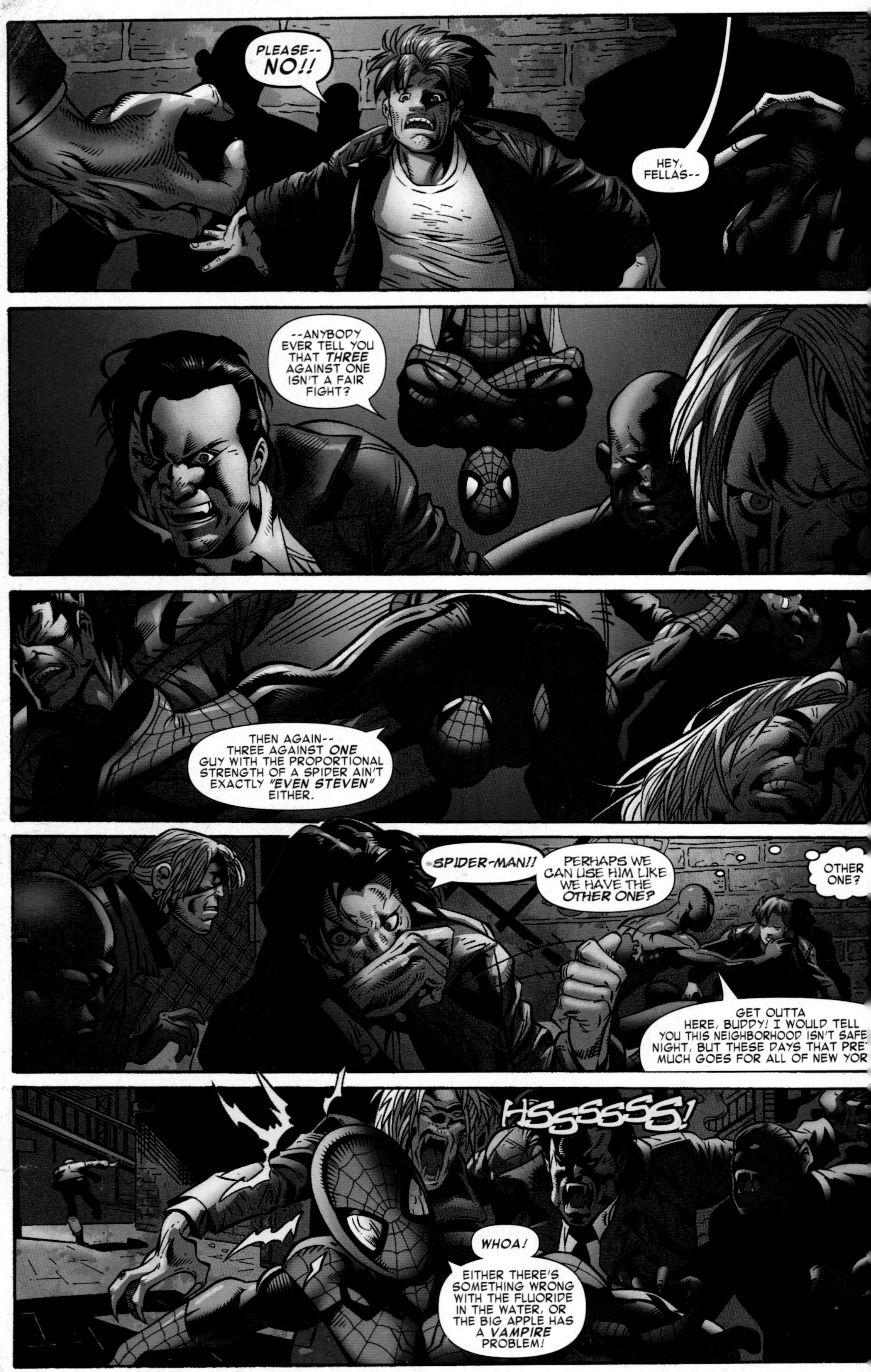
PLEASE--
NO!!
HEY, FELLAS--
--ANYBODY EVER TELL YOU THAT THREE AGAINST ONE ISN'T A FAIR FIGHT?
THEN AGAIN-- THREE AGAINST ONE GUY WITH THE PROPORTIONAL STRENGTH OF A SPIDER AIN'T EXACTLY "EVEN STEVEN" EITHER.
SPIDER-MAN!!
PERHAPS WE CAN USE HIM LIKE WE HAVE THE OTHER ONE?
OTHER ONE?
GET OUTTA HERE, BUDDY! I WOULD TELL YOU THIS NEIGHBORHOOD ISN'T SAFE NIGHT, BUT THESE DAYS THAT PRE MUCH GOES FOR ALL OF NEW YOR
HSSSSSS!
WHOA!
EITHER THERE'S SOMETHING WRONG WITH THE FLUORIDE IN THE WATER, OR THE BIG APPLE HAS A VAMPIRE PROBLEM!

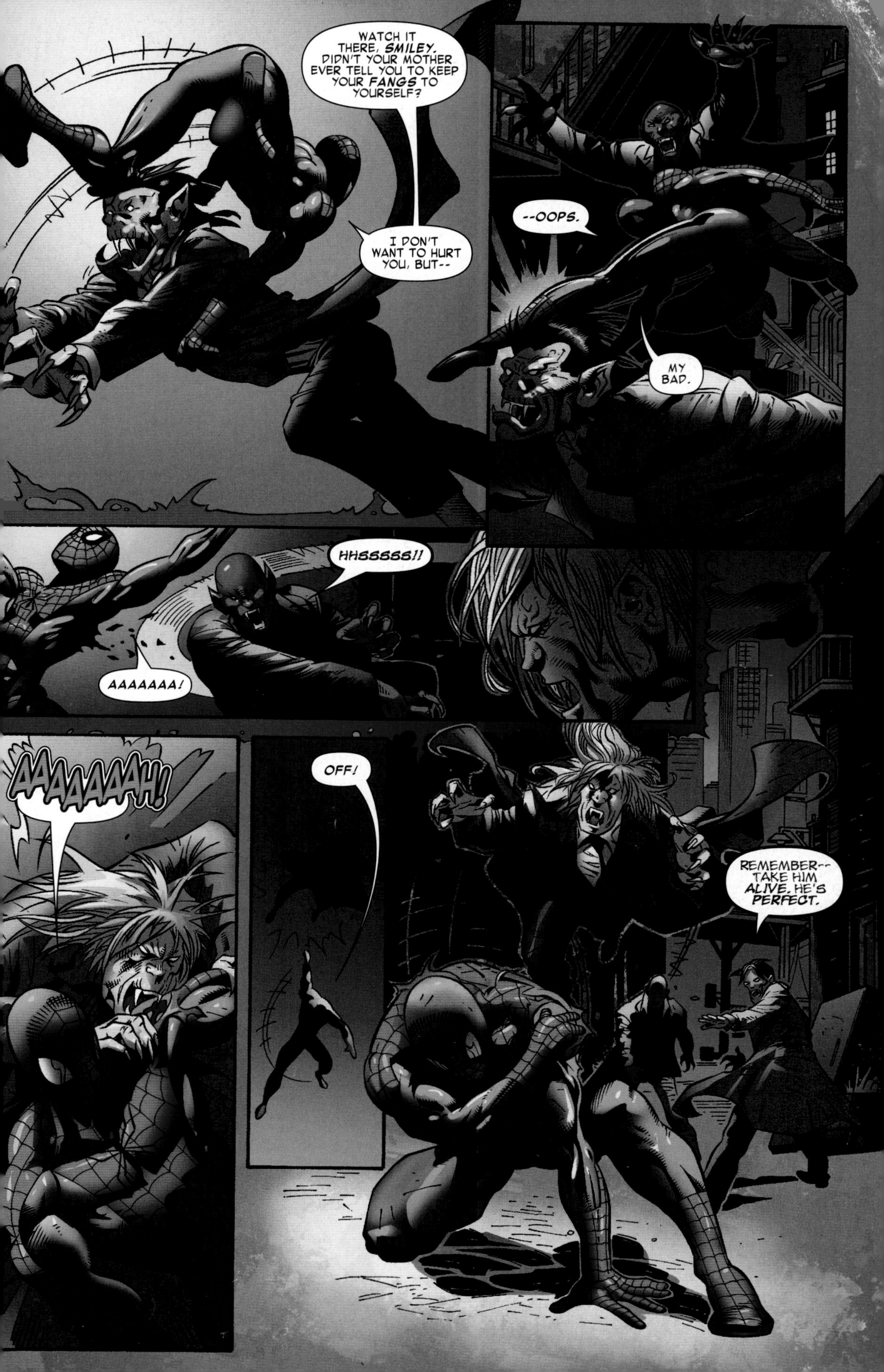
WATCH IT THERE, SMILEY. DIDN'T YOUR MOTHER EVER TELL YOU TO KEEP YOUR FANGS TO YOURSELF?
I DON'T WANT TO HURT YOU, BUT--
--OOPS.
MY BAD.
HHSSSSS!!
AAAAAAA!
AAAAAAAH!
OFF!
REMEMBER-- TAKE HIM ALIVE. HE'S PERFECT.

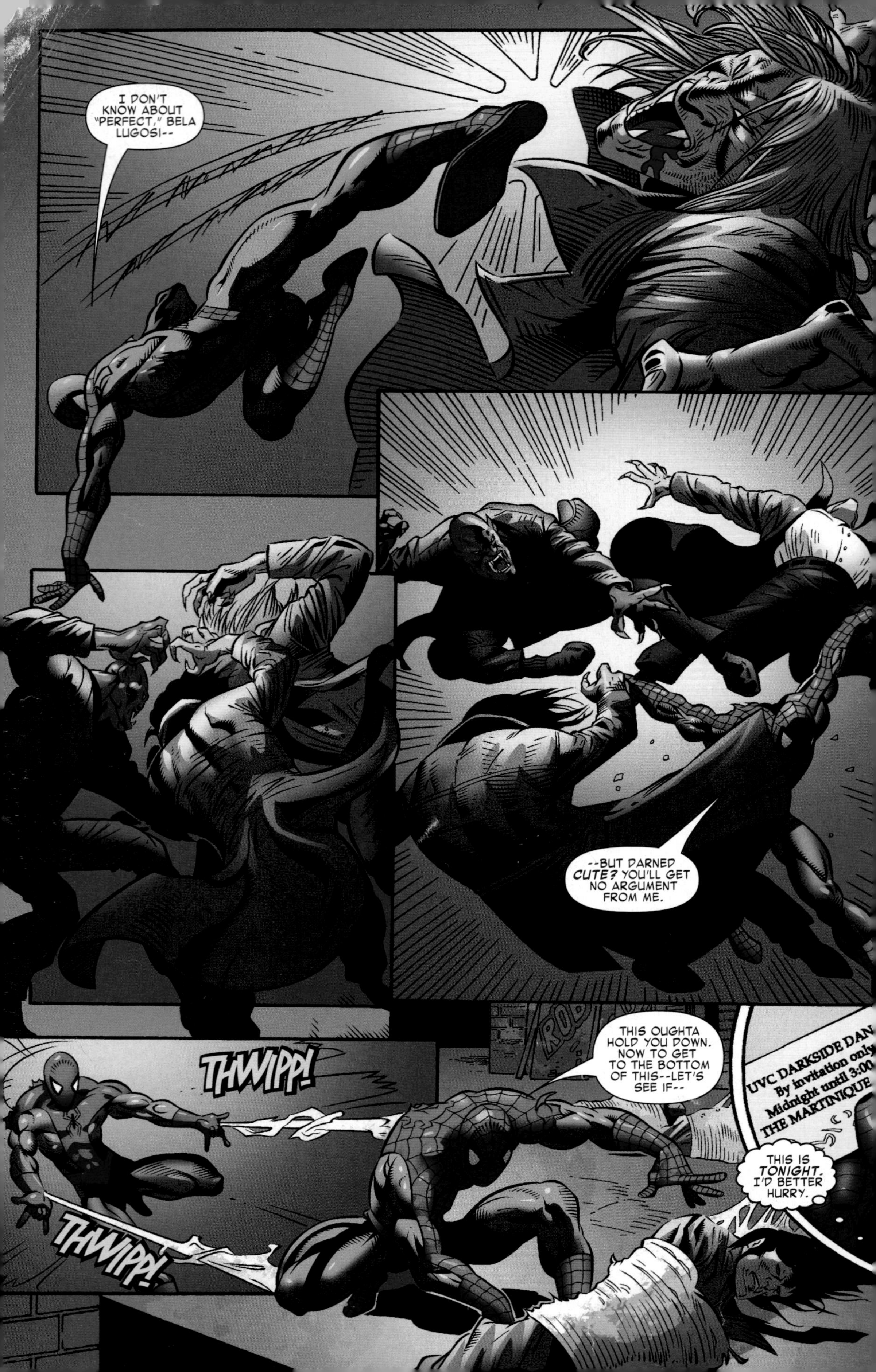
I DON'T KNOW ABOUT "PERFECT," BELA LUGOSI--
--BUT DARNED *CUTE?* YOU'LL GET NO ARGUMENT FROM ME.
THWIPP!
THWIPP!
THIS OUGHTA HOLD YOU DOWN. NOW TO GET TO THE BOTTOM OF THIS--LET'S SEE IF--
UVC DARKSIDE DAN
By invitation only
Midnight until 3:00
THE MARTINIQUE
THIS IS *TONIGHT.* I'D BETTER HURRY.

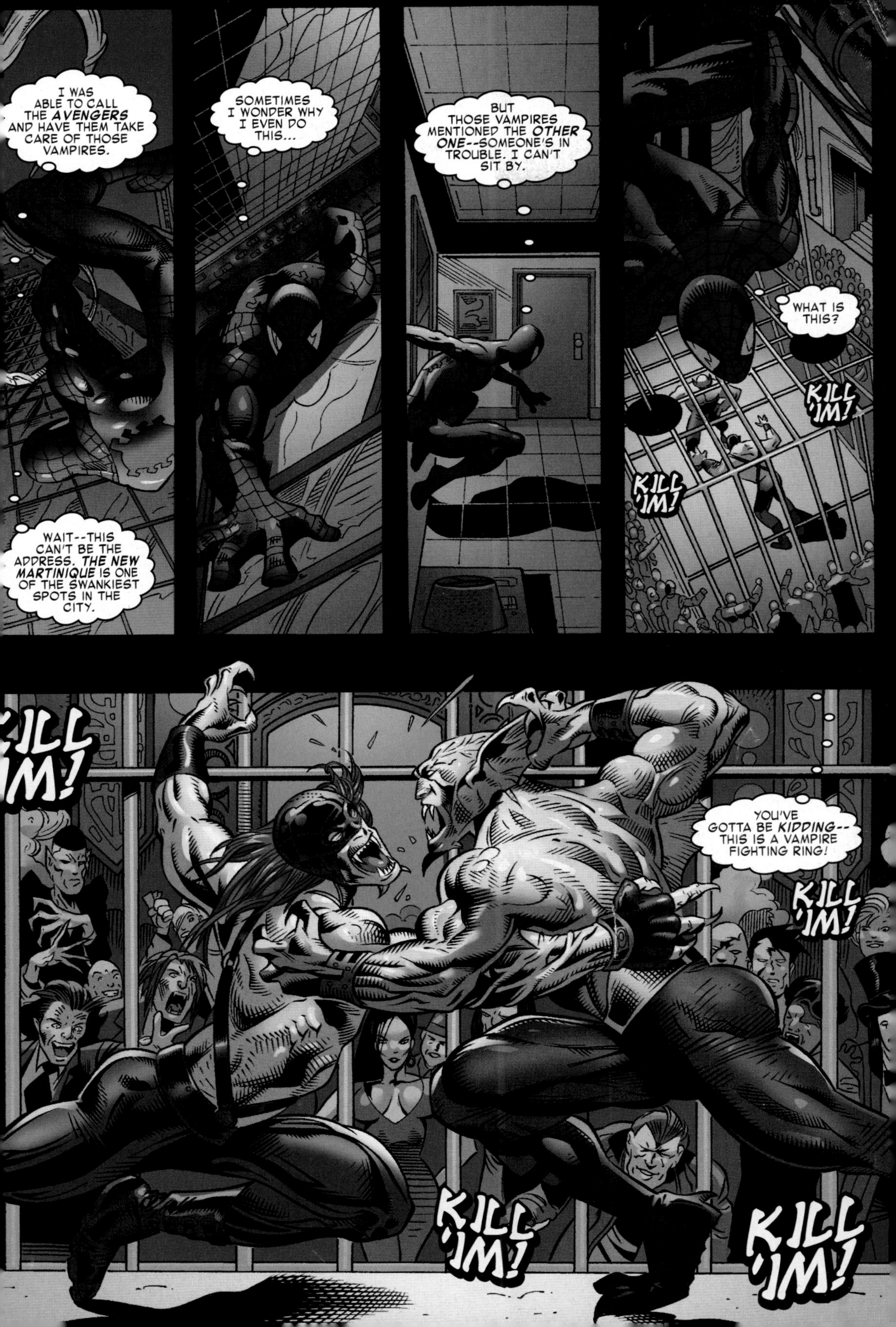

I WAS ABLE TO CALL THE AVENGERS AND HAVE THEM TAKE CARE OF THOSE VAMPIRES.
WAIT--THIS CAN'T BE THE ADDRESS. THE NEW MARTINIQUE IS ONE OF THE SWANKIEST SPOTS IN THE CITY.
SOMETIMES I WONDER WHY I EVEN DO THIS...
BUT THOSE VAMPIRES MENTIONED THE OTHER ONE--SOMEONE'S IN TROUBLE. I CAN'T SIT BY.
WHAT IS THIS?
KILL 'IM!
KILL 'IM!
KILL 'IM!
YOU'VE GOTTA BE KIDDING--THIS IS A VAMPIRE FIGHTING RING!
KILL 'IM!
KILL 'IM!
KILL 'IM!

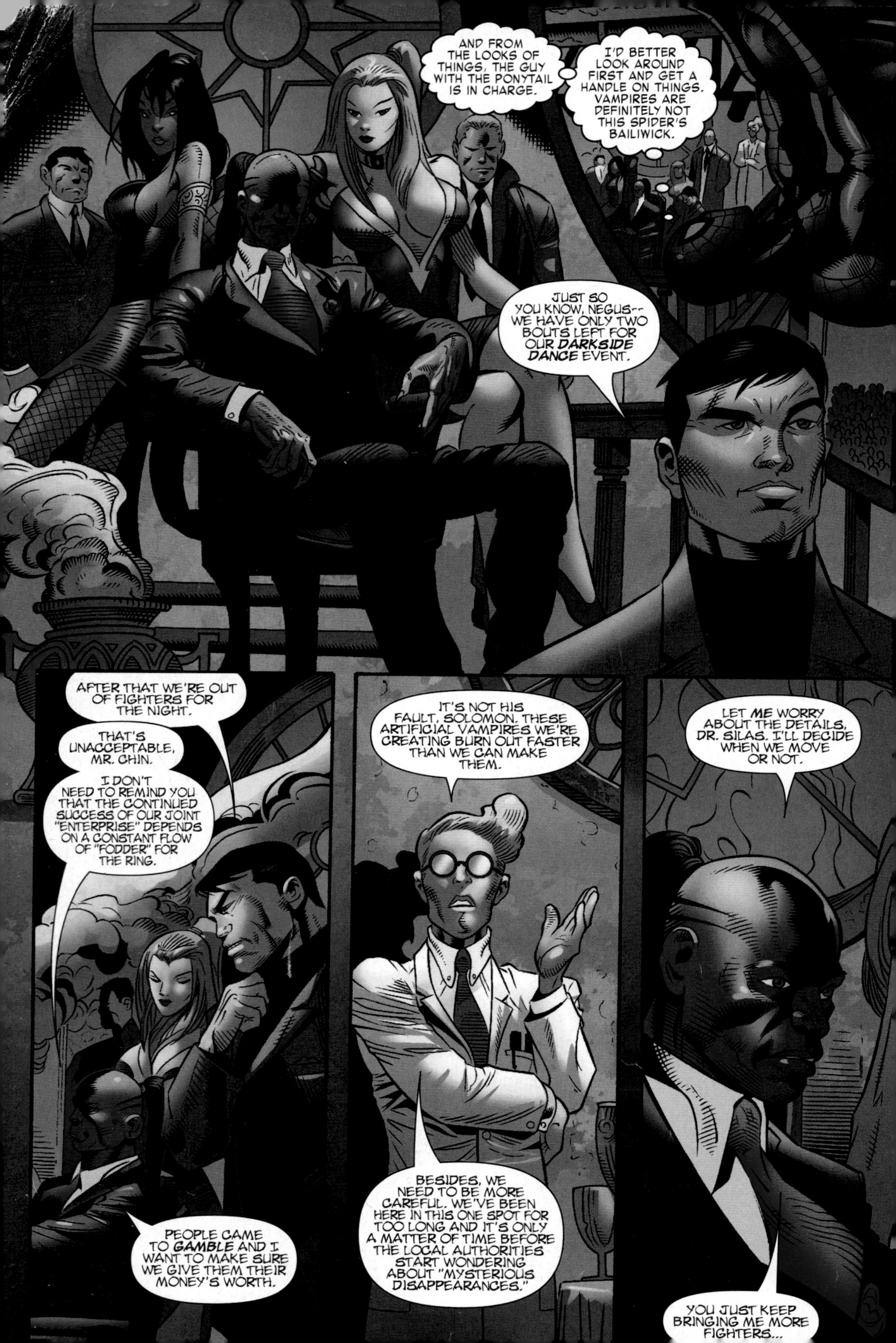
AND FROM THE LOOKS OF THINGS, THE GUY WITH THE PONYTAIL IS IN CHARGE.
I'D BETTER LOOK AROUND FIRST AND GET A HANDLE ON THINGS. VAMPIRES ARE DEFINITELY NOT THIS SPIDER'S BAILIWICK.
JUST SO YOU KNOW, NEGUS-- WE HAVE ONLY TWO BOUTS LEFT FOR OUR DARKSIDE DANCE EVENT.
AFTER THAT WE'RE OUT OF FIGHTERS FOR THE NIGHT.
THAT'S UNACCEPTABLE, MR. CHIN.
I DON'T NEED TO REMIND YOU THAT THE CONTINUED SUCCESS OF OUR JOINT "ENTERPRISE" DEPENDS ON A CONSTANT FLOW OF "FODDER" FOR THE RING.
PEOPLE CAME TO GAMBLE AND I WANT TO MAKE SURE WE GIVE THEM THEIR MONEY'S WORTH.
IT'S NOT HIS FAULT, SOLOMON. THESE ARTIFICIAL VAMPIRES WE'RE CREATING BURN OUT FASTER THAN WE CAN MAKE THEM.
BESIDES, WE NEED TO BE MORE CAREFUL. WE'VE BEEN HERE IN THIS ONE SPOT FOR TOO LONG AND IT'S ONLY A MATTER OF TIME BEFORE THE LOCAL AUTHORITIES START WONDERING ABOUT "MYSTERIOUS DISAPPEARANCES."
LET ME WORRY ABOUT THE DETAILS, DR. SILAS. I'LL DECIDE WHEN WE MOVE OR NOT.
YOU JUST KEEP BRINGING ME MORE FIGHTERS...

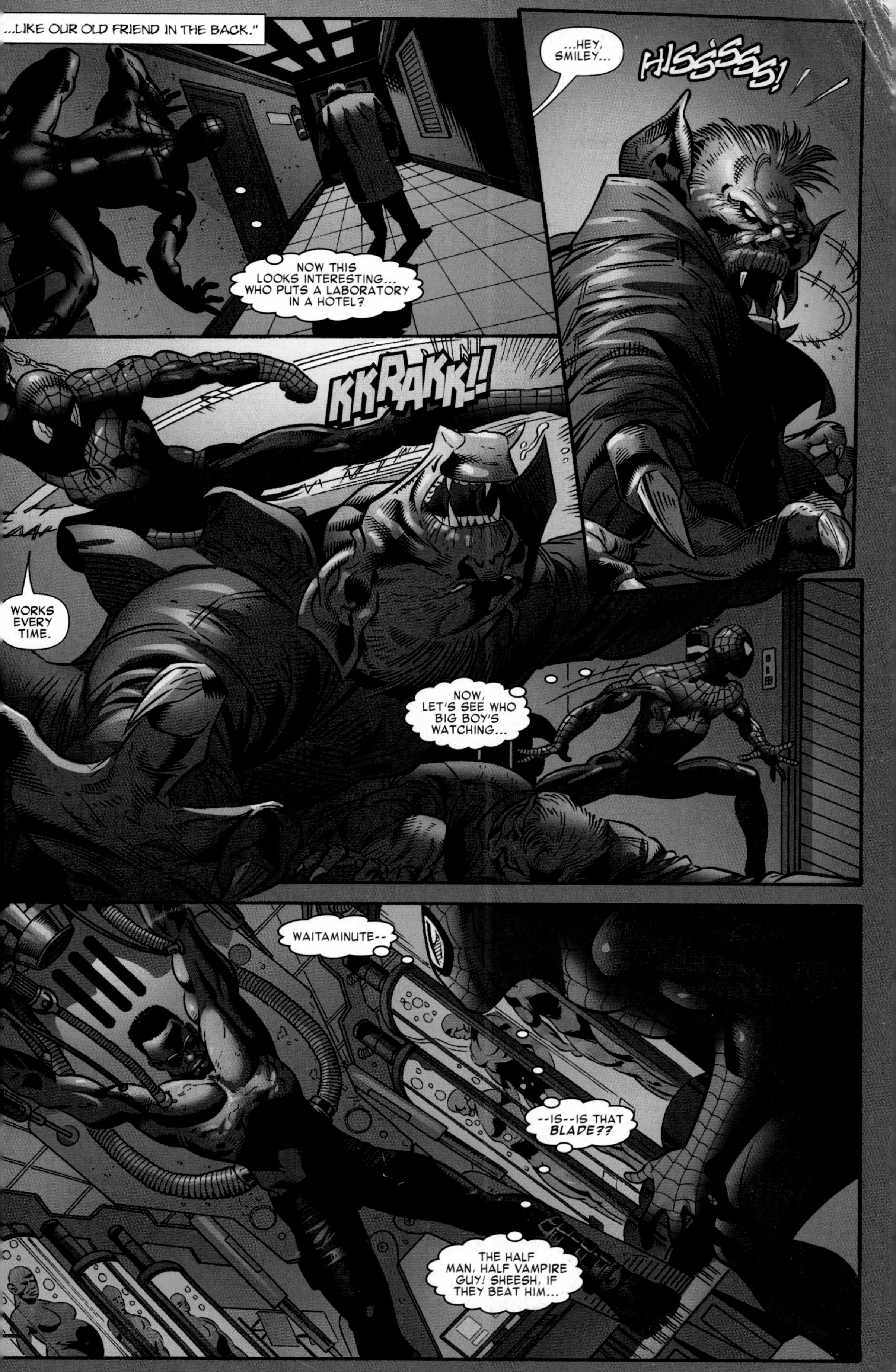
...LIKE OUR OLD FRIEND IN THE BACK."
NOW THIS LOOKS INTERESTING... WHO PUTS A LABORATORY IN A HOTEL?
...HEY, SMILEY...
HISSSSS!
KKRAKK!!
WORKS EVERY TIME.
NOW, LET'S SEE WHO BIG BOY'S WATCHING...
WAITAMINUTE--
--IS--IS THAT BLADE??
THE HALF MAN, HALF VAMPIRE GUY! SHEESH, IF THEY BEAT HIM...

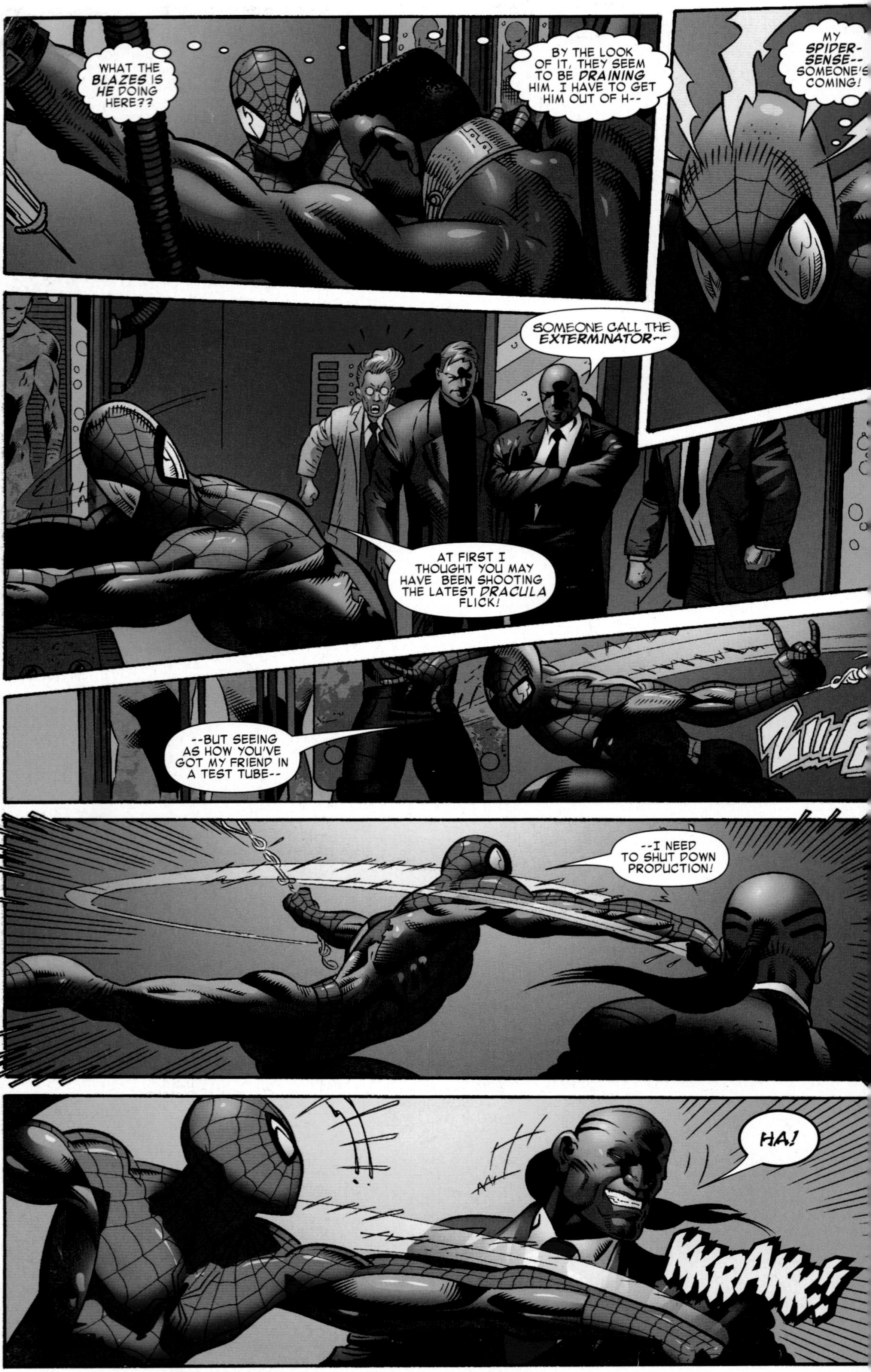

WHAT THE BLAZES IS HE DOING HERE??
BY THE LOOK OF IT, THEY SEEM TO BE DRAINING HIM. I HAVE TO GET HIM OUT OF H--
MY SPIDER-SENSE-- SOMEONE'S COMING!
SOMEONE CALL THE EXTERMINATOR--
AT FIRST I THOUGHT YOU MAY HAVE BEEN SHOOTING THE LATEST DRACULA FLICK!
--BUT SEEING AS HOW YOU'VE GOT MY FRIEND IN A TEST TUBE--
--I NEED TO SHUT DOWN PRODUCTION!
HA!
KKRAKK!!

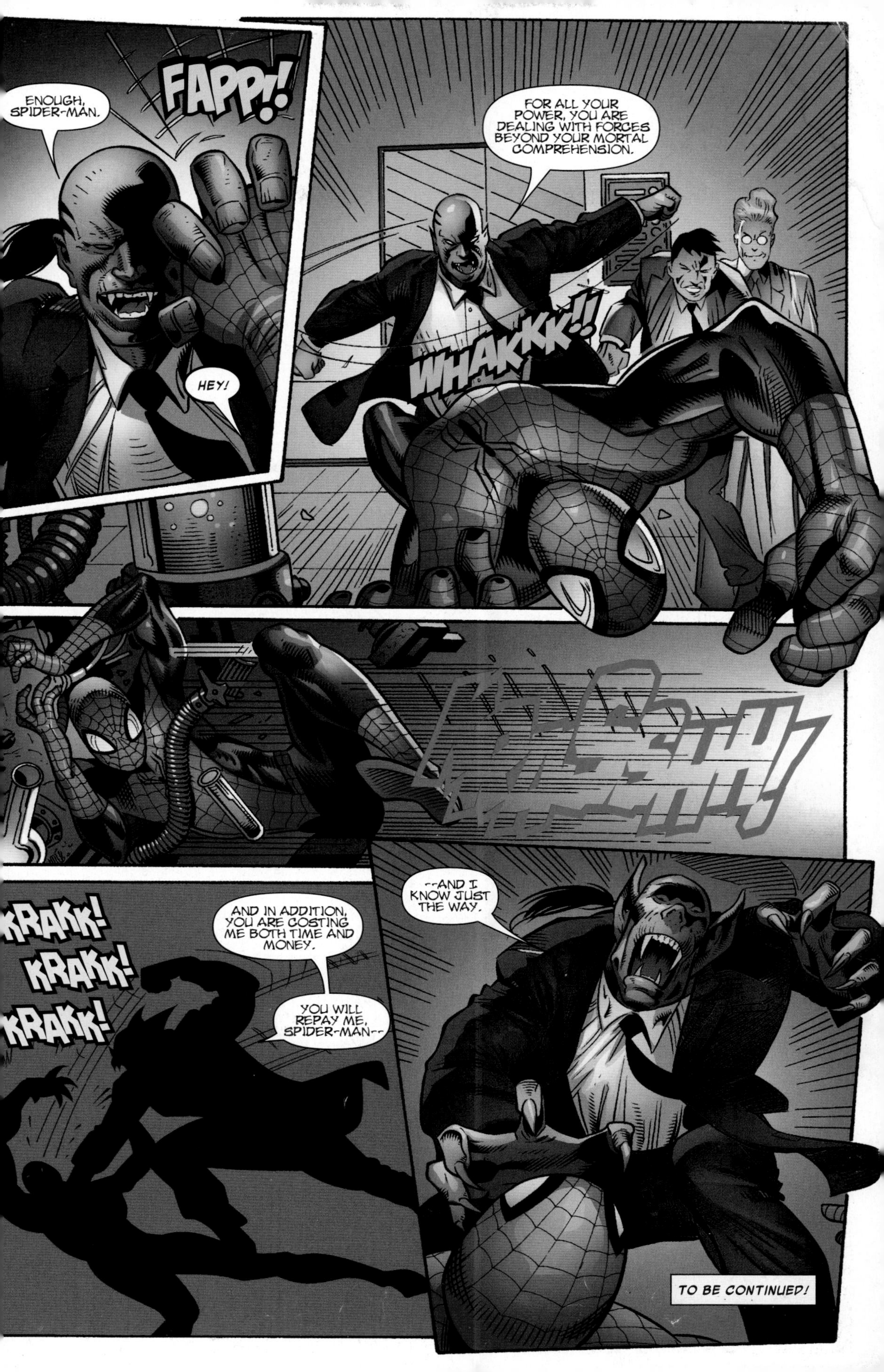

FAPP!!
ENOUGH, SPIDER-MAN.
HEY!
FOR ALL YOUR POWER, YOU ARE DEALING WITH FORCES BEYOND YOUR MORTAL COMPREHENSION.
WHAKKK!!
KRAKK!
KRAKK!
KRAKK!
AND IN ADDITION, YOU ARE COSTING ME BOTH TIME AND MONEY.
YOU WILL REPAY ME, SPIDER-MAN--
--AND I KNOW JUST THE WAY.
TO BE CONTINUED!

THE SPIDER & THE SWORD

CHAPTER

2

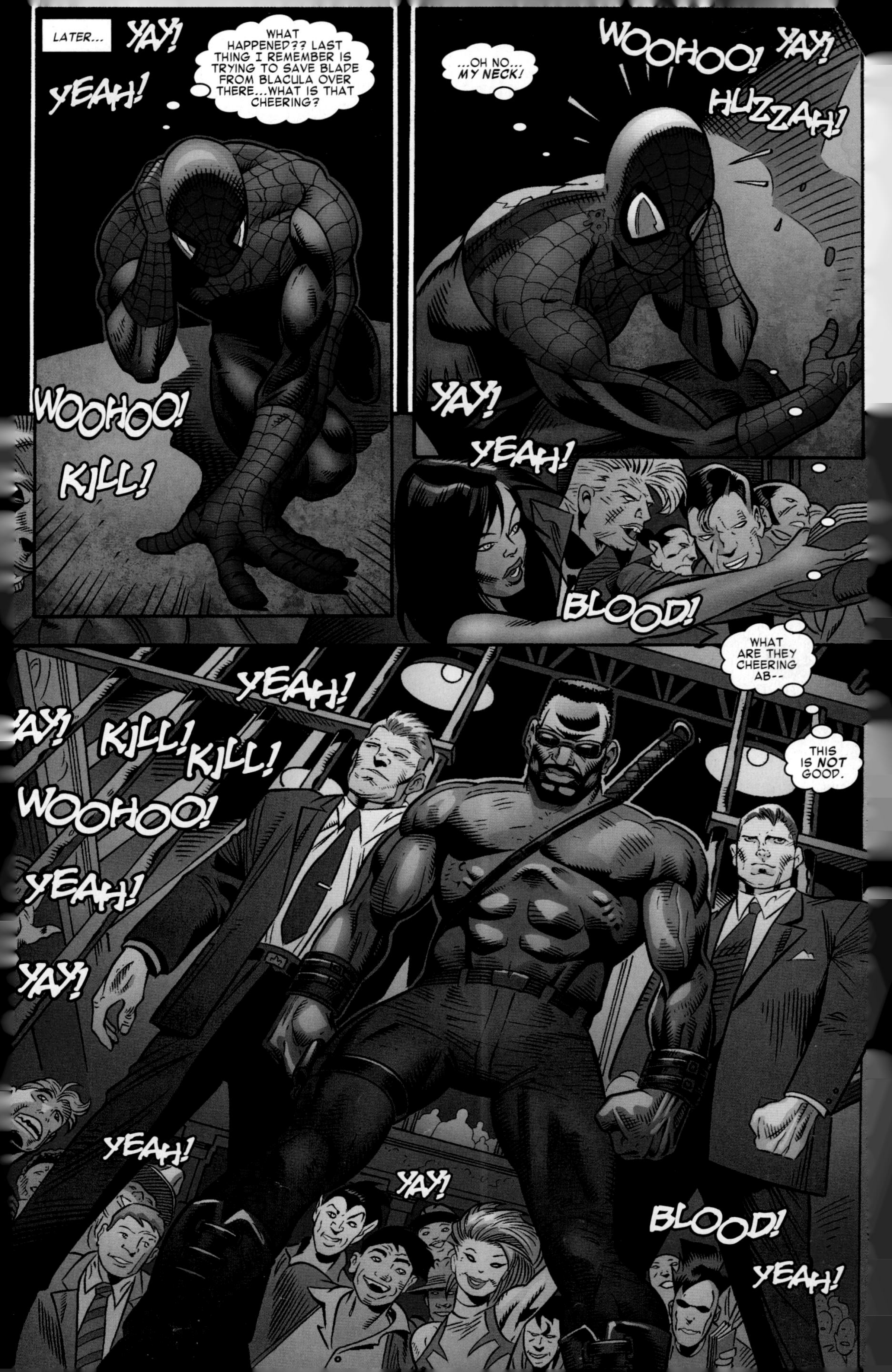
LATER...
YAY!
YEAH!
WHAT HAPPENED?? LAST THING I REMEMBER IS TRYING TO SAVE BLADE FROM BLACULA OVER THERE...WHAT IS THAT CHEERING?
WOOHOO!
KILL!
...OH NO... MY NECK!
WOOHOO!
YAY!
HUZZAH!
YAY!
YEAH!
BLOOD!
YEAH!
YAY!
KILL!
KILL!
WOOHOO!
YEAH!
YAY!
WHAT ARE THEY CHEERING AB--
THIS IS NOT GOOD.
YEAH!
YAY!
BLOOD!
YEAH!

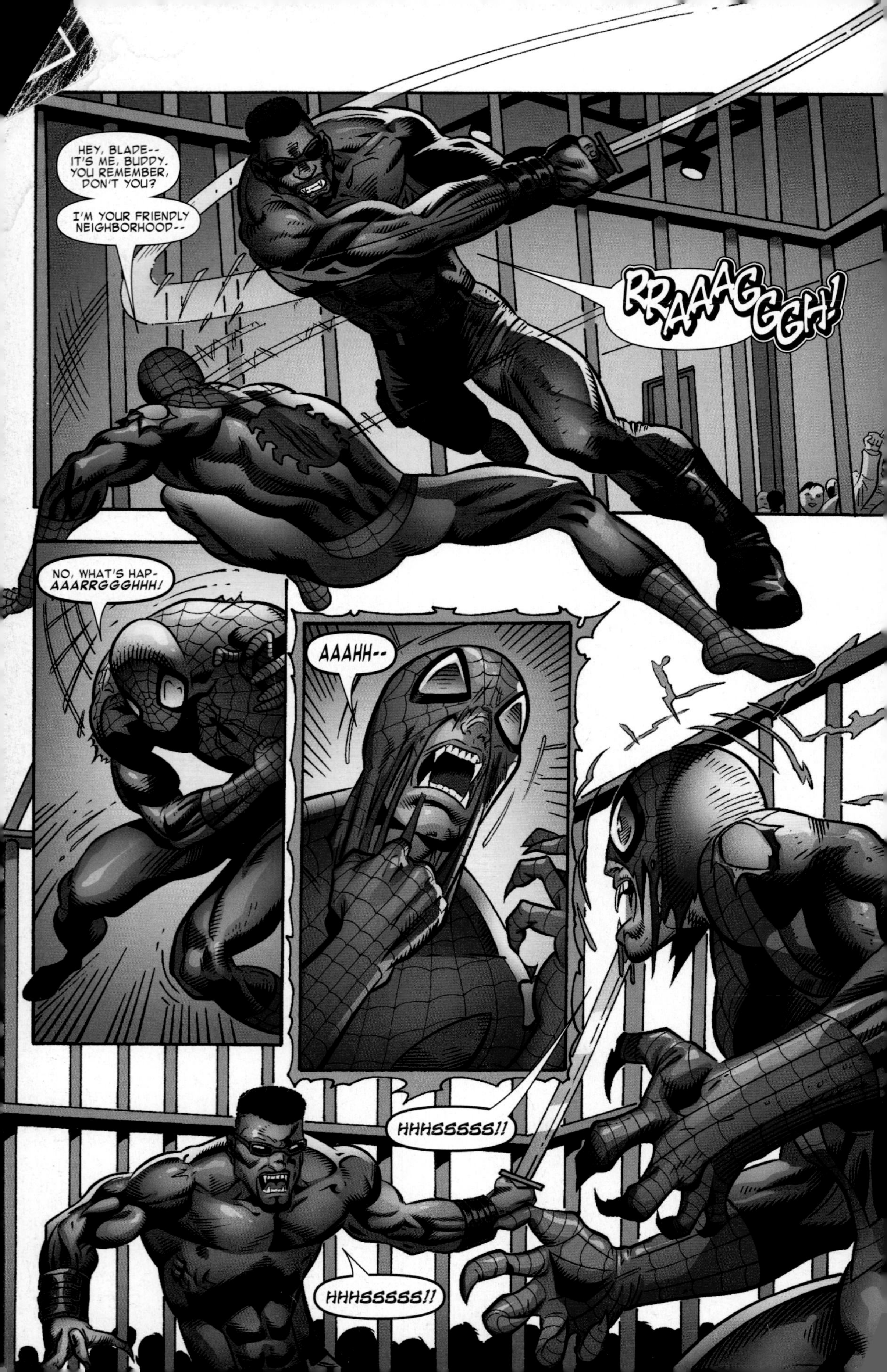
HEY, BLADE--
IT'S ME, BUDDY.
YOU REMEMBER,
DON'T YOU?
I'M YOUR FRIENDLY
NEIGHBORHOOD--
RRAAAAGGGH!
NO, WHAT'S HAP-
AAARRGGGHHH!
AAAHH--
HHHSSSSSS!!
HHHSSSSSS!!

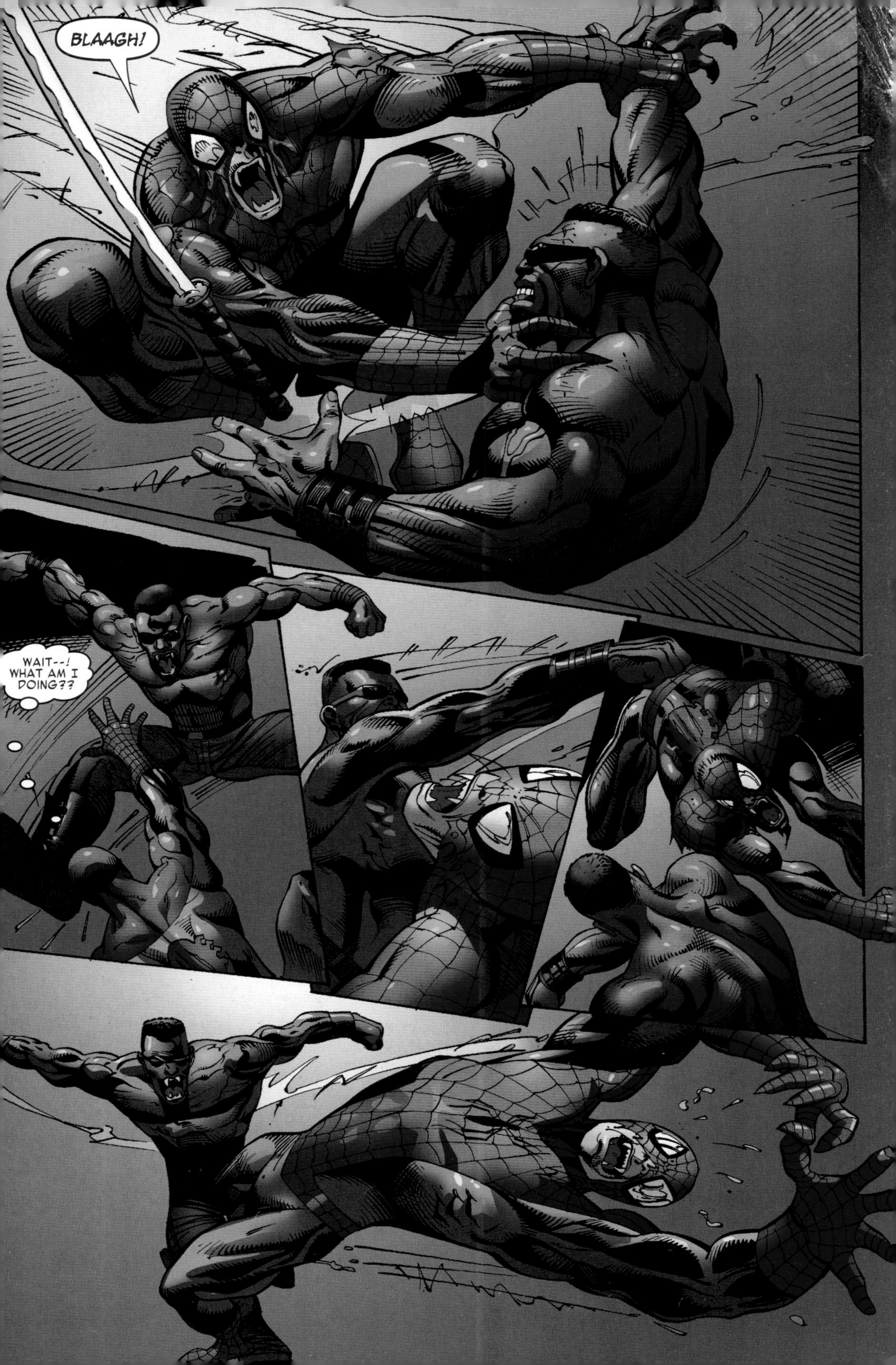
BLAAGH!
WAIT--! WHAT AM I DOING??

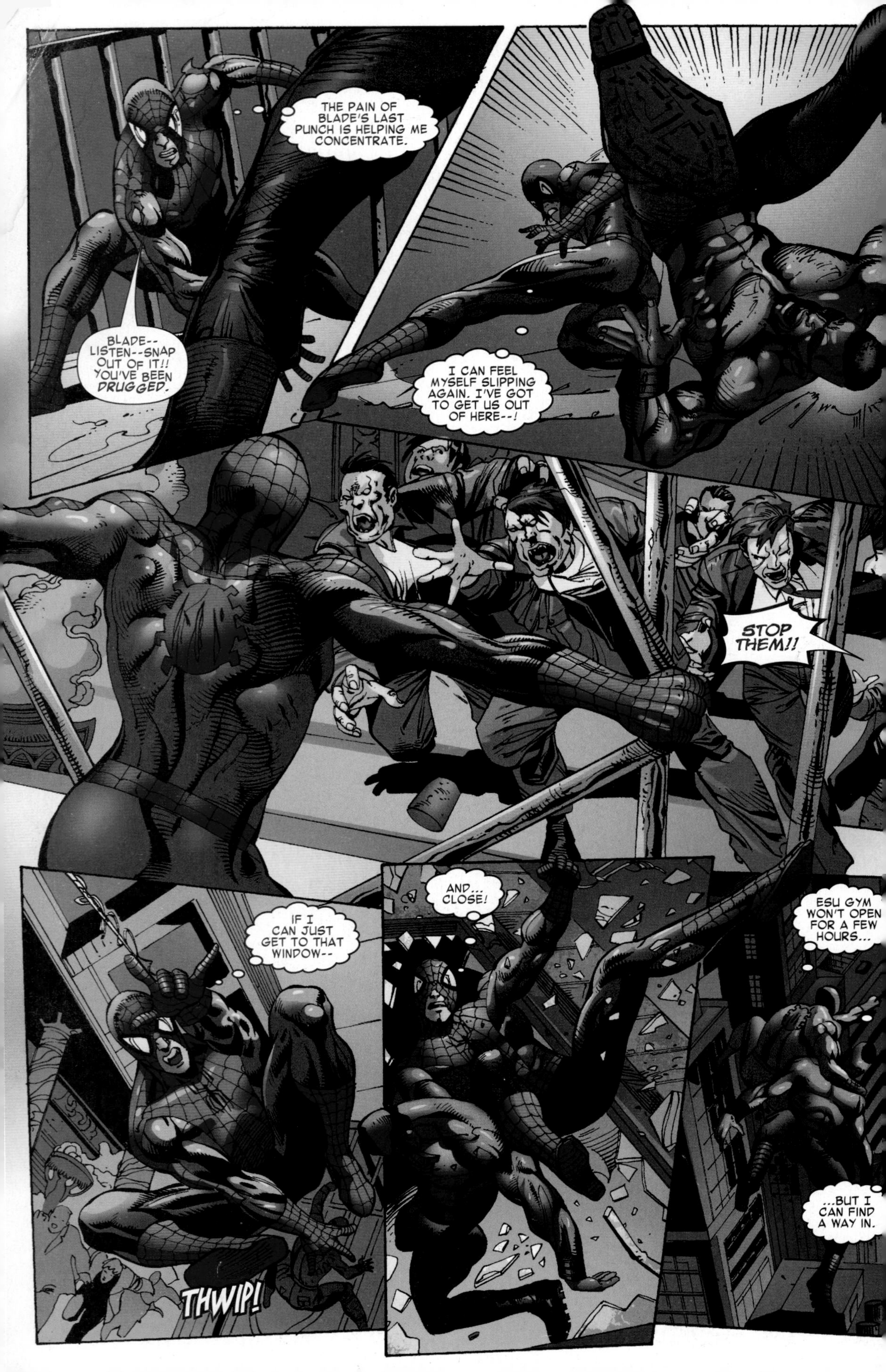
THE PAIN OF BLADE'S LAST PUNCH IS HELPING ME CONCENTRATE.
BLADE-- LISTEN--SNAP OUT OF IT!! YOU'VE BEEN DRUGGED.
I CAN FEEL MYSELF SLIPPING AGAIN. I'VE GOT TO GET US OUT OF HERE--!
STOP THEM!!
IF I CAN JUST GET TO THAT WINDOW--
THWIP!
AND... CLOSE!
ESU GYM WON'T OPEN FOR A FEW HOURS...
...BUT I CAN FIND A WAY IN.

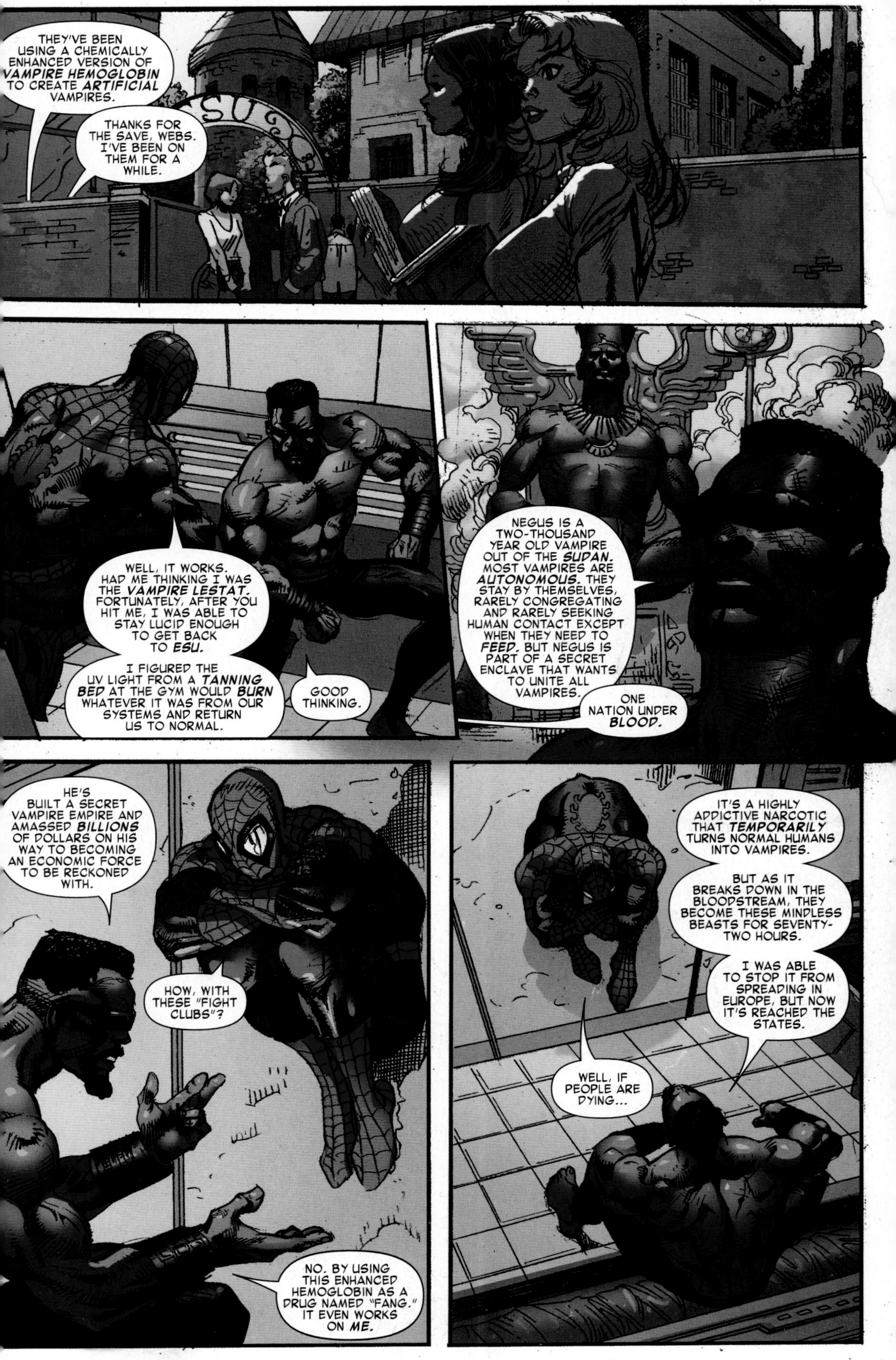
THEY'VE BEEN USING A CHEMICALLY ENHANCED VERSION OF VAMPIRE HEMOGLOBIN TO CREATE ARTIFICIAL VAMPIRES.
THANKS FOR THE SAVE, WEBS. I'VE BEEN ON THEM FOR A WHILE.
ESU
WELL, IT WORKS. HAD ME THINKING I WAS THE VAMPIRE LESTAT. FORTUNATELY, AFTER YOU HIT ME, I WAS ABLE TO STAY LUCID ENOUGH TO GET BACK TO ESU.
I FIGURED THE UV LIGHT FROM A TANNING BED AT THE GYM WOULD BURN WHATEVER IT WAS FROM OUR SYSTEMS AND RETURN US TO NORMAL.
GOOD THINKING.
NEGUS IS A TWO-THOUSAND YEAR OLD VAMPIRE OUT OF THE SUDAN. MOST VAMPIRES ARE AUTONOMOUS. THEY STAY BY THEMSELVES, RARELY CONGREGATING AND RARELY SEEKING HUMAN CONTACT EXCEPT WHEN THEY NEED TO FEED. BUT NEGUS IS PART OF A SECRET ENCLAVE THAT WANTS TO UNITE ALL VAMPIRES.
ONE NATION UNDER BLOOD.
HE'S BUILT A SECRET VAMPIRE EMPIRE AND AMASSED BILLIONS OF DOLLARS ON HIS WAY TO BECOMING AN ECONOMIC FORCE TO BE RECKONED WITH.
HOW, WITH THESE "FIGHT CLUBS"?
NO. BY USING THIS ENHANCED HEMOGLOBIN AS A DRUG NAMED "FANG." IT EVEN WORKS ON ME.
IT'S A HIGHLY ADDICTIVE NARCOTIC THAT TEMPORARILY TURNS NORMAL HUMANS INTO VAMPIRES.
BUT AS IT BREAKS DOWN IN THE BLOODSTREAM, THEY BECOME THESE MINDLESS BEASTS FOR SEVENTY-TWO HOURS.
I WAS ABLE TO STOP IT FROM SPREADING IN EUROPE, BUT NOW IT'S REACHED THE STATES.
WELL, IF PEOPLE ARE DYING...

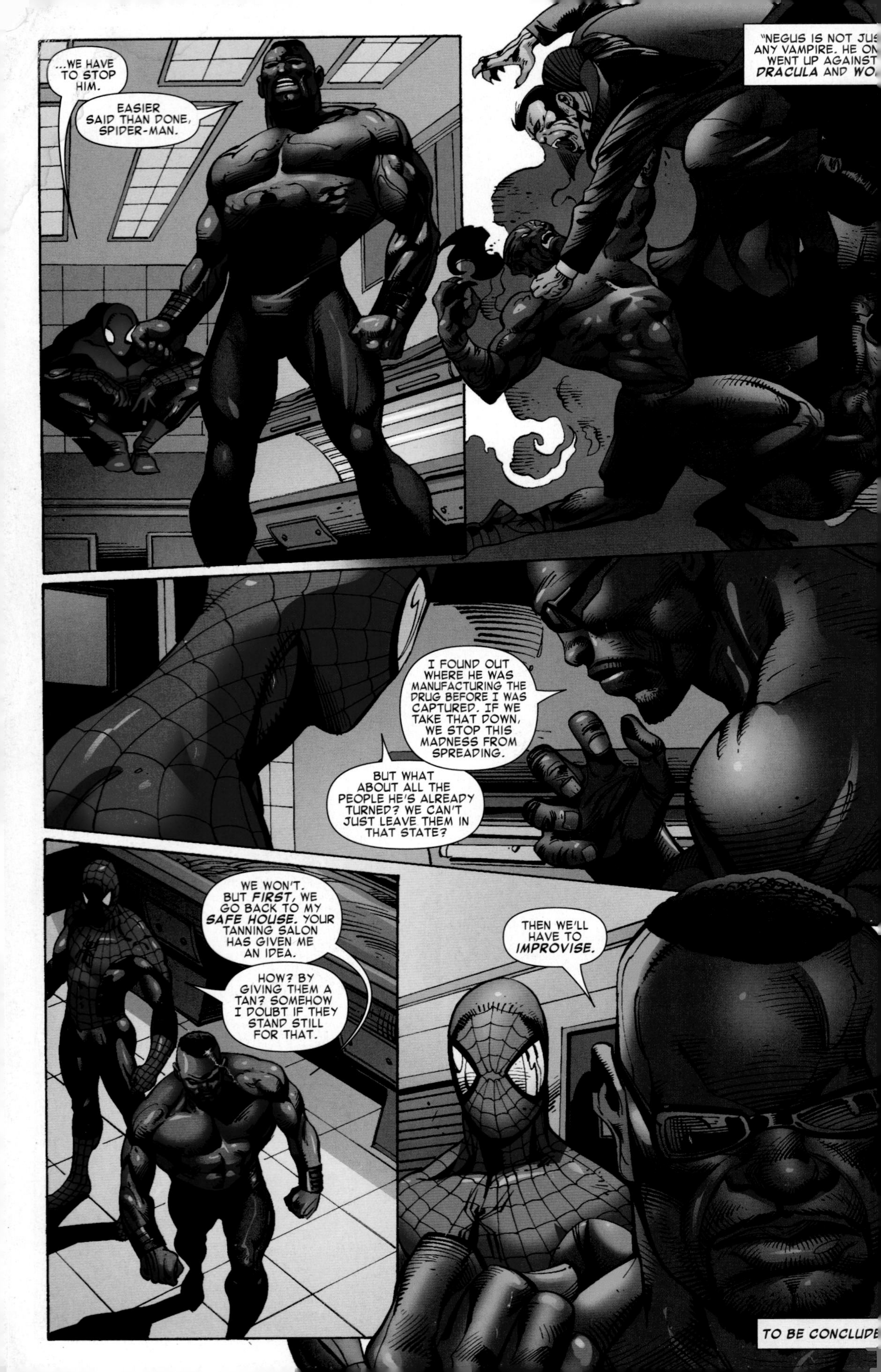
...WE HAVE TO STOP HIM.
EASIER SAID THAN DONE, SPIDER-MAN.
"NEGUS IS NOT JUS ANY VAMPIRE. HE ON WENT UP AGAINST DRACULA AND WO
I FOUND OUT WHERE HE WAS MANUFACTURING THE DRUG BEFORE I WAS CAPTURED. IF WE TAKE THAT DOWN, WE STOP THIS MADNESS FROM SPREADING.
BUT WHAT ABOUT ALL THE PEOPLE HE'S ALREADY TURNED? WE CAN'T JUST LEAVE THEM IN THAT STATE?
THEN WE'LL HAVE TO IMPROVISE.
WE WON'T. BUT FIRST, WE GO BACK TO MY SAFE HOUSE. YOUR TANNING SALON HAS GIVEN ME AN IDEA.
HOW? BY GIVING THEM A TAN? SOMEHOW I DOUBT IF THEY STAND STILL FOR THAT.
TO BE CONCLUDE

THE SPIDER & THE SWORD

CHAPTER

3

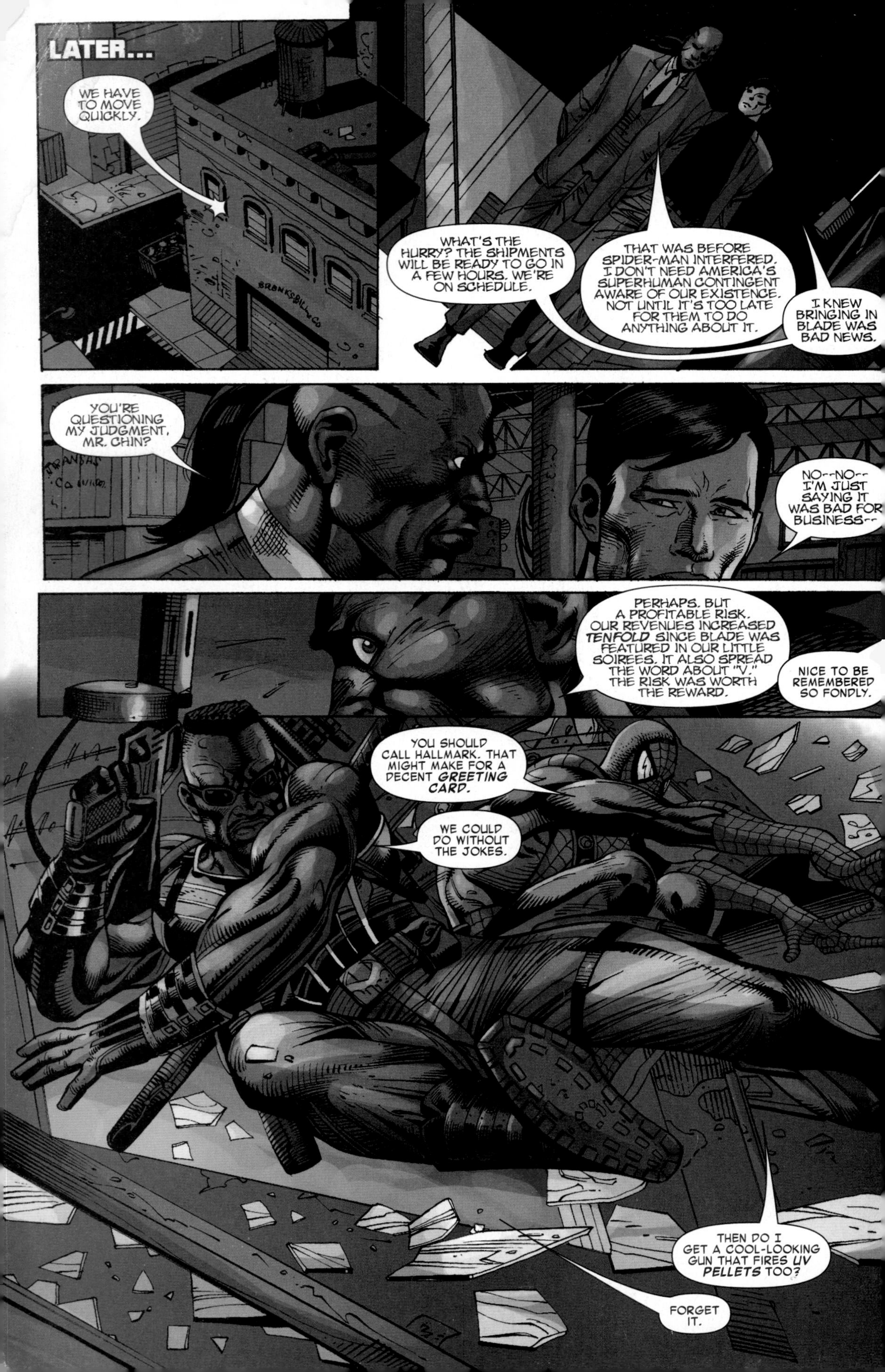
LATER...
WE HAVE TO MOVE QUICKLY.
BRONKS BILL & CO
WHAT'S THE HURRY? THE SHIPMENTS WILL BE READY TO GO IN A FEW HOURS. WE'RE ON SCHEDULE.
THAT WAS BEFORE SPIDER-MAN INTERFERED. I DON'T NEED AMERICA'S SUPERHUMAN CONTINGENT AWARE OF OUR EXISTENCE. NOT UNTIL IT'S TOO LATE FOR THEM TO DO ANYTHING ABOUT IT.
I KNEW BRINGING IN BLADE WAS BAD NEWS.
YOU'RE QUESTIONING MY JUDGMENT, MR. CHIN?
NO--NO--I'M JUST SAYING IT WAS BAD FOR BUSINESS--
PERHAPS. BUT A PROFITABLE RISK. OUR REVENUES INCREASED TENFOLD SINCE BLADE WAS FEATURED IN OUR LITTLE SOIREES. IT ALSO SPREAD THE WORD ABOUT "V." THE RISK WAS WORTH THE REWARD.
NICE TO BE REMEMBERED SO FONDLY.
YOU SHOULD CALL HALLMARK. THAT MIGHT MAKE FOR A DECENT GREETING CARD.
WE COULD DO WITHOUT THE JOKES.
THEN DO I GET A COOL-LOOKING GUN THAT FIRES UV PELLETS TOO?
FORGET IT.

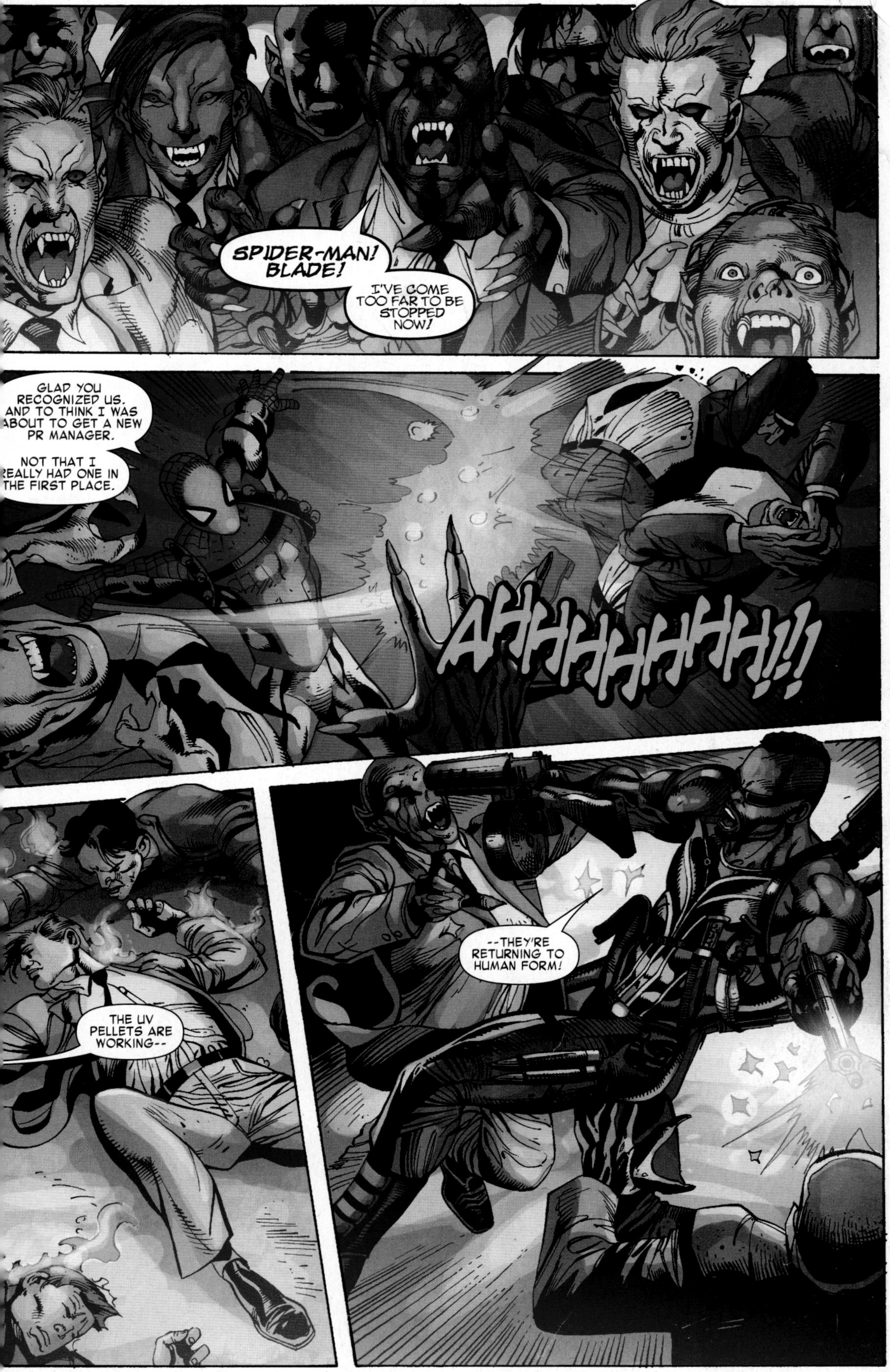
SPIDER-MAN! BLADE!
I'VE COME TOO FAR TO BE STOPPED NOW!
GLAD YOU RECOGNIZED US. AND TO THINK I WAS ABOUT TO GET A NEW PR MANAGER.
NOT THAT I REALLY HAD ONE IN THE FIRST PLACE.
AHHHHHHH!!!
THE UV PELLETS ARE WORKING--
--THEY'RE RETURNING TO HUMAN FORM!

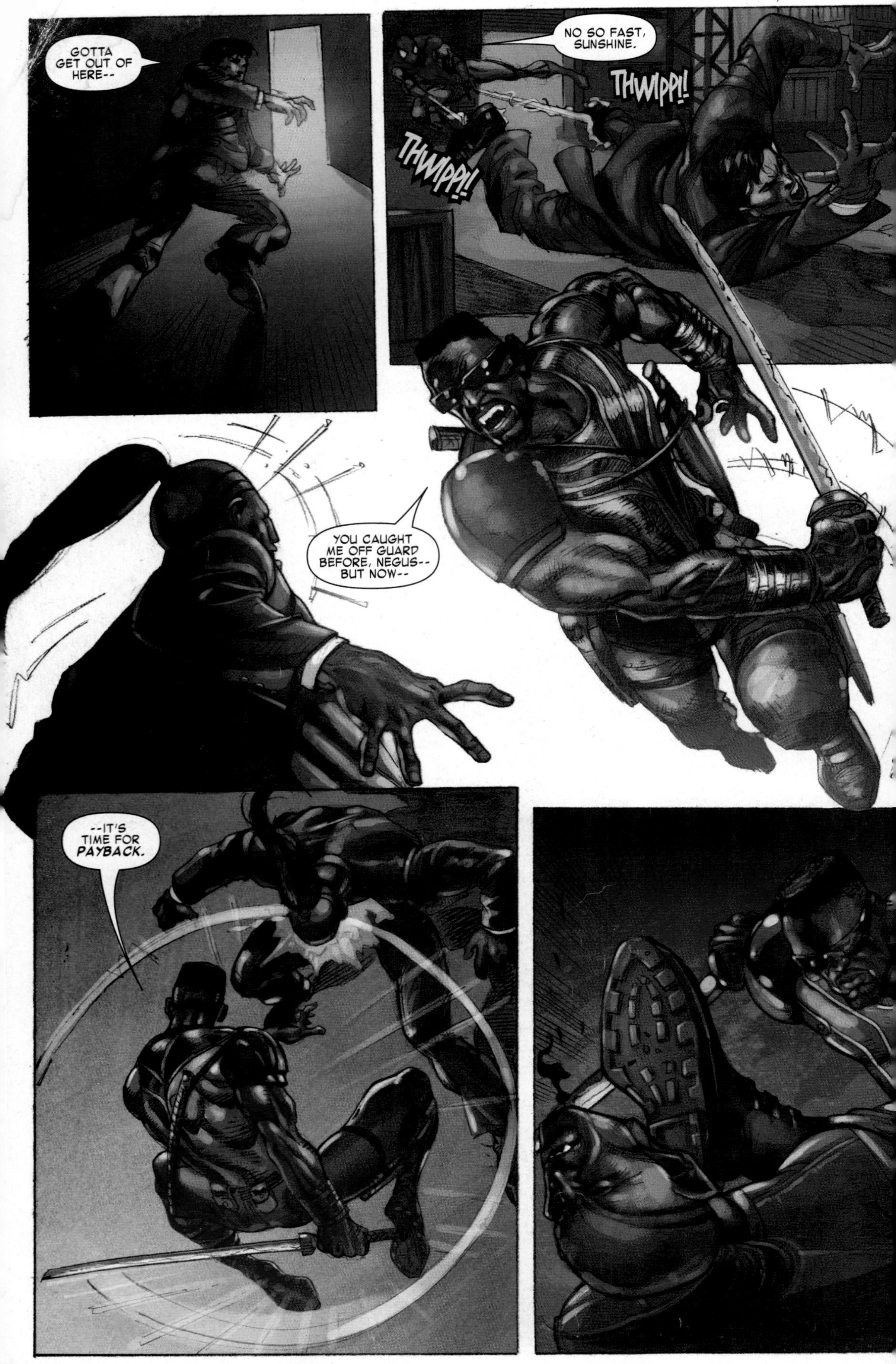
GOTTA GET OUT OF HERE--
NO SO FAST, SUNSHINE.
THWIPP!!
THWIPP!!
YOU CAUGHT ME OFF GUARD BEFORE, NEGUS-- BUT NOW--
--IT'S TIME FOR PAYBACK.

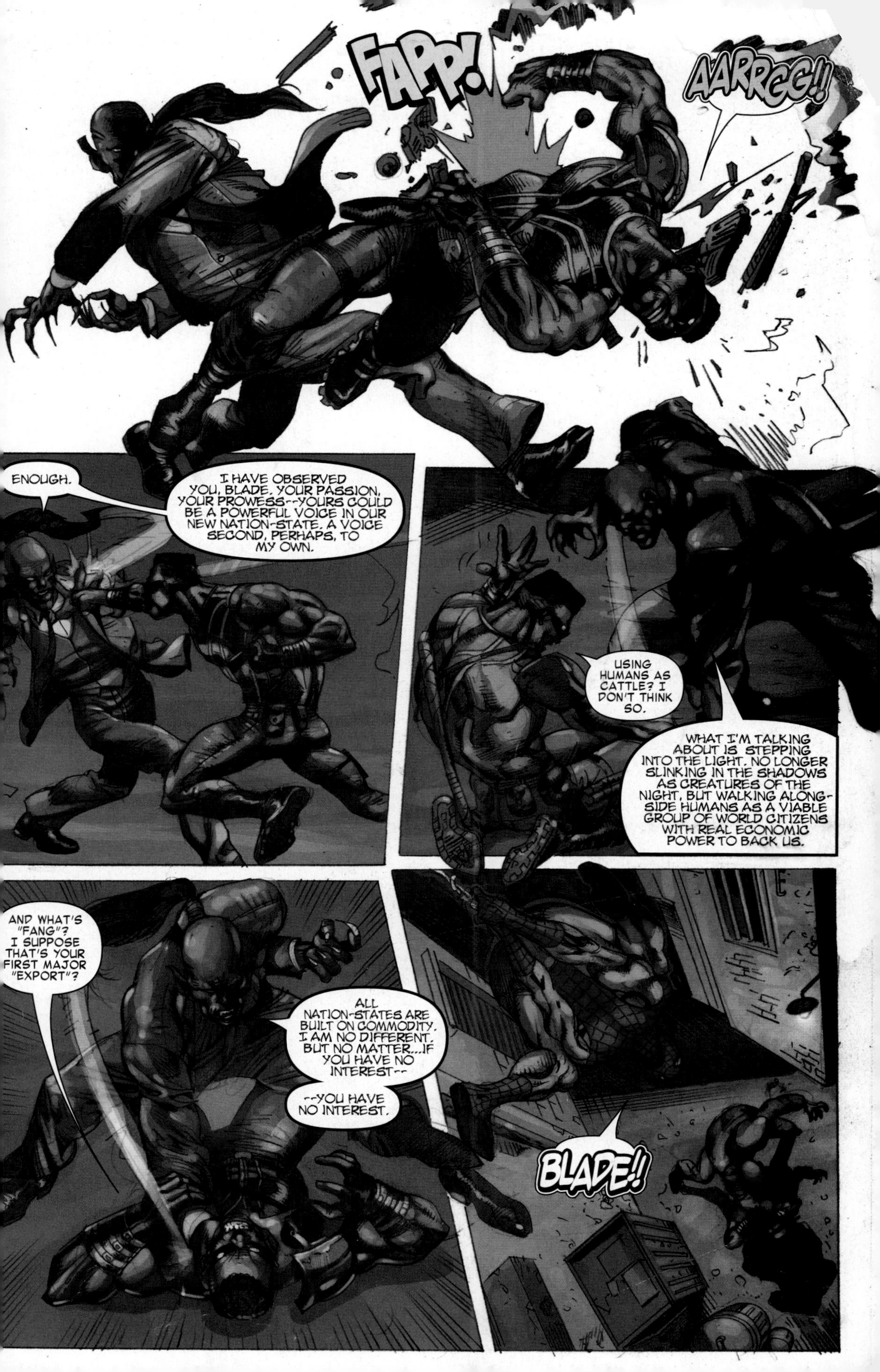
FAPP!
AARRGG!!
ENOUGH.
I HAVE OBSERVED YOU, BLADE. YOUR PASSION, YOUR PROWESS--YOURS COULD BE A POWERFUL VOICE IN OUR NEW NATION-STATE. A VOICE SECOND, PERHAPS, TO MY OWN.
USING HUMANS AS CATTLE? I DON'T THINK SO.
WHAT I'M TALKING ABOUT IS STEPPING INTO THE LIGHT. NO LONGER SLINKING IN THE SHADOWS AS CREATURES OF THE NIGHT, BUT WALKING ALONG-SIDE HUMANS AS A VIABLE GROUP OF WORLD CITIZENS WITH REAL ECONOMIC POWER TO BACK US.
AND WHAT'S "FANG"? I SUPPOSE THAT'S YOUR FIRST MAJOR "EXPORT"?
ALL NATION-STATES ARE BUILT ON COMMODITY. I AM NO DIFFERENT. BUT NO MATTER...IF YOU HAVE NO INTEREST--
--YOU HAVE NO INTEREST.
BLADE!!

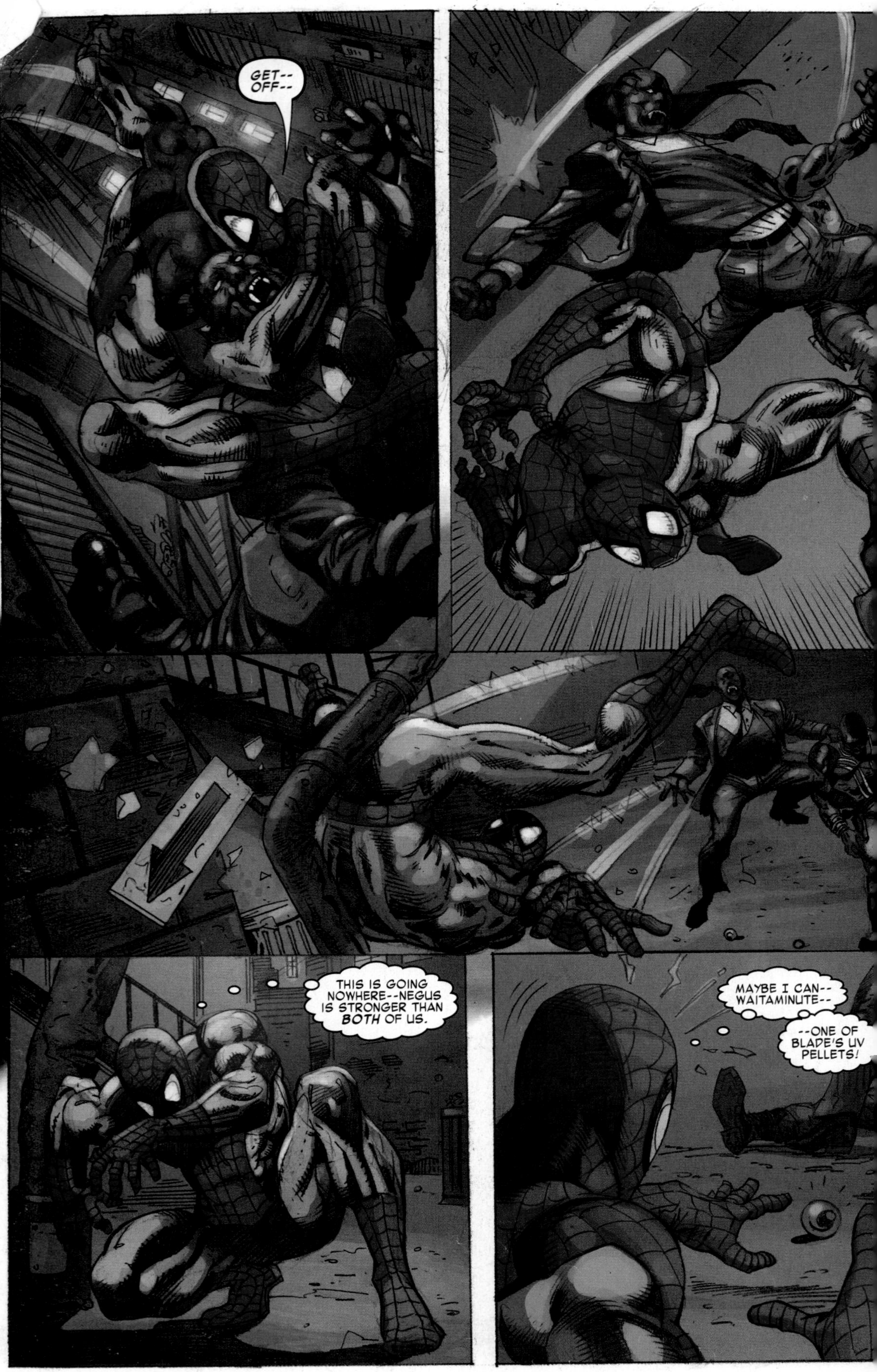
GET-- OFF--
THIS IS GOING NOWHERE--NEGUS IS STRONGER THAN BOTH OF US.
MAYBE I CAN-- WAITAMINUTE--
--ONE OF BLADE'S UV PELLETS!

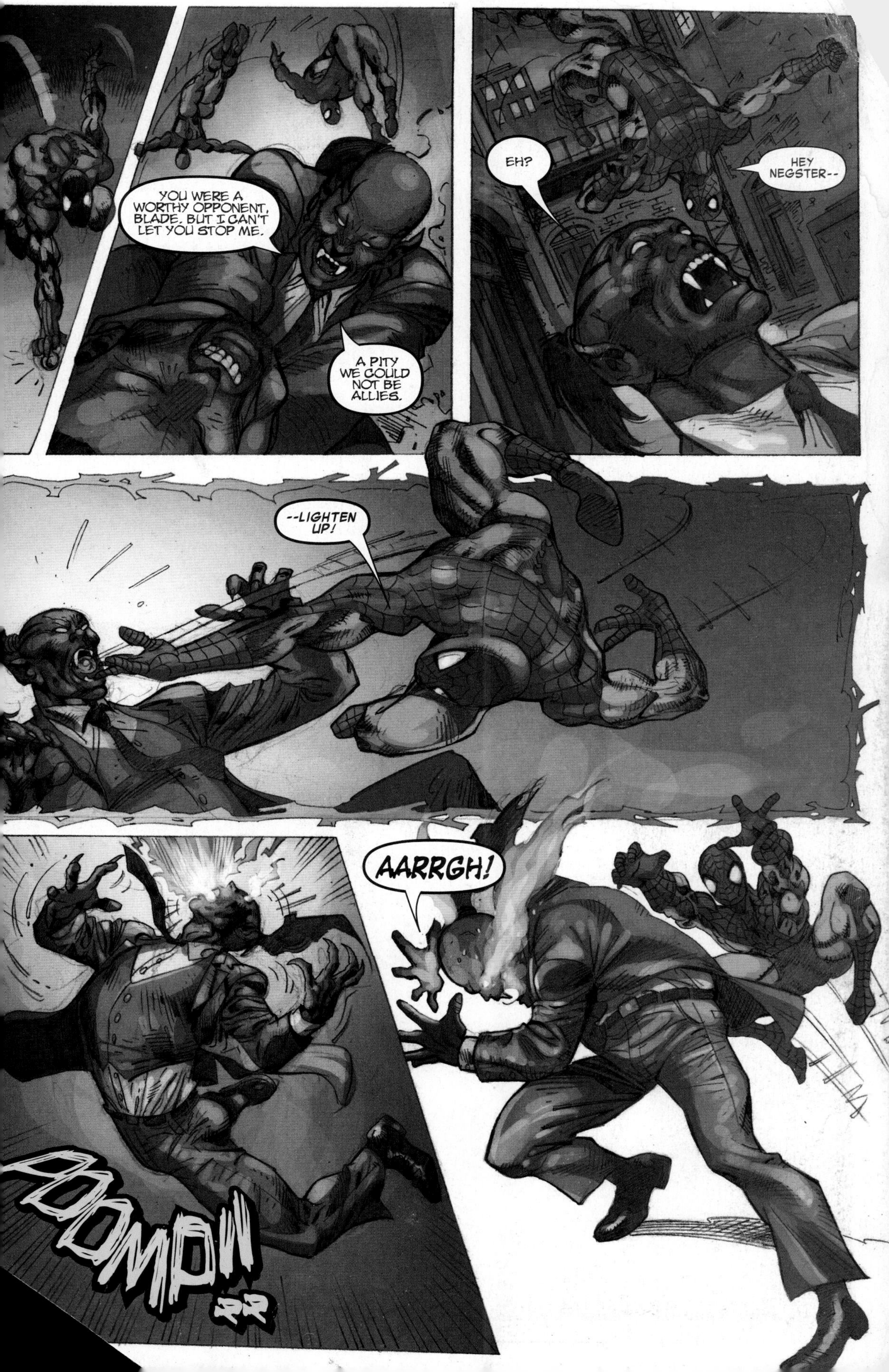
YOU WERE A WORTHY OPPONENT, BLADE. BUT I CAN'T LET YOU STOP ME.
A PITY WE COULD NOT BE ALLIES.
HEY NEGSTER--
EH?
--LIGHTEN UP!
AARRGH!

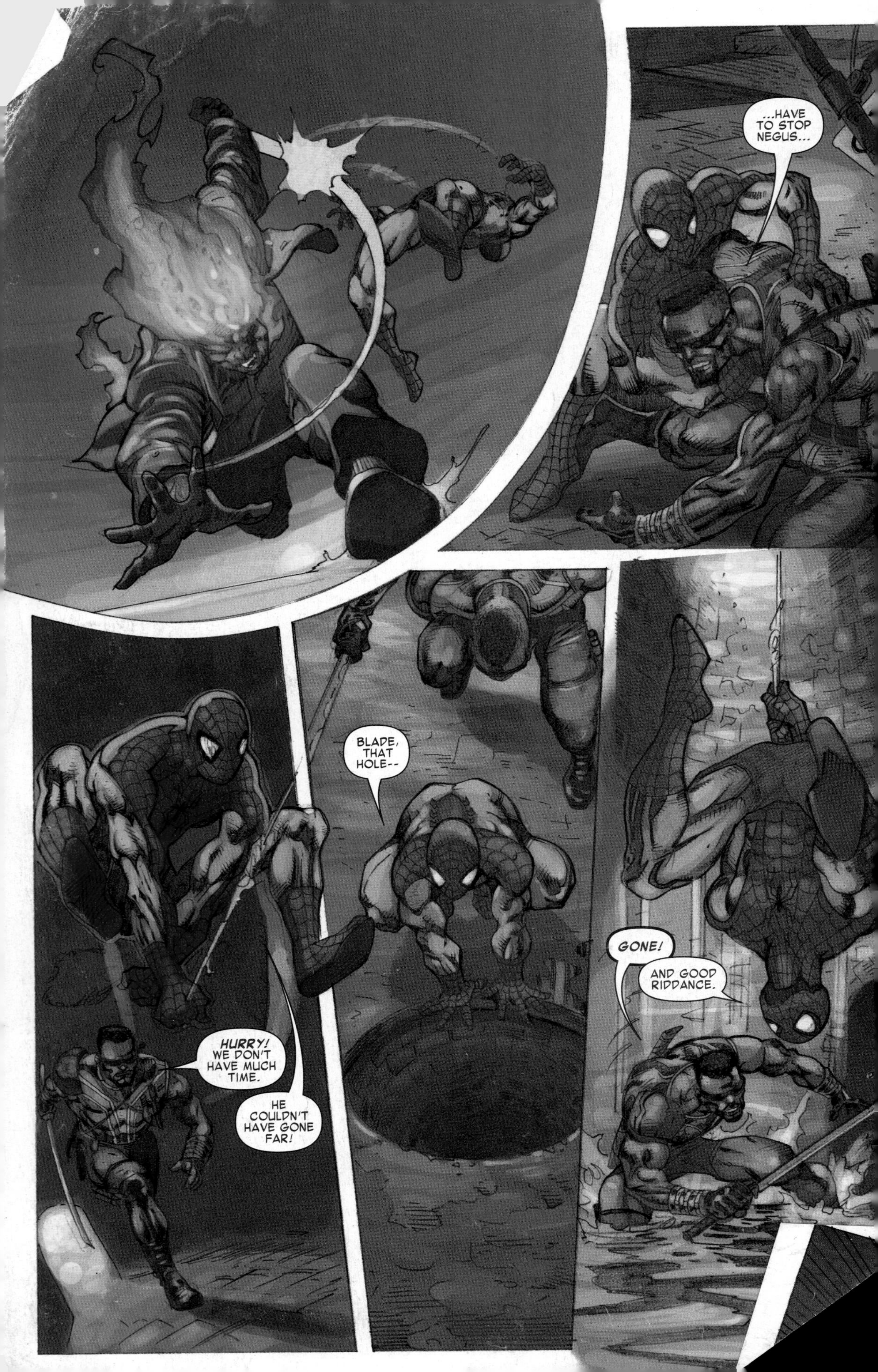
...HAVE TO STOP NEGUS...
HURRY! WE DON'T HAVE MUCH TIME.
HE COULDN'T HAVE GONE FAR!
BLADE, THAT HOLE--
GONE!
AND GOOD RIDDANCE.

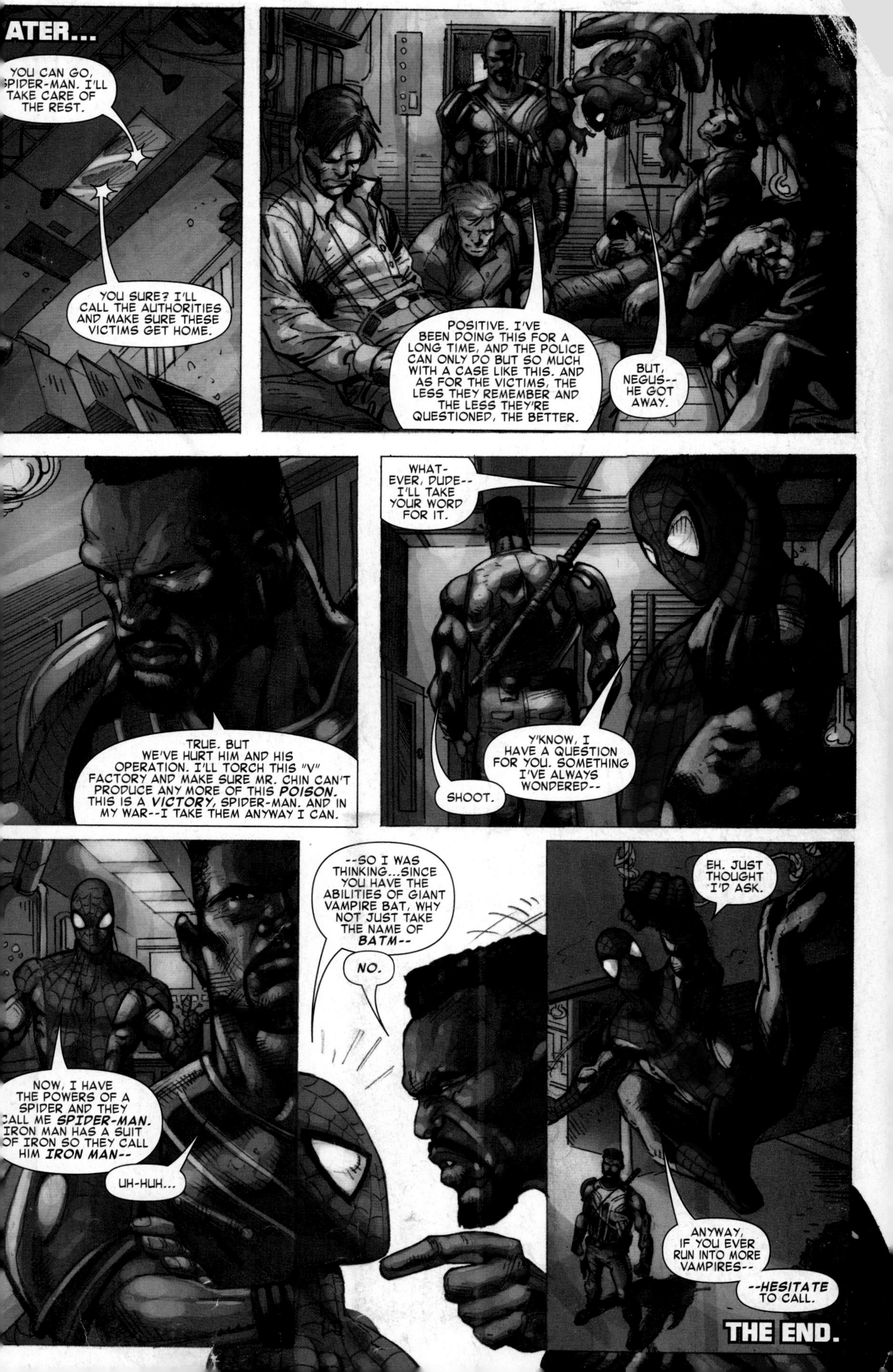

ATER...
YOU CAN GO, SPIDER-MAN. I'LL TAKE CARE OF THE REST.
YOU SURE? I'LL CALL THE AUTHORITIES AND MAKE SURE THESE VICTIMS GET HOME.
POSITIVE. I'VE BEEN DOING THIS FOR A LONG TIME, AND THE POLICE CAN ONLY DO BUT SO MUCH WITH A CASE LIKE THIS. AND AS FOR THE VICTIMS, THE LESS THEY REMEMBER AND THE LESS THEY'RE QUESTIONED, THE BETTER.
BUT, NEGUS-- HE GOT AWAY.
TRUE. BUT WE'VE HURT HIM AND HIS OPERATION. I'LL TORCH THIS "V" FACTORY AND MAKE SURE MR. CHIN CAN'T PRODUCE ANY MORE OF THIS POISON. THIS IS A VICTORY, SPIDER-MAN. AND IN MY WAR--I TAKE THEM ANYWAY I CAN.
WHAT-EVER, DUDE-- I'LL TAKE YOUR WORD FOR IT.
Y'KNOW, I HAVE A QUESTION FOR YOU. SOMETHING I'VE ALWAYS WONDERED--
SHOOT.
NOW, I HAVE THE POWERS OF A SPIDER AND THEY CALL ME SPIDER-MAN. IRON MAN HAS A SUIT OF IRON SO THEY CALL HIM IRON MAN--
UH-HUH...
--SO I WAS THINKING...SINCE YOU HAVE THE ABILITIES OF GIANT VAMPIRE BAT, WHY NOT JUST TAKE THE NAME OF BATM--
NO.
EH. JUST THOUGHT I'D ASK.
ANYWAY, IF YOU EVER RUN INTO MORE VAMPIRES--
--HESITATE TO CALL.
THE END.

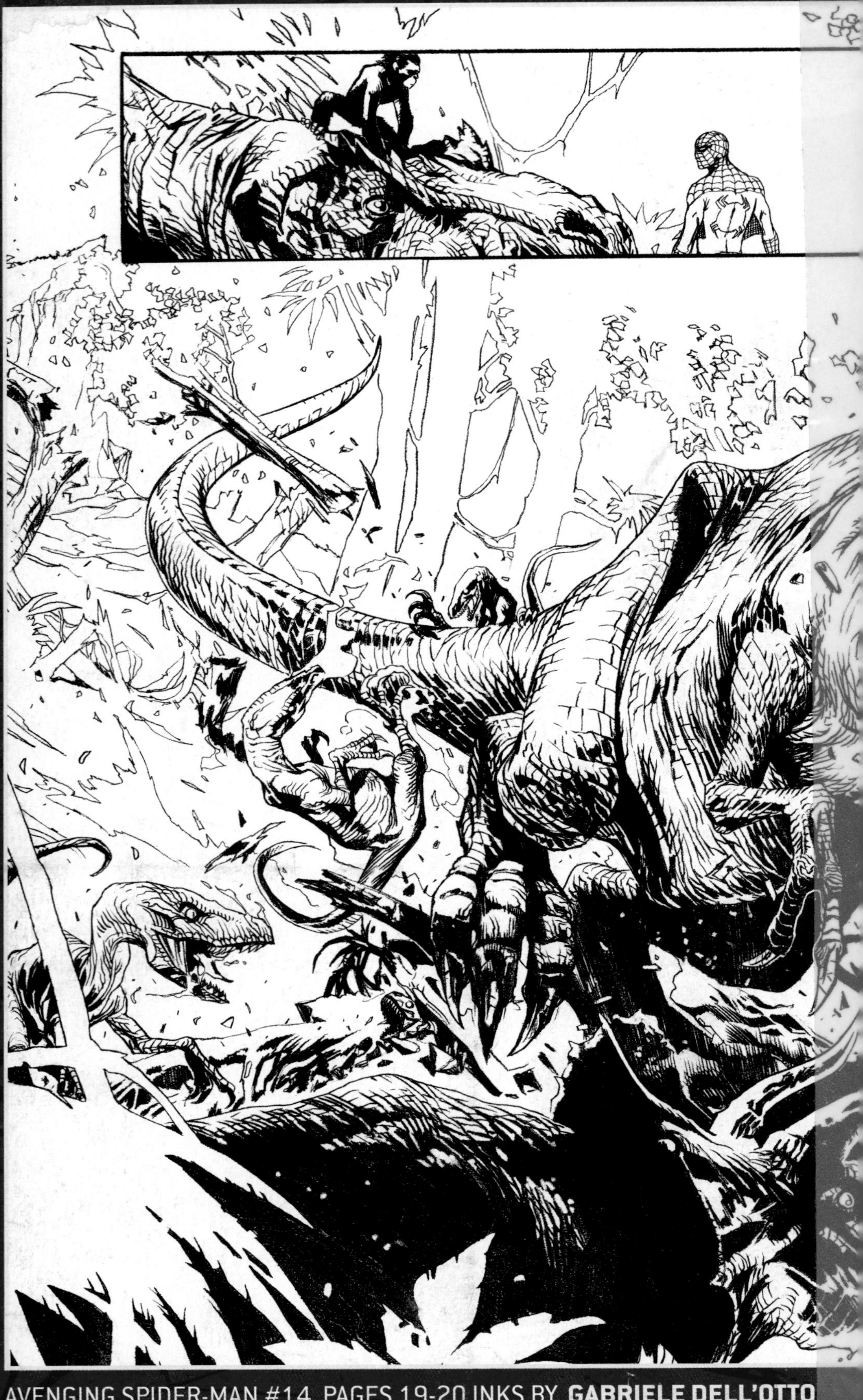

AVENGING SPIDER-MAN #14, PAGES 19-20 INKS BY **GABRIELE DELL'OTTO**

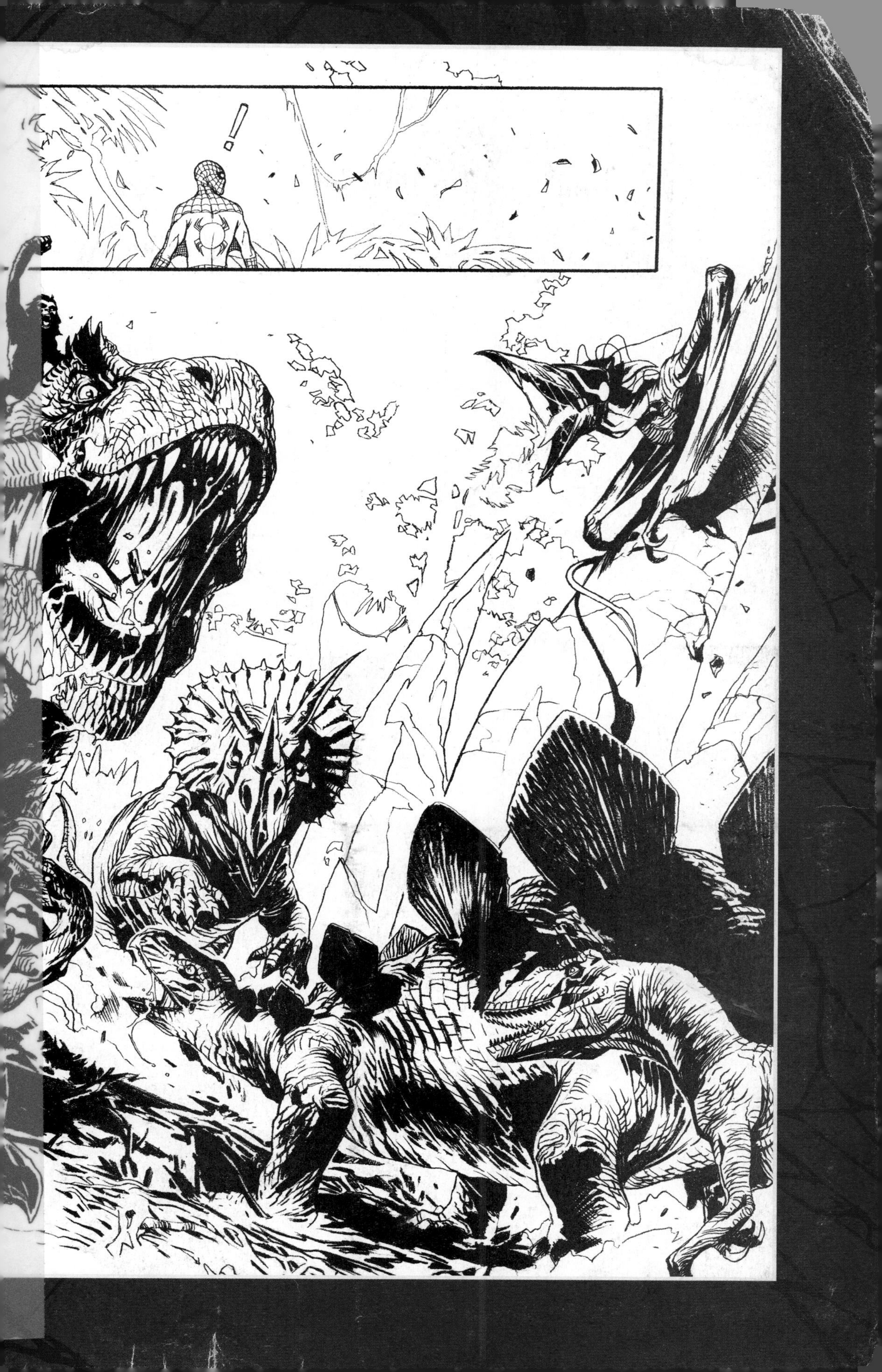
!

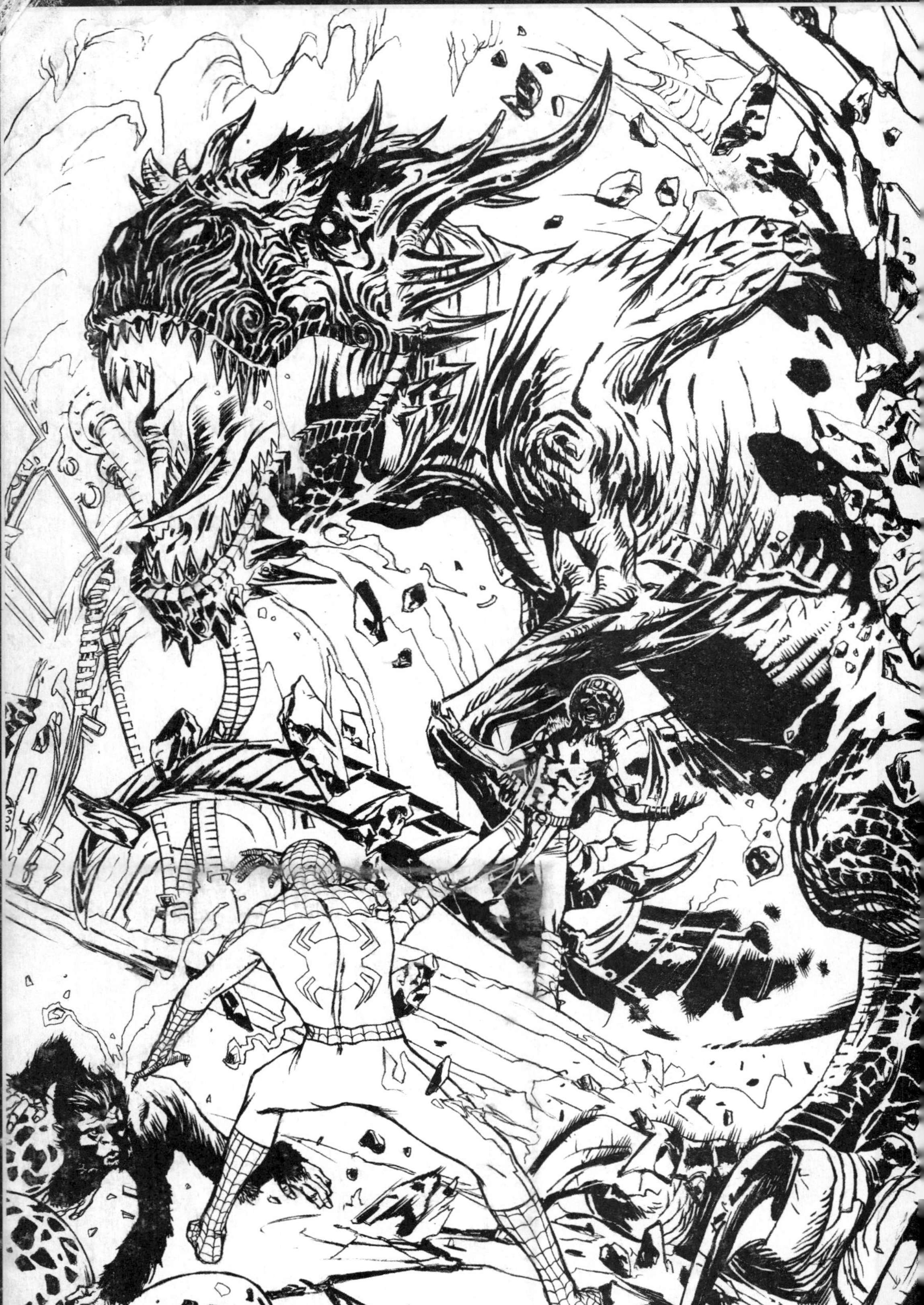

AVENGING SPIDER-MAN #14, PAGE 12 INKS BY **GABRIELE DELL'OTTO**